EJB 3.0 Database Persistence with Oracle Fusion Middleware 11g

A complete guide to EJB 3.0 database persistence with Oracle Fusion Middleware 11g

Deepak Vohra

[PACKT] PUBLISHING enterprise

professional expertise distilled

BIRMINGHAM - MUMBAI

EJB 3.0 Database Persistence with Oracle Fusion Middleware 11*g*

First published: August 2010

Production Reference: 1190810

Published by Packt Publishing Ltd.
32 Lincoln Road
Olton
Birmingham, B27 6PA, UK.

ISBN 978-1-849681-56-8

www.packtpub.com

Cover Image by Tina Negus (tina_manthorpe@sky.com)

Credits

Author
Deepak Vohra

Reviewers
Maxence Button
Niall C. Commiskey
Balamurali Kothandaraman
Frank Nimphius

Acquisition Editor
Amey Kanse

Development Editor
Wilson D'souza

Technical Editors
Arani Roy
Conrad Sardinha
Kavita Iyer

Indexer
Monica Ajmera Mehta

Editorial Team Leader
Mithun Sehgal

Project Team Leader
Lata Basantani

Project Coordinator
Srimoyee Ghoshal

Proofreader
Sandra Hopper

Production Coordinator
Alwin Roy

Cover Work
Alwin Roy

About the Author

Deepak Vohra is a consultant and a principal member of the NuBean.com software company. Deepak is a Sun Certified Java Programmer and Web Component Developer, and has worked in the fields of XML and Java programming and J2EE for over five years. Deepak is the co-author of the Apress book *Pro XML Development with Java Technology* and was the technical reviewer for the O'Reilly book *WebLogic: The Definitive Guide*. Deepak was also the technical reviewer for the Course Technology PTR book *Ruby Programming for the Absolute Beginner*, and the technical editor for the Manning Publications book *Prototype and Scriptaculous in Action*. Deepak is also the author of the Packt Publishing books *JDBC 4.0 and Oracle JDeveloper for J2EE Development* and *Processing XML documents with Oracle JDeveloper 11g*.

About the Reviewers

Maxence Button started to work with Java in 2000. He has worked as a developer, architect, and more recently as a consultant for BEA, then Oracle. This position allowed him to specialize in the WebLogic and AquaLogic lines of products, then in the Oracle Fusion Middleware stack.

After three years working as a principal consultant on Oracle | BEA technology, he started his own company in March, 2010 and now advises his clients, in the pure spirit of independence.

> I would like to thank my wife for her patience throughout the whole process, which held me stuck in front of my PC for a few evenings :)

Niall Commiskey works as a Senior Principal Technologist with Oracle Corporation. He is part of the PTS group within Oracle, which assists Oracle partners in getting the most out of Oracle technologies. In his previous role within the organization, Niall worked for Oracle Consulting Services in Germany. He has over 20 years of IT development experience, ranging from mainframe assembler to SOA developer. He works for Oracle, which is the world's largest enterprise software company.

> Thanks to my wife Renate and children, Lucia and Phillip, for teaching me what life is really about.

Balamurali Kothandaraman [Bala] has over 14 years of experience in IT Architecture, including full Blue-print of Reference and Enterprise Architecture. He has been involved in product development, design, consultation, project mentoring, product readiness, technology mentoring, solution design, and architecture on various technologies like Java, Java EE, C, C++, and so on, including SOA-based application frameworks. He is currently working as a Principal Instructor with Oracle Corporation involved in assisting customers with implementing their Enterprise Architecture using Oracle Fusion Middleware product suites. He worked for more than seven years with BEA Systems Inc. as a Senior Delivery Technologist involved in assisting various customers with designing and implementing Service-Oriented Architecture for their enterprise using the BEA WebLogic and AquaLogic Product suites. Prior to BEA, he worked for many consulting houses, such as 3i Infotech, and Technosoft, HCL Technologies where he designed, developed, and implemented Enterprise Solutions for various organizations.

Bala is a globally recognized speaker and workshop modulator on various major events covering hot topics such as SOA, Event-Driven Architecture, and Enterprise Architecture Principles and Methodologies. He has presented at JavaOne, BEAWorld conferences, BEA Support Webinars, and WebLogic User Groups. Bala also published technical articles with various journals and web sites, such as WebLogic Developers Journal, BEA Dev2Dev, and so on. Bala constantly blogs about WebLogic Server at `http://weblogicserver.blogspot.com`.

Frank Nimphius is a Senior Principal Product Manager for Oracle JDeveloper and Oracle Application Development Framework (ADF) within the Oracle Application Development Tool Product Management group. In his current job role, Frank actively presents the Oracle development team at Oracle and non-Oracle conferences around the world and recently co-authored the Oracle Press book: *Oracle Fusion Developer Guide: Building Rich Internet Applications with Oracle ADF Business Components and Oracle ADF Faces.*

Table of Contents

Preface

EJB (Enterprise JavaBeans) 3.0 entity beans is a commonly used database persistence technology. EJB 3.0 has simplified the development of EJBs with an annotations-based API that does not require remote/local interfaces, home/local home interfaces, or deployment descriptors. Developing entity EJBs requires an application server and a relational database, and optionally a Java EE IDE to simplify the process of development. The objective of the JSR-000220 Enterprise JavaBeans 3.0 specification (`http://jcp.org/aboutJava/communityprocess/final/jsr220/index.html`) is to improve the EJB architecture by reducing its complexity from the developer's point of view. EJB 3.0 has introduced some new features, which include support for metadata annotations, default values for configuration, simplified access to environment variables, simplified session and entity beans, interceptors, enhanced support for checked exceptions, and elimination of callback interfaces.

A number of books are available on EJB 3.0, but none cover EJB 3.0 on the Oracle Fusion Middleware (11*g*) platform. Most of the EJB 3.0 books are GlassFish server based, which has only 10percent of the application server market. Welcome to *EJB 3.0 Database Persistence with Oracle Fusion Middleware 11g*, a book that will teach you how to leverage EJB 3.0 persistence on Oracle Fusion Middleware 11*g*. Oracle Fusion Middleware 11*g* includes many components such as the SOA/BPM Suite, WebCenter, and Oracle Identity Management. All of these components run on Oracle Weblogic Server 11*g*. The main development tool (IDE) for Oracle Fusion Middleware is Oracle JDeveloper. In respect of EJB 3.0, JDeveloper provides wizard support to reverse engineer database tables as EJB 3.0 entity beans. JDeveloper 11*g* also provides a wizard for creating session beans. The JPA persistence provider used in JDeveloper 11*g* is the EclipseLink persistence provider. JDeveloper comes with its own embedded/integrated Weblogic Server instance, which makes it very easy to develop and test within the one environment. We shall be using the embedded WebLogic Server 11*g* in some of the chapters and the standalone WebLogic Server in others.

The objective of the book is to discuss the support of EJB 3.0 database persistence in Oracle Fusion Middleware 11*g*. While JDeveloper is the main Java IDE used in the book, one of the chapters leverages the Oracle Enterprise Pack for Eclipse. The book covers all aspects of EJB 3.0 database persistence including:

- Creating EJB 3.0 entity beans from database tables
- Creating session bean façades for entity beans
- Entity beans with session beans
- Creating EJB 3.0 entity relationships
- Creating JSF and ADF Faces user interfaces (UIs) on top of EJB 3.0 database persistence
- Using EJB 3.0 database persistence in combination with Ajax and web services

What this book covers

In *Chapter 1, What's New in EJB 3.0*, we discuss the new features in the EJB 3.0 specification, such as support for metadata annotations, default values for configuration, simplified session and entity beans, and enhanced support for checked exceptions.

In *Chapter 2, Converting an EJB 2.0 Entity to an EJB*, we convert an example EJB 2.0 entity bean to an EJB 3.0 entity bean. We also generate the session bean façade for the EJB 3.0 entity bean. XSLT transformation is used for converting the EJB 2.0 entity bean to an EJB 3.0 entity bean.

In *Chapter 3, EclipseLink JPA Persistence Provider*, we discuss the JPA framework and the EclipseLink persistence provider.

In *Chapter 4, Building an EJB 3.0 Persistence Model with Oracle JDeveloper*, we discuss EJB 3.0 database persistence with JDeveloper 11*g*, WebLogic Server 11*g*, and Oracle Database 10*g*. We create an EJB 3.0 entity bean from a database table, create a session bean façade, and finally create a JSP test client. Using the test client, we create, retrieve, and delete entity bean instances.

In *Chapter 5, EJB 3.0 Persistence with Oracle Enterprise Pack for Eclipse*, we discuss the same example we covered in Chapter 4, but with the Oracle Enterprise Pack for Eclipse, WebLogic Server, and the open source MySQL database, which has been acquired by Oracle.

In *Chapter 6, EJB 3.0 with ADF Faces UI*, we discuss using an ADF Faces client for EJB 3.0 database persistence. We create an entity bean using data input from an ADF Faces user interface (UI). Subsequently, we find an entity bean instance using data input from an ADF Faces UI.

In *Chapter 7, Creating EJB 3.0 Entity Relationships*, we discuss EJB 3.0 entity relationships using, as an example, three entity beans that have inter-relationships. We also discuss the significance of a fetch strategy.

In *Chapter 8, EJB 3.0 Database Persistence with Ajax in the UI*, we discuss EJB 3.0 database persistence in combination with Ajax in the user interface (UI). We demonstrate data validation and autocompletion with Ajax.

In *Chapter 9, Using JSF with Entity Relationships*, we discuss adding JSFs to EJB 3.0 database persistence to create and persist entity bean instances that have entity relationships between them.

In *Chapter 10, Creating an EJB 3.0 Web Service*, we create a JAX-WS Web Service from an EJB 3.0 entity bean, create a web service client, package and deploy the web service to WebLogic Server, and test the Web Service using the WebLogic console.

What you need for this book

The book is based on Oracle JDeveloper 11*g* Studio Edition for Windows and Oracle WebLogic Server 11*g*, Windows version, which are the two main components of Oracle Fusion Middleware 11*g* and may be downloaded from `http://www.oracle.com/technology/software/products/middleware/index.html`. If you have Linux installed, the book may still be used (though the source code and samples have not been tested with Linux); just download and install the Linux versions of Oracle JDeveloper 11*g* and Oracle WebLogic Server 11*g*. Slight modifications may be required with the Linux install; for example, the directory paths on Linux would be different than the Windows directory paths used in the book. For one of the chapters, you would need to download and install Oracle Enterprise pack for Eclipse from `http://www.oracle.com/tools/enterprise-eclipse-pack.html`. For database, you would need to download and install Oracle Database 10*g*/11g from `http://www.oracle.com/technology/software/products/database/index.html`. For another chapter, you would need to download and install the open source MySQL 5.x database from `http://www.mysql.com/downloads/mysql/`. The annotations used in EJB 3.0 are a J2SE 5.0 feature; therefore, you need to install J2SE 5.0 or later.

Who this book is for

The target audience of the book is EJB 3.0 application developers who want to learn about the practical use of EJB 3.0 database persistence with Oracle Fusion Middleware 11*g*. Those who are already using EJB 3.0 database persistence will learn about using EJB 3.0 database persistence with Oracle Fusion Middleware 11*g*. We won't be discussing the EJB 3.0 specification in much detail but you can refer - JSR-000220 (`http://jcp.org/aboutJava/communityprocess/final/jsr220/index.html`) for more information. This book is suitable for professional Java EE developers. The book is also suitable for an intermediate/advanced level course in EJB 3.0. The target audience is expected to have prior, albeit beginner's, knowledge about Java EE, EJBs, EJB 3.0, JSF, ADF Faces, Ajax, Web Services, and XML. The book also requires some familiarity with WebLogic Server and Java EE IDEs, JDeveloper, and Eclipse.

Conventions

In this book, you will find a number of styles of text that distinguish between different kinds of information. Here are some examples of these styles, and an explanation of their meaning.

Code words in text are shown as follows: "The `Catalog` entity bean has `properties` `id` and `journal`".

A block of code is set as follows:

```
@Resources({
  @Resource(name="ds1", type="javax.sql.DataSource"),
  @Resource(name="ds2", type="javax.sql.DataSource")
})
```

New terms and **important words** are shown in bold. Words that you see on the screen, in menus or dialog boxes for example, appear in the text like this: "In the **New Gallery** window, select **Categories:General | XML** and **Items:XSL Style Sheet** and click on **OK**".

Warnings or important notes appear in a box like this.

Tips and tricks appear like this.

Reader feedback

Feedback from our readers is always welcome. Let us know what you think about this book—what you liked or may have disliked. Reader feedback is important for us to develop titles that you really get the most out of.

To send us general feedback, simply send an e-mail to feedback@packtpub.com, and mention the book title via the subject of your message.

If there is a book that you need and would like to see us publish, please send us a note in the **SUGGEST A TITLE** form on www.packtpub.com or e-mail suggest@packtpub.com.

If there is a topic that you have expertise in and you are interested in either writing or contributing to a book, see our author guide on www.packtpub.com/authors.

Customer support

Now that you are the proud owner of a Packt book, we have a number of things to help you to get the most from your purchase.

Downloading the example code for this book

You can download the example code files for all Packt books you have purchased from your account at http://www.PacktPub.com. If you purchased this book elsewhere, you can visit http://www.PacktPub.com/support and register to have the files e-mailed directly to you.

Errata

Although we have taken every care to ensure the accuracy of our content, mistakes do happen. If you find a mistake in one of our books—maybe a mistake in the text or the code—we would be grateful if you would report this to us. By doing so, you can save other readers from frustration and help us improve subsequent versions of this book. If you find any errata, please report them by visiting http://www.packtpub.com/support, selecting your book, clicking on the **errata submission form** link, and entering the details of your errata. Once your errata are verified, your submission will be accepted and the errata will be uploaded on our website, or added to any list of existing errata, under the Errata section of that title. Any existing errata can be viewed by selecting your title from http://www.packtpub.com/support.

Piracy

Piracy of copyright material on the Internet is an ongoing problem across all media. At Packt, we take the protection of our copyright and licenses very seriously. If you come across any illegal copies of our works, in any form, on the Internet, please provide us with the location address or website name immediately so that we can pursue a remedy.

Please contact us at `copyright@packtpub.com` with a link to the suspected pirated material.

We appreciate your help in protecting our authors, and our ability to bring you valuable content.

Questions

You can contact us at `questions@packtpub.com` if you are having a problem with any aspect of the book, and we will do our best to address it.

1
What's New in EJB 3.0

The main objective of the **Enterprise JavaBeans** (**EJB**) 3.0 specification is to improve the EJB architecture by reducing its complexity from the developer's point of view. EJB 3.0 has simplified the development of EJBs with the introduction of some new features. The new features include support for metadata annotations, default values for a configuration, simplified access of environmental dependencies and external resources, simplified session and entity beans, interceptors, enhanced support for checked exceptions, and elimination of callback interfaces. The persistence and object/relational model has been revised and enhanced in EJB 3.0. The persistence and object/relational model in EJB 3.0 is the **Java Persistence API** (**JPA**). We shall discuss and introduce these new features in this chapter.

Metadata annotations

Metadata annotations were introduced in JDK 5.0 as a means to provide data about an application. Annotations are used for the following purposes:

- Generating boilerplate code (code that is repeated in different sections of a Java program) automatically.

- Replacing configuration information in configuration files such as deployment descriptors.

- Replacing comments in a program.

- Informing the compiler about detecting errors and generating or suppressing warnings. The `@Deprecated` annotation is used to inform the compiler about a deprecated feature, on detecting which the compiler generates a warning. The `@Override` annotation informs the compiler about an overridden element. If the element is not overridden properly, the compiler generates an error. The `@SuppressWarnings` annotation is used to inform the compiler to suppress specific warnings.

- Runtime processing of annotations by annotating the annotations with the `@Retention(RetentionPolicy.RUNTIME)` annotation.

EJB 3.0 specification has introduced some metadata annotations for annotating EJB 3.0 applications. EJB 3.0 metadata annotations have reduced the number of classes and interfaces a developer is required to implement. Also, the metadata annotations have eliminated the requirement for an EJB deployment descriptor. Three types of metadata annotations are used in EJB 3.0: EJB 3.0 annotations, object/relational mapping annotations, and annotations for resource injection and security. Though annotations follow a different semantic than Java code, they help in reducing code lines and — in the case of EJB — increase cross-platform portability. The EJB 3.0 annotations are defined in the javax.ejb package. For example, the `@Stateless` annotation specifies that an EJB is a Stateless Session Bean:

```
import javax.ejb.Stateless;

@Stateless
public class HelloBean implements Hello {
  public void hello() {
    System.out.println("Hello EJB 3.0!");
  }
}
```

For all the new EJB 3.0, annotations, refer to the EJB 3.0 specification document EJBCore (ejb-3_0-fr-spec-ejbcore.pdf). Persistence annotations are defined in the javax.ejb.persistence package. For example, the `@Entity` annotation specifies that the EJB is an Entity Bean:

```
import javax.persistence.*;

@Entity
@Table(name = "Catalog")
public class Catalog implements Serializable {
  private long id;

  @Id
  public long getId() {
```

```
    return id;
    }
    public void setId(long id) {
    this.id = id;
    }
}
```

The resource injection and security annotations are defined in the Common Annotations for the Java Platform specification, and are in the `javax.annotation` and `javax.annotation.security` packages. For example, the `@Resource` injection may be used to inject a `javax.sql.DataSource` resource. First, configure a data source in a Java EE container. Subsequently, inject a data source handle by annotating a declaration for a variable of type javax.sql.DataSource with the `@Resource` annotation.

```
@Resource
private  javax.sql.DataSource mysqlDS;

public getCatalogEntry(){
   Connection conn = mysqlDS.getConnection();
}
```

Data source injection using the `@Resource` annotation precludes the requirement for JNDI lookup using an `InitialContext` object. The security annotations are presented in the following table.

Annotation	Description
DeclareRoles	Declares references to security roles
RolesAllowed	Declares the methods that are allowed to invoke the methods of the entity bean
PermitAll	Specifies that all security roles are allowed to invoke the specified methods.
DenyAll	Specifies that no security roles are allowed to invoke the specified methods.
RunAs	Specify a security role as the bean's run-as property.

Configuration defaults

Common expected behaviors and requirements for the EJB container are not required to be specified by a developer. For example, by default an EJB 3.0 container provides Container-Managed persistence and **Container-Managed Transaction (CMT)** demarcation. Default metadata values and programmatic defaults are provided by the EJB 3.0 implementation. A "configuration by exception" approach is taken rather than explicit configuration. Relationship Mapping Defaults are defined in the persistence API. Object/relational mapping defaults are also defined. For example, an Entity bean is mapped to a database table name of the same name as the capitalized entity class name. Therefore, an Entity class `Catalog` is mapped to database table `CATALOG` by default. Similarly, the default column name is the property or field name. The entity name defaults to the entity class name.

Environmental dependencies and JNDI Access

An enterprise bean's context may be divided into 3 components:

- Container context
- Resources
- Environment context

The container may be used to supply references to resources and environment entries. Environmental dependencies and JNDI access may be encapsulated with dependency annotations, a dependency injection mechanism, and a simple lookup mechanism. Dependency injection implies that the EJB container automatically supplies/injects a bean's variable or setter method with a reference to a resource or environment entry in the bean's context. Alternatively, you would have to use the `javax.ejb.EJBContext` or JNDI APIs to access the environment entries and resources. Dependency injection is implemented by annotating a bean's variable or setter method with one of the following annotations:

- `@javax.ejb.EJB` is used to specify dependency on another EJB.

- `@javax.annotation.Resource` is used to specify dependency on an external resource such as a JDBC datasource, a JMS destination, or a JMS connection factory. The `@Resource` annotation is not specific to EJB 3, and may be also used with other Java EE components.

For accessing multiple resources, use the corresponding grouping annotations `@javax.ejb.EJBs` and `@javax.annotation.Resources`. An example of injecting dependency on an EJB into a bean's variable using the `@javax.ejb.EJB` annotation is as follows:

```
import javax.ejb.EJB;

@Stateful
public class CatalogBean implements Catalog {
  @EJB(beanName = "HelloBean")
  private Hello hello;

  public void helloFromCatalogBean() {
    hello.hello();
  }
}
```

In the preceding example, the `hello` variable is injected with the EJB `HelloBean`. The type of the `hello` variable is `Hello`, which is the `HelloBean`'s business interface that it implements. Subsequently, we invoked the `hello()` method of the `HelloBean`. A resource may also be injected into a setter method. If the resource type can be determined from the parameter type, the resource type is not required to be specified in the `@Resource` annotation. In the following code snippet, the setter method is annotated with the `@Resource` annotation. In the setter method, the `dataSource` property is set to a JNDI resource of type `javax.sql.DataSource` with value as `catalogDB`.

```
private javax.sql.DataSource dataSource;

@Resource(name="catalogDB")
public void setDataSource (DataSource jndiResource) {
  this.dataSource = jndiResource;
}
```

The setter method must follow the JavaBean conventions: the method name begins with `set`, returns `void`, and has only one parameter. If the name of the resource is the same as the property name, the resource name is not required to be specified in the `@Resource` annotation. The JNDI name of the resource is of the format `class_name/catalogDB`, `class_name` being the class name.

```
private javax.sql.DataSource catalogDB;

@Resource
public void setCatalogDB (DataSource jndiResource) {
  this.catalogDB = jndiResource;
}
```

Setter injection methods are invoked by the container before any business methods on the bean instance. Multiple resources may be injected using the `@Resources` annotation. For example, in the following code snippet two resources of type `javax.sql.DataSource` are injected.

```
@Resources({
    @Resource(name="ds1", type="javax.sql.DataSource"),
    @Resource(name="ds2", type="javax.sql.DataSource")
})
```

JNDI resources injected with the dependency mechanism may be looked up in the `java:comp/env` namespace. For example, if the JNDI name of a resource of type `javax.sql.DataSource` is `catalogDB`, the resource may be looked up as follows.

```
InitialContext ctx = new InitialContext();
Javax.sql.DataSource ds = ctx.lookup("java:comp/env/catalogDB");
```

Simplified Session Beans

In EJB 2.x, a session bean is required to implement the `SessionBean` interface. An EJB 3.0 session bean class is a **POJO (Plain Old Java Object)** and does not implement the `SessionBean` interface.

An EJB 2.x session bean class includes one or more `ejbCreate` methods, the callback methods `ejbActivate`, `ejbPassivate`, `ejbRemove`, and `setSessionContext`, and the business methods defined in the local/remote interface. An EJB 3.0 session bean class includes only the business methods.

In EJB 3.0, EJB component interfaces and home interfaces are not required for session beans. A remote interface in an EJB 2.x session EJB extends the `javax.ejb.EJBObject` interface; a local interface extends the `javax.ejb.EJBLocalObject` interface. A home interface in an EJB 2.x session EJB extends the `javax.ejb.EJBHome` interface; a local home interface extends the `javax.ejb.EJBLocalHome` interface. In EJB 3.0 the home/local home and remote/local interfaces are not required. The EJB interfaces are replaced with a **POJI (Plain Old Java Interface)** business interface. If a business interface is not included with the session bean class, a POJI business interface gets generated from the session bean class by the EJB server.

An EJB 2.x session EJB includes a deployment descriptor that specifies the EJB name, the bean class name, and the interfaces. The deployment descriptor also specifies the bean type of Stateless/Stateful. In EJB 3.0, a deployment descriptor is not required for a session bean. An example EJB 2.x session bean, which implements the `SessionBean` interface, is listed next:

```
import javax.ejb.SessionBean;
import javax.ejb.SessionContext;

public class CatalogBean implements SessionBean {
  private SessionContext ctx;

  public String getJournal(String publisher) {
    if (publisher.equals("Oracle Publisher"))
      return new String("Oracle Magazine");
    if (publisher.equals("OReilly"))
      return new String("dev2dev");
}

  public void ejbCreate() {
  }

  public void ejbRemove() {
  }

  public void ejbActivate() {
  }

  public void ejbPassivate() {
  }

  public void setSessionContext(SessionContext ctx) {
    this.ctx = ctx;
  }
}
```

In EJB 3.0, metadata annotations are used to specify the session bean type and local and remote business interfaces. A stateless session bean is specified with the annotation @Stateless, a stateful session bean with the annotation @Stateful. Component and home interfaces are not required for a session bean. A session bean is required to implement a business interface. The business interface, which is a POJI, may be a local or remote interface. A local interface is denoted with the annotation @Local and a remote interface is denoted with the annotation @Remote. A session bean may implement one or both (local and remote) of the interfaces. If none of the interfaces is specified, a local business interface gets generated. The remote and local business interface class may be specified in the @Local and @Remote annotations. For example, a local business interface may be specified as @Local ({CatalogLocal.class}).

The EJB 3.0 session bean corresponding to the EJB 2.x stateless session bean is annotated with the metadata annotation @Stateless. The EJB 3.0 bean class does not implement the SessionBean interface. The EJB 3.0 session bean implements a business interface. The @Local annotation specifies the local business interface for the session bean. The EJB 3.0 session bean corresponding to the EJB 2.x example session bean is listed next:

```
import javax.ejb.*;
@Stateless
@Local( { CatalogLocal.class })
public class CatalogBean implements CatalogLocal {
  public String getJournal(String publisher) {
    if (publisher.equals("Oracle Publisher"))
      return new String("Oracle Magazine");
    if (publisher.equals("OReilly"))
      return new String("java.net");
  }
}
```

In EJB 3.0, the component and home interfaces of EJB 2.x are replaced with a business interface. The business interfaces for the session bean are POJIs, and do not extend the EJBLocalObject or the EJBObject. A local business interface is denoted with the annotation @Local. A remote business interface is denoted with the annotation @Remote. A remote business interface does not throw the RemoteException. The local business interface corresponding to the session bean class is listed next:

```
import javax.ejb.*;
@Local
public interface CatalogLocal {
  public String getJournal(String publisher);
}
```

A client for an EJB 2.x session bean gets a reference to the session bean with JNDI. The JNDI name for the CatalogBean session bean is CatalogLocalHome. The local/remote object is obtained with the create() method. The client class for the EJB 2.x session bean is listed.

```
import javax.naming.InitialContext;
public class CatalogBeanClient {
  public static void main(String[] argv) {
    try {
      InitialContext ctx = new InitialContext();
      Object objref = ctx.lookup("CatalogLocalHome");
      CatalogLocalHome catalogLocalHome = (CatalogLocalHome) objref;
      CatalogLocal catalogLocal = (CatalogLocal) catalogLocalHome

      .create();
      String publisher = "OReilly";
      String journal = catalogLocal.getJournal(publisher);
      System.out.println("Journal for Publisher: " + publisher + " "
                                                                 +
      journal);
```

```
    } catch (Exception e) {
      System.err.println(e.getMessage());
    }
  }
 }
}
```

In EJB 3.0, a reference to a resource may be obtained with a dependency injection with the @EJB annotation. JNDI lookup and create() method invocation is not required in EJB 3.0. The client class for the EJB 3.0 session bean is listed next:

```
public class CatalogClient {

  @EJB
  CatalogBean catalogBean;
  String publisher="OReilly";
  String journal=catalogBean.getJournal(publisher);
  System.out.println("Journal for Publisher: "+publisher +"
"+journal);
}
```

Simplified entity beans

An EJB 2.x Entity EJB bean class must implement the javax.ejb.
EntityBean interface, which defines callback methods setEntityContext, unsetEntityContext, ejbActivate, ejbPassivate, ejbLoad, ejbStore, and ejbRemove that are called by the EJB container. An EJB 2.x provides implementation for the callback methods in the interface. An EJB 2.x entity bean also includes the ejbCreate and ejbPostCreate callback methods corresponding to one create method in the home interface. An EJB 2.x entity bean's component and home interfaces extend the EJBObject/EJBLocalObject and EJBHome/EJBLocalHome interfaces respectively. In comparison, an EJB 3.0 entity bean class is a POJO which does not implement the EntityBean interface. The callback methods are not implemented in the EJB 3.0 entity bean class. Also, the component and home interfaces and deployment descriptors are not required in EJB 3.0. The EJB configuration information is included in the Entity bean POJO class using metadata annotations. An EJB 2.1 entity bean also consists of getter/setter **CMP (Container Managed Persistence)** field methods, and getter/setter **CMR (Container Managed Relationships)** field methods. An EJB 2.x entity bean also defines finder and ejbSelect methods in the home/local home interfaces for EJB-QL queries. An example EJB 2.x entity bean is listed next:

```
import javax.ejb.EntityBean;
import javax.ejb.EntityContext;

public class CatalogBean implements EntityBean {
```

```
    private EntityContext ctx;
    public abstract void setCatalogId();
    public abstract String getCatalogId();
    public abstract void setJournal();
    public abstract String getJournal();
    public String ejbCreate(String catalogId) {
      setCatalogId(catalogId);
      return null;
    }
    public void ejbRemove() {
    }
    public void ejbActivate() {
    }
    public void ejbPassivate() {
    }
    public void ejbLoad() {
    }
     public void ejbStore() {
     }
     public void setEntityContext(EntityContext ctx) {
           this.ctx = ctx;
     }
     public void unsetEntityContext() {
           ctx = null;
     }
  }
```

In EJB 2.x, the `ejb-jar.xml` deployment descriptor defines the EJB-QL for finder methods. An example finder method is specified in the `ejb-jar.xml` as follows:

```
<query>
  <query-method>
    <method-name>findByJournal</method-name>
    <method-params>
      <method-param>java.lang.String</method-param>
    </method-params>
  </query-method>
  <ejb-ql>
  <![CDATA[SELECT DISTINCT OBJECT(obj)  FROM Catalog obj WHERE obj.
journal =
```

```
?1 ]]>
   </ejb-ql>
</query>
```

An EJB 3.0 entity bean is a POJO class annotated with the `@Entity` annotation. The finder methods are specified in the entity bean class itself using the `@NamedQuery` annotation. The EJB 3.0 entity bean persistence annotations are defined in the `javax.persistence` package. Some of the EJB 3.0 persistence annotations are presented in the following table:

Annotation	Description
@Entity	Specifies an entity bean.
@Table	Specifies the entity bean table.
@SecondaryTable	Specifies a secondary table for an entity class for which data is stored across multiple tables.
@Id	Specifies an identifier property.
@Column	Specifies the database table column for a persistent entity bean property.
@NamedQueries	Specifies a group of named queries.
@NamedQuery	Specifies a named query or a query associated with a finder method.
@OneToMany	Specifies a one-to-many CMR relationship.
@OneToOne	Specifies a one-to-one CMR relationship.
@ManyToMany	Specifies a many-to-many CMR relationship.

The EJB 3.0 entity bean class corresponding to the EJB 2.x entity bean class is annotated with the metadata annotation `@Entity`. The finder method `findByJournal` in the EJB 2.x bean class is specified in the EJB 3.0 POJO class with the `@NamedQuery` annotation. The `@Id` annotation specifies the identifier property `catalogId`. The `@Column` annotation specifies the database column corresponding to the identifier property `catalogId`. If a `@Column` annotation is not specified for a persistent entity bean property, the column name is the same as the entity bean property name. Transient entity bean properties are specified with the `@Transient` annotation. The EJB 3.0 entity bean POJO class corresponding to the EJB 2.x entity bean is listed next:

```
import javax.persistence.Entity;
import javax.persistence.NamedQuery;
import javax.persistence.Id;
import javax.persistence.Column;

@Entity
@NamedQuery(name = "findByJournal", queryString = "SELECT DISTINCT
OBJECT(obj)  FROM Catalog obj WHERE obj.journal = ?1")
public class CatalogBean {
  public CatalogBean() {
```

```
    }
    public CatalogBean(String catalogId) {
        this.catalogId = catalogId;
    }

    private String catalogId;
    private String journal;

    @Id
    @Column(name = "CatalogId", primaryKey = "true")
    public String getCatalogId() {
    return catalogId;
    }

     public void setCatalogId(String catalogId) {
            this.catalogId = catalogId;
     }
    public void setJournal(String journal) {
      this.journal = journal;
    }
    public String getJournal() {
      return journal;
    }
}
```

An EJB 2.x entity bean instance is created with the create() method in the entity bean home/local home interface. A client for an EJB 2.x entity bean obtains a reference for the entity bean with JNDI lookup; CatalogLocalHome is the JNDI name of the CatalogBean entity bean:

```
InitialContext ctx=new InitialContext();
Object objref=ctx.lookup("CatalogLocalHome");
CatalogLocalHome catalogLocalHome=(CatalogLocalHome)objref;

//Create an instance of Entity bean
CatalogLocal catalogLocal=(CatalogLocal)catalogLocalHome.
create(catalogId);
```

To access the getter/setter methods of an entity bean, the remote/local object in EJB 2.x is obtained with the finder methods:

```
CatalogLocal catalogLocal =
    (CatalogLocal) catalogLocalHome.findByPrimaryKey(catalogId);
```

An entity bean instance is removed with the remove() method:

```
catalogLocal.remove();
```

In EJB 3.0, persistence and lookup are provided by the `EntityManger` class. In a session bean client class for the EJB 3.0 entity bean, dependency injection is used to inject an `EntityManager` object using the `@PersistenceContext` annotation:

```
@PersistenceContext
private EntityManager em;
```

An entity bean instance is created by invoking `new` on the `CatalogBean` class and persisted with the `persist()` method of the `EntityManager` class:

```
CatalogBean catalogBean=new CatalogBean(catalogId);
em.persist(catalogBean);
```

An entity bean instance is obtained with the `find()` method:

```
CatalogBean catalogBean=(CatalogBean)em.find("CatalogBean",
catalogId);
```

A `Query` object for a finder method is obtained with the `createNamedQuery` method:

```
Query query=em.createNamedQuery("findByJournal");
```

An entity bean instance is removed with the `remove()` method of the `EntityManager` class:

```
CatalogBean catalogBean;
em.remove(catalogBean);
```

The client class for the EJB 3.0 entity bean is listed next:

```
import javax.ejb.Stateless;
import javax.ejb.Resource;
import javax.persistence.EntityManager;
import javax.persistence.Query;

@Stateless
public class CatalogClient implements CatalogLocal {
  @Resource
  private EntityManager em;
  public void create(String catalogId) {
    CatalogBean catalogBean = new CatalogBean(catalogId);
    em.persist(catalogBean);
  }
  public CatalogBean findByPrimaryKey(String catalogId) {
    return (CatalogBean) em.find("CatalogBean", catalogId);
  }
  public void remove(CatalogBean catalogBean) {
```

```
        em.remove(catalogBean);
    }
}
```

Java Persistence API

The **Java Persistence API (JPA)** is the persistence component of EJB 3.0. "An EJB 3.0 entity is a lightweight persistent domain object." As discussed in the previous section, the entity class is a POJO annotated with the @Entity annotation. The relationship modeling annotations @OneToOne, @OneToMany, @ManyToOne, and @ManyToMany, are used for object/relational mapping of entity associations. EJB 3.0 specifies the object/relational mapping defaults for entity associations.

The annotations for object/relational mapping are defined in the javax.persistence package. An entity instance is created with the new operator and persisted using the EntityManager API. An EntityManager is injected into an entity bean using the @PersistenceContext annotation:

```
@PersistenceContext
EntityManager  em;
```

An entity instance is persisted using the persist() method:

```
CatalogBean catalogBean=new CatalogBean();
em.persist(catalogBean);
```

The EntityManager is also used to remove entity instances using the remove() method:

```
em.remove(catalogBean);
```

EntityManager is also used to find entities by their primary key with the find method:

```
CatalogBean catalogbean=(CatalogBean)(em.find("CatalogBean",
catalogId));
```

The @NamedQuery annotation is used to specify a named query in the Java Persistence Query language, which is an extension of EJB-QL. The Java Persistence Query language further adds operations for bulk update and delete, JOIN operations, GROUP BY, HAVING, and subqueries, and also supports dynamic queries and named parameters. Queries may also be specified in native SQL.

```
@NamedQuery(
  name="findAllBlogsByName",
  query="SELECT b FROM Blog b WHERE b.name LIKE :blogName"
)
```

The `EntityManager` is used to query entities using a `Query` object created from a named query:

```
Query query = em.createNamedQuery("findAllBlogsByName");
```

The named query parameters are set using the `setParameter()` method:

```
query.setParameter("blogName", "Smythe");
```

A `SELECT` query is run using the `getResultList()` method. A `SELECT` query that returns a single result is run using the `getSingleResult()` method. An `UPDATE` or `DELETE` statement is run using the `executeUpdate()` method. For a query that returns a list, the maximum number of results may be set using the `setMaxResults()` method.

```
List blogs=query.getResultList();
```

A persistence unit defines a set of entities that are mapped to a single database and managed by an `EntityManager`. A persistence unit is defined in the `persistence.xml` deployment descriptor, which is packaged in the `META-INF` directory of an entity bean JAR file. The root element of the `persistence.xml` file is `persistence`, which has one or more `persistence-unit` sub-elements. The `persistence-unit` element consists of the name and `transaction-type` attributes and subelements `description`, `provider`, `jta-data-source`, `non-jta-data-source`, `mapping-file`, `jar-file`, `class`, `exclude-unlisted-classes`, and `properties`. Only the `name` attribute is required; the other attributes and subelements are optional. The `jta-data-source` and `non-jta-data-source` are used to specify the global JNDI name of the data source to be used by the persistence provider. For all the elements in the `persistence.xml` and a detailed discussion on Java Persistence API, refer to the EJB 3.0 specification (ejb-3_0-fr-spec-persistence.pdf).

Interceptors

An interceptor is a method that intercepts a business method invocation or a lifecycle callback event. In EJB 2.x, runtime services such as transaction and security are applied to bean objects at the method's invocation time, using method interceptors that are managed by the EJB container. EJB 3.0 has introduced the Interceptor feature with which the interceptors may be managed by a developer. EJB interceptors are methods annotated with the `@javax.ejb.AroundInvoke` annotation. Interceptors may be used with business methods of session beans and message-driven beans. Interceptor methods may be defined in the bean class or an external interceptor class with a maximum of one interceptor method per class.

Simplified checked exceptions

Checked exceptions are exceptions that are not a subclass of the `java.lang.RuntimeException`. In EJB 2.1, if a bean method performs an operation that results in a checked exception that the bean method cannot recover, the bean method should throw the `javax.ejb.EJBException` that wraps the original exception. In EJB 3.0, application exceptions that are checked exceptions may be defined as such by being declared in the `throws` clause of the methods of the bean's business interface, home interface, component interface, and web service endpoint. `AroundInvoke` methods are allowed to throw checked exceptions that the business methods allow in the `throws` clause.

Callback Interfaces

As we discussed in the previous sections, callback interfaces `javax.ejb.SessionBean`, and `javax.ejb.EntityBean` are not implemented by the session beans and entity beans respectively. The callback methods of these methods are not implemented by the session and entity beans. Any method may be made a callback method using the callback annotations such as `PostActivate`, `PrePassivate`, `PreDestroy`, and `PostConstruct`. The callback methods may be specified in a callback listener class instead of the bean class.

Summary

In this chapter, we discussed the new features in EJB 3.0. We compared the EJB 3.0 features with EJB 2.0 features and discussed how EJB 3.0 is different from EJB 2.0. EJB 3.0 metadata annotations reduce the code required and make the deployment descriptors redundant. The local/remote and local home/home interfaces are not required in EJB 3.0 entity beans, and only a POJO class is required for an entity bean. The Java Persistence API provides an object-relational mapping model. Interceptors, simplified checked exceptions, and callback interfaces are some of the other new features in EJB 3.0.

In the next chapter, we shall convert an example EJB 2.x entity bean to an EJB 3.0 entity bean.

2
Converting an EJB 2.0 Entity to an EJB 3.0 Entity

The **Enterprise JavaBeans (EJB)** 3.0 specification has facilitated the development of EJBs by providing an annotations-based API in which the remote/local and home/ local home interfaces are not required. The deployment descriptors that form the basis of an EJB 2.0 entity bean are also not required for deploying an EJB 3.0 entity bean. In Chapter 1, we discussed the new features in EJB 3.0. This chapter covers the procedure to convert an EJB 2.0 Entity to an EJB 3.0 Entity.

The EJB 3.0 entity bean classes are simplified in comparison to the EJB 2.0 specification classes. The EJB 3.0 entity class is a **Plain Old Java Object (POJO)** instead of a class implementing the `EntityBean` interface. The component interfaces in EJB 2.0, which were required to extend the `EJBLocalObject`/`EJBObject` and home interfaces, which were required to extend the `EJBLocalHome`/`EJBHome` interfaces, are replaced with the `javax.persistence.EntityManager` API to create, find, and update entity bean instances.

Setting the environment

We shall be creating an EJB 3.0 entity by transforming the EJB 2.0 deployment descriptor (`ejb-jar.xml`) using XSL stylesheets. This chapter uses the built-in XSL transformation tool in Oracle JDeveloper 11*g* to provide the XSLT transformation for converting the EJB 2.0 entity deployment descriptor to the EJB 3.0 entity class. Download and install Oracle JDeveloper 11*g* from `http://www.oracle.com/ technology/software/products/middleware/index.html`.

Adding an Application

First, create a new application in JDeveloper. To do so, click on **New Application**, as shown next:

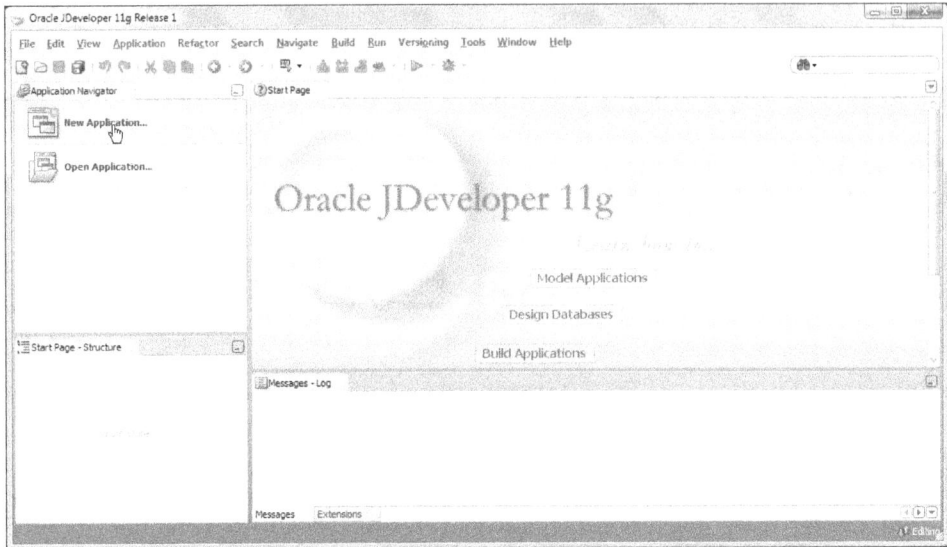

In the **New Application** wizard, specify an **Application Name** (for example EJB2toEJB3). Select **Application Template** as **Generic Application** and click on **Next**, as shown in the following screenshot:

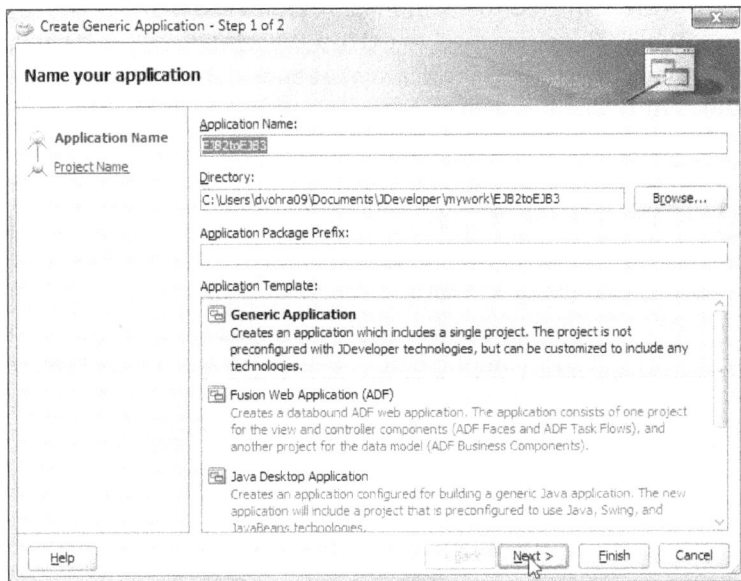

Next, specify a **Project Name** (EJB2toEJB3 for example). Select **XML** as a project technology and click on **Finish**.

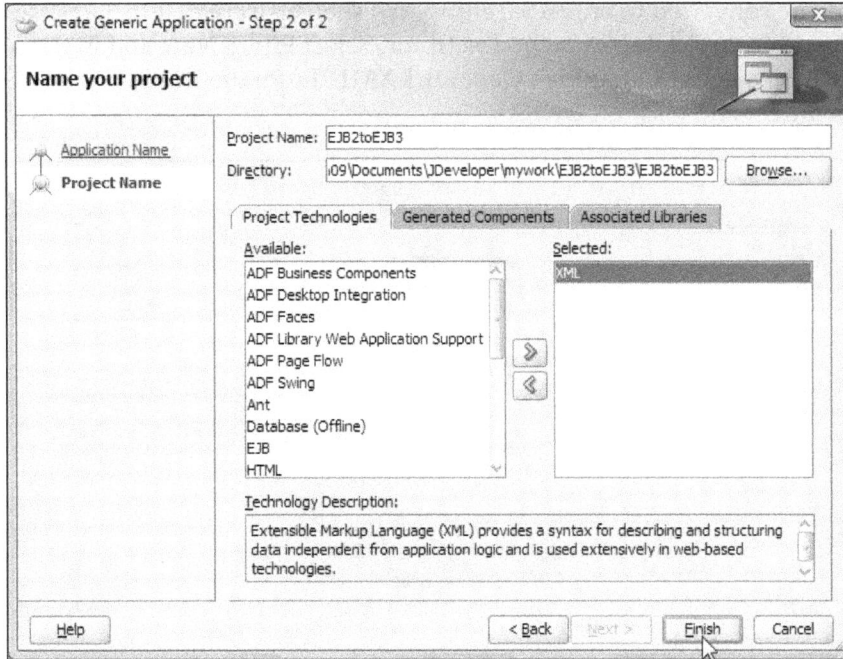

An application and a project get added to the **Application Navigator**, as shown next:

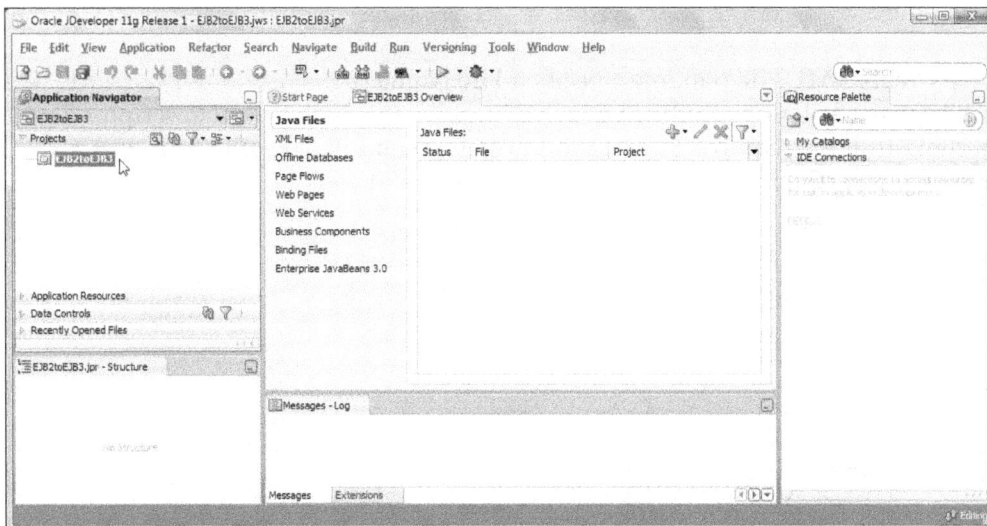

Creating an XML deployment descriptor

Next, we create an XML document for the EJB 2.0 entity deployment descriptor, which is to be converted to anEJB 3.0 entity. We shall also create EJB 3.0 Session bean façade classes from the deployment descriptor. Select **File | New** and in the **New Gallery** window select **Categories:General | XML**. From the **Items:** window, select **XML Document** and click on **OK**.

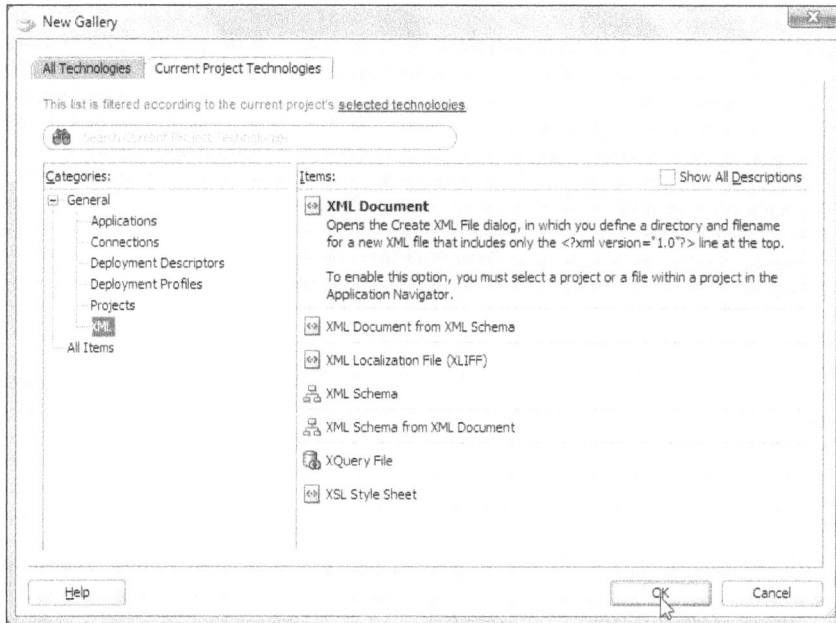

In the **Create XML File** window, specify a **File Name** (ejb-jar-modified.xml). We shall be using a slightly modified ejb-jar.xml, as the deployment descriptor does not contain all the required information to convert an EJB 2.0 entity to an EJB 3.0 entity. Click on **OK**.

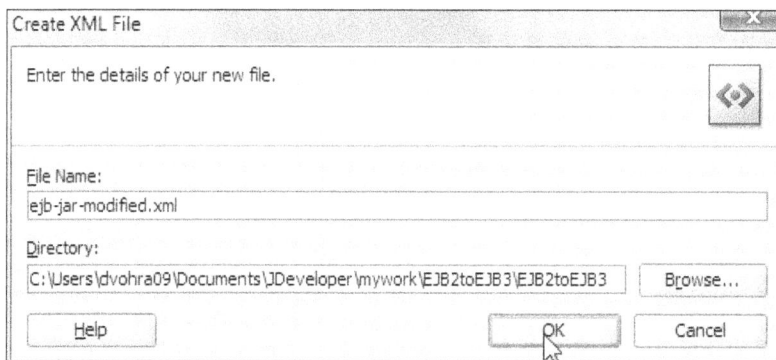

Creating stylesheets

We also need to create the XSL stylesheets to transform the EJB 2.0 entity deployment descriptor to EJB 3.0 entity class and façade classes. In the **New Gallery** window, select **Categories:General | XML** and **Items:XSL Style Sheet** and click on **OK**.

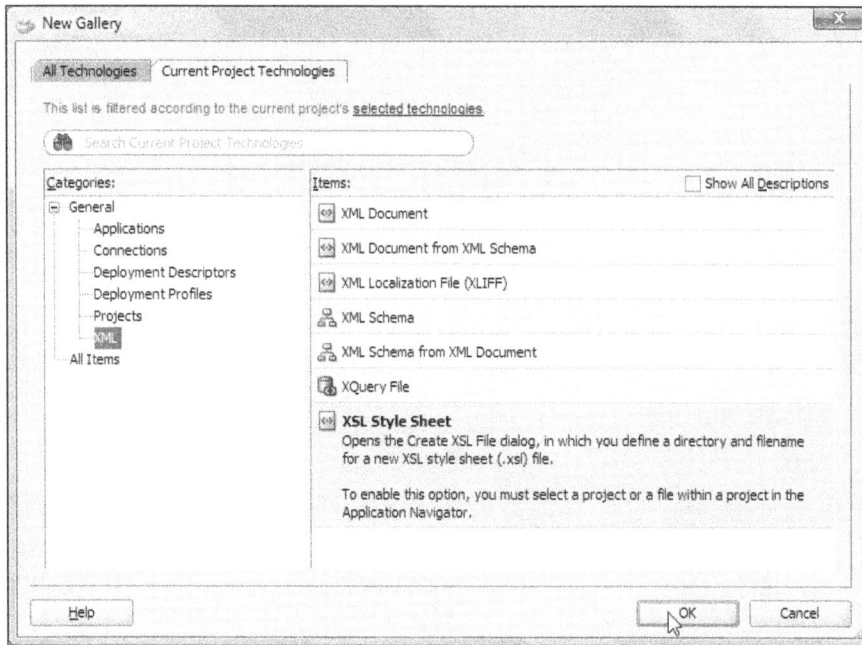

In the **Create XSL File** window specify an XSL **File Name** (entity-bean.xsl) and click on **OK**. The XSL version is set to **XSL 2.0** by default.

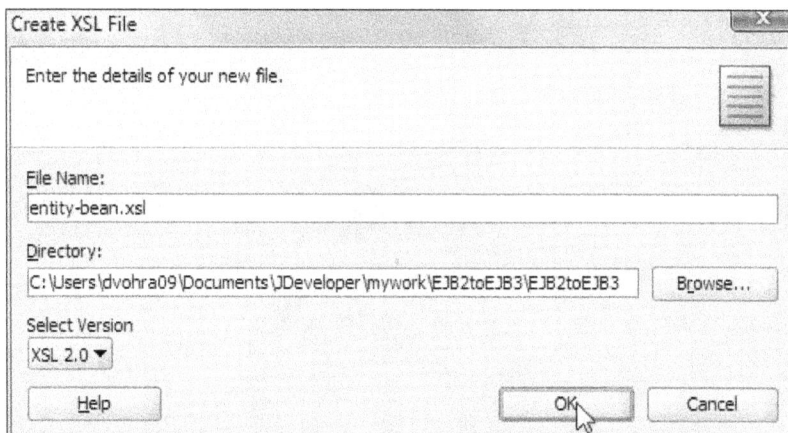

The XSL stylesheet `entity-bean.xsl` gets added to the `EJB2toEJB3` project. The following illustration shows the stylesheet copied from a later listing in this chapter.

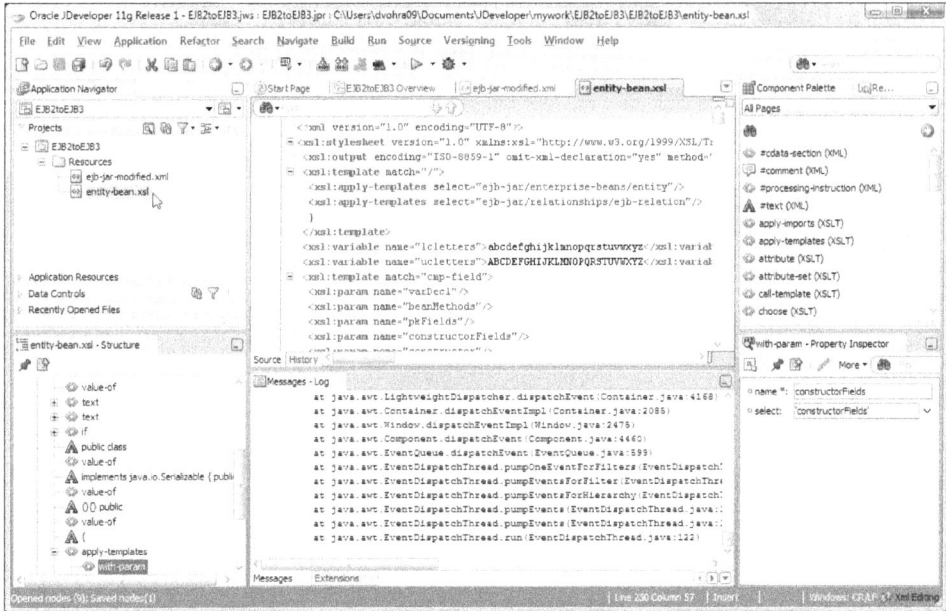

Similarly, add XSL stylesheets `façade.xsl` and `façade-bean.xsl` to generate EJB 3.0 façade classes with.

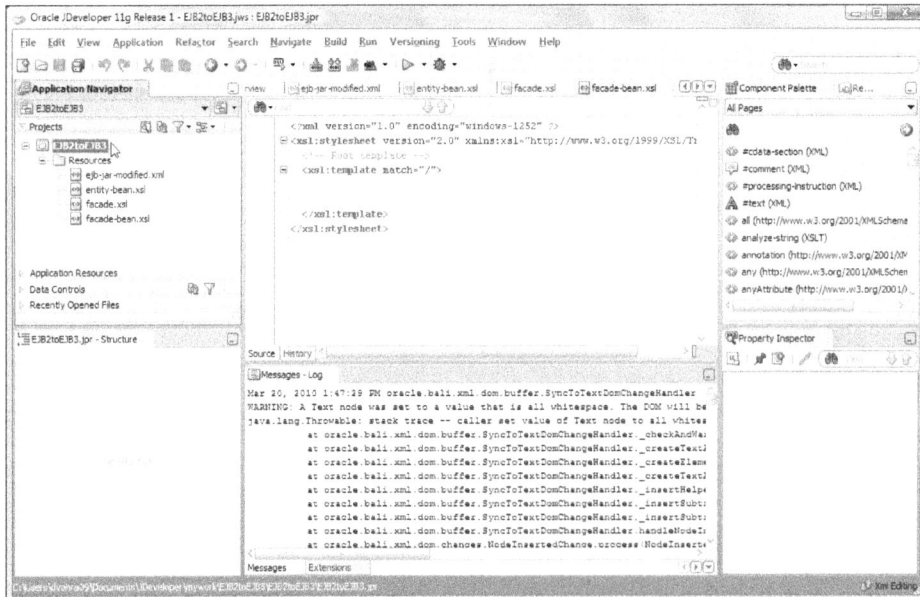

To test that the EJB 3.0 entity classes generated using XSL transformation comply with the EJB 3.0 API, add libraries EJB 3.0, Java EE 1.5, and Java EE 1.5 API to the project in the **Project Properties** window. First, select **Tools | Project Properties**. Subsequently, add the required libraries with the **Add Library** button. These libraries are pre-configured in JDeveloper and only need to be selected and added. Click on **OK**.

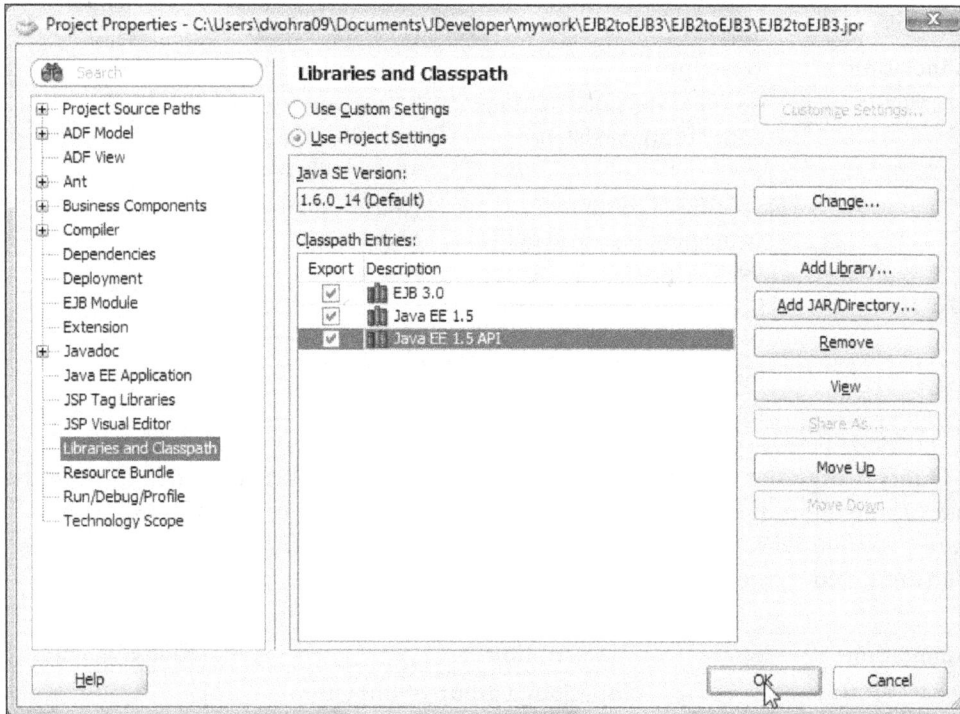

Converting the entity class

The EJB 3.0 entity class is a non-abstract POJO class with implementations for the getter/setter methods, in comparison to the EJB 2.0 entity bean class, which is abstract with abstract getter/setter methods. EJB 3.0 does not require component and home interfaces. The entity bean class may implement a business interface, though is not required to.

In the EJB 3.0 specification, the `EntityManager` class is used to create, find, and update an entity bean instance. In EJB 3.0, deployment descriptors are not required and are replaced with metadata annotations. When deployment descriptors are supplied, their values override annotations. An entity bean is specified with the `@Entity` annotation. The table name, column name, and primary key column properties are specified with the metadata annotations listed in the following table:

Annotation	Description	Annotation Elements
`@Table`	Specifies the table used for entity bean persistence.	Name (if the name element is not specified, the EJB class name is used as the table name).
`@Column`	Specifies a column corresponding to an entity bean property.	Name, nullable, length, updatable, and unique.
`@Id`	Specifies a primary key column property.	
`@Transient`	Specifies a property that is not persistent.	

EJB **Query Language (QL)** queries in the EJB 2.0 specification are specified with the `<query/>` element in the `ejb-jar.xml` deployment descriptor. EJB QL queries in EJB 3.0 are specified with the metadata annotations `@NamedQuery` and `@NamedQueries`, which are listed in the following table:

Annotation	Description	Annotation Elements
`@NamedQueries`	Specifies a group of EJB QL queries	
`@NamedQuery`	Specifies an EJB QL query	`name="query name"` `query="SQL query"`

The entity bean container-managed relationship (CMR) relationships in EJB 2.0 are specified with the `<ejb-relation/>` elements in the `ejb-jar.xml` deployment descriptor, and the entity bean CMR relationships in EJB 3.0 are specified in the bean class. The metadata annotations used to specify the entity bean CMR relationships are listed in the following table:

Annotation	Description
`@OneToMany`	One-to-many entity bean CMR relationship.
`@OneToOne`	One-to-one entity bean CMR relationship.
`@ManyToOne`	Many-to-one entity bean CMR relationship.
`@ManyToMany`	Many-to-many entity bean CMR relationship.

The EJB 2.0 entity

The EJB 2.0 entity class being migrated to EJB 3.0 in this chapter is as shown next:

```java
import javax.ejb.*;
abstract public class CatalogBean implements EntityBean {
  private EntityContext ctx;
  public CatalogBean() {
  };
  public void setEntityContext(EntityContext ctx) {
    this.ctx = ctx;
  }
  public void unsetEntityContext() {
    this.ctx = null;
  }
  abstract public String getCatalogId();
  abstract public void setCatalogId(String catalogId);
  abstract public String getJournal();
  abstract public void setJournal(java.lang.String journal);
  abstract public String getPublisher();
  abstract public void setPublisher(String publisher);
  public void ejbActivate() {
  }
  public void ejbPassivate() {
  }
  public void ejbLoad() {
  }
  public void ejbStore() {
  }
  public void ejbRemove() throws RemoveException {
  }
  public String ejbCreate(String catalogId, String journal,
                          String publisher)
    throws CreateException {
      setCatalogId(catalogId);
      setJournal(journal);
      setPublisher(publisher);

      return null;
  }

  public void ejbPostCreate(String catalogId, String journal,
                            String publisher) {

  }
}
```

The chapter is about converting an EJB 2 entity to EJB 3.0. We are not migrating, which would have involved taking sections of the EJB 2 entity and creating the corresponding EJB 3 entity. We are converting using an XSLT transformation and we need to modify slightly the starting deployment descriptor `ejb-jar.xml`. The EJB 2.0 entity `ejb-jar.xml` deployment descriptor does not include enough information to generate an EJB 3.0 entity from. Modify the `ejb-jar.xml` deployment descriptor for the example entity to include elements for the table name, field type, and EJB QL query collection type for multi-entity return values. Add the `<table-name/>`, `<field-type/>`, and `<collection-type/>` elements to `ejb-jar.xml`. The modified `ejb-jar.xml` deployment descriptor for the example entity bean is as follows:

```
<?xml version="1.0"?>
<!DOCTYPE ejb-jar PUBLIC
        "-//Sun Microsystems, Inc.//DTD Enterprise JavaBeans 2.0//EN"
        "http://java.sun.com/dtd/ejb-jar_2_0.dtd">
<ejb-jar>
  <enterprise-beans>
    <entity>
      <table-name>Catalog</table-name>
      <ejb-name>Catalog</ejb-name>
      <local-home>CatalogHome</local-home>
      <local>Catalog</local>
      <ejb-class>CatalogBean</ejb-class>
      <persistence-type>Container</persistence-type>
      <prim-key-class>CatalogPK</prim-key-class>
      <reentrant>False</reentrant>
      <cmp-version>2.x</cmp-version>
      <abstract-schema-name>CatalogBean</abstract-schema-name>
      <cmp-field>
        <field-name>catalogId</field-name>
        <field-type>String</field-type>
      </cmp-field>
      <cmp-field>
        <field-name>journal</field-name>
        <field-type>String</field-type>
      </cmp-field>
      <cmp-field>
        <field-name>publisher</field-name>
        <field-type>String</field-type>
      </cmp-field>
      <primkey-field>catalogId</primkey-field>
      <query>
        <query-method>
```

```
        <method-name>findByCatalogId</method-name>
        <method-params>
          <method-param>java.lang.String</method-param>
        </method-params>
      </query-method>
      <ejb-ql>
      <![CDATA[SELECT OBJECT(a) FROM CatalogBean AS a WHERE
                                            a.catalogId = ?1
      </ejb-ql>

    </query>
    <query>
      <query-method>
        <method-name>findByJournal</method-name>
        <method-params>
          <method-param>java.lang.String</method-param>
        </method-params>
      </query-method>
      <ejb-ql>
        <![CDATA[SELECT OBJECT(a) FROM CatalogBean AS a WHERE
                                            a.journal= ?1
      </ejb-ql>
      <collection-type>java.util.Collection</collection-type>
    </query>
  </entity>
 </enterprise-beans>
</ejb-jar>
```

Copy the modified deployment descriptor to the `ejb-jar-modified.xml` file in JDeveloper.

The XSLT stylesheet

Next, convert the modified `ejb-jar.xml` to an EJB 3.0 entity bean with an XSLT stylesheet. The EJB 3.0 entity bean class is generated using the built-in XSLT transformation tool in JDeveloper. The XSLT stylesheet `entity-bean.xsl` used to generate the EJB 3.0 entity is listed next:

```
<?xml version="1.0" encoding="UTF-8"?>
<xsl:stylesheet version="1.0"
  xmlns:xsl="http://www.w3.org/1999/XSL/Transform">
  <xsl:output encoding="ISO-8859-1" omit-xml-declaration="yes"
    method="text" />
  <xsl:template match="/">
```

```xsl
    <xsl:apply-templates select="ejb-jar/enterprise-beans/entity" />
    <xsl:apply-templates select="ejb-jar/relationships/ejb-relation"
    />
}
</xsl:template>
<xsl:variable name="lcletters">
  abcdefghijklmnopqrstuvwxyz
</xsl:variable>
<xsl:variable name="ucletters">
  ABCDEFGHIJKLMNOPQRSTUVWXYZ
</xsl:variable>
<xsl:template match="cmp-field">
  <xsl:param name="varDecl" />
  <xsl:param name="beanMethods" />
  <xsl:param name="pkFields" />
  <xsl:param name="constructorFields" />
  <xsl:param name="constructor" />
  <xsl:param name="constructorPK" />
  <xsl:param name="primKeyField" />
  <xsl:param name="fieldName" select="field-name" />
```

Create a constructor with primary key field as parameter:

```xsl
<xsl:if test="$constructor='constructor'">
  <xsl:if test="$primKeyField=$fieldName">
    this.
    <xsl:value-of
      select="translate((substring(field-name,
                                    1,1)),$ucletters,$lcletters)" />
    <xsl:value-of select="substring(field-name,2)" />
    =
    <xsl:value-of
      select="translate((substring(field-name, 1,1)),
                        $ucletters,$lcletters)" />
    <xsl:value-of select="substring(field-name,2)" />
      ;
  </xsl:if>
</xsl:if>
<xsl:if test="$varDecl='varDecl'">
  private
  <xsl:value-of select="field-type" />
  <xsl:text> </xsl:text>
  <xsl:value-of select="field-name" />
  ;
  <xsl:text disable-output-escaping="yes">
```

```
    </xsl:text>
  </xsl:if>
  <xsl:if test="$constructorFields='constructorFields'">
    <xsl:if test="$primKeyField=$fieldName">
      <xsl:value-of select="field-type" />
      <xsl:text> </xsl:text>
      <xsl:value-of
        select="translate((substring(field-name, 1,1)),
                          $ucletters,$lcletters)" />
      <xsl:value-of select="substring(field-name,2)" />
    </xsl:if>
  </xsl:if>
```

Create getter and setter methods for the primary key field:

```
  <xsl:if test="$beanMethods='beanMethods'">
    <xsl:if test="$primKeyField=$fieldName">
      <xsl:text disable-output-escaping="yes">@Id</xsl:text>
      <xsl:text disable-output-escaping="yes">
      </xsl:text>
      <xsl:text disable-output-escaping="yes">@Column(name="</xsl:text>
      <xsl:value-of
        select="translate((substring(field-name, 1)),
                          $lcletters,$ucletters)" />
      <xsl:text disable-output-escaping="yes">", unique=true)</xsl:text>
    </xsl:if>
    public
    <xsl:value-of select="field-type" />
    get
    <xsl:value-of
      select="translate((substring(field-name, 1,1)),
                        $lcletters,$ucletters)" />
    <xsl:value-of select="substring(field-name,2)" />
    () {return
    <xsl:value-of
      select="translate((substring(field-name, 1,1)),
                        $ucletters,$lcletters)" />
    <xsl:value-of select="substring(field-name,2)" />
    ;}
    <xsl:text>    </xsl:text>
    public void set
    <xsl:value-of
      select="translate((substring(field-name, 1,1)),
                        $lcletters,$ucletters)" />
    <xsl:value-of select="substring(field-name,2)" />
```

```
        (
        <xsl:value-of select="field-type" />
        <xsl:text> </xsl:text>
        <xsl:value-of
          select="translate((substring(field-name, 1,1)),
                              $ucletters,$lcletters)" />
        <xsl:value-of select="substring(field-name,2)" />
        ){this.
        <xsl:value-of
            select="translate((substring(field-name, 1,1)),
                                $ucletters,$lcletters)" />
        <xsl:value-of select="substring(field-name,2)" />
        =
        <xsl:value-of
          select="translate((substring(field-name, 1,1)),
                              $ucletters,$lcletters)" />
        <xsl:value-of select="substring(field-name,2)" />
        ;}
        </xsl:if>
    </xsl:template>
```

Create getter and setter methods for entity relationships:

```
    <xsl:template match="ejb-relation">
      <xsl:variable name="src1"
        select="ejb-relationship-role[position()=1]/
                                      relationship-role-source/ejb-
    name" />
      <xsl:variable name="src2"
        select="ejb-relationship-role[position()=2]/
                                      relationship-role-source/ejb-
    name" />
      <xsl:variable name="multiplicity1"
        select="ejb-relationship-role[position()=1]/multiplicity" />
      <xsl:variable name="multiplicity2"
        select="ejb-relationship-role[position()=2]/multiplicity" />
      <xsl:variable name="cmr1"
        select="ejb-relationship-role[position()=1]/cmr-field/cmr-field-
    name" />
      <xsl:variable name="cmrType1"
        select="ejb-relationship-role[position()=1]/cmr-field/cmr-field-
    type" />
      <xsl:variable name="cmr2"
        select="ejb-relationship-role[position()=2]/cmr-field/cmr-field-
    name" />
```

```
<xsl:if test="$multiplicity2='Many'">
  private
  <xsl:value-of select="$cmrType1" />
  <xsl:text disable-output-escaping="yes">&lt;</xsl:text>
  <xsl:value-of select="$src2" />
  <xsl:text disable-output-escaping="yes">&gt; </xsl:text>
  <xsl:value-of select="$cmr1"/>
  ;
</xsl:if>
<xsl:if test="$multiplicity2='One'">
  private
  <xsl:value-of select="$src2"/>
  <xsl:text> </xsl:text>
  <xsl:value-of select="$cmr1"/>
  ;
</xsl:if>
<xsl:if test="$multiplicity1='One' and $multiplicity2='Many'">
  <xsl:text disable-output-escaping="yes">@OneToMany</xsl:text>
  <xsl:text>   </xsl:text>
  public
  <xsl:value-of select="$cmrType1"/>
  <xsl:text disable-output-escaping="yes">&lt;</xsl:text>
  <xsl:value-of select="$src2"/>
  <xsl:text disable-output-escaping="yes">&gt; </xsl:text>
  get
  <xsl:value-of select="translate((substring($cmr1, 1, 1)),
                                  $lcletters,$ucletters)"/>
  <xsl:value-of select="substring($cmr1,2)"/>
  (){return
  <xsl:value-of select="$cmr1"/>
  ;} public void set
  <xsl:value-of select="translate((substring($cmr1, 1, 1)),
                                  $lcletters,$ucletters)"/>
  <xsl:value-of select="substring($cmr1,2)"/>
  (
  <xsl:value-of select="$cmrType1"/>
  <xsl:text disable-output-escaping="yes">&lt;</xsl:text>
  <xsl:value-of select="$src2"/>
  <xsl:text disable-output-escaping="yes">&gt; </xsl:text>
  <xsl:text>  </xsl:text>
  <xsl:value-of select="$cmr1"/>
  ){ this.
  <xsl:value-of select="$cmr1"/>
  =
```

```
        <xsl:value-of select="$cmr1"/>
        ; }
    </xsl:if>
    <xsl:if test="$multiplicity1='One' and $multiplicity2='One'">
        <xsl:text disable-output-escaping="yes">@OneToOne</xsl:text>
        <xsl:text>   </xsl:text>
        public
        <xsl:text disable-output-escaping="yes">&lt;</xsl:text>
        <xsl:value-of select="$src2"/>
        <xsl:text disable-output-escaping="yes">&gt; </xsl:text>
        get
        <xsl:value-of select="translate((substring($cmr1, 1, 1)),
                                        $lcletters,$ucletters)"/>
        <xsl:value-of select="substring($cmr1,2)"/>
        (){return
        <xsl:value-of select="$cmr1"/>
        ;} public void set
        <xsl:value-of select="translate((substring($cmr1, 1, 1)),
                                        $lcletters,$ucletters)"/>
        <xsl:value-of select="substring($cmr1,2)"/>
        (
        <xsl:value-of select="$src2"/>
        <xsl:text>   </xsl:text>
        <xsl:value-of select="$cmr1"/>
        ){ this.
        <xsl:value-of select="$cmr1"/>
        =
        <xsl:value-of select="$cmr1"/>
        ; }
    </xsl:if>
    <xsl:if test="$multiplicity1='Many' and $multiplicity2='One'">
        <xsl:text disable-output-escaping="yes">@ManyToOne</xsl:text>
        <xsl:text>   </xsl:text>
        public
        <xsl:value-of select="$src2"/>
        get
        <xsl:value-of select="translate((substring($cmr1, 1, 1)),
                                        $lcletters,$ucletters)"/>
        <xsl:value-of select="substring($cmr1,2)"/>
        (){return
        <xsl:value-of select="$cmr1"/>
        ;} public void set
        <xsl:value-of select="translate((substring($cmr1, 1, 1)),
                                        $lcletters,$ucletters)"/>
```

```
      <xsl:value-of select="substring($cmr1,2)"/>
      (
      <xsl:value-of select="$src2"/>
      <xsl:text> </xsl:text>
      <xsl:value-of select="$cmr1"/>
      ){ this.
      <xsl:value-of select="$cmr1"/>
      =
      <xsl:value-of select="$cmr1"/>
      ; }
  </xsl:if>
  <xsl:if test="$multiplicity1='Many' and $multiplicity2='Many'">
      <xsl:text disable-output-escaping="yes">@ManyToMany</xsl:text>
      <xsl:text>    </xsl:text>
      public
      <xsl:value-of select="$cmrType1"/>
      <xsl:text disable-output-escaping="yes">&lt;</xsl:text>
      <xsl:value-of select="$src2"/>
      <xsl:text disable-output-escaping="yes">&gt; </xsl:text>
      get
      <xsl:value-of select="translate((substring($cmr1, 1, 1)),
                                      $lcletters,$ucletters)"/>
      <xsl:value-of select="substring($cmr1,2)"/>
      (){return
      <xsl:value-of select="$cmr1"/>
      ;} public void set
      <xsl:value-of select="translate((substring($cmr1, 1, 1)),
                                      $lcletters,$ucletters)"/>
      <xsl:value-of select="substring($cmr1,2)"/>
      (
      <xsl:value-of select="$cmrType1"/>
      <xsl:text disable-output-escaping="yes">&lt;</xsl:text>
      <xsl:value-of select="$src2"/>
      <xsl:text disable-output-escaping="yes">&gt; </xsl:text>
      <xsl:text> </xsl:text>
      <xsl:value-of select="$cmr1"/>
      ){ this.
      <xsl:value-of select="$cmr1"/>
      =
      <xsl:value-of select="$cmr1"/>
      ; }
  </xsl:if>
</xsl:template>
```

Add `import` statements:

```
<xsl:template match="entity">
  import javax.persistence.Entity; import javax.persistence.Id; import
  javax.persistence.Column; import javax.persistence.NamedQueries;
import
  javax.persistence.NamedQuery;
  import javax.persistence.OneToMany; import javax.persistence.
OneToOne; import
  javax.persistence.ManyToOne; import javax.persistence.ManyToMany;
import
  javax.persistence.Table;
```

Add annotations for the entity and entity table:

```
<xsl:text disable-output-escaping="yes">@Entity</xsl:text>
  <xsl:text disable-output-escaping="yes">
</xsl:text>
  <xsl:text disable-output-escaping="yes">@Table(name="</xsl:text>
  <xsl:value-of select="table-name"/>
  <xsl:text disable-output-escaping="yes">")</xsl:text>

  <xsl:text disable-output-escaping="yes">
</xsl:text>
```

Add annotation for named queries:

```
 <xsl:if test="query">
   <xsl:text disable-output-escaping="yes">@NamedQueries({</xsl:text>
   <xsl:apply-templates select="query"/>
   <xsl:text disable-output-escaping="yes">})</xsl:text>
 </xsl:if>
```

Add a class declaration and class constructor:

```
  public class
  <xsl:value-of select="ejb-class"/>
  implements java.io.Serializable { public
  <xsl:value-of select="ejb-class"/>
  (){} public
  <xsl:value-of select="ejb-class"/>
  (
    <xsl:apply-templates select="cmp-field">
      <xsl:with-param name="constructorFields"
select="'constructorFields'"/>
      <xsl:with-param name="primKeyField" select="primkey-field"/>
    </xsl:apply-templates>
```

```
){
    <xsl:apply-templates select="cmp-field">
      <xsl:with-param name="constructor" select="'constructor'"/>
      <xsl:with-param name="primKeyField" select="primkey-field"/>
    </xsl:apply-templates>
  }
  <xsl:apply-templates select="cmp-field">
    <xsl:with-param name="varDecl" select="'varDecl'"/>
  </xsl:apply-templates>
  <xsl:text disable-output-escaping="yes">
  </xsl:text>
  <xsl:apply-templates select="cmp-field">
    <xsl:with-param name="beanMethods" select="'beanMethods'"/>
    <xsl:with-param name="primKeyField" select="primkey-field"/>
  </xsl:apply-templates>
</xsl:template>
```

Add named queries:

```
<xsl:template match="query">
  <xsl:text disable-output-escaping="yes">@NamedQuery(name="</
xsl:text>
  <xsl:value-of select="translate((substring(query-method/method-name,

1,1)),$lcletters,$ucletters)"/>
  <xsl:value-of select="substring(query-method/method-name,2)"/>
  <xsl:text disable-output-escaping="yes">",query="</xsl:text>
  <xsl:value-of select="ejb-ql"/>
  <xsl:text disable-output-escaping="yes">")</xsl:text>
  <xsl:if test="position() != last()">,</xsl:if>
  <xsl:text disable-output-escaping="yes">
  </xsl:text>
  </xsl:template>
</xsl:stylesheet>
```

Copy the stylesheet to the `entity-bean.xsl` file in JDeveloper.

Generating the EJB 3.0 entity

To transform the modified deployment descriptor (`ejb-jar-modified.xml`) to an EJB 3.0 entity bean class, right-click on `entity-bean.xsl` and select **Run**.

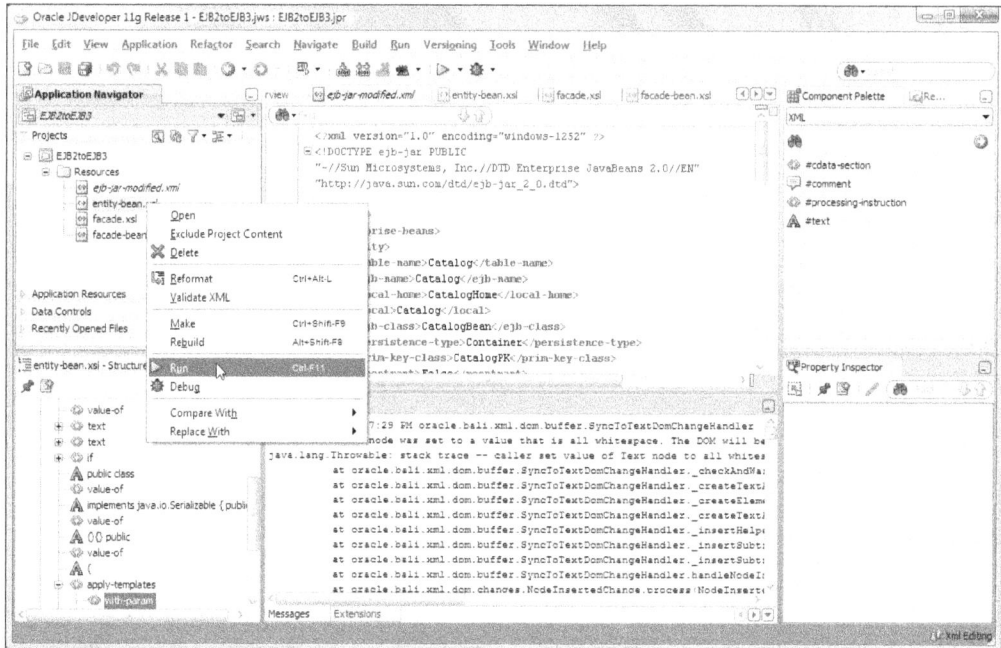

In the **XSLT Settings** window select **Input XML File** as `ejb-jar-modified.xml` and specify **Output File** as `CatalogBean.java`. Click on **OK**.

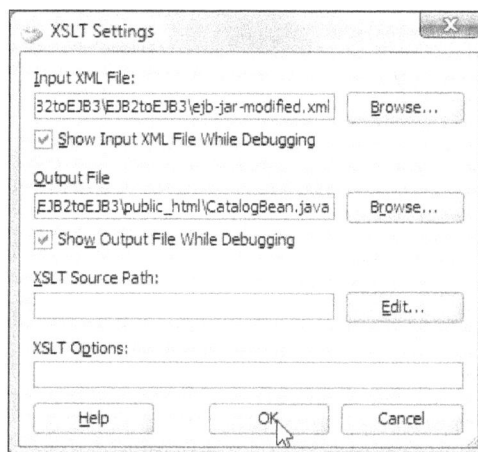

The **XSLT Settings** wizard is displayed only the first time an XSLT stylesheet is run. For subsequent runs of the stylesheet or running other stylesheets, the input XML document and the output file are required to be configured in the **Project Properties** window. Select **Run/Debug/Profile** in **Project Properties**, select the **Run Configuration | Default,** and click on **Edit**.

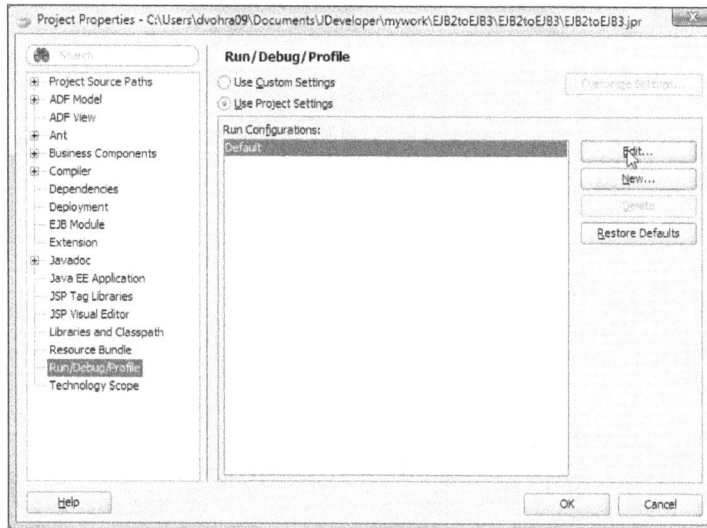

In the **Edit Run Configuration** window, select **Launch Settings | XSLT**. Specify the **Input XML File** and the **Output File** and click on **OK**.

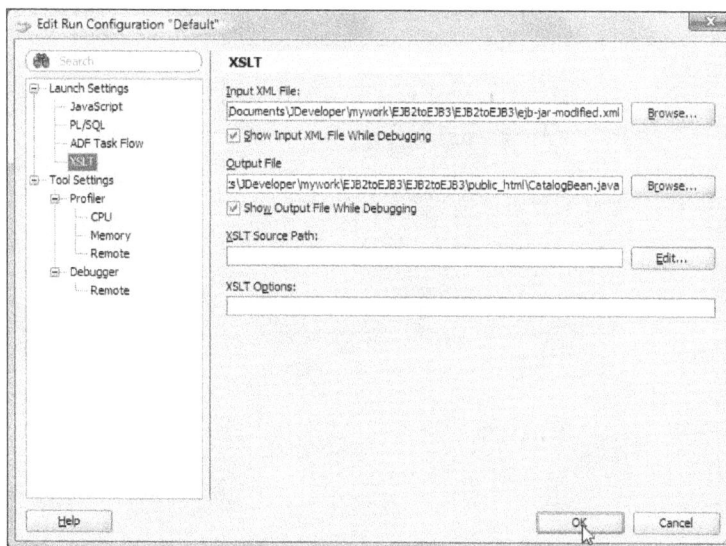

Using either method to set the input XML file and the output file, generate the output file `CatalogBean.java`. Add the output file to the project with **View | Refresh**. Alternatively, import the generated file with **File | Import**. In the **Import** window, select **Java Source** and click on **OK**.

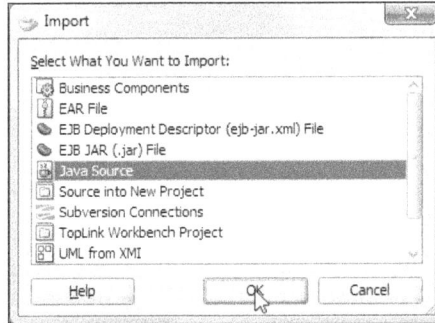

In **Choose Directory,** select the `public_html` directory. In the **Java Source** window, the Java source file and the to directory gets specified. Click on **OK**.

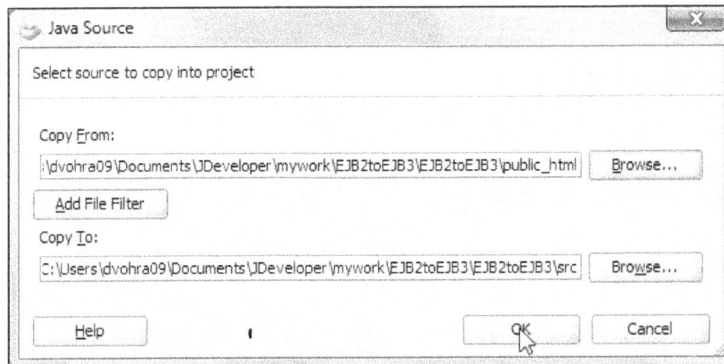

The `CatalogBean.java` gets added to the project:

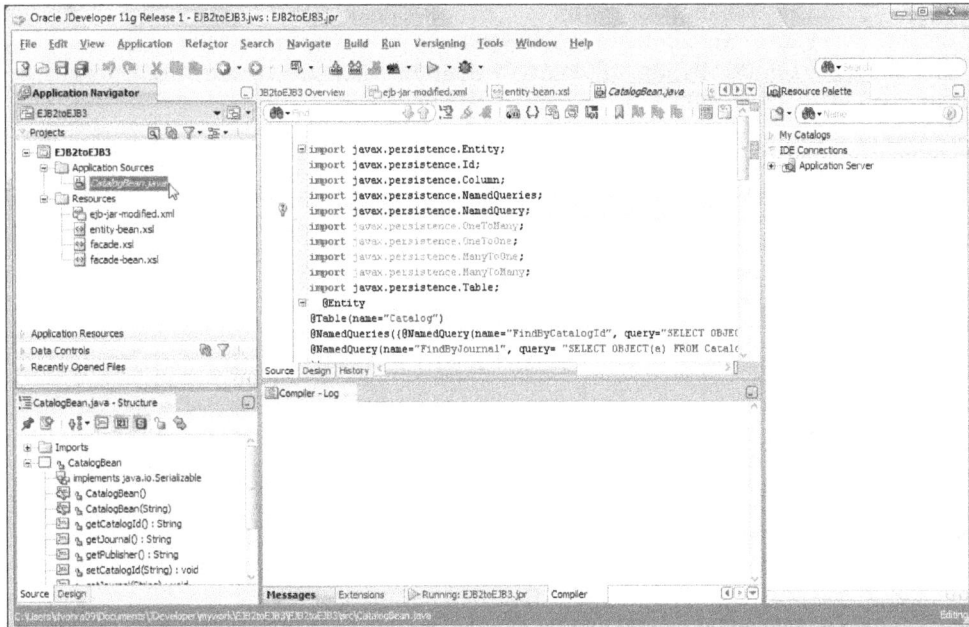

The EJB 3.0 entity bean generated from the EJB 2.0 entity bean is listed below. First, the import statements are specified.

```
import javax.persistence.Entity;
import javax.persistence.Id;
import javax.persistence.Column;
import javax.persistence.NamedQueries;
import javax.persistence.NamedQuery;
import javax.persistence.OneToMany;
import javax.persistence.OneToOne;
import javax.persistence.ManyToOne;
import javax.persistence.ManyToMany;
import javax.persistence.Table;
```

The @Entity annotation specifies the class to be an entity class. And, the @Table annotation specifies the table name.

```
@Entity
@Table(name="Catalog")
```

The named queries are grouped with the @NamedQueries annotation and each named query is specified with the @NamedQuery annotation. The name attribute specifies the named query name that may be used with EntityManager when creating query objects. The query attribute specifies the query string in the Java Persistence query language.

```
@NamedQueries({@NamedQuery(name="FindByCatalogId", query="SELECT
OBJECT(a) FROM CatalogBean AS a WHERE a.catalogId = ?1"),
@NamedQuery(name="FindByJournal", query= "SELECT OBJECT(a) FROM
CatalogBean AS a WHERE a.journal= ?1 ")
})
```

The entity class declaration and the properties declarations are specified next.

```
public class
CatalogBean implements java.io.Serializable {
    public CatalogBean(){} public CatalogBean
(
String catalogId
){

  this.catalogId=catalogId;

}

 private String catalogId;

 private String journal;

 private String publisher;
```

The id property is specified with the @Id annotation and the column is specified with the @Column annotation. The getter/setter methods for the id property are also specified.

```
@Id
@Column(name="CATALOGID", unique=true)
    public String getCatalogId() {return catalogId;}

    public void setCatalogId(String catalogId){this.
catalogId=catalogId;}
```

The getter/setter methods for the entity properties are specified next.

```
public String getJournal() {return journal;}

public void setJournal
(
String journal
){this.journal=journal;}

public String getPublisher() {return publisher;}
```

```
        public void setPublisher(String publisher){
            this.publisher=publisher; }

    }
```

The XSL transformation generated entity class may require some reformatting or/ and debugging depending on the complexity of the initial EJB 2.0 entity. The EJB 3.0 entity generated in this chapter requires only slight reformatting. The EJB 3.0 entity class has the import statements for the `javax.persistence` package classes. The `@Entity` annotation specifies the class as an entity EJB class. The `@Table` annotation specifies the database table name for the entity EJB, the `@NamedQueries` annotation specifies the named queries, the `@Id` annotation specifies the identifier property/ primary key field, and the `@Column` annotation specifies the database column corresponding to the identifier property. The EJB 2.0-to-EJB 3.0 conversion XSLT also includes the conversion of entity bean CMR relationships.

Developing a session façade for an entity

In EJB 2.0, an entity bean is created with the `create` method in the `home/local` home interface and the entity bean fields are modified with the getter/setter methods in the `local/remote` interface. In EJB 3.0, an entity bean is created and modified with the `EntityManager` API. The `EntityManager` class provides methods for finding, persisting, and removing an entity bean instance. This section covers generation of a session bean that implements the `EntityManager` API.

In the session bean class, the `EntityManager` is obtained with the `@Resource` annotation:

```
    @Resource private EntityManager em;
```

Some of the commonly used methods of the `EntityManager` class are listed in the following table:

EntityManager Method	Description
persist(Object entity)	Saves an entity bean instance in the database. The persist method returns the entity bean that is persisted in the database.
find(String entityName, Object primaryKey)	Finds an entity bean instance with a primary key.
remove(Object entityBean)	Removes an entity bean from the database.
createQuery(String ejbQlString)	Creates an EJB QL query.
createNamedQuery(String queryName)	Creates a @NamedQuery query.

A stateless session bean class is annotated with the `@Stateless` annotation. In the session bean class, an entity bean is created with the `create()` method. For example, the `create()` method corresponding to the identifier property `catalogId` is as follows:

```
public void create(String catalogId)
    {   CatalogBean catalogBean = new CatalogBean(catalogId);
    em.persist(catalogBean);
    }
```

The `create()` method is a custom method as opposed to the `create()` method of the EJB 2.0 specification; the method naming in the session bean façade may be modified. The `persist()` method of the `EntityManager` class saves a new entity in the database. The `remove()` method of the `EntityManager` class is used to remove an entity:

```
public void remove(CatalogBean  catalogBean) {
    em.remove(catalogBean);
    }
```

The `find()` method of the `EntityManager` class is used to find an entity bean. In the session EJB, add finder methods for the named queries defined in the EJB bean class. The `createNamedQuery()` method is used to obtain a query object for a named query. For example, the finder method corresponding to the named query `FindByCatalogId`, which is defined in the entity class, is as follows:

```
public CatalogBean findByCatalogId(java.lang.String param1)
    {Query query=em.createNamedQuery("FindByCatalogId");
    query.setParameter(0, param1);
    return (CatalogBean)(query.getSingleResult());
    }
```

In the `findByCatalogId()` method, a `javax.persistence.Query` object is obtained from the named query `FindByCatalogId`. The parameter values are set on the query object. An entity EJB bean instance is obtained with the `getSingleResult()` method of the query object. The named query `FindByCatalogId` returns a single entity of the entity EJB bean. A named query may also return a collection of entities. For example, the named query `FindByJournal` returns a collection. The finder method corresponding to the `FindByJournal` named query is as follows.

```
public java.util.List<CatalogBean> findByJournal(java.lang.String
param1)
    {   Query query= em.createNamedQuery("FindByJournal");
    query.setParameter(0, param1);
```

```
    return query.getResultList();
}
```

In the `findByJournal()` method, a query object is obtained from the named query and a `java.util.List` of entity beans is obtained with the `getResultList()` method of the query object.

The XSLT stylesheet

The XSL stylesheet (`façade-bean.xsl`) used to generate the session bean façade class is listed below.

```
<?xml version="1.0" encoding="UTF-8"?>
<xsl:stylesheet version="1.0" xmlns:xsl="http://www.w3.org/1999/XSL/
Transform">
 <xsl:output encoding="ISO-8859-1" omit-xml-declaration="yes"
method="text"/>
 <xsl:template match="/">
  <xsl:apply-templates select="ejb-jar/enterprise-beans/entity"/>
 </xsl:template>
 <xsl:template match="package">
  package
  <xsl:value-of select="."/>;
 </xsl:template>
 <xsl:variable name="lcletters">abcdefghijklmnopqrstuvwxyz</
xsl:variable>
 <xsl:variable name="ucletters">ABCDEFGHIJKLMNOPQRSTUVWXYZ</
xsl:variable>
 <xsl:template match="entity">
```

Add the `import` statements:

```
    import javax.persistence.EntityManager; import javax.persistence.
Query; import
    javax.annotation.Resource; import javax.ejb.Stateless;
```

Add the annotation to specify a `Stateless` bean:

```
    <xsl:text disable-output-escaping="yes">@</xsl:text>
    Stateless
```

Add the session bean class declaration:

```
    <xsl:text> public class </xsl:text>
    <xsl:value-of select="ejb-name"/>
    FaçadeBean implements
    <xsl:value-of select="ejb-name"/>
```

```
        Façade{
```
Inject an `EntityManager` resource.

```
        <xsl:text disable-output-escaping="yes">@Resource
    </xsl:text>
        <xsl:text>private EntityManager em;</xsl:text>
```

The create() method is used to create and persist an entity instance.

```
        public void create(
        <xsl:apply-templates select="cmp-field">
         <xsl:with-param name="paramPK" select="'paramPK'"/>
         <xsl:with-param name="primKeyField" select="primkey-field"/>
        </xsl:apply-templates>
        ) {
        <xsl:value-of select="ejb-class"/>
        <xsl:text> </xsl:text>
        <xsl:value-of select="translate((substring(ejb-class,
    1,1)),$ucletters,$lcletters)"/>
        <xsl:value-of select="substring(ejb-class,2)"/>
        = new
        <xsl:value-of select="ejb-class"/>
        (
        <xsl:apply-templates select="cmp-field">
         <xsl:with-param name="pkField" select="'pkField'"/>
         <xsl:with-param name="primKeyField" select="primkey-field"/>
        </xsl:apply-templates>
        ); em.persist(
        <xsl:value-of select="translate((substring(ejb-class,
    1,1)),$ucletters,$lcletters)"/>
        <xsl:value-of select="substring(ejb-class,2)"/>
        ); }
```

The remove() method is used to remove an entity instance.

```
        public void remove(
          <xsl:value-of select="ejb-class"/>
          <xsl:text>   </xsl:text>
          <xsl:value-of select="translate((substring(ejb-class,
    1,1)),$ucletters,$lcletters)"/>
          <xsl:value-of select="substring(ejb-class,2)"/>
          ) { em.remove(
          <xsl:value-of select="translate((substring(ejb-class,
    1,1)),$ucletters,$lcletters)"/>
          <xsl:value-of select="substring(ejb-class,2)"/>
          ); }
```

```
    <xsl:apply-templates select="query"/>
    }
  </xsl:template>
```

Next, Create and use named query objects.

```
  <xsl:template match="query">
   <xsl:if test="collection-type">
    public java.util.List
    <xsl:text disable-output-escaping="yes">&lt;</xsl:text>
    <xsl:value-of select="../ejb-class"/>
    <xsl:text disable-output-escaping="yes">&gt;  </xsl:text>
    <xsl:value-of select="query-method/method-name"/>
    (
    <xsl:apply-templates select="query-method/method-params/method-
param">
      <xsl:with-param name="finderParam" select="'finderParam'"/>
    </xsl:apply-templates>
    ){ Query query= em.createNamedQuery
    <xsl:text disable-output-escaping="yes">("</xsl:text>
    <xsl:value-of select="translate((substring(query-method/method-
name, 1,1)),$lcletters,$ucletters)"/>
    <xsl:value-of select="substring(query-method/method-name,2)"/>
    <xsl:text disable-output-escaping="yes">")</xsl:text>
    ;
    <xsl:apply-templates select="query-method/method-params/method-
param">
      <xsl:with-param name="queryParam" select="'queryParam'"/>
    </xsl:apply-templates>
    return query.getResultList(); }
   </xsl:if>
   <xsl:if test="not(collection-type)">
    public
    <xsl:value-of select="../ejb-class"/>
    <xsl:text>  </xsl:text>
    <xsl:value-of select="query-method/method-name"/>
    (
    <xsl:apply-templates select="query-method/method-params/method-
param">
      <xsl:with-param name="finderParam" select="'finderParam'"/>
    </xsl:apply-templates>
    ) { Query query=em.createNamedQuery
    <xsl:text disable-output-escaping="yes">("</xsl:text>
    <xsl:value-of select="translate((substring(query-method/method-
name, 1,1)),$lcletters,$ucletters)"/>
```

```
    <xsl:value-of select="substring(query-method/method-name,2)"/>
    <xsl:text disable-output-escaping="yes">)</xsl:text>
    ;
    <xsl:apply-templates select="query-method/method-params/method-
param">
      <xsl:with-param name="queryParam" select="'queryParam'"/>
    </xsl:apply-templates>
    return (
    <xsl:value-of select="../ejb-class"/>
    )(query.getSingleResult()); }
  </xsl:if>
</xsl:template>
<xsl:template match="cmp-field">
 <xsl:param name="paramPK"/>
 <xsl:param name="pkField"/>
 <xsl:param name="primKeyField"/>
 <xsl:param name="fieldName" select="field-name"/>
 <xsl:if test="$paramPK='paramPK'">
  <xsl:if test="$primKeyField=$fieldName">
   <xsl:value-of select="field-type"/>
   <xsl:text>  </xsl:text>
   <xsl:value-of select="field-name"/>
  </xsl:if>
 </xsl:if>
 <xsl:if test="$pkField='pkField'">
  <xsl:if test="$primKeyField=$fieldName">
   <xsl:value-of select="field-name"/>
  </xsl:if>
 </xsl:if>
</xsl:template>
<xsl:template match="method-param">
 <xsl:param name="finderParam"/>
 <xsl:param name="queryParam"/>
 <xsl:if test="$finderParam='finderParam'">
  <xsl:value-of select="."/>
  <xsl:text> </xsl:text>
  param
  <xsl:value-of select="position()"/>
  <xsl:if test="position() != last()">,</xsl:if>
 </xsl:if>
 <xsl:if test="$queryParam='queryParam'">
  query.setParameter(
  <xsl:value-of select="position()-1"/>
   param
```

```
    <xsl:value-of select="position()"/>
    );
   </xsl:if>
  </xsl:template>
  <xsl:template match="text()">
   <value-of select="." disable-output-escaping="yes"/>
  </xsl:template>
 </xsl:stylesheet>
```

Generating the session Façade

Next, generate the EJB 3.0 session bean class that implements the `EntityManager` API with XSLT transformation. Set the input XML file and the output file in the Default Run Configuration as discussed earlier. Specify **Input XML File** as `ejb-jar-modified.xml` and **Output File** as `CatalogFaçadeBean.java`.

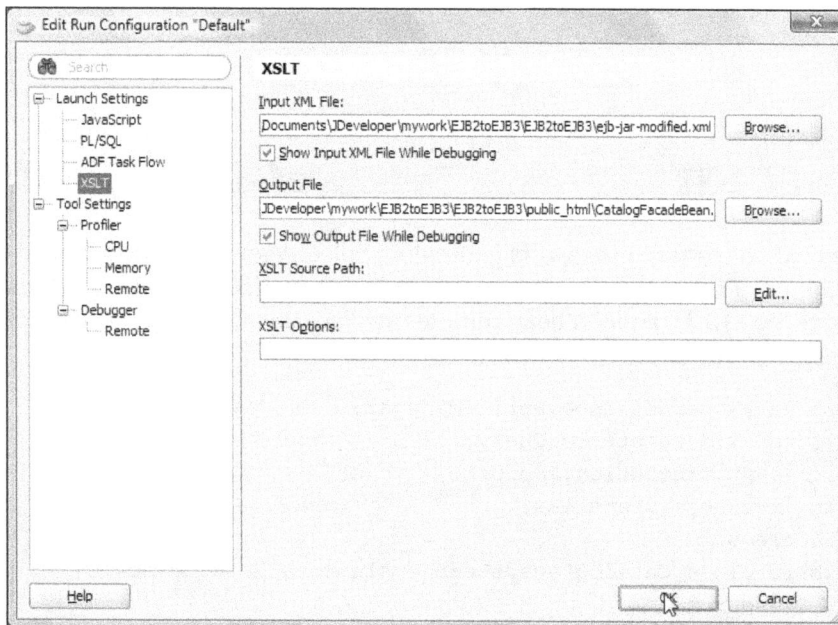

Right-click on `façade-bean.xsl` and select **Run**.

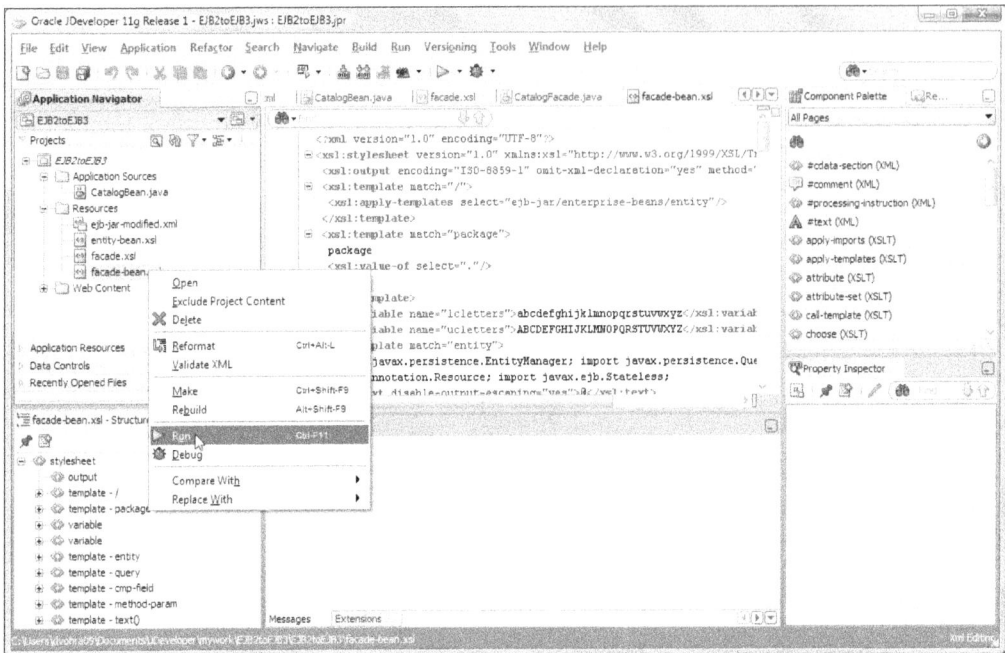

The `CatalogFaçadeBean.java` gets generated. Select **View | Refresh** to add the `CatalogFaçadeBean.java` class to the project. The EJB 3.0 session bean class implements the EJB 3.0 session bean remote interface `CatalogFaçade`. The session bean class generated is shown below:

```
import javax.persistence.EntityManager;
import javax.persistence.Query;
import javax.annotation.Resource;
import javax.ejb.Stateless;
  @Stateless
    public class CatalogFaçadeBean implements CatalogFaçade{
       @Resource
private EntityManager em;
          public void create(String  catalogId) {
                 CatalogBean catalogBean= new CatalogBean(catalogId);
                 em.persist(catalogBean); }
public void remove(CatalogBean  catalogBean) {
                 em.remove(catalogBean); }
public CatalogBean  findByCatalogId(java.lang.String param1) {
Query query=em.createNamedQuery("FindByCatalogId");
          query.setParameter(0, param1);
```

```
                return (CatalogBean)(query.getSingleResult()); }
    public java.util.List <CatalogBean> findByJournal
(java.lang.String param1){ Query query= em.createNamedQuery("FindByJo
urnal");
                    query.setParameter(0, param1 );
            return query.getResultList(); }
    }
```

We also need to generate an interface, `CatalogFaçade.java`, for the session bean class. The façade interface has the abstract method definitions for the methods implemented in the session bean façade. The XSLT stylesheet, `façade.xslt`, used to generate the session bean interface is listed next:

```
<?xml version="1.0" encoding="UTF-8"?>
<xsl:stylesheet version="1.0"
  xmlns:xsl="http://www.w3.org/1999/XSL/Transform">
  <xsl:output encoding="ISO-8859-1" omit-xml-declaration="yes"
    method="text" />
  <xsl:template match="/">
    <xsl:apply-templates select="ejb-jar/enterprise-beans/entity" />
  </xsl:template>
  <xsl:variable name="lcletters">
    abcdefghijklmnopqrstuvwxyz
  </xsl:variable>
  <xsl:variable name="ucletters">
    ABCDEFGHIJKLMNOPQRSTUVWXYZ
  </xsl:variable>
  <xsl:template match="entity">
    import javax.ejb.Remote;
    <xsl:text disable-output-escaping="yes">@</xsl:text>
      Remote
    <xsl:text> public interface </xsl:text>
    <xsl:value-of select="ejb-name" />
    Façade{ void create(
      <xsl:apply-templates select="cmp-field">
      <xsl:with-param name="paramPK" select="'paramPK'" />
      <xsl:with-param name="primKeyField" select="primkey-field" />
      </xsl:apply-templates>
    ); void remove(
      <xsl:value-of select="ejb-class" />
      <xsl:text>  </xsl:text>
      <xsl:value-of
        select="translate((substring(ejb-class,
                                     1,1)),$ucletters,$lcletters)" />
      <xsl:value-of select="substring(ejb-class,2)" />
```

```
        );
        <xsl:apply-templates select="query" />
        }
    </xsl:template>
    <xsl:template match="query">
      <xsl:if test="collection-type">
        java.util.List
        <xsl:text disable-output-escaping="yes">&lt;</xsl:text>
        <xsl:value-of select="../ejb-class" />
        <xsl:text disable-output-escaping="yes">&gt;  </xsl:text>
        <xsl:text>  </xsl:text>
        <xsl:value-of select="query-method/method-name"/>
        (
          <xsl:apply-templates select="query-method/method-params/
                                                            method-
param">
            <xsl:with-param name="finderParam" select="'finderParam'"/>
          </xsl:apply-templates>
        );
        <xsl:text disable-output-escaping="yes">
        </xsl:text>
      </xsl:if>
      <xsl:if test="not(collection-type)">
        <xsl:value-of select="../ejb-class"/>
        <xsl:text>  </xsl:text>
        <xsl:value-of select="query-method/method-name"/>
        (
          <xsl:apply-templates select="query-method/method-params/
                                                            method-
param">
            <xsl:with-param name="finderParam" select="'finderParam'"/>
          </xsl:apply-templates>
        );
        <xsl:text disable-output-escaping="yes">
        </xsl:text>
      </xsl:if>
    </xsl:template>
    <xsl:template match="cmp-field">
      <xsl:param name="primKeyField"/>
      <xsl:param name="fieldName" select="field-name"/>
      <xsl:param name="paramPK"/>
      <xsl:param name="pkField"/>
      <xsl:if test="$paramPK='paramPK'">
        <xsl:if test="$primKeyField=$fieldName">
```

```xml
              <xsl:value-of select="field-type"/>
              <xsl:text>  </xsl:text>
              <xsl:value-of select="field-name"/>
            </xsl:if>
          </xsl:if>
          <xsl:if test="$pkField='pkField'">
            <xsl:if test="$primKeyField=$fieldName">
              <xsl:value-of select="field-name"/>
            </xsl:if>
          </xsl:if>
        </xsl:template>
        <xsl:template match="method-param">
          <xsl:param name="finderParam"/>
          <xsl:param name="queryParam"/>
          <xsl:if test="$finderParam='finderParam'">
            <xsl:value-of select="."/>
            <xsl:text> </xsl:text>
            param
            <xsl:value-of select="position()"/>
            <xsl:if test="position() != last()">,</xsl:if>
          </xsl:if>
          <xsl:if test="$queryParam='queryParam'">
            query.setParameter(
              <xsl:value-of select="position()"/>
              , param
              <xsl:value-of select="position()"/>
            );
          </xsl:if>
        </xsl:template>
        <xsl:template match="text()">
          <value-of select="." disable-output-escaping="yes"/>
        </xsl:template>
</xsl:stylesheet>
```

Copy the façade.xsl to the EJB2toEJB3 project in JDeveloper. Set the **Input XML File** to ejb-jar-modified.xml and **Output File** to CatalogFacade.java in the **Default Run Configuration**.

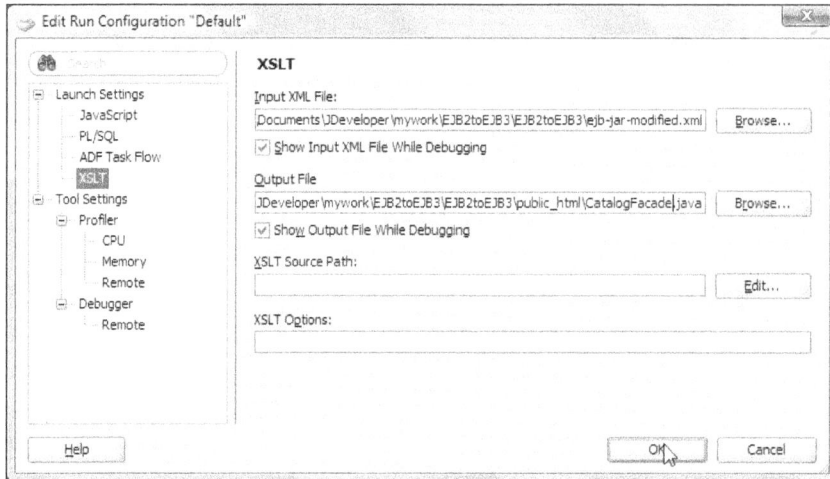

Right-click on façade.xsl and select **Run** to transform the modified EJB 2.0 deployment descriptor to an EJB 3.0 session bean façade interface.

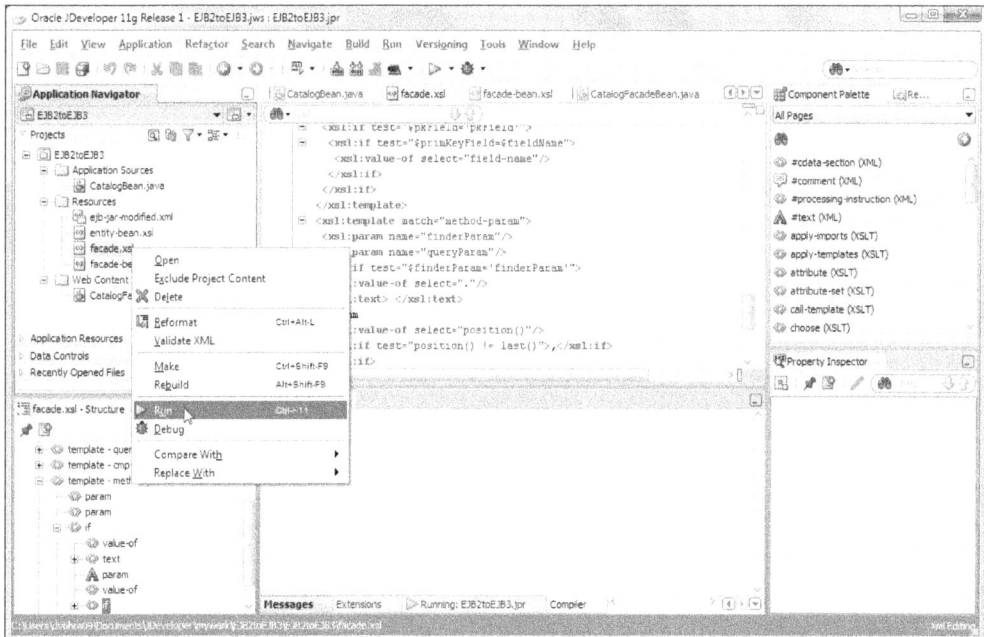

The session bean façade interface `CatalogFaçade.java` gets generated. The `@Remote` annotation specifies a remote interface. `CatalogFaçade.java` is listed next:

```
import javax.ejb.Remote;
@Remote
 public interface CatalogFaçade{
    void create(String  catalogId);
    void remove(CatalogBean  catalogBean);
    CatalogBean  findByCatalogId(java.lang.String param1 );
java.util.List <CatalogBean>    findByJournal(java.lang.String
param1);

 }
```

Select **View** | **Refresh** to add the session bean interface to the `EJB2toEJB3` conversion project. The session bean façade class and façade interface may require some reformatting.

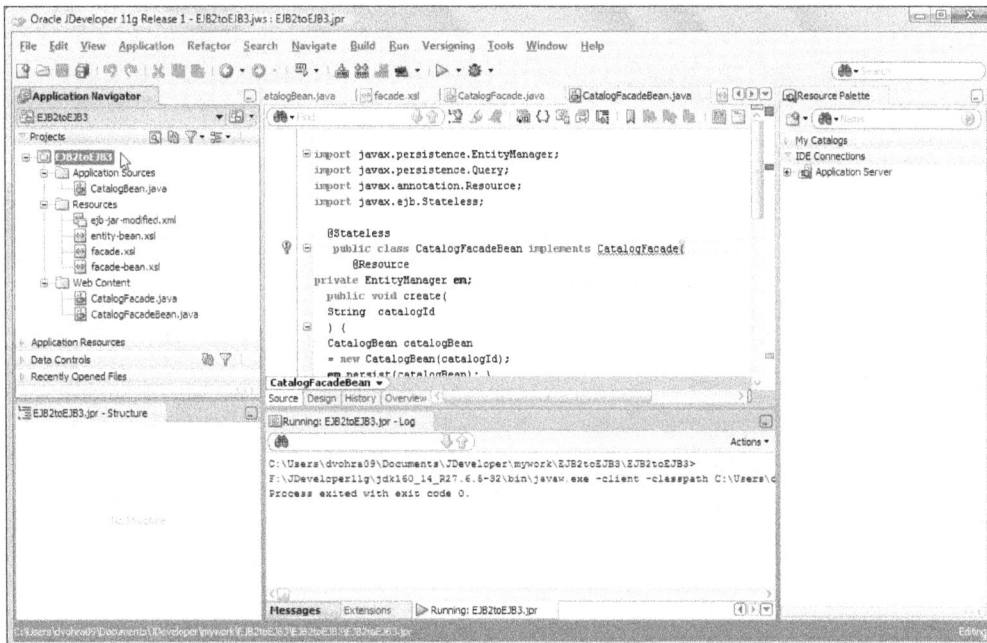

Summary

In this chapter, we converted an EJB 2.0 entity bean to an EJB 3.0 entity bean using XSLT transformation. We used the built-in JDeveloper XSLT transformation tool for the XSLT transformations. The XSL stylesheets may be modified to convert entity EJBs developed with earlier versions of EJB specifications to entity beans for later versions of the EJB specification. For example, an EJB 2.1 entity may also be converted to an EJB 3.0 entity.

3

EclipseLink JPA Persistence Provider

The **Java Persistence API (JPA)** is a component of EJB 3.0 and replaces CMP and JDO. Oracle's strategic Java persistence implementation within Oracle Fusion Middleware 11*g* is Oracle TopLink 11*g*, which is based on the open source EclipseLink. EclipseLink is based on an older version of TopLink, which Oracle contributed to Eclipse. The EclipseLink version in Oracle Fusion Middleware 11*g* supports the JPA 1.0 specification. In this chapter, we shall discuss the JPA framework and the EclipseLink JPA persistence provider.

What is a JPA persistence provider? A JPA persistence provider is an implementation of the JPA; JPA is just a specification. Various JPA persistence providers such as Hibernate, Apache OpenJPA, and JPA for WebSphere Application Server are available, but we shall be discussing the persistence provider in Oracle Fusion Middleware: the EclipseLink JPA persistence provider. This section is not meant to be a repetition of the JPA specification (`http://jcp.org/en/jsr/detail?id=220`), or the EclipseLink JPA documentation (`http://wiki.eclipse.org/Category:JPA`), but a primer and an introduction to some of the features/values used in this book. In this chapter, we shall discuss the following:

- How to specify the EclipseLink persistence provider?
- The JPA framework
    - ○ The advantages of JPA
    - ○ What is required for JPA?

- Types of Entity Managers
    - ○ Container-managed entity manager
    - ○ Application-managed entity manager

- EclipseLink JPA
    - Metadata annotations
    - XML mapping metadata
    - Entity identity
    - Entity relationships

- EclispeLink JPA persistence unit properties

Specifying the EclipseLink persistence provider

The minimum required configuration to start using the EclipseLink persistence provider is to specify the persistence provider in the configuration file `persistence.xml`. The persistence provider is specified in the `META-INF/persistence.xml` configuration file in the `provider` sub-element of the `persistence-unit` element.

```xml
<?xml version="1.0" encoding="Cp1252" ?>
<persistence xmlns:xsi="http://www.w3.org/2001/XMLSchema-instance"
xsi:schemaLocation="http://java.sun.com/xml/ns/persistence http://
java.sun.com/xml/ns/persistence/persistence_1_0.xsd"
            xmlns="http://java.sun.com/xml/ns/persistence"
version="1.0">
<persistence-unit name="em">
<provider>org.eclipse.persistence.jpa.PersistenceProvider</provider>
<jta-data-source>java:/app/jdbc/jdbc/OracleDBConnectionDS</jta-data-
source>
<class>model.Catalog</class>
    <properties>
      ...
    </properties>
  </persistence-unit>
</persistence>
```

The JPA framework

The Java Persistence API (JPA) is a lightweight Java persistence framework based on Plain Old Java Object (POJO). JPA provides an **object relational mapping (ORM)** standard in Java, using which Java objects may be mapped to relational databases. The object relational mapping in JPA is based on metadata annotations that were introduced in Java SE 5. JPA may be used to create, query, update, and delete database table rows using Java objects. JPA is included with the Java EE 5 platform and may also be used with Java SE 5. JPA supports a SQL-like query language for dynamic and static queries. JPA also supports pluggable third-party persistence providers, which implies that a EJB container that conforms to the Enterprise JavaBeans 3.0 JPA specification can be used with any JPA persistence provider that also conforms to the Enterprise JavaBeans 3.0 JPA specification. JPA is based on entities. An entity is a Java object with the following properties:

- An entity can be made persistent.

- An entity has a persistent identity with a representation of it in a data store.

- An entity instance can be created and modified outside a transaction, but a transaction is required to persist the entity instance to a database.

- An entity mapping to a database is described by metadata. Metadata can be expressed as metadata annotations or an XML mapping file.

An entity is persisted to a database using an entity manager. An entity manager is required to create, read, and persist an entity. A non-persistent Java object may be created without an entity manager, but an entity manager requires to obtain a reference to the Java object to make it a persistent Java object that may be mapped to a relational database. The set of entities managed by an entity manager is called a persistence context and each entity in a persistence context has a unique persistent identity. An entity manager can be configured to manage a particular type of object, map to a particular database, or be implemented by a particular persistence provider. The persistence provider provides the backing JPA implementation. The `javax.persistence` package provides the metadata annotations that may be used to map JPA objects (the managed Java objects) to a database using a `persistence.xml` configuration file, which is discussed in a subsequent section. The `javax.persistence` package provides the classes and interfaces a persistence provider uses to manage the managed entities of the JPA. The following are the main interfaces in the JPA:

- `EntityManagerFactory`
- `EntityManager`
- `Query`
- `EntityTransaction`

The `EntityManagerFactory` is used within an application to create an entity manager. An `EntityManager` instance is created using the `EntityManagerFactory` and is associated with a persistence context, which is a collection of persistent entity instances, each of which have a unique persistent identity. The `EntityManager` is used to create and remove persistent entity instances, find entities by their primary key, and query entities. The collection of entities that can be managed by an `EntityManager` instance and that are mapped to a single database is defined by a persistence unit. A persistence unit is defined in the `persistence.xml` configuration file. The `EntityManager` interface is the main runtime API of the JPA. An `EntityManager` can be injected directly into a class using dependency injection or can be obtained from an `EntityManagerFactory` instance that has been injected using dependency injection. The Query interface is used in query execution and is created from an `EntityManager` instance. The `EntityTransaction` interface is used to manage resource-local transactions. We shall discuss the types of transactions supported by an entity manager in a subsequent section.

Advantages of JPA

JPA has several advantages over the entity persistence provided in the EJB 2.1 specification. The following are the main advantages:

- Persistent objects are POJOs; as a result fewer classes and interfaces are required.

- Object relational mapping is simplified with the use of metadata annotations (including annotation defaults), which replace the deployment descriptors.

- EJB 3.0 entities can be created and persisted outside the EJB container as they are not bound to the container via interfaces and container-managed EJB relationships as EJB 2.x entities were. Only a bean class containing annotations, which is a POJO, and a `persistence.xml` configuration file, which maps the bean class to a database, are required. Using an application-managed entity manager and resource-local transactions, EJB 3.0 entities can be created and persisted using only the J2SE 5 API.

- Persistent entity instances represent database rows, and entities and entity relationships can be queried using the query framework without requiring reference to foreign keys and database columns.

- Queries may be specified statically in the metadata or constructed dynamically. The Java persistence query language is an enhanced EJB-QL and includes some of the features lacking in EJB-QL.

- JPA can be used with pluggable third-party persistence providers.

- JNDI is replaced with resource injection, also called dependency injection.

What is required for JPA?

The following components are required for JPA:

- A relational database. We shall be using the Oracle database 10*g* or XE. But, any database may be used. The databases supported by EclipseLink JPA shall be discussed in the next section.

- Entity classes. An Entity class is just a POJO annotated with the `@Entity` annotation:

```
@Entity
public class Catalog implements Serializable {
...}
```

  We shall discuss in a later chapter why the class is implementing the `Serializable` interface.

- A `persistence.xml` configuration file. The `persistence.xml` file specifies the target database, the target server, the entities that are mapped to the database, and other properties, which we shall discuss in a later section.

- Metadata. Object relational mapping in EJB 3.0 is implemented using metadata, which may be specified using metadata annotations or in an object relational mapping XML file that conforms to the `http://java.sun.com/xml/ns/persistence/orm_1_0.xsd` XML Schema. If metadata annotations are used an XML mapping file is not required, but if the XML mapping file is included, in addition to the metadata annotations, the XML mapping file overrides the metadata annotations. Metadata annotations are easier to use as they are specified inline with the source code not requiring source code context replication. XML mapping is complex and requires source code context replication of where the metadata applies. For their ease of use and no major disadvantage other than the coupling of the source code with the metadata, we shall use metadata annotations in this book.

- Persistence provider. The persistence provider provides the JPA implementation. Oracle Fusion Middleware 11*g* uses the EclipseLink JPA persistence provider. The persistence provider manages the object relational mappings of entities and entity relationships.

- Entity manager. An entity manager is required to manage the entities. In the next section, we discuss the entity managers.

Types of entity managers

There are two types of entity managers available, depending on the Java environment in which the entity manager is obtained.

Container-managed entity manager

In the Java EE environment, the container manages the entity manager. The entity manager can be injected into a session bean, servlet, or JSP using dependency injection with the `@PersistenceContext` annotation, as shown next:

```
@PersistenceContext
  public EntityManager em;
```

Alternatively, the entity manager can be looked up using JNDI in the environment referencing context:

```
@PersistenceContext(name="CatalogEM", unitName="em")
    @Resource
    SessionContext ctx;

    EntityManager em = (EntityManager)ctx.lookup("CatalogEM");
```

We shall be using the simpler of the two methods—the dependency injection method. Transactions define when entities are synchronized with the database. Container-managed entity managers always use JTA transactions, the transactions of the Java EE server.

Application-managed entity manager

In a Java SE environment, the application manages the entity manager. The entity manager is created using the `createEntityManager()` method of the `EntityManagerFactory` class. An `EntityManagerFactory` object is obtained from the `Persistence` class using a persistence unit defined in the `persistence.xml` file (the `persistence.xml` is still required):

```
EntityManagerFactory emf =Persistence.createEntityManagerFactory("
pu");
EntityManager em = emf.createEntityManager();
.....
em.close();
emf.close();
```

The entity manager factory and the entity manager are required to be explicitly closed, as the container is not managing the entity manager. In a Java EE environment, an application-managed entity manager can be obtained by injecting an `EntityManagerFactory` instance using dependency injection and the `@PersistenceUnit` annotation and subsequently obtaining the entity manager from the `EntityManagerFactory` object. The `@PersistenceUnit` annotation can only be used in a session bean, servlet, or JSP.

```
@PersistenceUnit
  EntityManagerFactory emf;
```

```
EntityManager em = emf.createEntityManager();
```

Application-managed entity managers use either JTA transactions or resource-local transactions. The transaction type can be specified in the `persistence.xml` file. The default transaction type of entity managers in the Java EE server environment is JTA. In the Java SE environment only the resource-local transactions can be used, as we are not using an EJB container. The application explicitly manages the resource-local transactions using an `EntityTransaction` object acquired from the entity manager:

```
EntityManager em = emf.createEntityManager();
EntityTransaction tx = em.getTransaction();
//Begin the transaction
 tx.begin();
// Create and persist new entities
...
// Commit the transaction
tx.commit();
```

EclipseLink JPA

EclipseLink in Oracle Fusion Middleware 11*g* provides a complete implementation of JPA 1.0. EclipseLink implements all the mandatory features, some of the optional features and some additional features.

Metadata annotations

An annotation annotates a Java class/method/property with metadata that is compiled into the Java class file in which the annotation is specified. The compiled metadata is interpreted at runtime by the JPA persistence provider (EclipseLink JPA) to manage the persistence implementation. Each annotation has a default value. Annotations can be applied at three levels: class level, method level, and field level. EclipseLink JPA also defines some proprietary annotations in the `org.eclipselink.annotations` package.

XML mapping metadata

The XML mapping metadata file is used to specify object relational mapping (ORM) metadata. The default ORM metadata file is `META-INF/orm.xml`, which is based on XML Schema `http://java.sun.com/xml/ns/persistence/orm_1_0.xsd`. In `orm.xml` all the object relational mapping metadata is contained within the root element `entity-mappings`. EclipseLink provides a native XML metadata file, `META-INF/eclipselink-orm.xml`. The ORM metadata in the `eclipselink-orm.xml` overrides the ORM metadata in JPA's XML metadata file.

Entity identity

A persistent entity maps to a database table and must have a persistent identity that is an equivalent of the primary key in the database table that stores the entity state. The EclipseLink persistence provider assumes that each entity has at least one field/property that is the primary key. A primary key field using the `@Id` annotation is specified as follows:

```
@Id
@GeneratedValue(strategy=GenerationType.AUTO)
private int id;
```

The `@GeneratedValue` annotation specifies that the EclipseLink persistence provider generate unique identifiers for entity primary keys. The strategy attribute is not required and the default value is AUTO. The `@GeneratedValue` annotation is not required and by default the EclipseLink JPA persistence provider chooses the most appropriate primary key generator. We shall be using the default primary key generator:

```
@Id
private int id;
```

Entity relationships

We shall be using the `@OneToMany`, `@ManyToOne`, and `@ManyToMany` annotations to specify relationships between entities. The fetch strategy in an entity relationship specifies if the associated entities are fetched when an entity is fetched, and its value may be `FetchType.LAZY` or `FetchType.EAGER`. For the `LAZY` strategy, associated entities are not fetched and for the `EAGER` strategy, associated entities are fetched. The default values are listed in the following table:

Relationship	Default Fetch Strategy
@OneToMany	LAZY
@ManyToOne	EAGER
@ManyToMany	LAZY

EclispeLink JPA Persistence unit properties

EclipseLink JPA provides some persistence unit properties that may be specified in `persistence.xml` to configure various aspects of database persistence such as the target database, the JDBC connection URL, and the JDBC connection pooling provided by the data source. We shall discuss some of the persistence unit properties in the following table:

Property	Description	Default Value
`eclipselink.exception-handler`	This specifies an EclipseLink exception handler class.	-
`eclipselink.jdbc.bind-parameters`	This specifies if Java persistence queries use parameter binding. Property applies in J2SE environment.	true
`eclipselink.jdbc.native-sql`	This specifies if generation of database-platform-specific SQL should be enabled. Property applies in both Java SE environment and Java EE environment.	false
`eclipselink.jdbc.batch-writing`	This specifies the use of batch writing to optimize transactions with multiple writes. The following values may be specified: JDBC:Use JDBC batch writing. Oracle-JDBC: Use JDBC batch writing and Oracle native platform batch writing. Buffered: Do not use either JDBC batch writing or native platform batch writing. None: Do not use batch writing.	None
`eclipselink.jdbc.cache-statements`	This specifies if EclispeLink internal statement caching is to be used. Value may be true or false.	false
`eclipselink.jdbc.cache-statements.size`	This specifies the size of the internal statements cache.	50
`eclipselink.jdbc.exclusive-connection.is-lazy`	This specifies if a write connection is acquired lazily. Value may be true or false.	true

Property	Description	Default Value
`eclipselink.jdbc.driver`	This specifies the JDBC driver class used. For Oracle database, specify as follows: `<property name="eclipselink.jdbc. driver" value="oracle.jdbc. OracleDriver"/>`	-
`eclipselink.jdbc. password`	This specifies the password for logging into the database.	-
`eclipselink.jdbc.url`	This specifies the connection URL. With default settings, the value for Oracle database is as follows: `<property name="eclipselink.jdbc.url" value="jdbc:oracle:thin:@ localhost:1521:ORCL"/>` For the XE database replace `ORCL` with `XE`.	-
`eclipselink.jdbc.user`	This specifies the user name. Property applies in Java SE environment or when resource-local persistence unit is used.	-
`eclipselink.jdbc.read-connections.max`	This specifies the maximum number of connections allowed in the JDBC read connection pool. Property applies when used in Java SE environment.	2
`eclipselink.jdbc.read-connections.min`	This specifies the minimum number of connections allowed in the JDBC read connection pool. Property applies when used in Java SE environment.	2
`eclipselink.jdbc.read-connections.shared`	This specifes if shared read connections are allowed. Value may be set to true or false. Property applies when used in Java SE environment.	False

Property	Description	Default Value
`eclipselink.jdbc.write-connections.max`	This specifies the maximum number of connections allowed in the JDBC write connection pool. Property applies when used in Java SE environment.	10
`eclipselink.jdbc.write-connections.min`	This specifies the minimum number of connections allowed in the JDBC write connection pool. Property applies when used in Java SE environment.	5

`eclipselink.logging.logger`	This specifies the type of logger to use. The following values may be specified:
	
	`DefaultLogger`
	
	`JavaLogger`
	
	`ServerLogger`
	
	class name of custom logger
		DefaultLogger

`eclipselink.logging.level`	This specifies the logging level. The following values may be specified. The following are some of the values used: OFF: This disables logging. It is recommended for production. SEVERE: This logs exceptions of level severe and terminates EclipseLink. It includes a stack trace. WARNING: This logs exceptions of type warning and does not terminate EclipseLink. It does not include a stack trace. INFO: This logs the info about login/logout.	Level.INFO
`eclipselink.logging.timestamp`	This specifies if timestamp is logged in each log entry.	True

Property	Description	Default Value
`eclipselink.logging.` `exceptions`	This specifies if exceptions are logged before returning the exception to the calling application and ensures that all exceptions are logged.	False
`eclipselink.logging.` `file`	This specifies a file location (relative or absolute path) for log output. Property applies when used in Java SE environment.	
`eclipselink.target-` `database`	This specifies the target database. For Oracle database, specify `<property name="eclipselink.target-database" value="Oracle"/>` A value of AUTO specifies that EclipseLink determine the target database from the JDBC metadata obtained by accessing the database. Applies to JDBC drivers that support the the database metadata. We shall be using a value of AUTO or Oracle.	AUTO

`eclipselink.target-`
`server`
	This specifies the target application server. For WebLogic Server specify
	
	`<property`
	`name="eclipselink.`
	`target-server"`
	`value="WebLogic_10"/>`
	
	A value of None implies that configure EclipseLink for no server.
		None

Property	Description	Default Value
`eclipselink.ddl-generation`	This specifies the DDL generation action. The following values may be specified: none: EclipseLink does not generate DDL create-tables: EclipseLink will attempt to create tables using `CREATE TABLE` for each table and if a table already exists, the table, is not re-created. drop-and-create-tables: EclipseLink will attempt to drop all tables with the `DROP` statement and re-create tables with the `CREATE TABLE` statement.	None
`eclipselink.application-location`	This specifies the location of output DDL files.	"."+File.separator
`eclipselink.create-ddl-jdbc-file-name`	This specifies the file name of the DDL file containing the `CREATE TABLE SQL` statements.	createDDL.jdbc
`eclipselink.drop-ddl-jdbc-file-name`	This specifies the DDL file name containing the `DROP TABLE SQL` statements.	dropDDL.jdbc
`eclipselink.ddl-generation.output-mode`	This specifies the DDL generation target. The following values may be specified: Database: This is to execute SQL on the database only. Do not generate DDL files. sql-script: This is to generate DDL files only. Do not execute SQL on the database. Both: This is to generate DDL files and execute SQL on the database.	sql-script

Summary

In this chapter, we briefly introduced the JPA framework, discussed the EclipseLink JPA persistence provider, and discussed some of the commonly used EclipseLink persistence unit properties. In the next chapter, we discuss EJB 3.0 database persistence with Oracle JDeveloper, Oracle WebLogic Server, and Oracle database.

4
Building an EJB 3.0 Persistence Model with Oracle JDeveloper

Oracle Fusion Middleware is a family name for a set of Java EE products that are integrated for SOA and web application deployment. **WebLogic Server (WLS)** is the Java EE container and Oracle JDeveloper the Java EE and SOA development IDE. In this chapter, we will use JDeveloper to create an EJB 3.0 application, and then we will deploy and test our application leveraging the embedded WebLogic Server that comes with JDeveloper. This makes it very easy for us to develop, deploy, and test our application.

WebLogic server 10.x provides some value-added features to facilitate EJB 3 development. WebLogic server 10.x supports automatic deployment of a persistence unit based on the injected variable's name. The `@javax.persistence.PersistenceContext` and `@javax.persistence.PersistenceUnit` annotations are used to inject the persistence context in an `EntityManager` or `EntityManagerFactory` variable. A persistence context is a set of entities that are mapped to a database with a global JNDI name. If the name of the injected variable is the same as the persistence unit, the `unitName` attribute of the `@PersistenceContext` or `@PersistenceUnit` is not required to be specified. The EJB container automatically deploys the persistence unit and sets its JNDI name to be the same as the persistence unit name in `persistence.xml`. For example, if the persistence unit name in the `persistence.xml` file is em, an `EntityManager` variable may be injected with the persistence context as follows:

```
@PeristenceContext
private EntityManager em;
```

We did not need to specify the `unitName` attribute in the `@PersistenceContext` because the variable name is the same as the persistence unit. Similarly, an `EntityManagerFactory` variable may be injected with the persistence context as follows, `emf` being also the persistence unit name:

```
@PersistenceUnit
private EntityManagerFactory emf;
```

Another value-added feature in WebLogic server 10.x is support for vendor-specific subinterfaces of the `EntityManager` interface. For example, the BEA Kodo persistence provider provides the `KodoEntityManager` subinterface, which may be injected with the persistence context as follows:

```
@PersistenceContext
private KodoEntityManager em;
```

Setting the environment

Before getting started, we need to install Oracle JDeveloper 11*g*, which may be downloaded from `http://www.oracle.com/technology/products/jdev/index.html`. Download the Studio Edition, which is the complete version of JDevloper with all the features. Oracle JDeveloper 11*g* is distributed as a GUI self-extractor application. Click on the `jdevstudio11110install` application. The Oracle Installer gets started. Click on **Next** in the Oracle Installer. Choose a middleware home directory and click on **Next**.

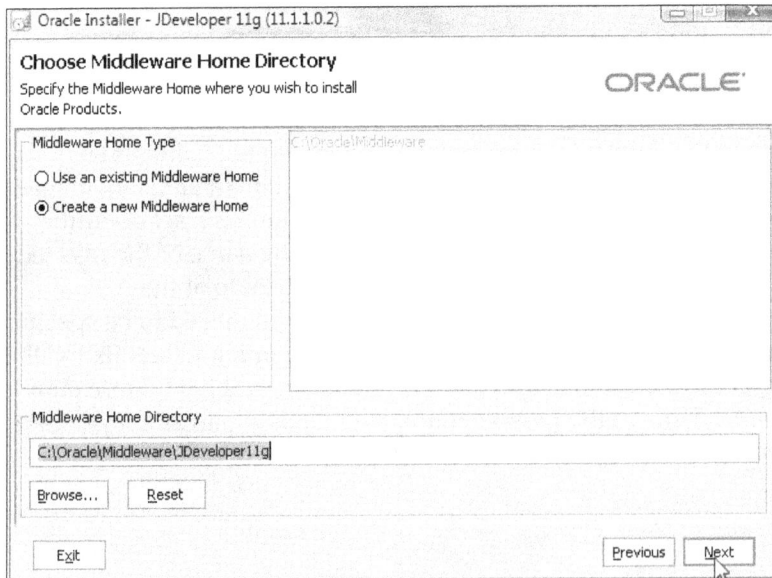

Choose the **Install Type** as **Complete**, which includes the integrated WebLogic Server, and click on **Next**.

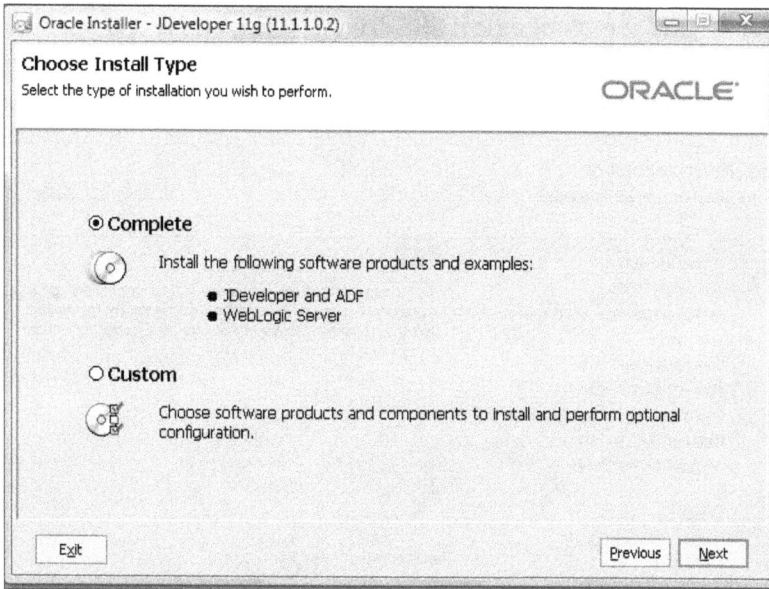

Confirm the default **Product Installation** directories and click on **Next**.

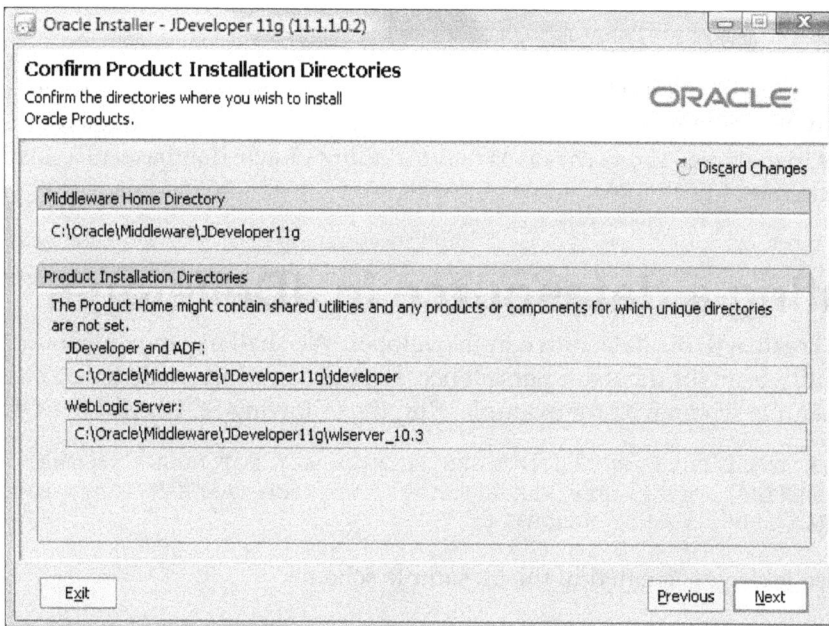

The WebLogic Server installation directory is the `wlserver_10.3` folder within the middleware home directory. Choose a shortcut location and click on **Next**. The **Installation Summary** lists the products that are installed, which include the WebLogic Server and the WebLogic JDBC drivers. Click on **Next** to install Oracle JDeveloper 11*g* and the integrated WebLogic Server 10.3.

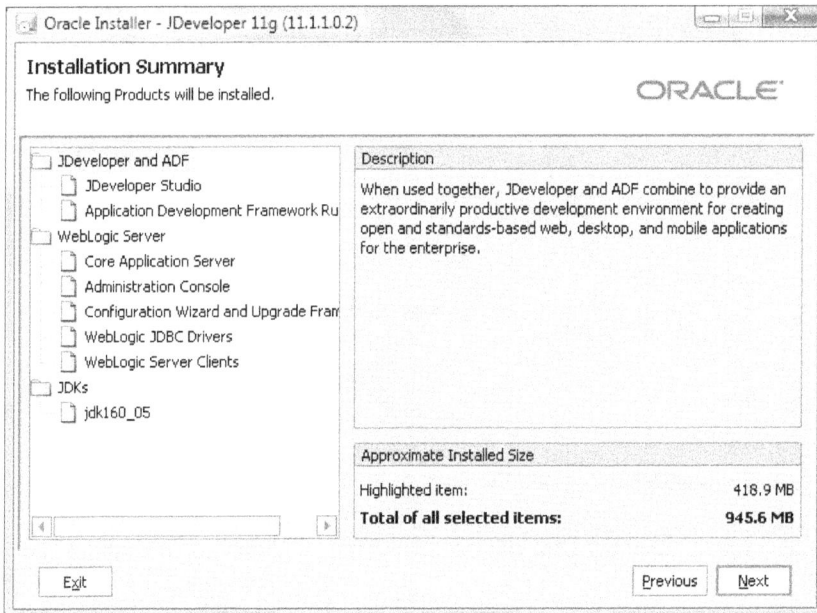

We also need to install the Oracle database 10*g*/11*g* or the lightweight Oracle XE, which may be downloaded from `http://www.oracle.com/technology/software/products/database/index.html`. When installing Oracle database, also install the sample schemas.

Creating a datasource in JDeveloper

Next, we create a JDBC datasource in JDeveloper. We shall use the datasource in the EJB 3.0 entity bean for database persistence. First, we need to create a database table in some sample schema, `OE` for example. Run the following SQL script in SQL *Plus:

```
CREATE TABLE Catalog (id INTEGER PRIMARY KEY NOT NULL, journal
VARCHAR(100), publisher VARCHAR(100), edition VARCHAR(100), title
VARCHAR(100), author VARCHAR(100));
```

A database table gets created in the `OE` sample schema.

Next, we need to create a JDBC connection in JDeveloper with Oracle database. Open the **Database Navigator** or select the **Database Navigator** tab if already open. Right-click on the **IDE Connections** node and select **New Connection**.

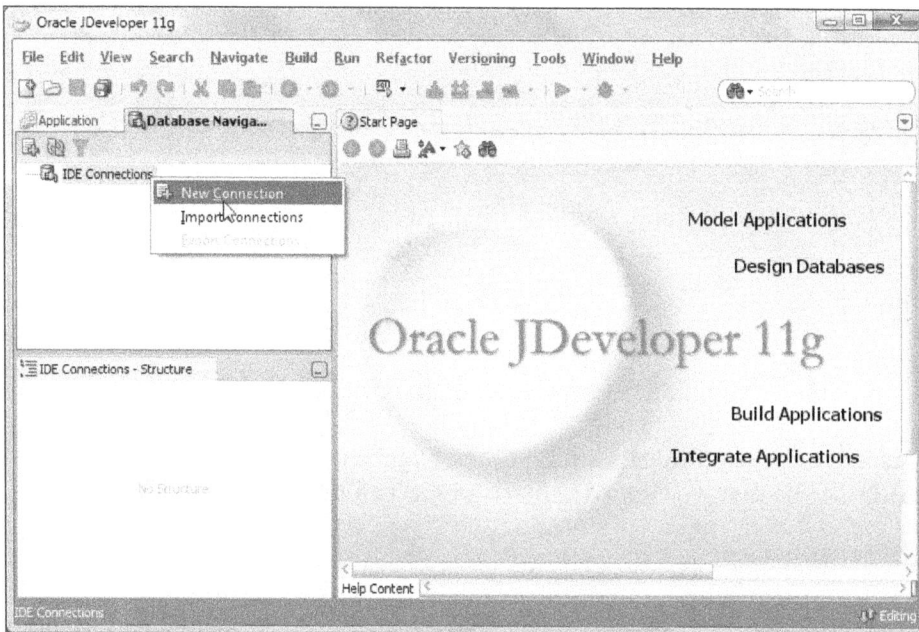

In the **Create Database Connection** window, specify a **Connection Name**, select **Connection Type** as **Oracle (JDBC)**, specify **Username** as **OE**, which is the schema in which the `Catalog` table is created, and specify the password for the **OE** schema. Select **Driver** as **thin**, **Host Name** as **localhost**, **SID** as **ORCL**, and **JDBC Port** as **1521**. Click on the **Test Connection** button to test the connection. If the connection gets established, click on **OK**.

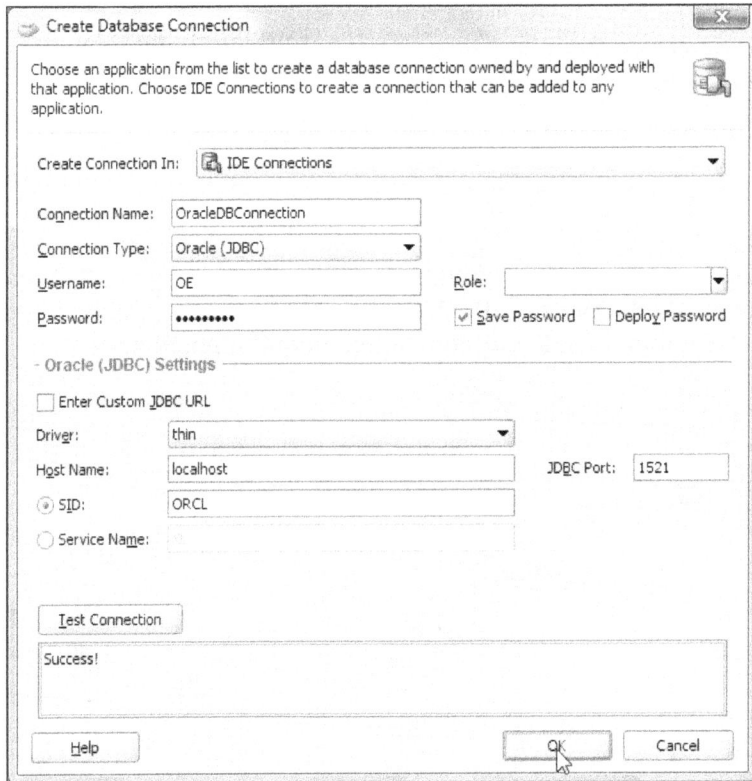

The **OracleDBConnection** gets added to the **Database Navigator** view. The **CATALOG** table that we created is listed in the **Tables**.

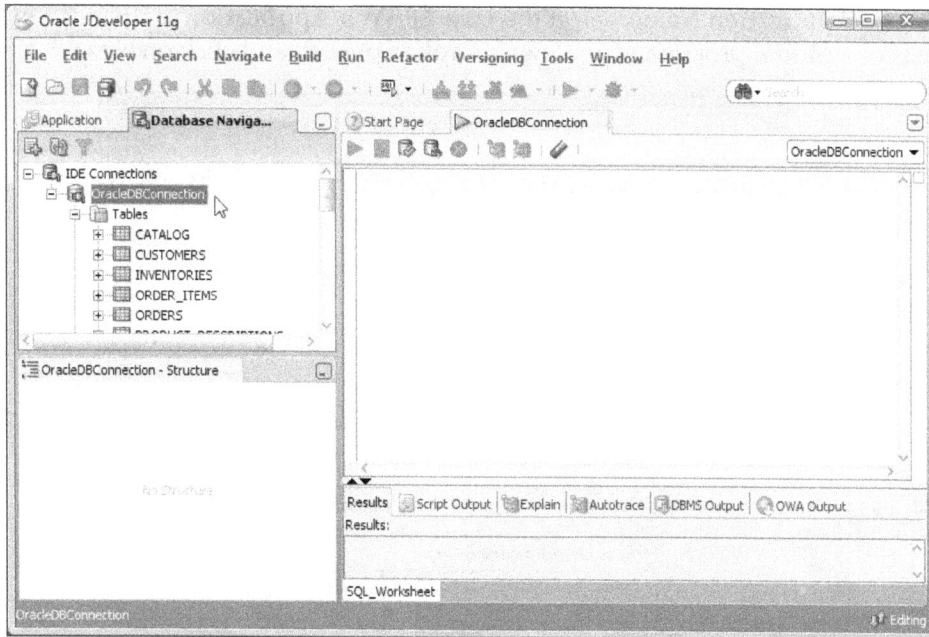

Creating an EJB 3 application

In this section, we create an EJB 3.0 application in JDeveloper. Select **New Application**.

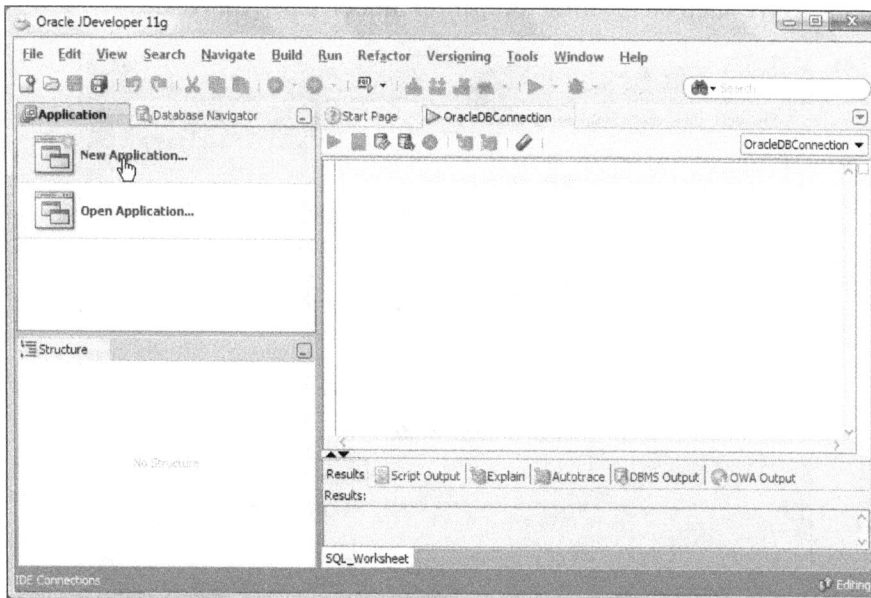

Specify an **Application Name**, select the **Java EE Web Application** template, which consists of a **Model** project and a **ViewController** project, and click on **Next**.

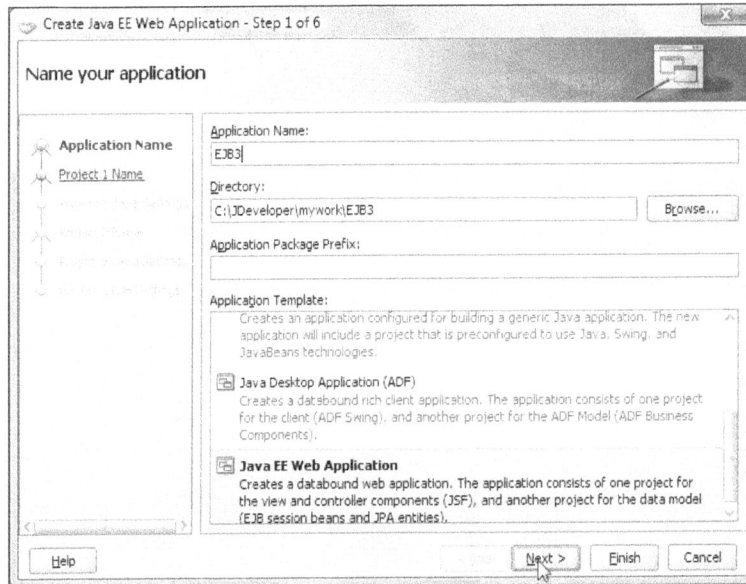

Next, specify the name (**EJB3ViewController**) for the View and Controller project. In the **Project Technologies** tab, transfer the **EJB** project technology from the **Available** list to the **Selected** list using the **>** button. We have selected the EJB project technology, as we shall be creating an EJB 3.0 model. Click on **Next**.

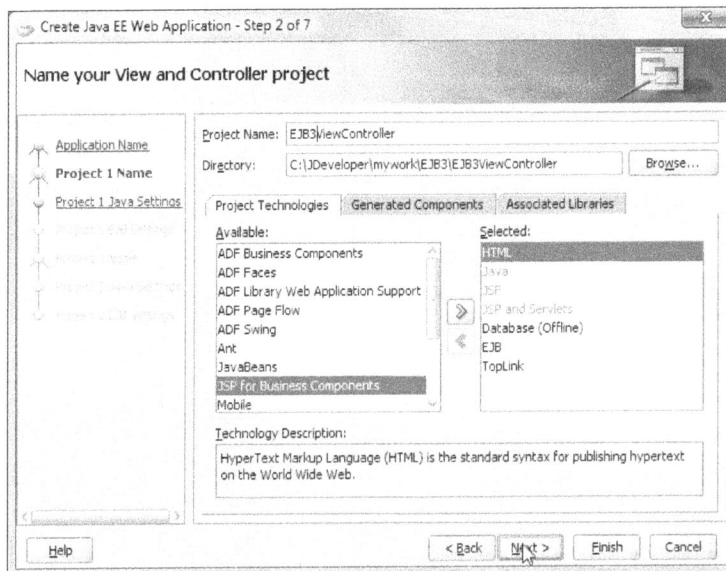

Select the default Java settings for the View project and click on **Next**.

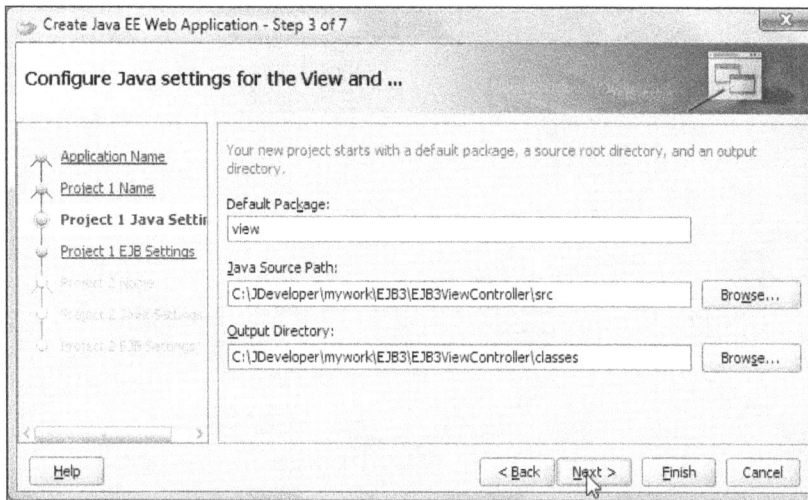

Configure the EJB Settings for the View project. Select **EJB Version** as **Enterprise JavaBeans 3.0** and select **Using Annotations**. Click on **Next**. Next, create the **Model** project. Specify the **Project Name** (**EJB3Model** for example), and in the **Project Technologies** tab transfer the **EJB** project technology from the **Available** list to the **Selected** list using the **>** button. We have added the EJB project technology, as the EJB 3.0 application client is created in the View project. Click on **Next**.

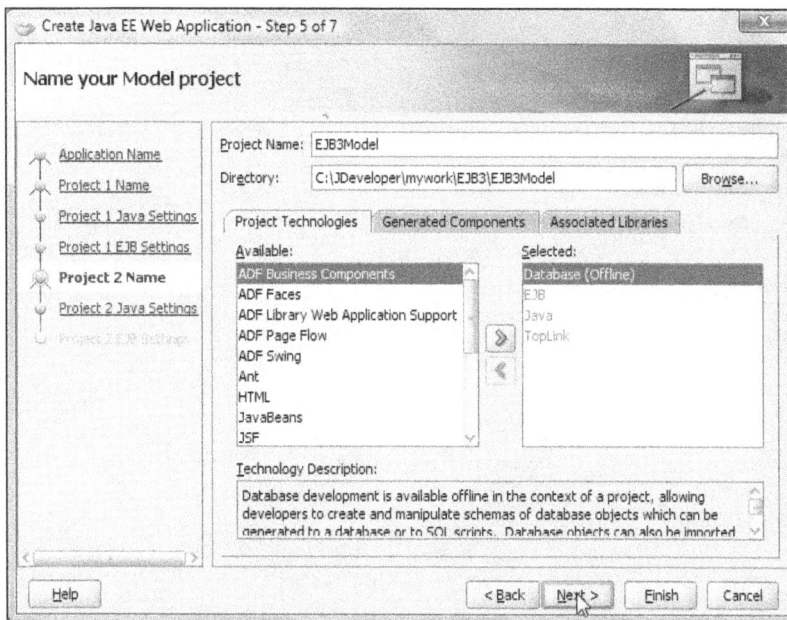

Select the default Java settings for the Model project and click on **Next**.

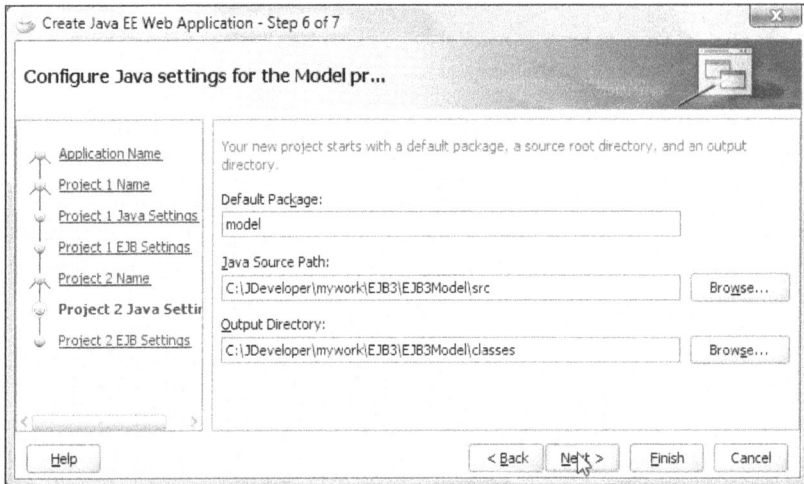

Similar to the View project, configure the EJB settings for the Model project. Select **EJB Version** as **Enterprise JavaBeans 3.0**, select **Using Annotations** and click on **Finish**. As we won't be using a `jndi.properties` file or an `ejb-jar.xml` file, we don't need to select the generate option for the `jndi.properties` file and the `ejb-jar.xml` file.

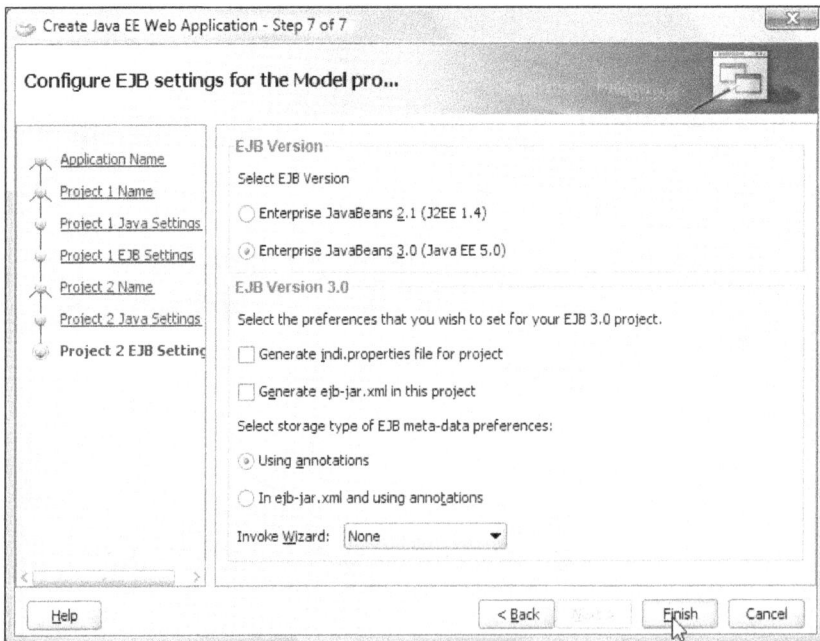

An EJB 3.0 application, which consists of a Model project and a `ViewController` project, get added in the **Application** tab.

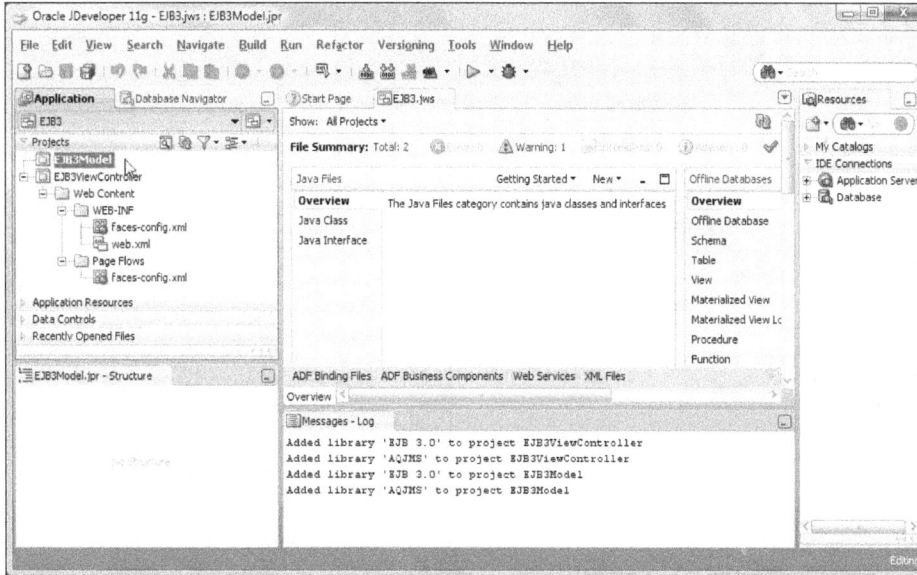

Select the **EJB3Model** project in the **Application** navigator and select **Tools | Project Properties**. In the **Project Properties** window, select the **Libraries and Classpath** node. The **EJB 3.0** library should be in the **Classpath Entries**.

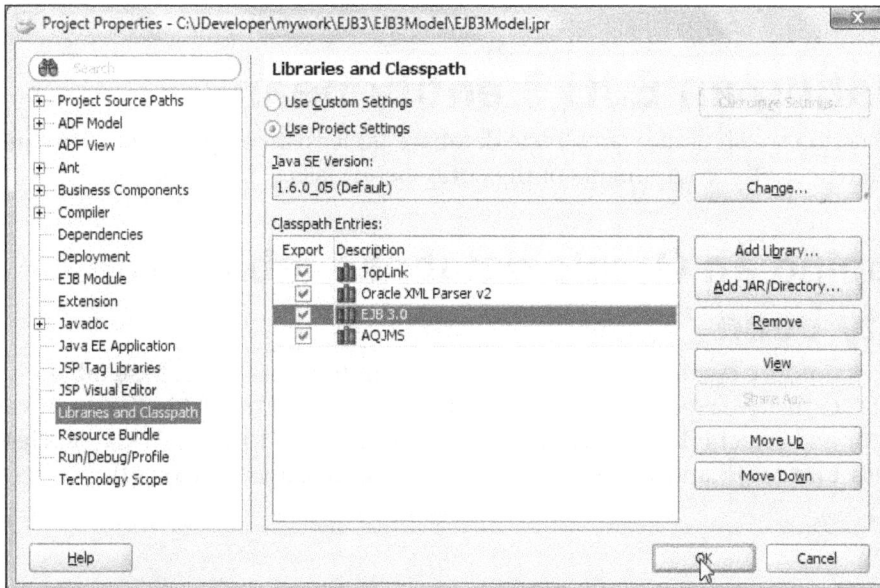

Select the **EJB Module** node and select the **OracleDBConnection** in the **Connection** drop-down list. The datasource corresponding to the **OracleDBConnection** is **jdbc/ OracleDBConnectionDS**.

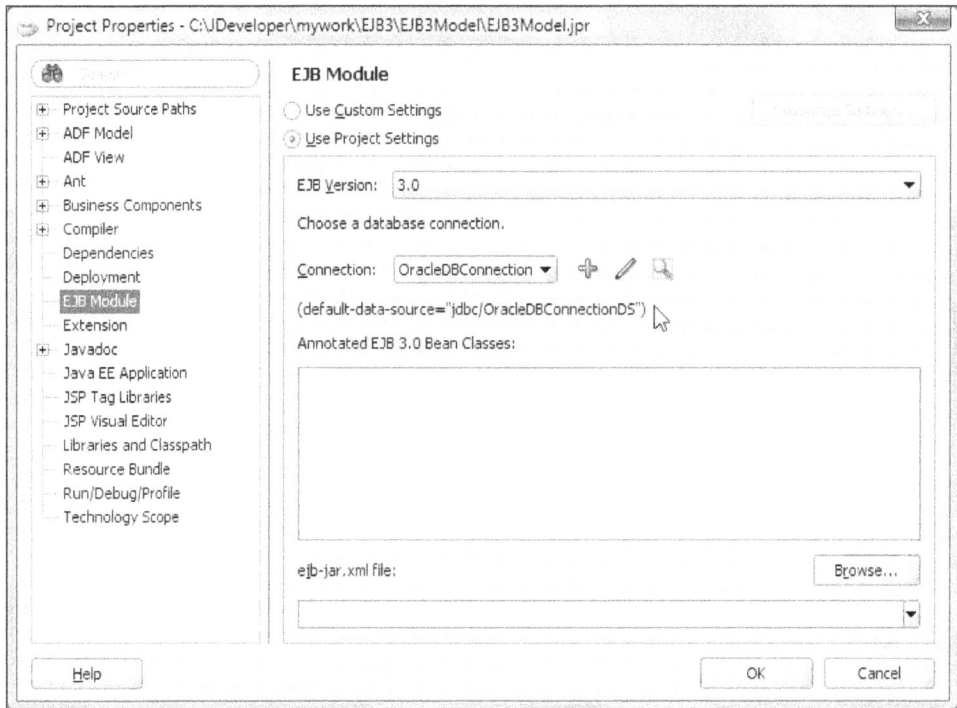

Creating an EJB 3 entity bean

In this section we shall map an Oracle database table to an entity bean. Subsequently we shall discuss the components of the entity bean class.

Mapping an Oracle database table to an entity bean

In this section, we create an EJB 3 entity bean from the Oracle database table **CATALOG** that we created earlier. Select the **EJB3Model** project in the **Application** navigator and select **File | New**. In the **New Gallery** window, select **Categories | Business Tier | EJB** and **Items | Entities from Tables,** and click on **OK**.

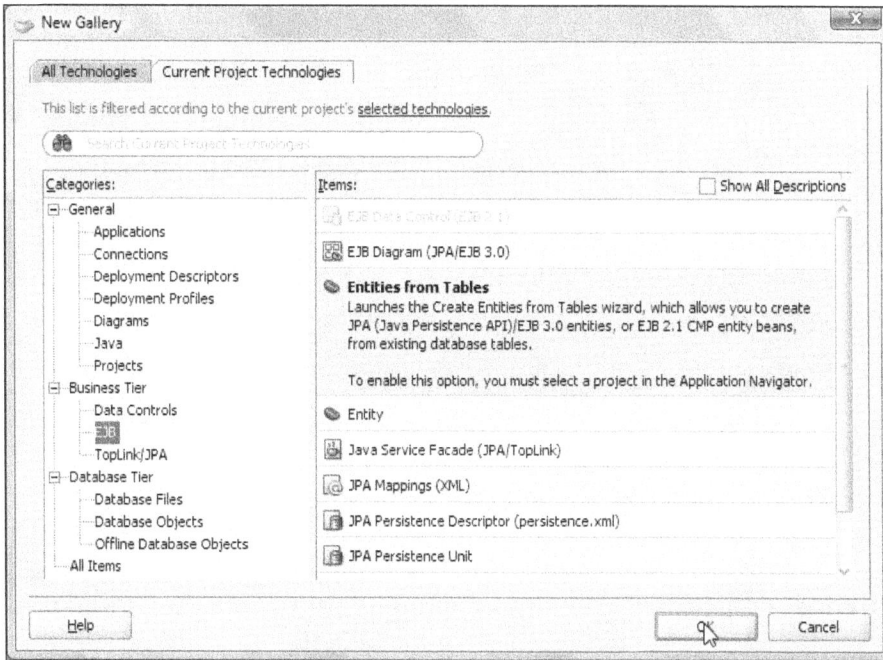

In the **Persistence Unit**, window, select **New** to create a new persistence unit. In the **New Persistence Unit** window specify a persistence unit name (**em**). Specify **JTA DataSource Name** as **jdbc/OracleDBConnectionDS**, which is the datasource name corresponding to the **OracleDBConnection** connection. Select the default settings for Toplink: **Server Platform** as **WebLogic 10**. Click on **OK**.

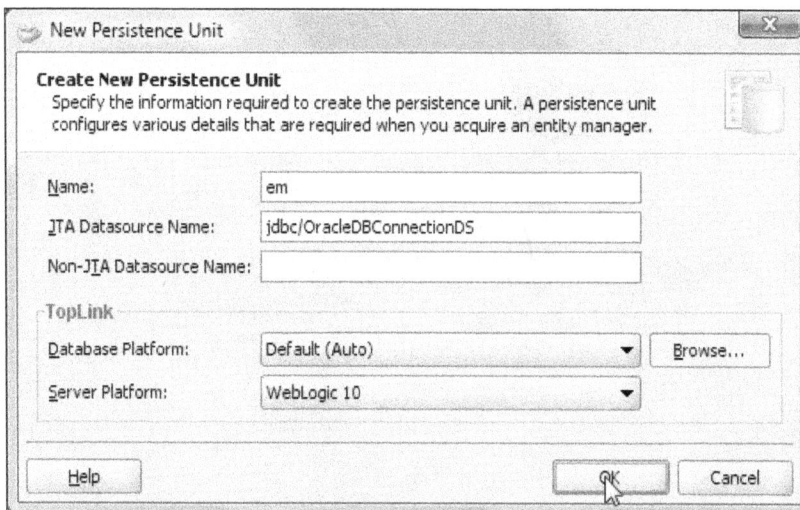

The em Persistence Unit gets created. Click on **OK** in the **Persistence Unit** window.

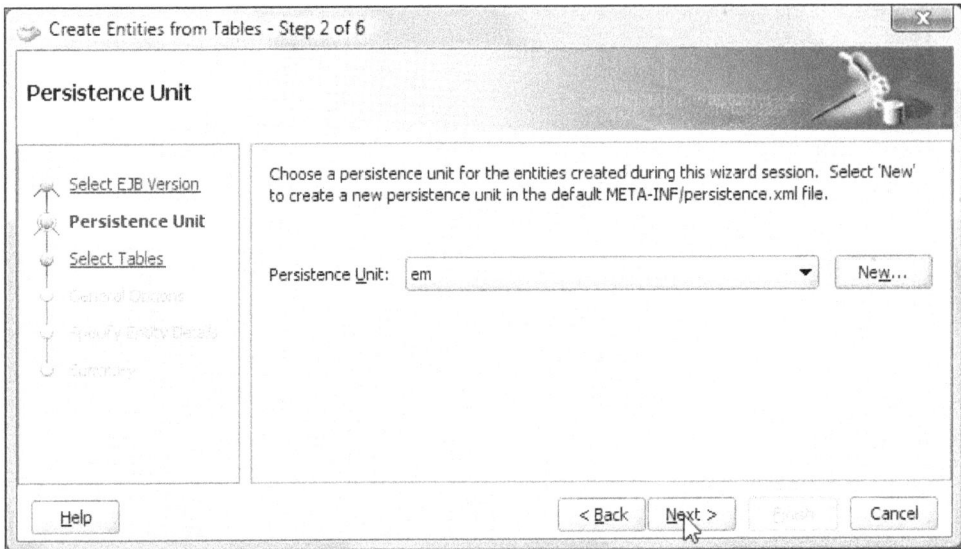

Select **Type of Connection** as **Online Database Connection** and click on **Next**.

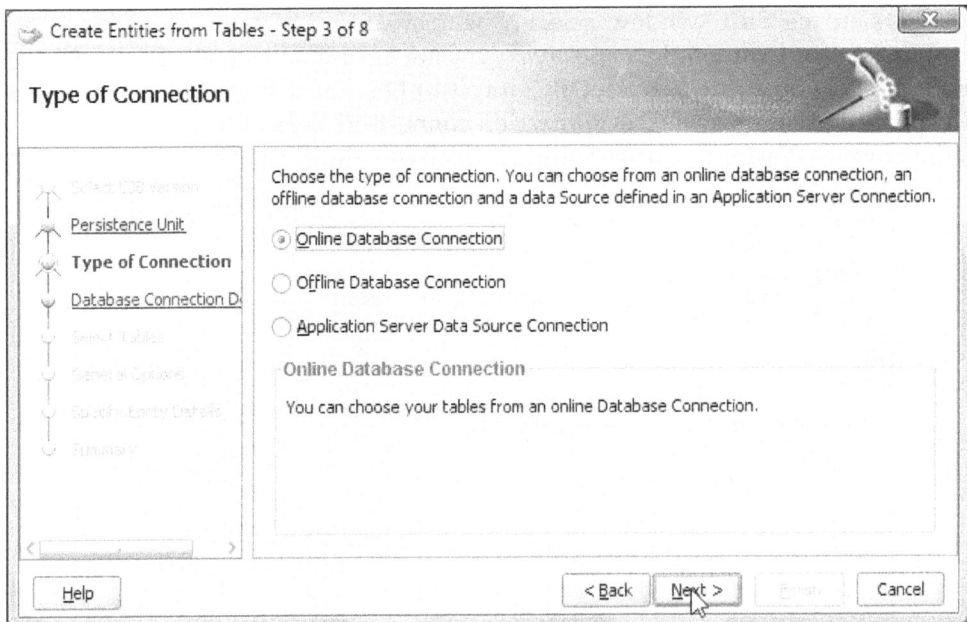

In the **Database Connection Details** window, select the **OracleDBConnection** and click on **Next**. We had configured a connection earlier, but the database connection can be created implicitly in the **Database Connection Details,** instead of explicitly.

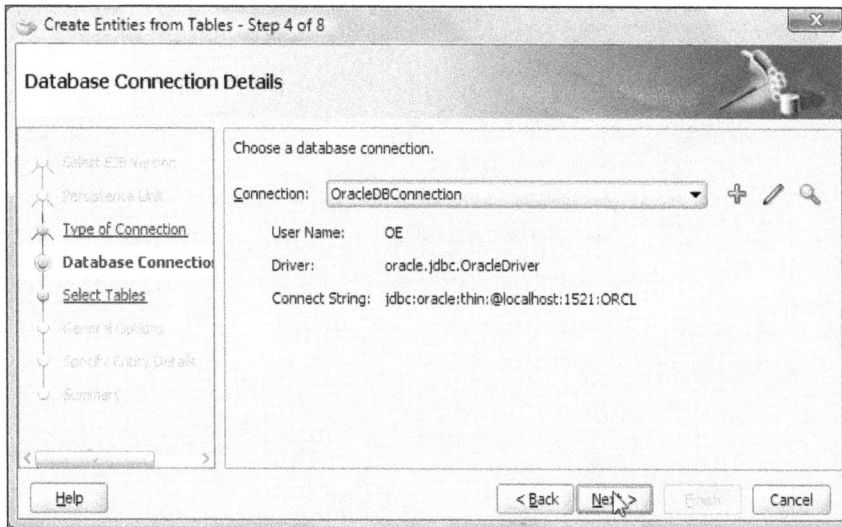

In the **Select Tables** window, select Schema as **OE**, **Name Filter** as %, and check the **Auto Query** checkbox. Select the **CATALOG** table and click on **Next**.

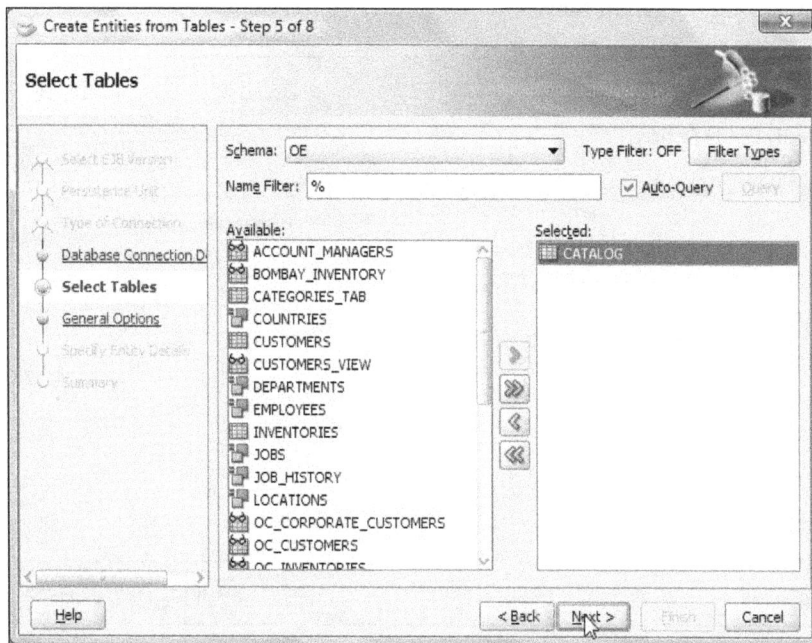

Select the default settings in the **General Options** window. The default package name is **model**. In the **Entity Class**, select **Place member-level annotations on as Fields**, and select the **Implement java.io.Serializable** checkbox. Click on **Next**.

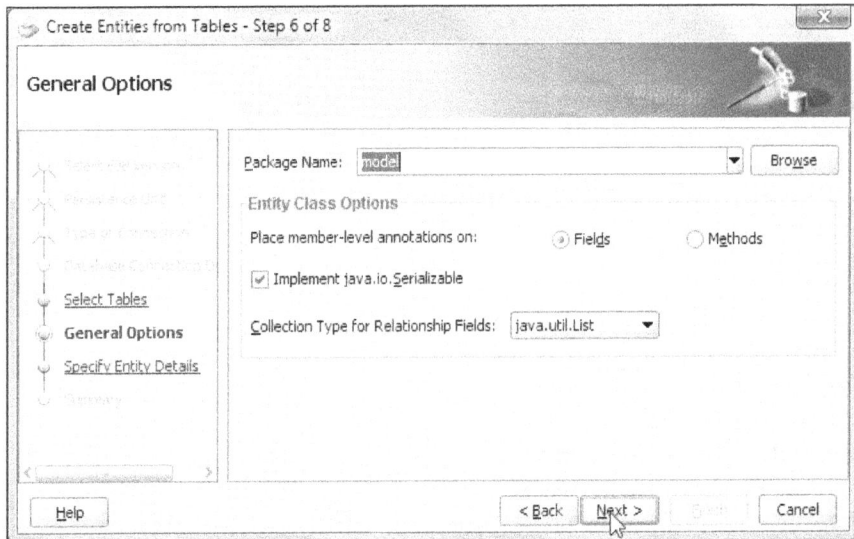

In the **Specify Entity Details** window, select **Table Name** as **OE.CATALOG**. As shown in the following screenshot, specify **Entity Name** as **Catalog** and **Entity Class** as **model.Catalog**. Click on **Next**.

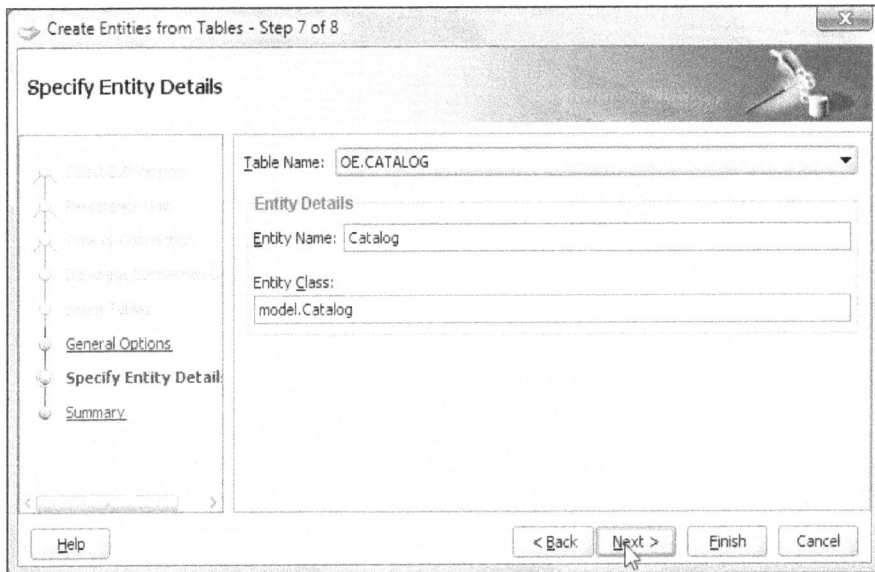

The **Summary** page lists the EJB 3.0 JPA Entity that will be generated. In the **Summary Page**, click on **Finish**.

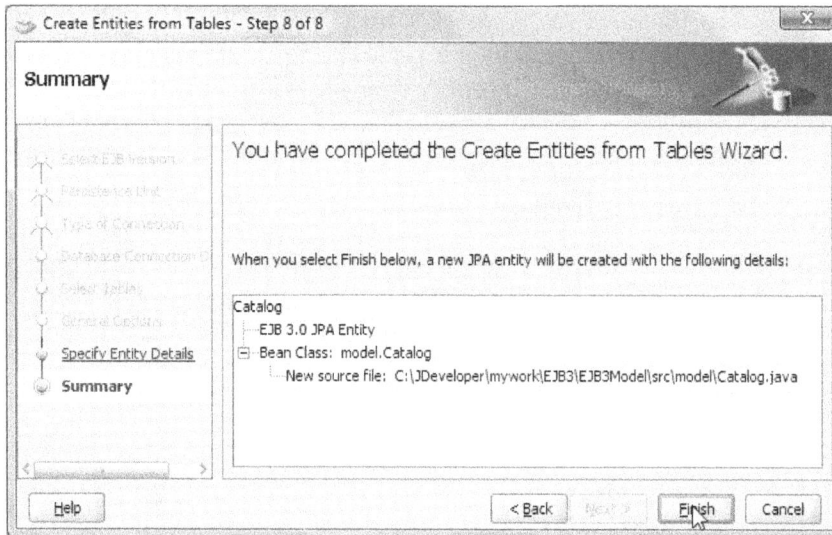

The CMP Entity bean class — `model.Catalog` — gets created. The `persistence.xml` deployment descriptor gets created in the `META-INF` directory.

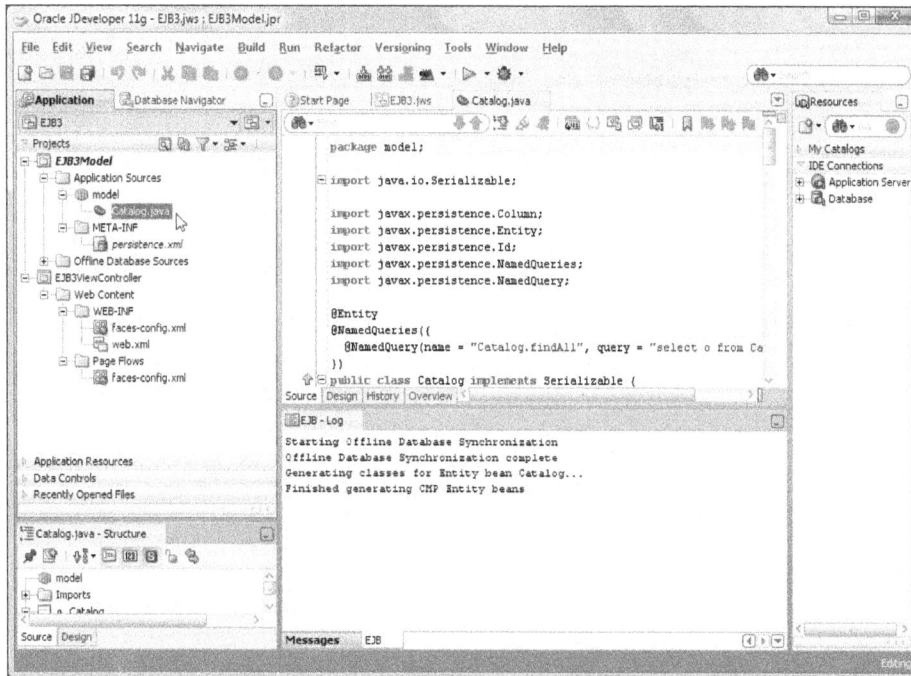

The entity bean class

The entity bean class is just a POJO class annotated with the @Entity annotation. A @NamedQuery specifies a findAll query, which selects all the entity instances. An entity bean that has caching enabled is persisted to a database; the entity bean is serialized by caches. Therefore, the entity bean class implements the java.io.Serializable interface. Specify a serialVersionUID variable that is used by serialization runtime to associate a version number with the serializable class:

```
private static final long serialVersionUID = 7422574264557894633L;
```

The database columns are mapped to entity bean properties, which are defined as private variables. The getter setter methods for the properties are also defined. The identifier property is specified with the @Id annotation. The @Column annotation specifies that the id column is not nullable:

```
@Id
@Column(nullable = false)
private long id;
```

By default the id column of type INTEGER is mapped to a field of type Long. Modify the id field to type long, as usually id values are of primitive type. The entity bean class is listed next:

```
package model;
import java.io.Serializable;

import javax.persistence.Column;
import javax.persistence.Entity;
import javax.persistence.Id;
import javax.persistence.NamedQueries;
import javax.persistence.NamedQuery;

@Entity
@NamedQueries({
  @NamedQuery(name = "Catalog.findAll", query = "select o from Catalog
o")
})
public class Catalog implements Serializable {
    private String author;
    private String edition;
    private static final long serialVersionUID = 7422574264557894633L;
    @Id
    @Column(nullable = false)
    private long id;
    private String journal;
    private String publisher;
```

```java
    private String title;
    public Catalog() {super();
    }
    public Catalog(String author, String edition, long id, String
journal,
                    String publisher, String title) {
        super();
        this.author = author;
        this.edition = edition;
        this.id = id;
        this.journal = journal;
        this.publisher = publisher;
        this.title = title;
    }
    public String getAuthor() {
        return author;
    }
    public void setAuthor(String author) {
        this.author = author;
    }
    public String getEdition() {
        return edition;
    }
    public void setEdition(String edition) {
        this.edition = edition;
    }
    public long getId() {
        return id;
    }
    public void setId(long id) {
        this.id = id;
    }
    public String getJournal() {
        return journal;
    }
    public void setJournal(String journal) {
        this.journal = journal;
    }
    public String getPublisher() {
        return publisher;
    }
```

```
    public void setPublisher(String publisher) {
        this.publisher = publisher;
    }
    public String getTitle() {
        return title;
    }
    public void setTitle(String title) {
        this.title = title;
    }
}
```

The `persistence.xml` file is used to define the persistence unit/s, which include a JTA datasource that is used for database persistence. The persistence provider is specified as `org.eclipse.persistence.jpa.PersistenceProvider`. The `jta-data-source` is defined as `java:/app/jdbc/jdbc/OracleDBConnectionDS`. The `eclipselink.target-server` property is specified as `WebLogic_10`. The `javax.persistence.jtaDataSource` property is specified as `java:/app/jdbc/jdbc/OracleDBConnectionDS`, which is just the default mapping JDeveloper uses for the JTA Data Source. The `java:/app/jdbc` prefix gets added to the JTA Data Source specified when creating the persistence unit. The `persistence.xml` configuration file is listed next:

```
<?xml version="1.0" encoding="windows-1252" ?>
<persistence xmlns:xsi="http://www.w3.org/2001/XMLSchema-instance"
  xsi:schemaLocation="http://java.sun.com/xml/ns/persistence
                 http://java.sun.com/xml/ns/persistence/
persistence_1_0.xsd"
  version="1.0" xmlns="http://java.sun.com/xml/ns/persistence">
  <persistence-unit name="em">
    <provider>
      org.eclipse.persistence.jpa.PersistenceProvider
    </provider>
    <jta-data-source>
      java:/app/jdbc/jdbc/OracleDBConnectionDS
    </jta-data-source>
    <class>
      model.Catalog
    </class>
    <properties>
      <property name="eclipselink.target-server" value="WebLogic_10"
      />
      <property name="javax.persistence.jtaDataSource"
              value="java:/app/jdbc/jdbc/OracleDBConnectionDS" />
    </properties>
  </persistence-unit>
</persistence>
```

Creating a session bean

One of the best practices in, developing an entity bean is to wrap it in a session bean for a client. The entity bean is not directly accessed by a client. To create a session bean select the **EJB3Model** project and select **File | New**. In the **New Gallery** window, select **Categories | Business Tier | EJB and Items | Session EJB**. Click on **OK**.

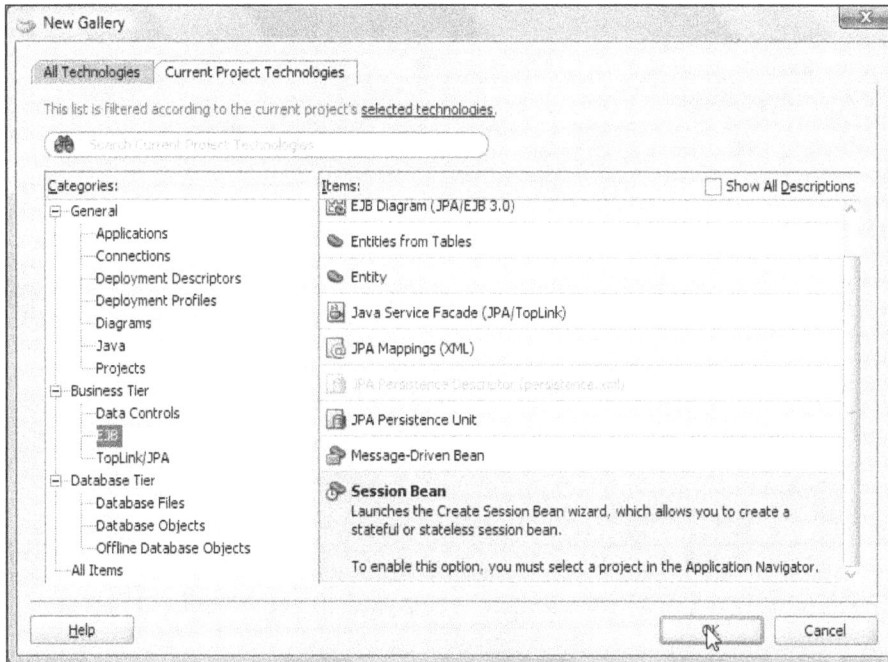

Specify the **EJB Name** as **CatalogTestSessionEJB**. Select **Session Type** as **Stateless** and **Transaction Type** as **Container**. We have selected the stateless session bean because stateless session beans are less resource-intensive due to the lack of the overhead to keep the state of a unique client-bean session. Select the default mapped name (**EJB3-SessionEJB**).

The **Generate Session Façade Methods** checkbox is selected by default. The **Entity Implementation** is **JPA Entities** by default. The persistence unit is **em**. Click on **Next**.

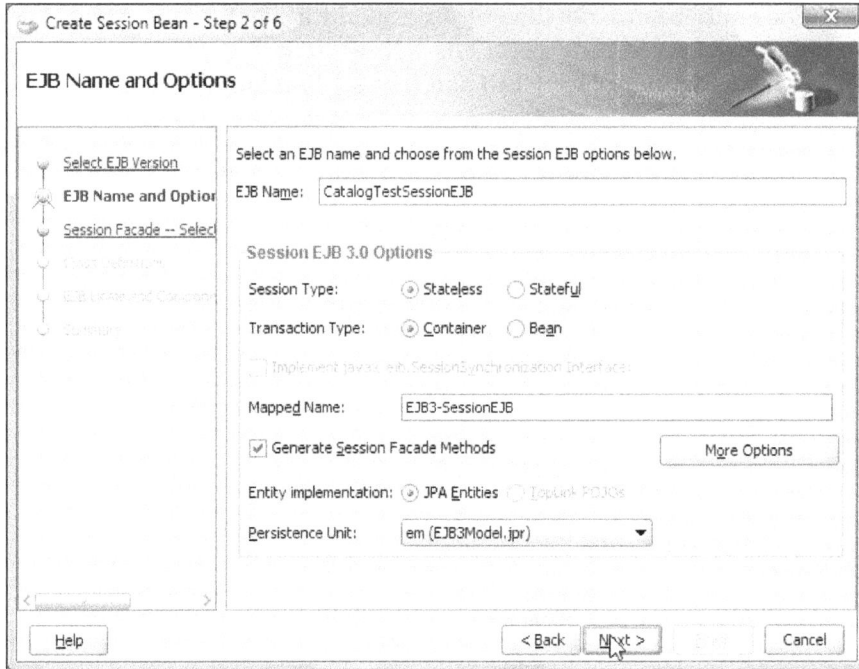

Select the default **JPA Entity Methods** to create and click on **Next**.

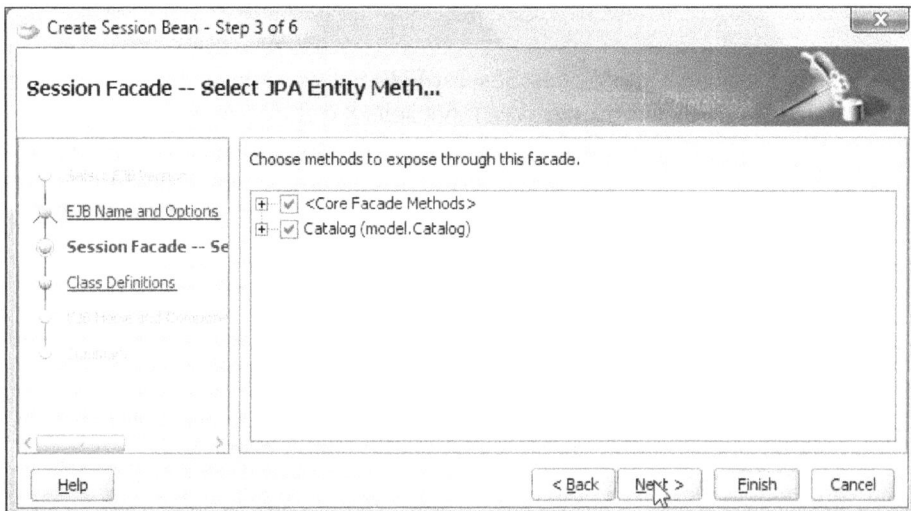

Specify the **Bean Class (model.CatalogTestSessionEJBBean)** and click on **Next**.

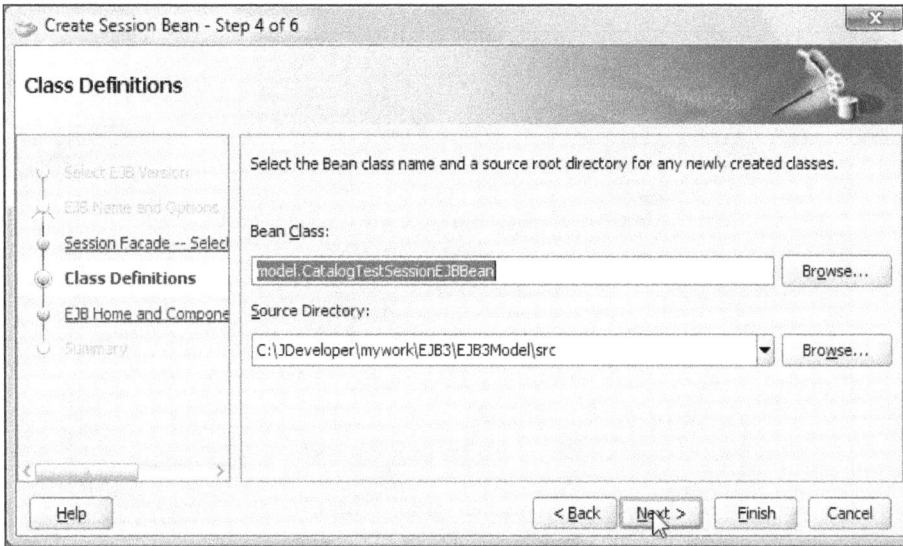

Select the EJB business interface to implement. Select the **Implement a Remote Interface** checkbox, specify the **Remote interface (model.CatalogTestSessionEJB)**. Click on **Next**. The remote interface may be used in a distributed environment, but if using the client and the EJB 3.0 model in the same JVM, the local client view may be used.

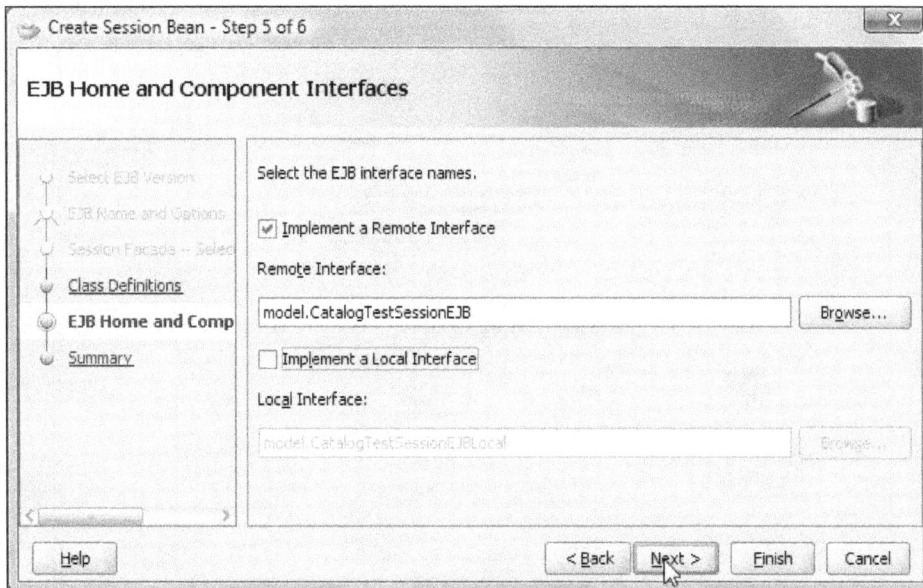

The **Summary** page lists the session bean and the corresponding bean and interface classes that will be generated. In the **Summary** window, click on **Finish**.

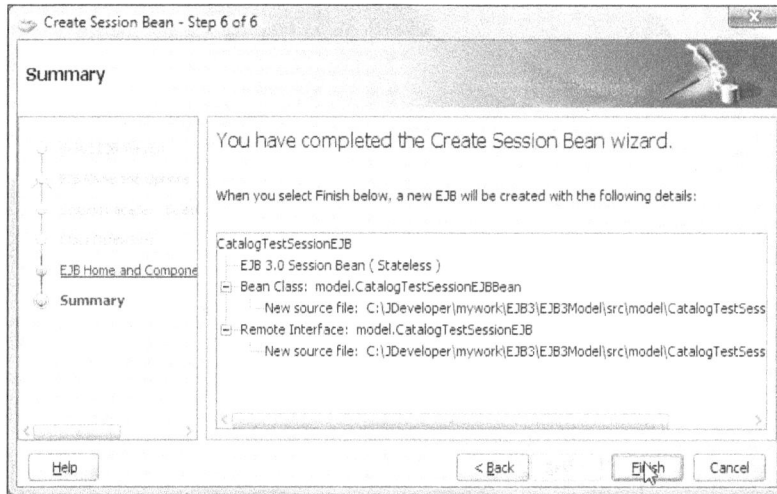

The session bean class

A session bean class **CatalogTestSessionEJBBean** gets added to the entity bean model project. The remote business interface for the session bean, **CatalogTestSessionEJB**, also gets created.

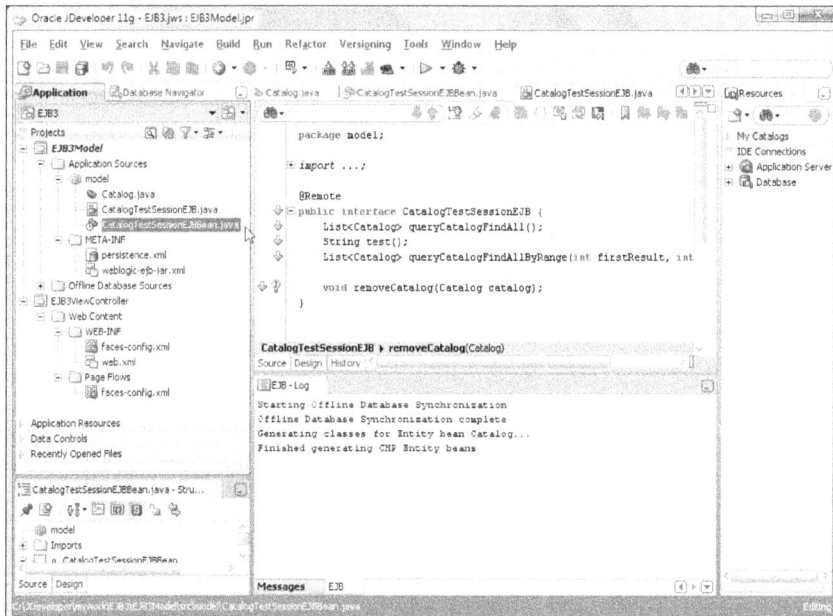

The `CatalogTestSessionEJBBean` class is annotated with the annotation
`@Stateless`. The `mappedName` attribute specifies the global JNDI for the session
bean. We shall use the mapped name in the test client to lookup the session bean and
invoke method/s on it. The `@Remote` annotation indicates that the session bean is a
remote interface.

```
@Stateless(name = "CatalogTestSessionEJB", mappedName = "EJB3-
SessionEJB")
@Remote
public class CatalogTestSessionEJBBean implements
CatalogTestSessionEJB { }
```

In the session bean an `EntityManager` is injected using the `@PersistenceContext`
annotation. The `unitName` is specified, but not required, as the `EntityManager`
variable name is the same as the persistence unit name.

```
@PersistenceContext(unitName = "em")
    private EntityManager em;
```

Add a method `test()` to the session bean and the remote interface. In the `test()`
method, create a `Catalog` entity instance with the `new` operator:

```
Catalog catalog =new Catalog("Kimberly Floss", "Nov-Dec 2004", new
Integer(1),"Oracle Magazine", "Oracle Publishing","Database Resource
Manager");
```

Invoke the `persistEntity(Object)` method to persist the entity bean instance:

```
persistEntity(catalog);
```

The `persistEntity` method invokes the persist method of the `EntityManager` to
persist the entity bean:

```
em.persist(entity);
```

Similarly, persist two more entity bean instances. Next, create an instance of the
`Query` object using the `createQuery` method to run a Java Persistence Query
Language statement. Bind an author name to the named parameter `:name` using
the `setParameter` method, and run the Java persistence query statement using the
`getResultList` method, which returns a `List`:

```
List catalogEntry =
            em.createQuery("SELECT c from Catalog c where
c.author=:name").setParameter("name","Jonas Jacobi").getResultList();
```

Iterate over the `List`, which is actually just one catalog entry, to output field values
for the `journal`, `publisher`, `edition`, `title`, and `author` fields:

```
for (Iterator iter = catalogEntry.iterator(); iter.hasNext(); )
```

```
{Catalog element = (Catalog)iter.next();
            retValue =retValue + "<br/>" + element.getJournal() +
"<br/>" + element.getPublisher() +
"<br/>" + element.getEdition() + "<br/>" +element.getTitle() + "<br/>"
+ element.getAuthor() +
                "<br/>";
    }
```

Similarly, run a query to list all titles. Remove an entity instance using the `remove` method of the `EntityManager`. Subsequently, run a query to list all the remaining entity instances.

```
em.remove(catalog2);
```

The `test` method returns a `String`, which consists of a catalog entry, a list of all the titles, and all the entity instances after removing an entity instance. The session bean class is listed next:

```
package model;
import java.util.Iterator;
import java.util.List;
import javax.ejb.Remote;
import javax.ejb.Stateless;
import javax.persistence.EntityManager;
import javax.persistence.PersistenceContext;
import javax.persistence.Query;

@Stateless(name = "CatalogTestSessionEJB",
          mappedName = "EJB3-SessionEJB")
@Remote
public class CatalogTestSessionEJBBean implements
CatalogTestSessionEJB {
  @PersistenceContext(unitName = "em")
  private EntityManager em;

  public CatalogTestSessionEJBBean() {
}

public String test() {
  Catalog catalog =
    new Catalog("Kimberly Floss", "Nov-Dec 2004", new Integer(1),
              "Oracle Magazine", "Oracle Publishing",
              "Database Resource Manager");
  persistEntity(catalog);
  Catalog catalog2 =
      new Catalog("Jonas Jacobi", "Nov-Dec 2004", new Integer(2),
              "Oracle Magazine", "Oracle Publishing",
```

```
                              "From ADF UIX to JSF");
        persistEntity(catalog2);
        Catalog catalog3 =
          new Catalog("Steve Muench", "March-April 2005", new Integer(3),
                      "Oracle Magazine", "Oracle Publishing",
                      "Starting with Oracle ADF");
        persistEntity(catalog3);
        String retValue = "<b>A catalog entry: </b>";
        List catalogEntry =
          em.createQuery("SELECT c from Catalog c where c.author=:name").
          setParameter("name", "Jonas Jacobi").getResultList();
        for (Iterator iter = catalogEntry.iterator(); iter.hasNext(); ) {
          Catalog element = (Catalog)iter.next();
          retValue = retValue + "<br/>" + element.getJournal() + "<br/>" +
                     element.getPublisher() + "<br/>" +
                     element.getEdition() + "<br/>" +
                     element.getTitle() + "<br/>" + element.getAuthor() +
                     "<br/>";
        }
        retValue = retValue + "<b>All Titles: </b>";
        List allTitles =
                  em.createQuery("SELECT c from Catalog c").getResultList();
        for (Iterator iter = allTitles.iterator(); iter.hasNext(); ) {
          Catalog element = (Catalog)iter.next();
          retValue = retValue + "<br/>" + element.getTitle() + "<br/>";
        }
        em.remove(catalog2);
        retValue = retValue + "<b>All Entries after removing an entry:
                              </b>";
        List allCatalogEntries =
                  em.createQuery("SELECT c from Catalog c").getResultList();
        for (Iterator iter = allCatalogEntries.iterator(); iter.hasNext(); )
        {
          Catalog element = (Catalog)iter.next();
          retValue = retValue + "<br/>" + element + "<br/>";
        }
        return retValue;
      }
```

```java
public Object mergeEntity(Object entity) {
    return em.merge(entity);
}

public Object persistEntity(Object entity) {
    em.persist(entity);
    return entity;
}
/** <code>select o from Catalog o</code> */
public List<Catalog> queryCatalogFindAll() {
    return em.createNamedQuery("Catalog.findAll").getResultList();
}



/** <code>select o from Catalog o</code> */
public List<Catalog> queryCatalogFindAllByRange(int firstResult,
                                                int maxResults) {
    Query query = em.createNamedQuery("Catalog.findAll");
    if (firstResult > 0) {
        query = query.setFirstResult(firstResult);
    }
    if (maxResults > 0) {
        query = query.setMaxResults(maxResults);
    }
    return query.getResultList();
}
public void removeCatalog(Catalog catalog) {
    catalog = em.find(Catalog.class, catalog.getId());
    em.remove(catalog);
}
}
```

The remote business interface is listed next:

```java
package model;
import java.util.List;
import javax.ejb.Remote;
@Remote
public interface CatalogTestSessionEJB {
    List<Catalog> queryCatalogFindAll();
    String test();
    List<Catalog> queryCatalogFindAllByRange(int firstResult,
                                             int maxResults);

    void removeCatalog(Catalog catalog);
}
```

Creating and testing a test client

In this section, we create a JSP client to test the entity bean using a wrapper session bean.

Creating a client

First, we need to create a JSP. Select the **EJB3ViewController** project and select **File>New**. In the **New Gallery** window, select **Categories | Web Tier | JSP** and **Items | JSP**. Click on **OK**.

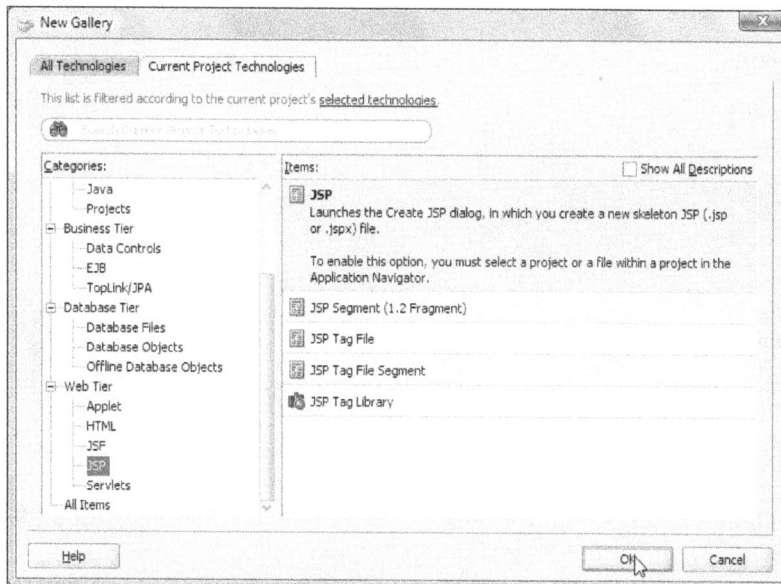

In the **Create JSP** window, specify a **FileName (EJB3Client)** and click on **OK**.

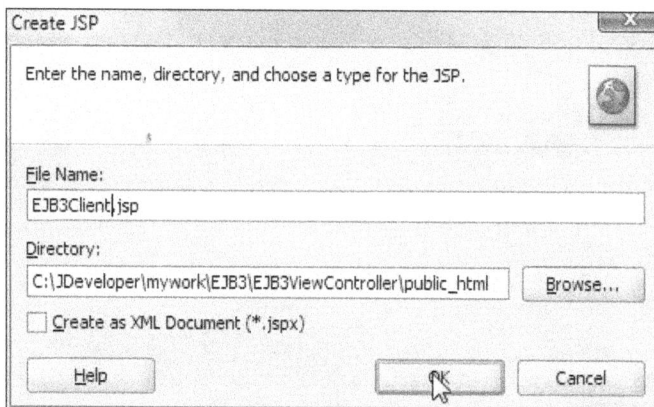

As we shall be invoking the entity bean, which is in the model project, from the JSP, which is in the **ViewController** project, we need to add a dependency in the **ViewController** project on the **Model** project. Select **Tools | Project Properties** and select **Dependencies**. Click on the **Edit Dependencies** button.

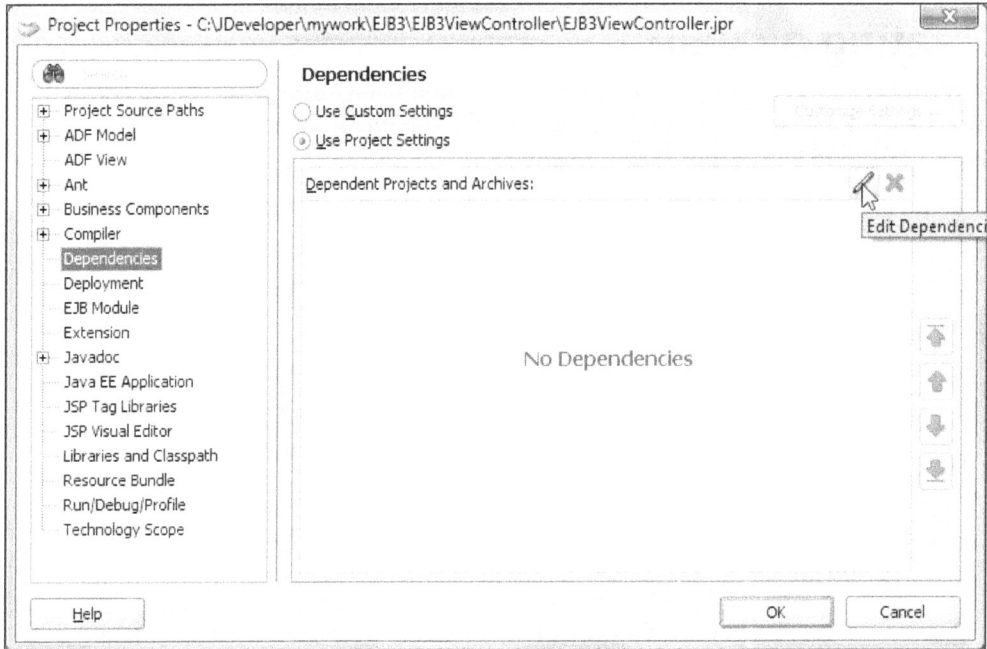

In the **Edit Dependencies** window, select **EJB3Model | Build Output** and click on **OK**, as shown:

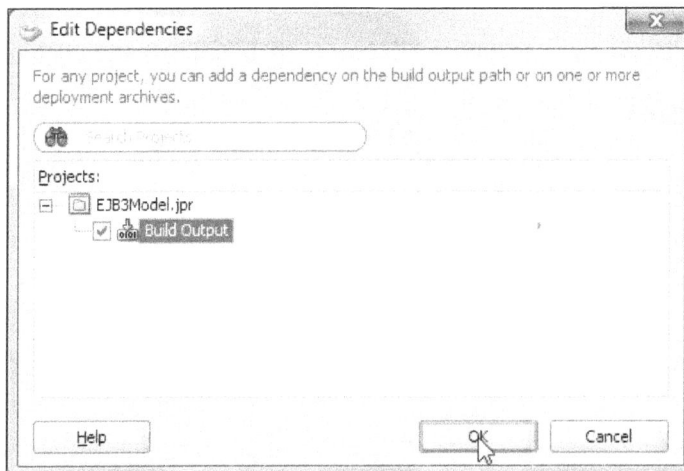

The **EJB3Model** project gets added to the **Dependencies**. Click on **OK**, as shown next:

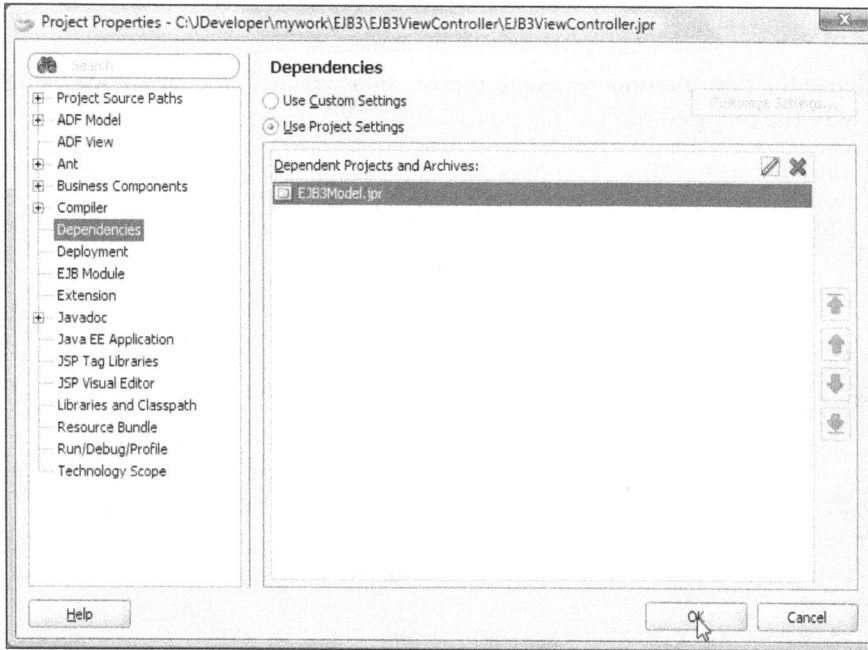

In the JSP client, we look up the session bean and invoke the `test()` method on it, which returns a `String`. First, we create an `InitialContext`:

```
InitialContext context = new InitialContext();
```

Two methods are available to look up a session bean using the remote business interface.

- Look up the session bean remote interface using the mapped name. The global JNDI name for a session bean remote business interface is derived from the remote business interface name. The format of the global JNDI name is `mappedName#qualified_name_of_businessInterface`.

- Specify the business interface JNDI name in the `weblogic-ejb-jar.xml` deployment descriptor. The global JNDI name is specified as follows:

```
<weblogic-enterprise-bean>
  <ejb-name>CatalogTestSessionEJBBean</ejb-name>
  <stateless-session-descriptor>
    <business-interface-jndi-name-map>
      <business-remote>CatalogTestSessionEJB
      </business-remote>
```

```
        <jndi-name>EJB3-SessionEJB</jndi-name>
      </business-interface-jndi-name-map>
    </stateless-session-descriptor>
  </weblogic-enterprise-bean>
```

We shall use the first method. Create a remote business interface instance using lookup with the mapped name:

```
CatalogTestSessionEJB beanRemote = (CatalogTestSessionEJB) context.
lookup("EJB3-SessionEJB#model.CatalogTestSessionEJB");
```

Invoke the `test()` method of the session bean:

```
String catalog=beanRemote.test();
```

Output the string returned by the `test` method:

```
<%=catalog %>
```

The `EJB3Client` is listed next:

```
<!DOCTYPE HTML PUBLIC "-//W3C//DTD HTML 4.01 Transitional//EN"
"http://www.w3.org/TR/html4/loose.dtd">
<%@ page import="model.*, javax.naming.*" %>
<%@ page
contentType="text/html;charset=windows-1252"%>
<html>
  <head>
    <meta http-equiv="Content-Type" content="text/html;
                                  charset=windows-1252" />
    <title>EJB3Client</title>
  </head>
  <body><% InitialContext context = new InitialContext();
    CatalogTestSessionEJB beanRemote = (CatalogTestSessionEJB)
    context.lookup("EJB3-SessionEJB#model.CatalogTestSessionEJB");
    String catalog=beanRemote.test(); %><%=catalog %></body>
</html>
```

Testing the client

To run the test client, right-click on, **EJB3Client.jsp** and select **Run**.

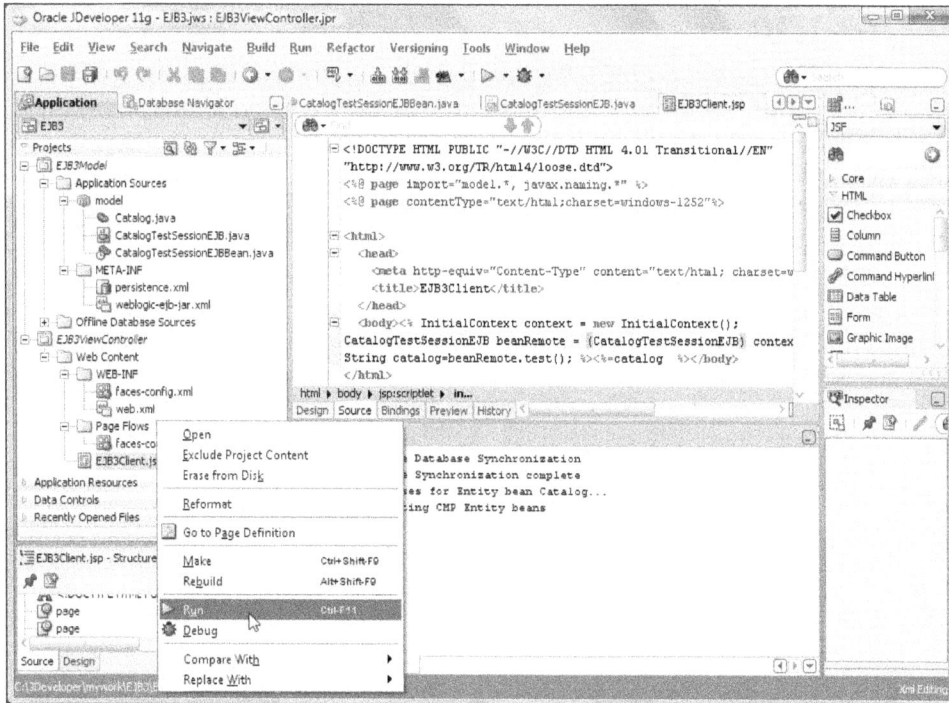

The output from the test client lists a catalog entry, all the titles, and all the entity instances after removing a catalog entry.

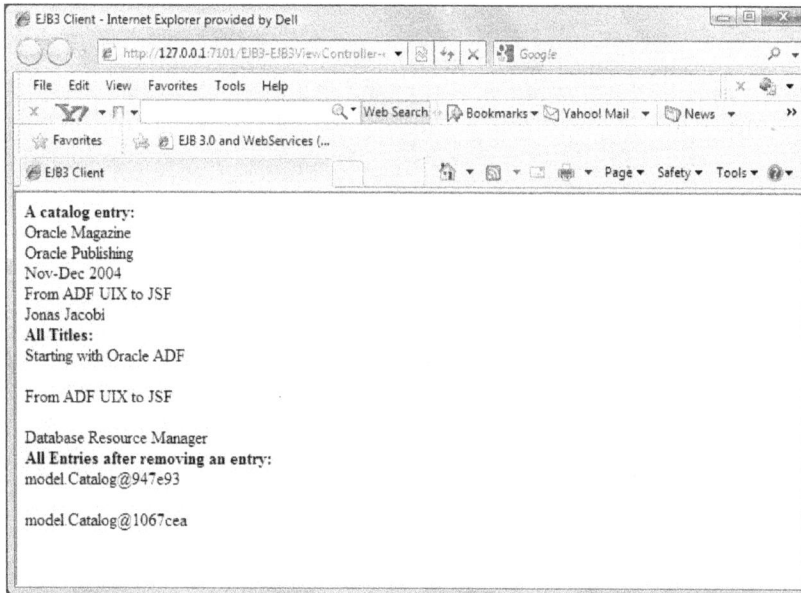

Summary

In this section, we created an EJB 3.0 entity bean in JDeveloper 11*g* from an Oracle database table. The Catalog entity bean is automatically created a database table CATALOG; the database table columns are mapped to entity bean properties. We created a wrapper session bean for the entity bean, including a remote business interface. We added a test method to the session bean for creating and persisting entity instances, querying entity instances, and removing an entity instance. We created a JSP test client to test the entity bean. We look up the session bean remote interface using the mapped name for the session bean and invoke the test method on the remote interface instance. In the next chapter, we shall discuss EJB 3.0 database persistence with Oracle Enterprise Pack for Eclipse and WebLogic server.

5
EJB 3.0 Persistence with Oracle Enterprise Pack for Eclipse

Developing Entity EJBs require an application server and a relational database, and, optionally, a Java IDE to improve productivity and simplify the development. Eclipse IDE is the most commonly used open source Java IDE and MySQL database is the most commonly used open source relational database. **Oracle Enterprise Pack for Eclipse (OEPE)** All-In-One edition bundles a pre-configured Eclipse and Eclipse plugins. Oracle has acquired the open source MySQL database. MySQL database is available under the GPL license; a commercial license is also available without the precondition to purchase support services from Oracle. In this chapter, we shall develop an EJB 3.0 entity using the Eclipse-WebLogic Server-MySQL combination; you will learn the following:

- Creating a MySQL database table
- Configuring WebLogic Server with MySQL database
- Creating a JPA project in Eclipse
- Creating an EJB 3.0 entity
- Creating a persistence configuration file
- Creating a session bean
- Creating a test client
- Deploying the EJB 3.0 entity in WebLogic Server
- Testing the EJB 3.0 entity client

Setting the environment

In the following sections, we will learn how to set up the environment.

Installing required products

First, download and install the following required products; when installing the MySQL database, select the option to add the MySQL `bin` directory to the Windows system `PATH` environment variable:

1. Oracle WebLogic Server 11*g* (`http://www.oracle.com/technology/software/products/ias/htdocs/wls_main.html`).

2. Oracle Enterprise Pack for Eclipse All-In-One edition (`http://www.oracle.com/technology/software/products/oepe/oepe_11113.html`).

3. MySQL 5.x database (`http://www.oracle.com/us/products/mysql/index.html`).

Creating a MySQL database table

Next, create a database table in the MySQL database as follows:

1. Log in to the MySQL database with the following command:
   ```
   >mysql
   ```

2. Set database as `test`:
   ```
   mysql>use test
   ```

3. Run the following SQL script, which creates a `Catalog` table for the EJB 3 entity:
   ```
   CREATE TABLE Catalog (id INT PRIMARY KEY NOT NULL, journal
   VARCHAR(100), publisher VARCHAR(100), date VARCHAR(100), title
   VARCHAR(100), author VARCHAR(100));
   ```

The output from the CREATE TABLE SQL script is shown in the following screenshot:

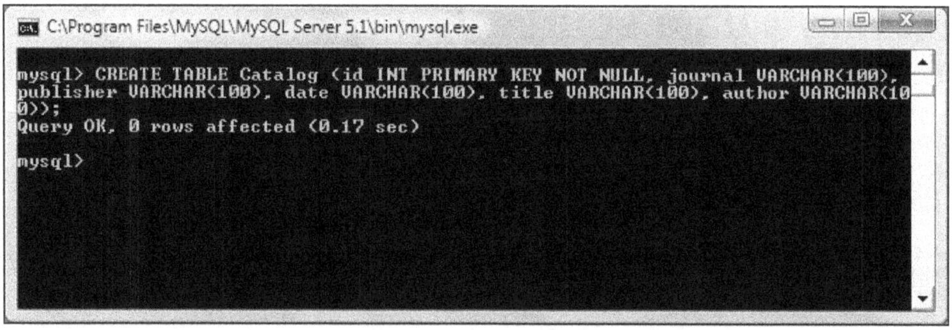

The table description may be listed with the `desc` command, as shown in the following illustration:

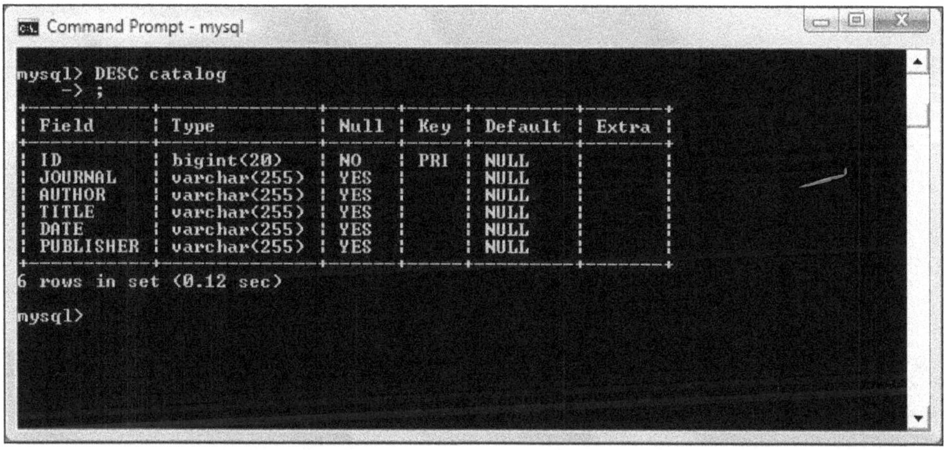

Configuring WebLogic Server with MySQL database

We shall be using a MySQL database for persistence. Therefore, we need to create a data source in WebLogic Server. Start the WebLogic Server and log in to the Administration Console.

Creating a data source

Select the **base_domain | Services | JDBC | Data Sources**. Click on **New** in the **Data Sources** table. Specify a data source name and a **JNDI Name** (**jdbc/MySQLDS**) for the data source. Select **Database Type** as **MySQL** and **Database Driver** as **MySQL's Driver (Type 4): com.mysql.jdbc.Driver**. Click on **Next**, as shown in the following screenshot:

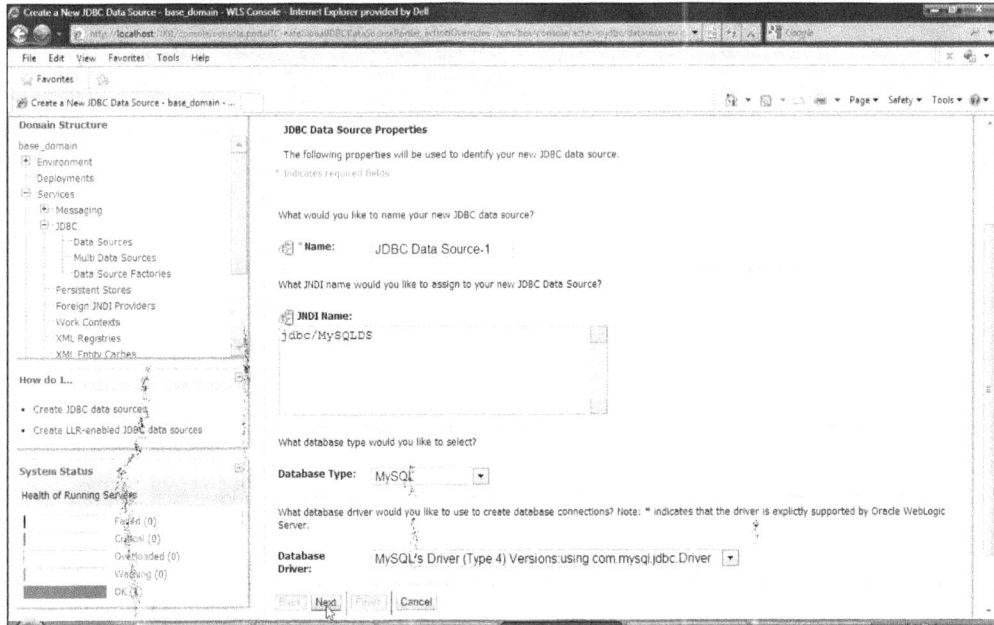

In the **Transaction Options** window, select **Supports Global Transactions** and **One-Phase Commit**. Click on **Next**, as shown in the following screenshot:

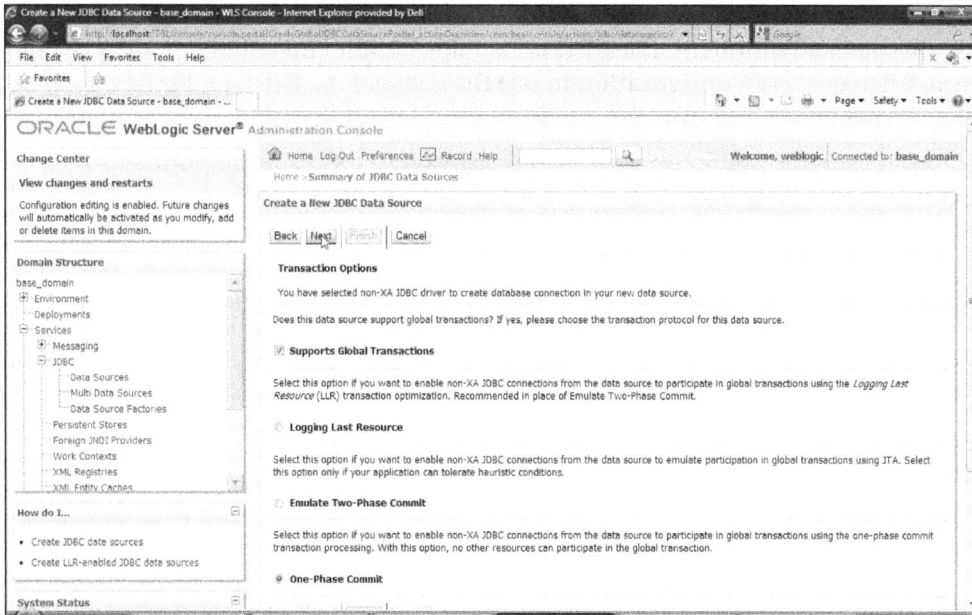

Specify the connection properties: **Database Name** as **test**, **Host Name** as **localhost**, **Port** as **3306**, and **Database User Name** as **root**. Specify the **Password** used when installing MySQL and click on **Next**, as shown in the following screenshot:

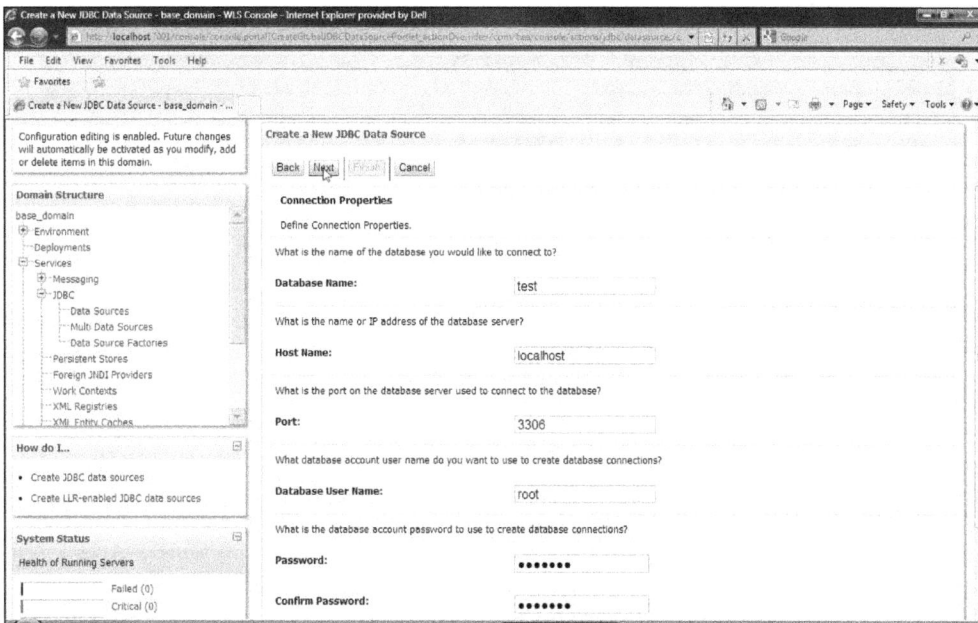

In the **Test Database Connection** window, the **Driver Class Name** and connection **URL** are specified, normally filled from the information you entered in the previous screen. Click on **Test Configuration** to test the connection. Click on **Finish**, as shown in the following screenshot:

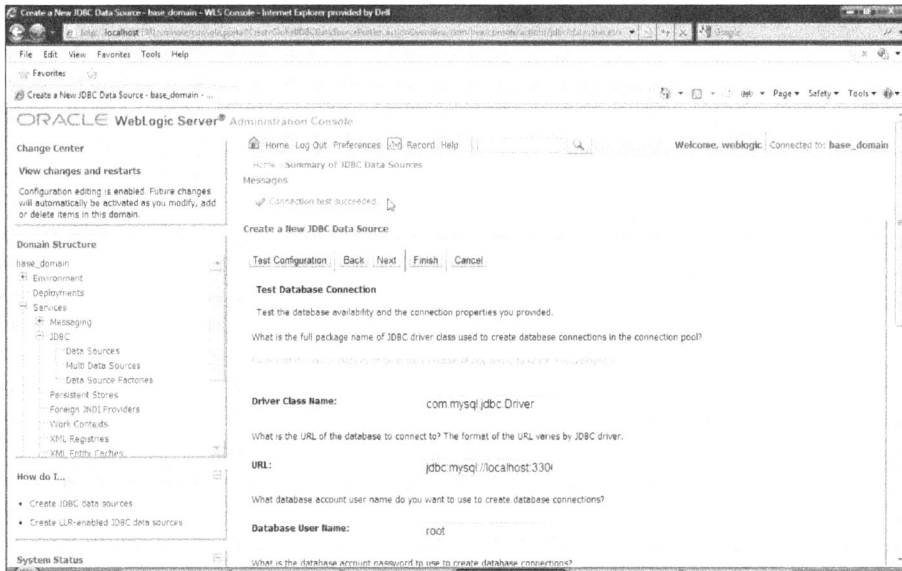

A data source gets added to the **Data Sources** table with its data source **JNDI Name** as **jdbc/MySQLDS**, as shown in the following screenshot:

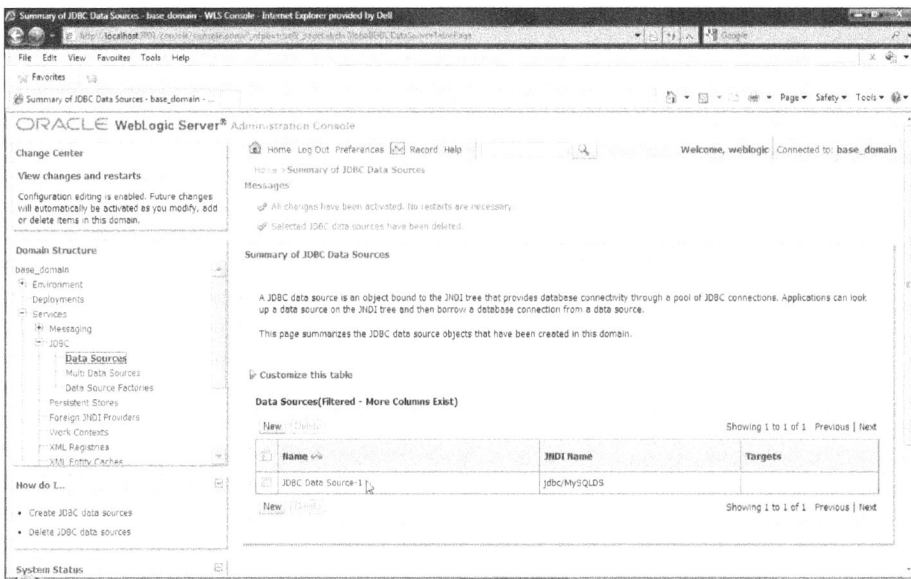

Deploying the data source

Next, we deploy the data source to a target server. Click on the data source link in the **Data Sources** table and select the **Targets** tab. Select the **AdminServer** checkbox and click on **Save,** as shown in the following screenshot:

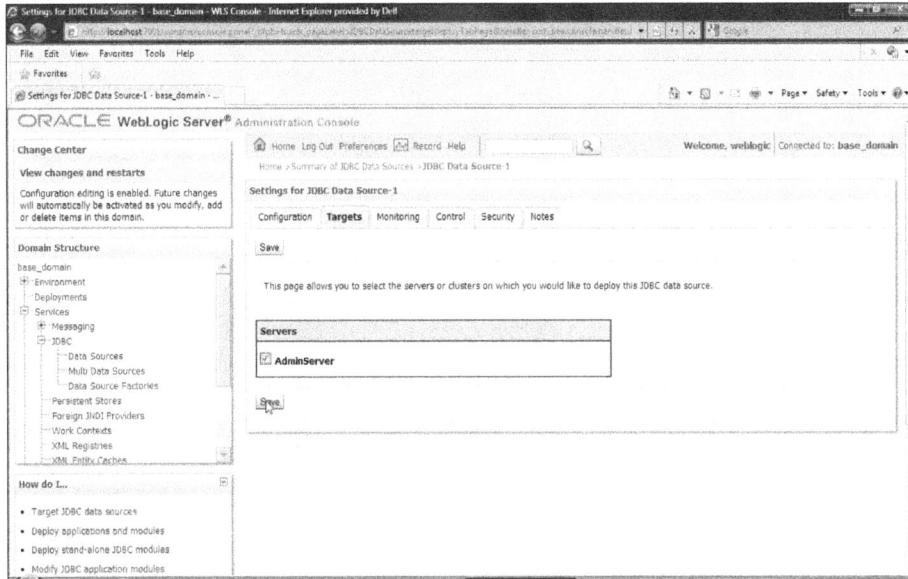

The target server changes get applied and saved:

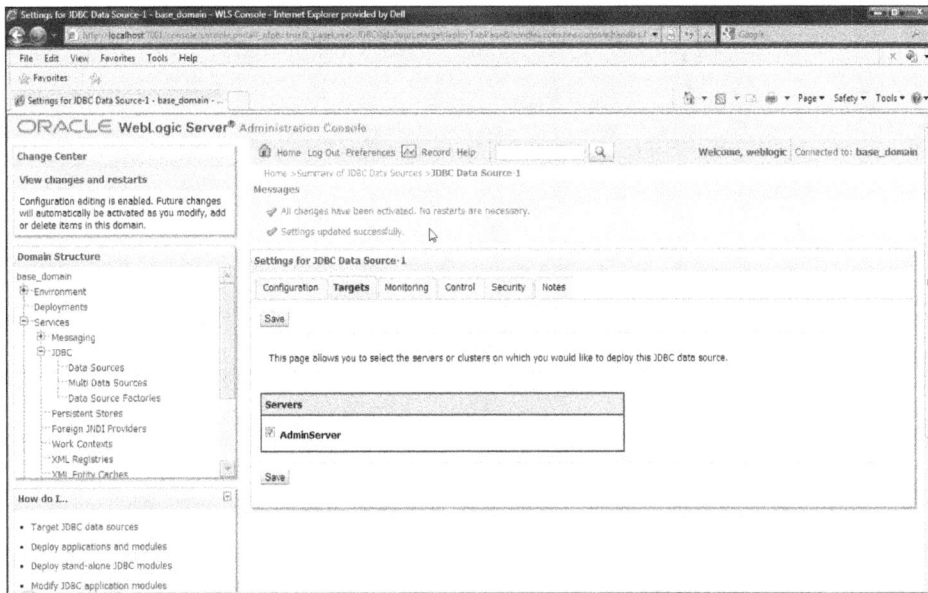

Testing the data source

To test the data source, click on **Test Data Source**. If the data source tests without an error, a message indicating the same gets displayed as shown next:

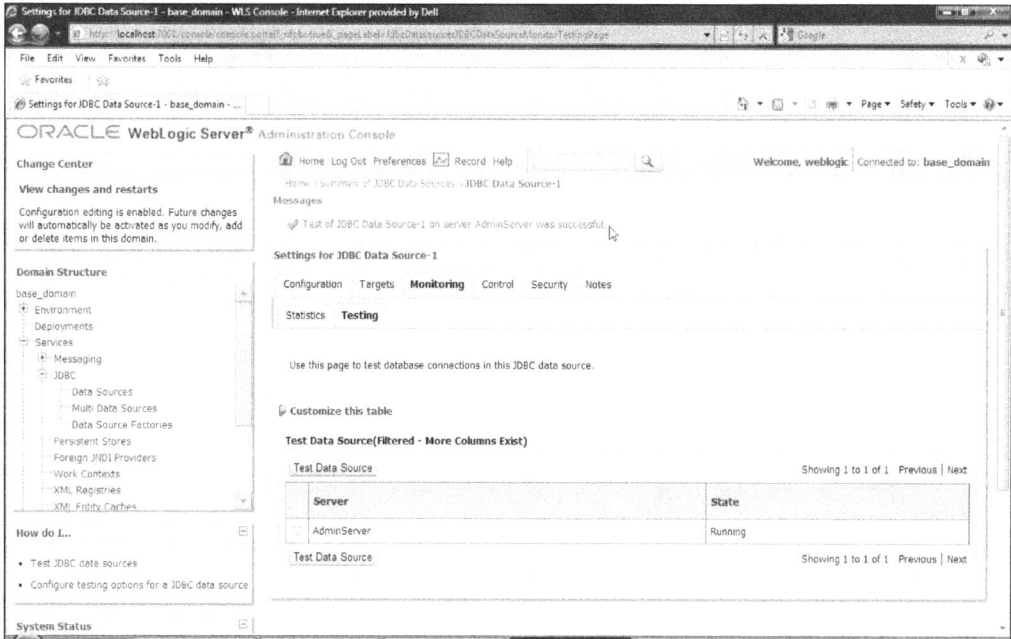

Creating a JPA project in Eclipse

For creating an EJB 3.0 entity bean we require Java Persistence API (JPA) project in Eclipse. Next, we create a JPA project in Eclipse. In the Eclipse IDE, select **File | New**. In the **New** window select **JPA | JPA Project** and click on **Next**, as shown below:

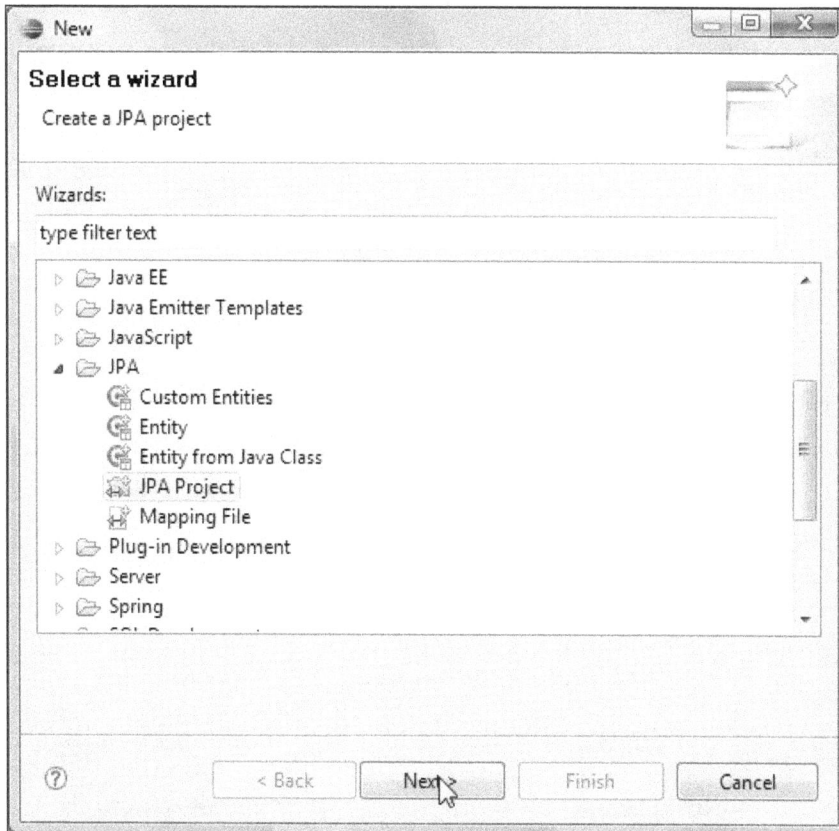

In the **New JPA Project** window, specify a **Project name**, select the default **Contents** directory, and select the **Utility JPA project with Java 5.0**. Click on **Next**:

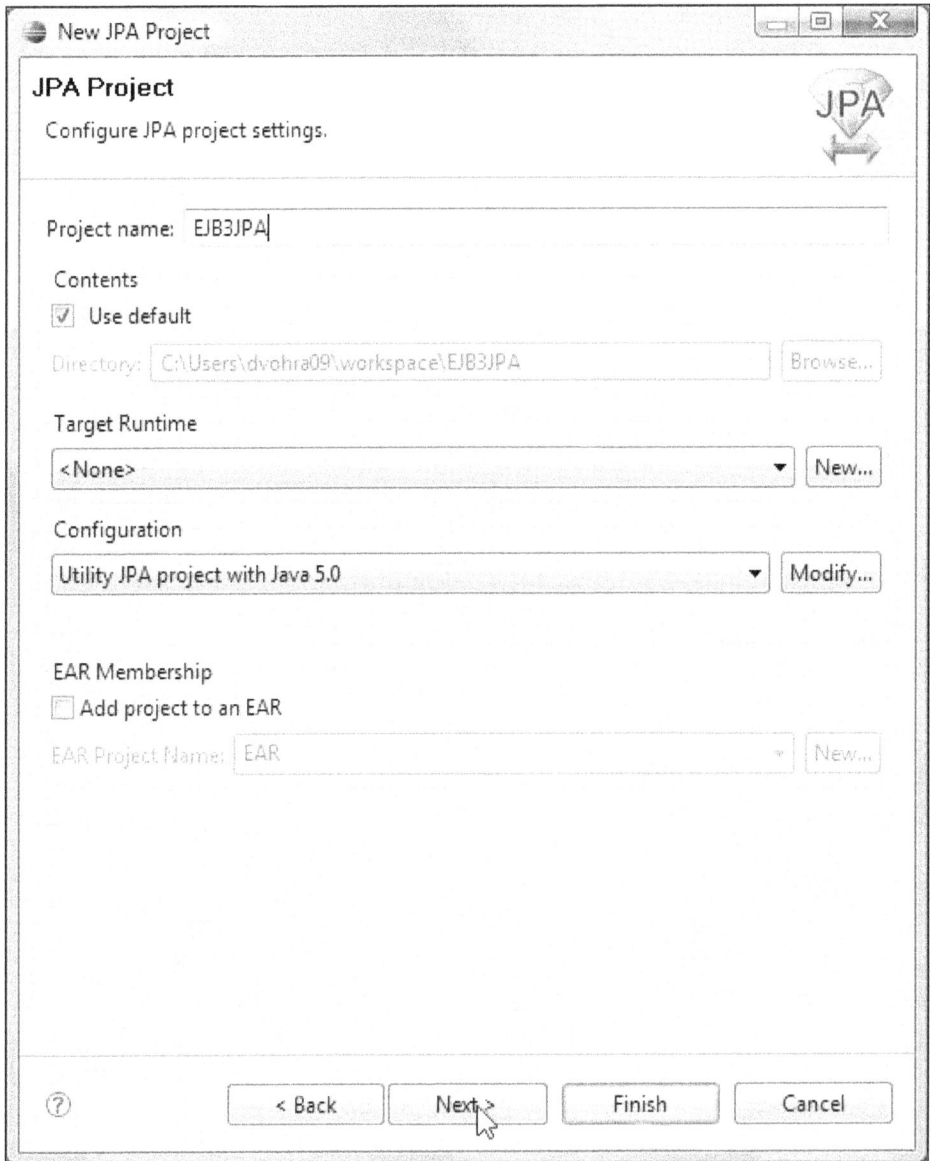

In the **New JPA Project** window, select a JPA persistence provider under **Platform**. We shall be using the **EclipseLink** JPA persistence provider. We need a database connection for database persistence. Click on the **Add connection** link adjacent to the **Connection** select list, as shown in the following screenshot:

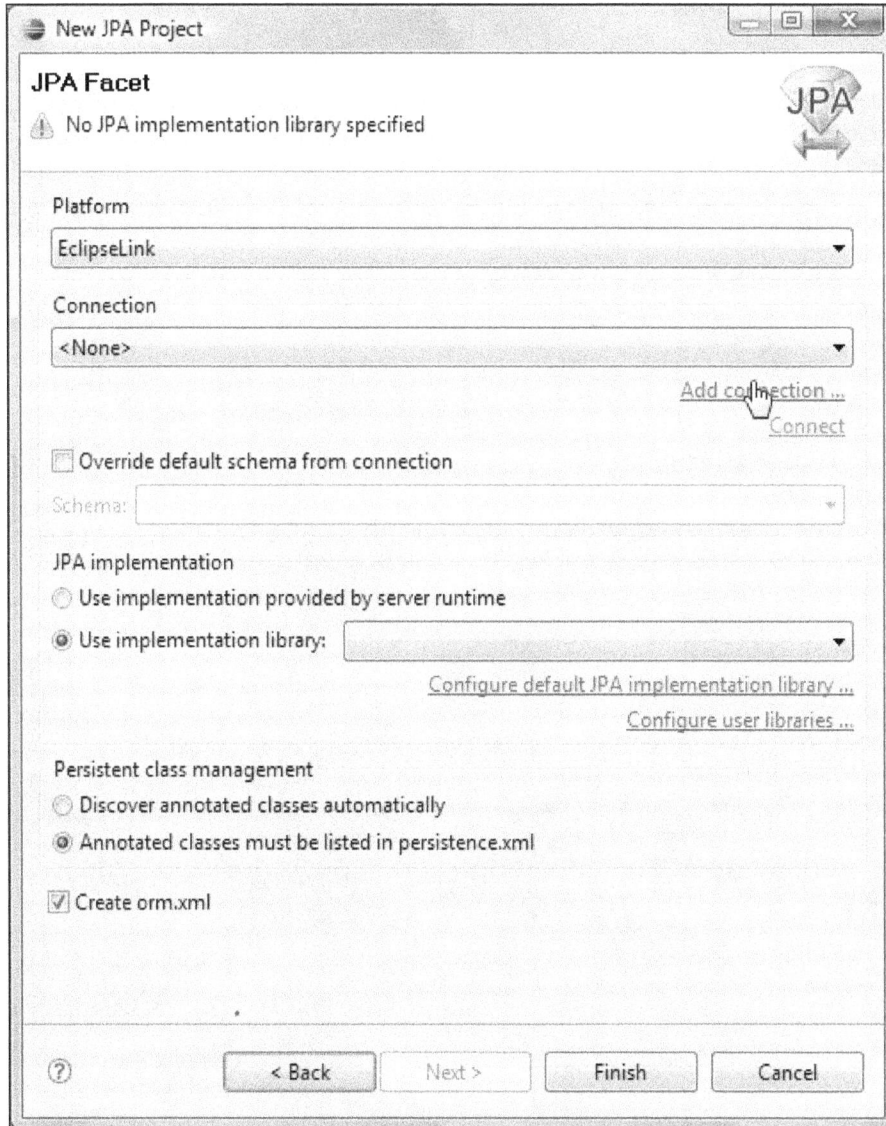

In the **New Connection Profile** window, select **Connection Profile Type** as **MySQL**, specify a connection profile name, and click on **Next**:

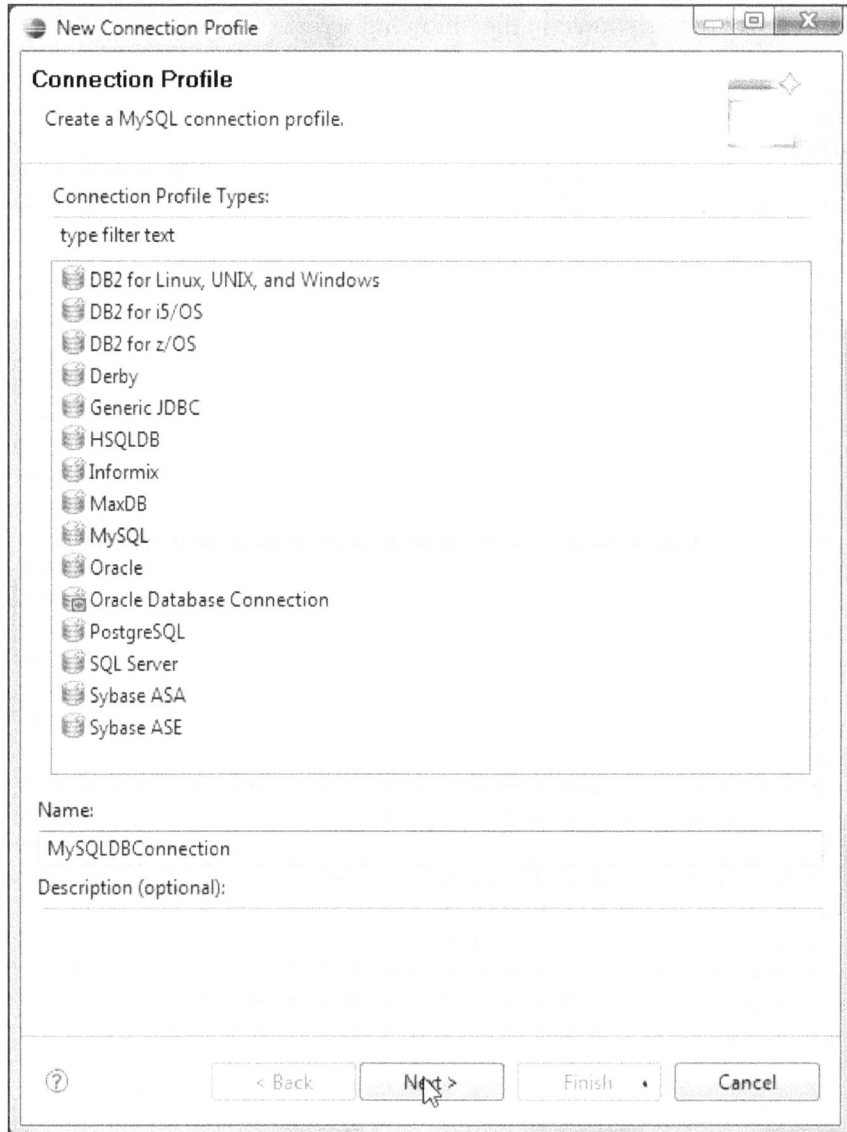

Next, specify a driver and other connection details. To add a new driver definition, click on the button adjacent to the **Drivers** select list, as shown next:

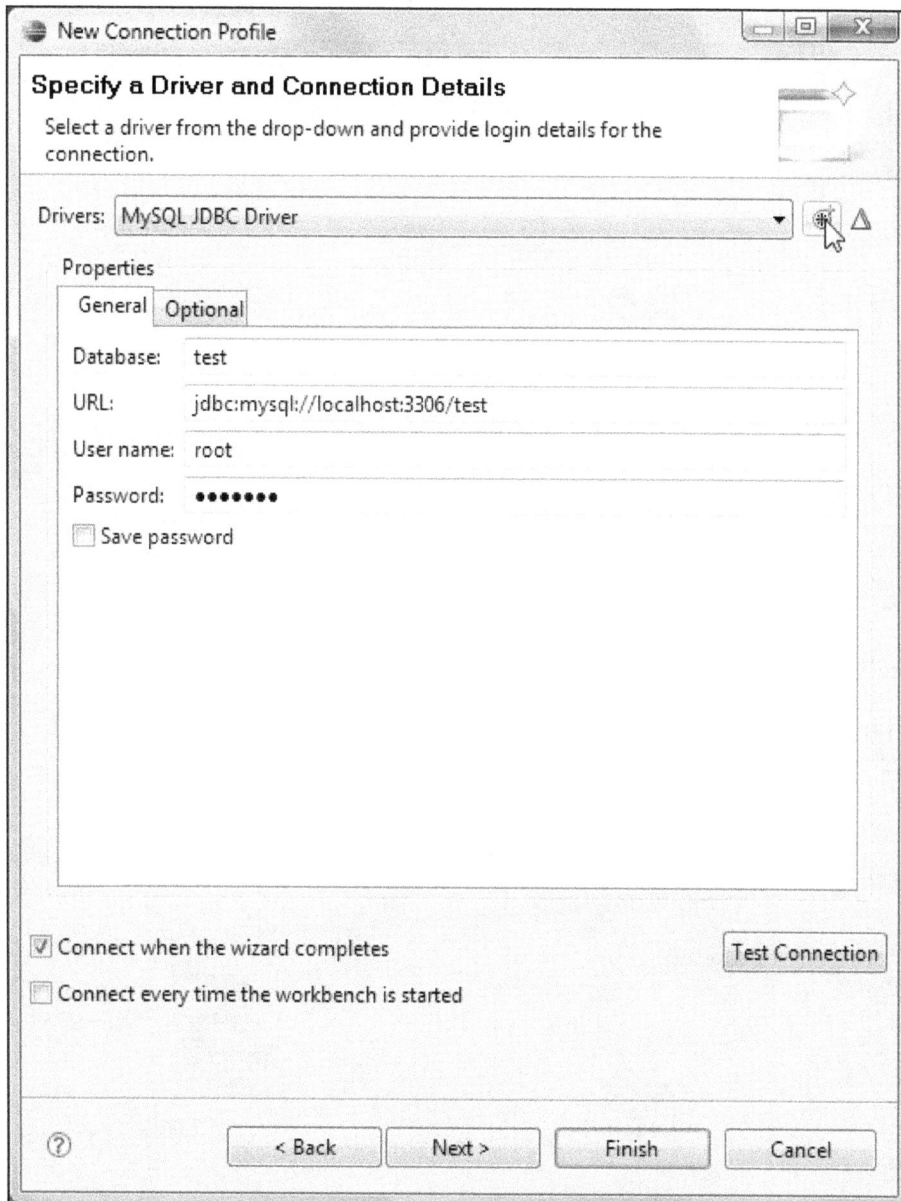

In the **New Driver Definition** window, select the **Driver** template as **MySQL JDBC Driver System Version 5.1**, and specify a **Driver name** (**MySQLJDBCDriver**). JAR files for the driver definition may need to be added, for which select the **Jar List** tab:

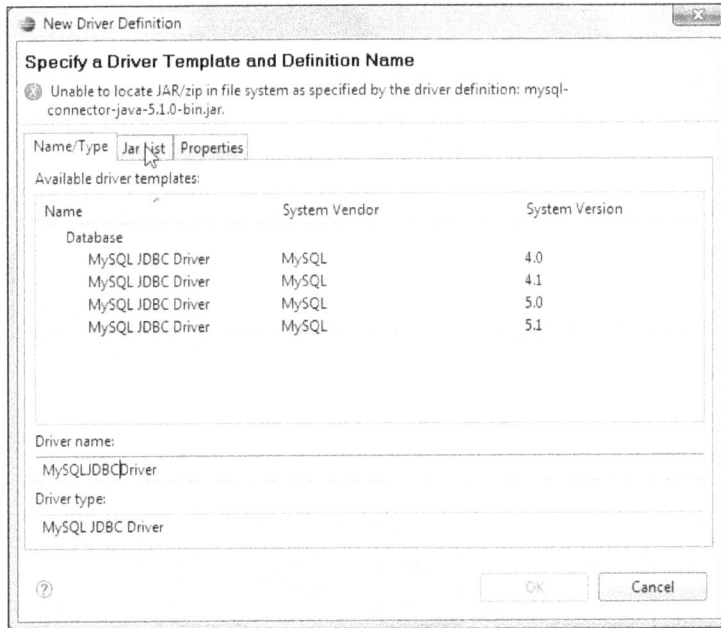

In the **Jar List** tab, add `mysql-connector-java-5.1.10.jar`, the MySQL 5.1 Connector-J JDBC JAR file, and click on **OK**.

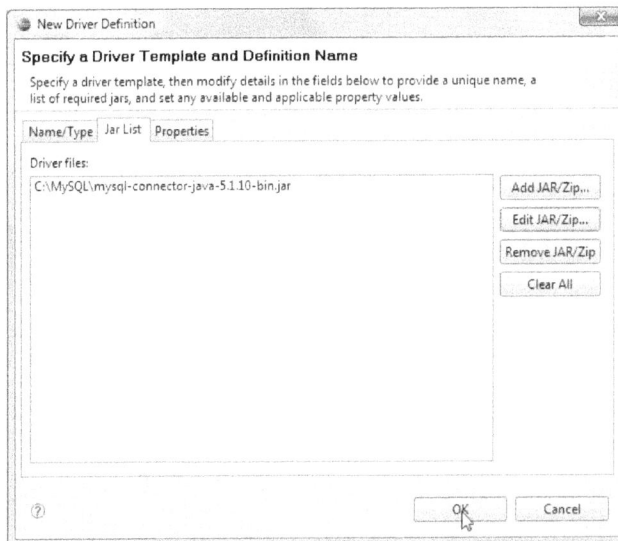

The driver definition (**MySQLJDBCDriver**) gets added to the **Drivers** select list and may be selected for creating a connection profile. Specify the connection details in **Properties**: **Database** as **test**, **URL** as **jdbc:mysql://localhost:3306/test**, **Username** as **root**, and **Password** for the **root** user. Click on **Test Connection** to test the connection.

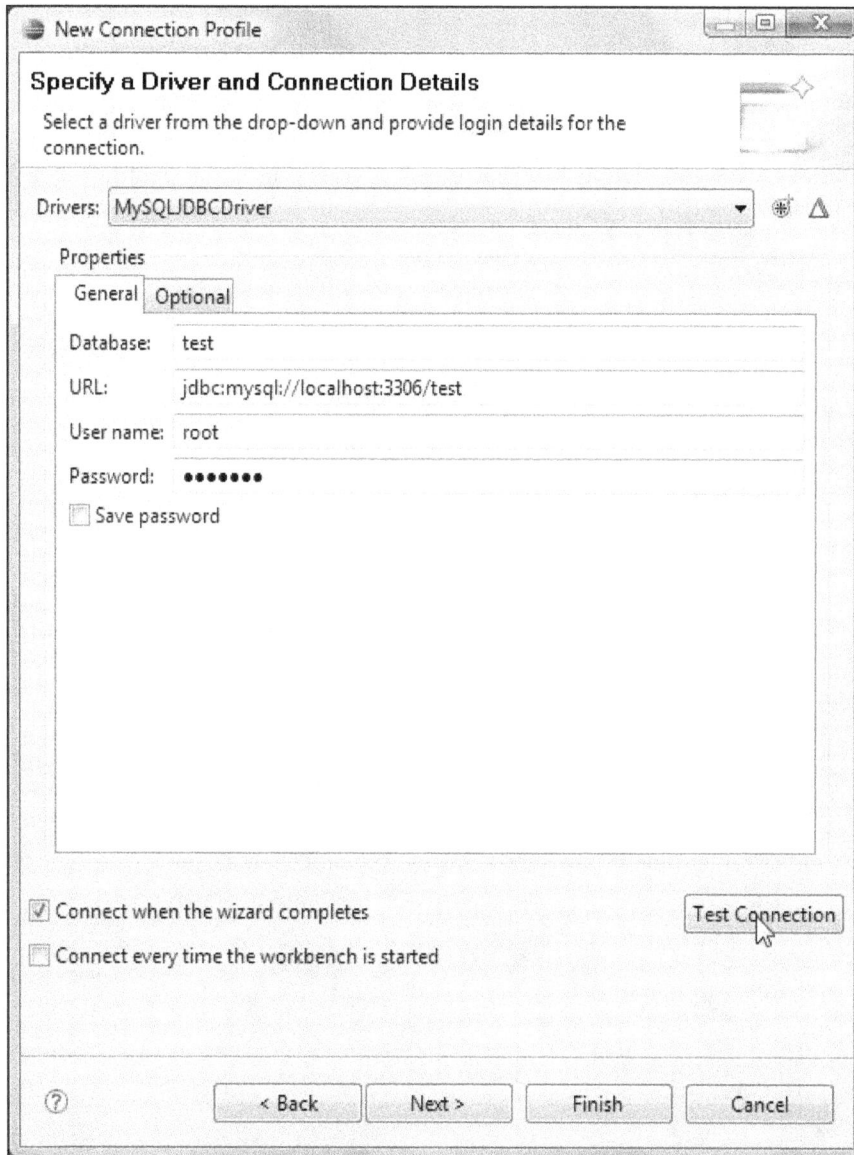

A **Ping succeeded!** message gets displayed if a connection gets established. Click on **Next** in the **New Connection Profile** window, as shown:

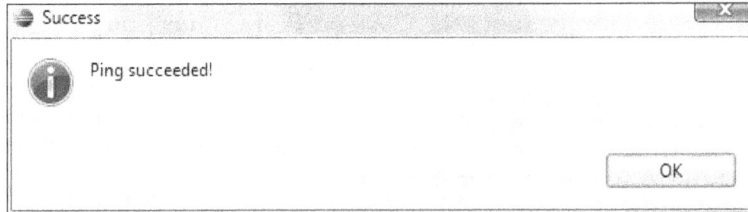

The **Summary** window displays the summary of the connection profile. Click on **Finish**, as shown next:

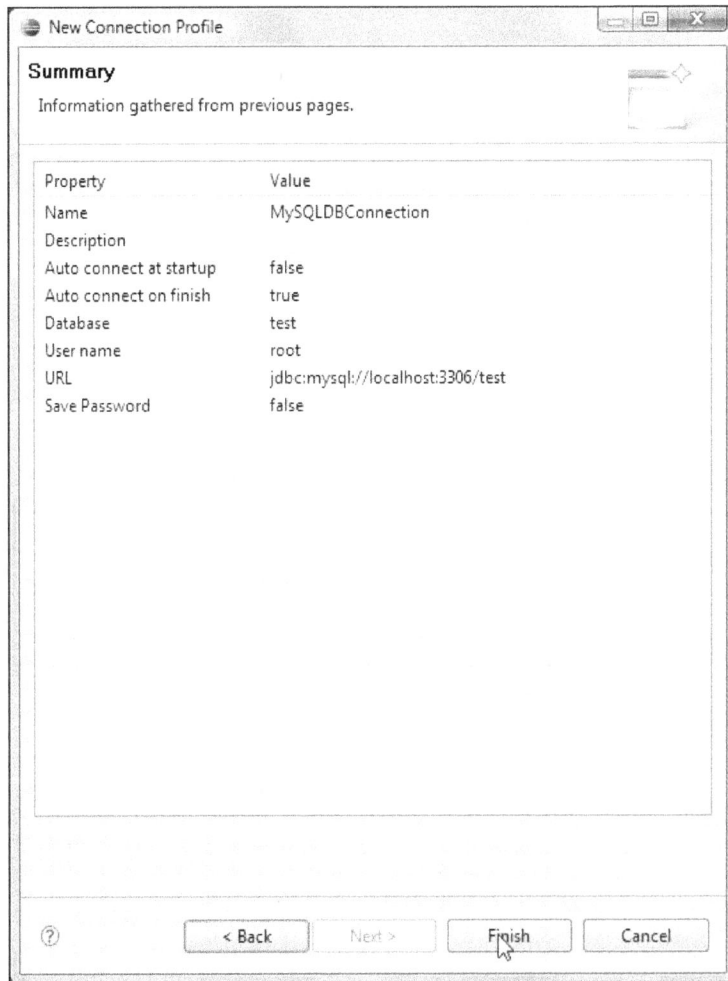

The connection profile gets added to the **Connection** select list. Next, select the **JPA implementation**. Select **Use implementation library: EJB 3.0**. In the **Persistent class management section**, select **Annotated classes must be listed in persistence.xml**. Click on **Finish,** as shown next:

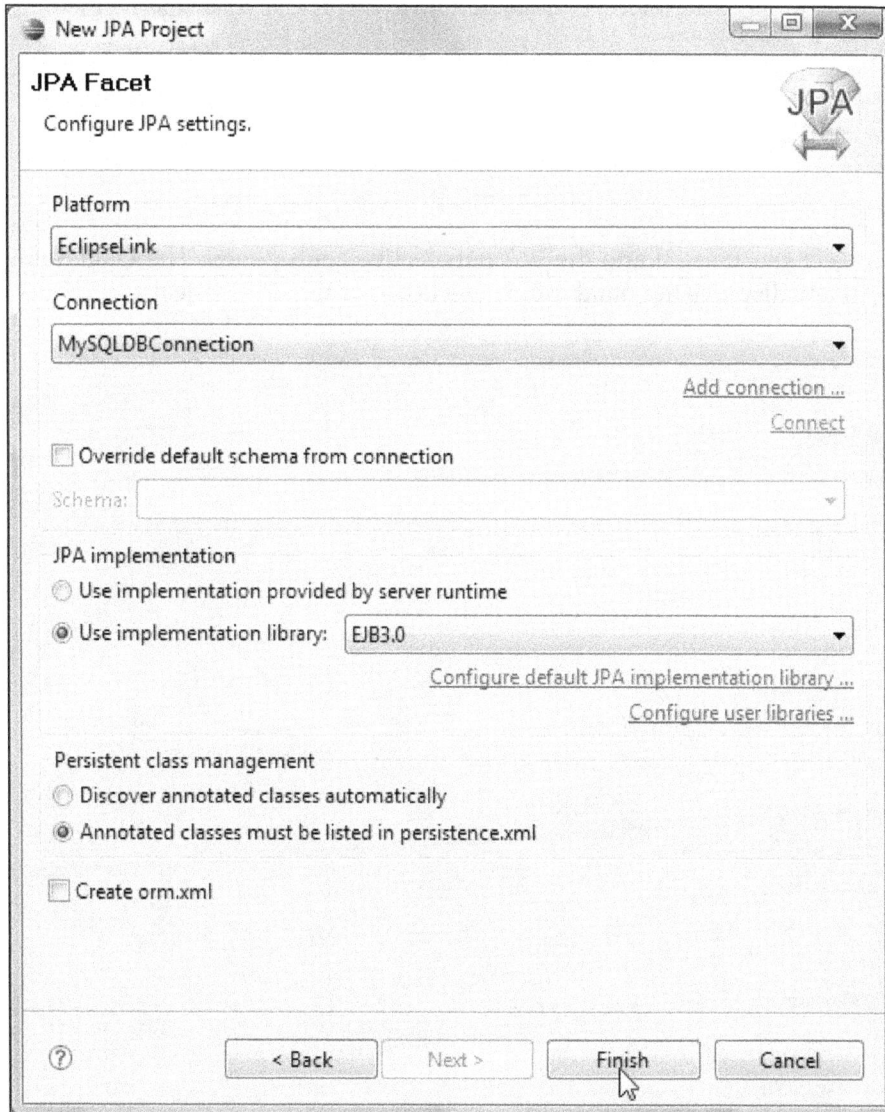

An **Open Associated Perspective?** message prompt gets displayed. To open the JPA perspective, click on **Yes**.

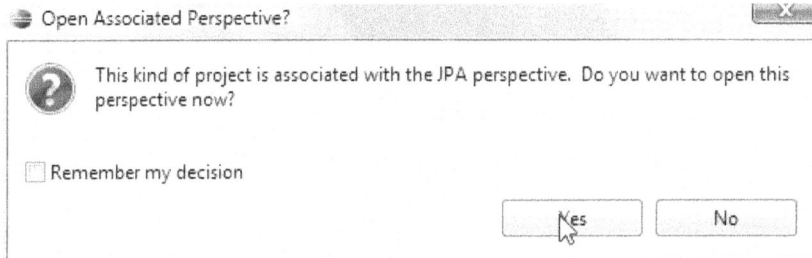

A JPA project gets created and the JPA perspective gets opened. The **Data Source Explorer** view displays the database connections for the JPA project.

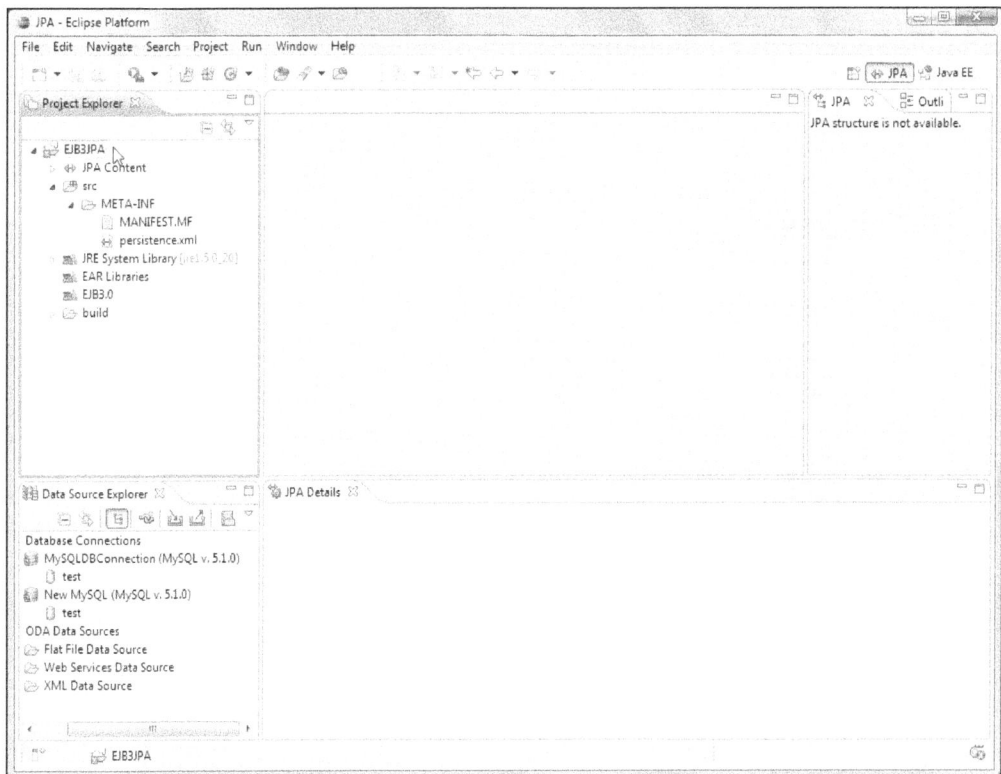

We need to have JRE 5.0 in the Build Path of the JPA project, as we shall be using JDK 5 features such as annotations. Right-click on the project node in **Project Explorer** and select **Project Properties**. In the **Properties** window, select the **Java Build Path** node and select the **Libraries** tab. Add a JRE 1.5 System library if not already added.

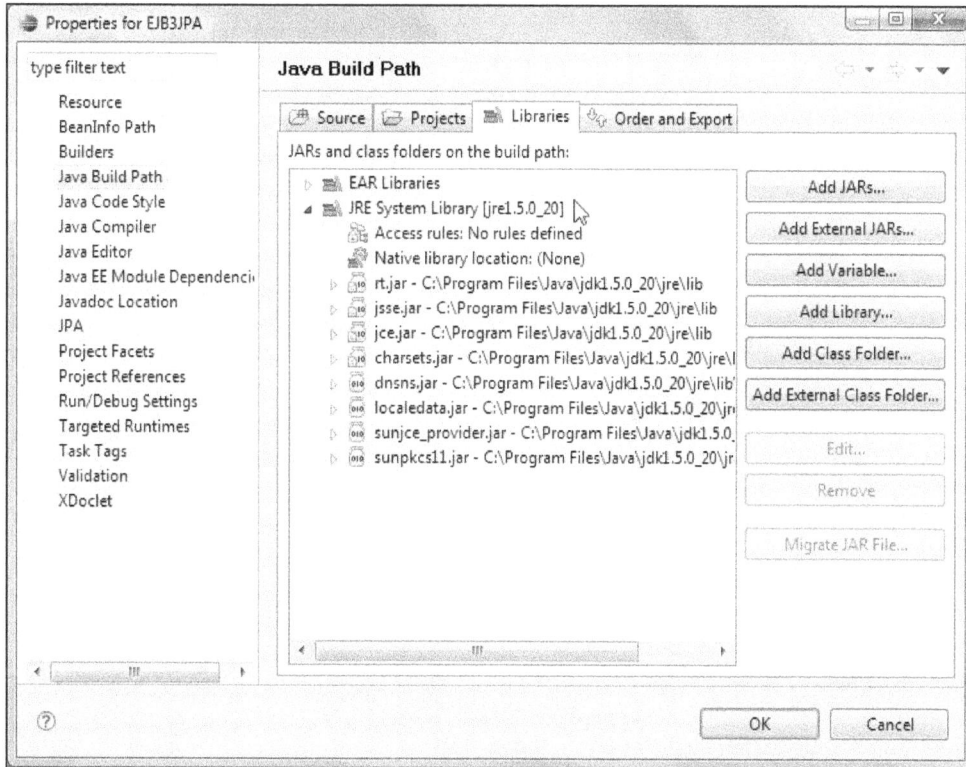

Creating an EJB 3.0 entity bean

In this section we create an EJB 3.0 entity bean. Select the JPA project node in **Project Explorer** and select **File | New**. In the **New** window, select **JPA | Entity** and click on **Next**.

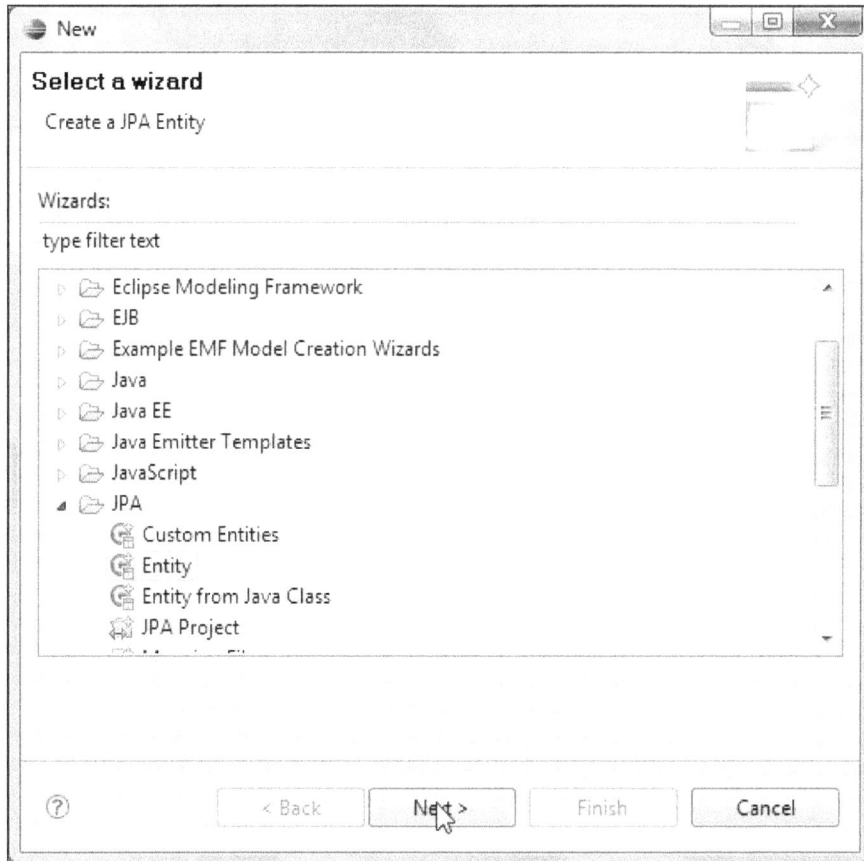

In the **New JPA Entity** window, we define an **Entity** class. Select the project in which the Entity class is to be created. Select the **Source folder**, specify a **Java package**, and specify a **Class name**. In **Inheritance**, select **Entity**. Click on **Next**, as shown in the following screenshot:

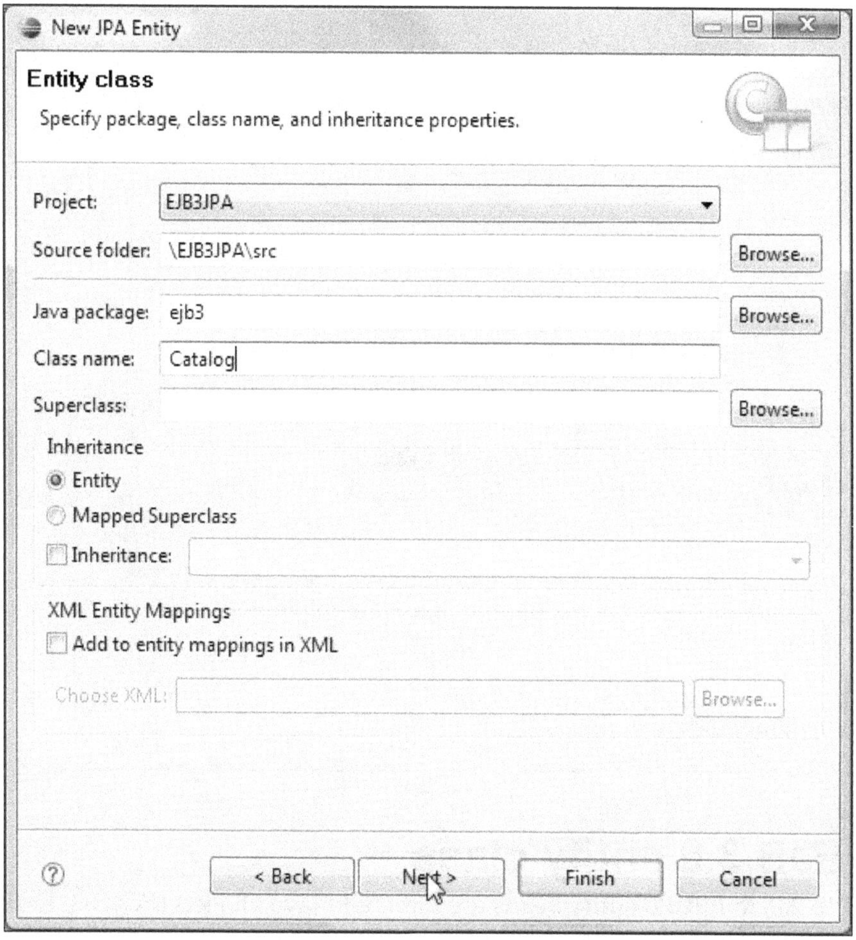

In the **Entity Properties** window, the **Entity Name**, **Table Name**, and **Entity Fields** are specified. Entity fields may be added with the **Add** button. Click on **Finish**. An EJB 3.0 entity bean class gets added to the JPA project. The Entity class `Catalog` is shown with code, which we shall discuss next:

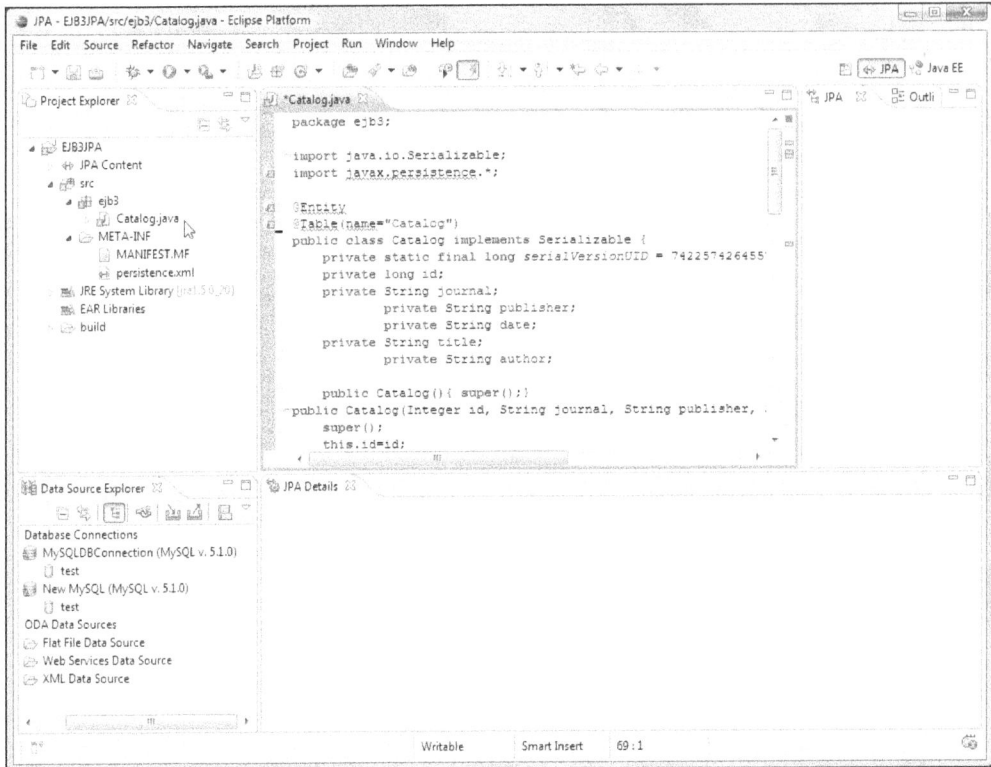

The EJB 3.0 entity class

Unlike EJB 2.0, in EJB 3.0 entity beans are Plain Old Java Objects (POJOs). Entity bean mappings are defined using annotations, which were introduced in JDK 5.0 and are in the `javax.persistence` package. A POJO class annotated with the `@Entity` annotation is an entity bean. The schema and table for the entity bean mapping is set at the class level using the `@Table` annotation. If the `@Table` annotation is not specified, the default table name is the entity bean class name. We shall create an entity bean `Catalog` that is mapped to `Catalog` table:

```
@Entity
@Table(name="Catalog")
public class Catalog implements Serializable {
...
}
```

If an entity bean that has caching enabled is persisted to a database via an entity manager, the entity bean is serialized by caches. Therefore, an entity bean is recommended to implement the `java.io.Serializable` interface. In the entity bean class, specify the POJO properties. Also, specify the `serialVersionUID`, which is used by the serialization runtime to associate a version number with the serializable class. Add the getter and setter methods for the entity bean properties. Specify the identifier property with the `@Id` annotation. We have used only some of the EJB 3.0 annotations that may be specified in an entity bean. For a complete reference to EJB 3.0 annotations, refer to, EJB 3.0 specification (`http://java.sun.com/products/ejb/docs.html`). The `Catalog` entity bean is listed next:

```
package ejb3;
import java.io.Serializable;
import javax.persistence.*;
@Entity
@Table(name="Catalog")
public class Catalog implements Serializable {
   private static final long serialVersionUID = 7422574264557894633L;
   private long id;
   private String journal;
   private String publisher;
   private String date;
   private String title;
   private String author;
   public Catalog(){ super();}
   public Catalog(Integer id, String journal, String publisher, String
                  date, String title, String author){
     super();
     this.id=id;
     this.journal=journal;
     this.publisher=publisher;
     this.date=date;
     this.title=title;
     this.author=author;
   }
   @Id
     public long getId() {
     return id;
   }
   public void setId(long id) {
     this.id = id;
   }
   public String getJournal() {
     return journal;
   }
   public void setJournal(String journal) {
     this.journal = journal;  }
```

```java
    public String getPublisher() {
      return publisher;
    }
    public void setPublisher(String publisher) {
      this.publisher = publisher;
    }
    public String getDate() {
      return date;
    }
    public void setDate(String date) {
      this.date = date;
    }

    public String getTitle() {
      return title;
    }
    public void setTitle(String title) {
      this.title = title;
    }
    public String getAuthor() {
      return author;
    }
    public void setAuthor(String author) {
      this.author = author;
    }
}
```

Creating a Persistence Configuration file

An EJB 3.0 entity bean is required to have a `persistence.xml` configuration file, which defines the database persistence properties. A `persistence.xml` file gets added to the `META-INF` folder when a JPA project is defined. Copy the following listing to the `persistence.xml` file in Eclipse:

```xml
<?xml version="1.0" encoding="UTF-8" ?>
<persistence xmlns:xsi="http://www.w3.org/2001/XMLSchema-instance"
        xsi:schemaLocation=
          "http://java.sun.com/xml/ns/persistence
           http://java.sun.com/xml/ns/persistence/persistence_1_0.xsd"
        xmlns="http://java.sun.com/xml/ns/persistence" version="1.0">
  <persistence-unit name="em">
  <provider>org.eclipse.persistence.jpa.PersistenceProvider</provider>
    <jta-data-source>jdbc/MySQLDS</jta-data-source>
    <class>ejb3.Catalog</class>
    <properties>
```

```
      <property name="eclipselink.target-server" value="WebLogic_10"
      />
      <property name="javax.persistence.jtaDataSource" value="jdbc/
                  MySQLDS" />
      <property name="eclipselink.ddl-generation"
                  value="create-tables" />
      <property name="eclipselink.target-database" value="MySQL" />
   </properties>
  </persistence-unit>
 </persistence>
```

The `persistence-unit` is required to be named and may be given any name. We had configured a JDBC data source with JNDI `jdbc/MySQLDS` in WebLogic Server. Specify the JNDI name in the `jta-data-source` element. The properties element specifies vendor-specific properties. The `eclipselink.ddl-generation` property is set to `create-tables`, which implies that the required database tables will be created unless they are already created . The `persistence.xml` configuration file is shown in the Eclipse project in the following illustration:

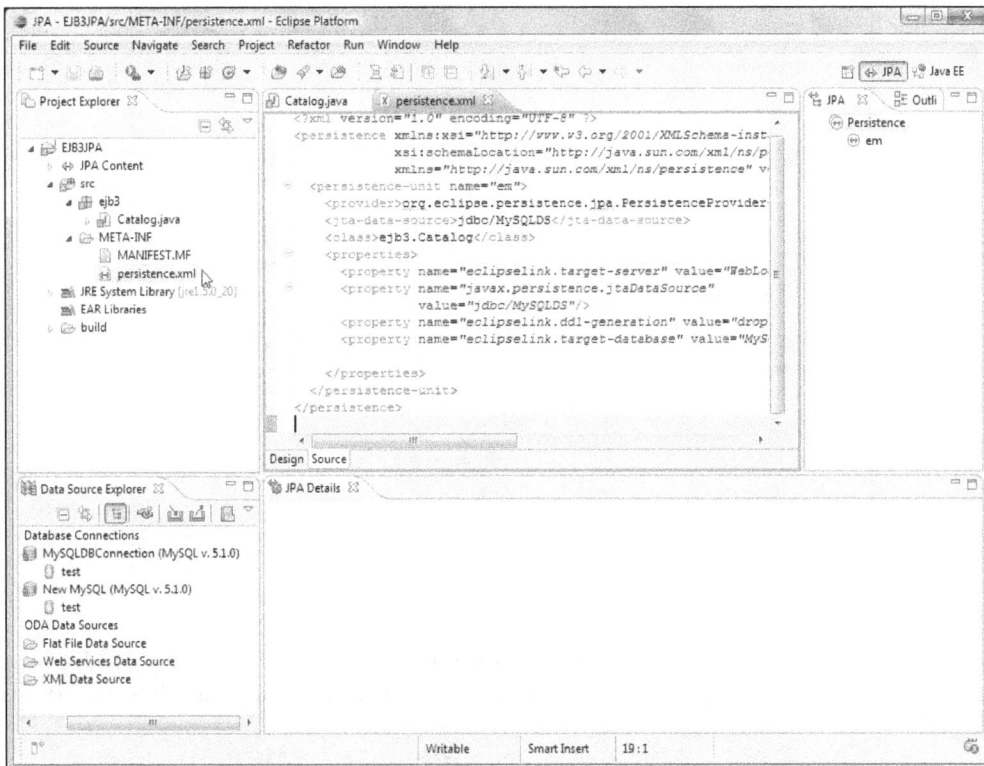

Creating a session bean

For better performance, one of the best practices in developing EJBs is to access entity beans from session beans. Wrapping an entity bean with a session bean reduces the number of remote method calls as a session bean may invoke an entity bean locally. If a client accesses an entity bean directly, each method invocation is a remote method call and incurs an overhead of additional network resources. We shall use a stateless session bean, which consumes less resources than a stateful session bean, to invoke entity bean methods. In this section, we create a session bean in Eclipse. A stateless session bean class is just a Java class annotated with the @Stateless annotation. Therefore, we create Java classes for the session bean and session bean remote interface in Eclipse. To create a Java class, select **File** | **New**. In the **New** window, select **Java** | **Class** and click on **Next>**

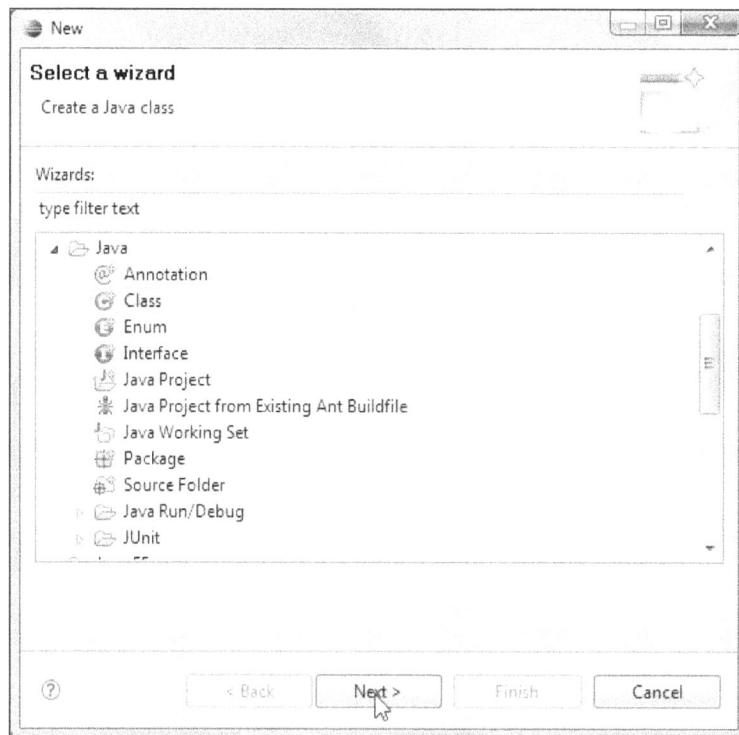

In the **New Java Class** window, select the **Source folder** as EJB3JPA/src, EJB3JPA being the project name. Specify **Class Name** as **CatalogTestBean** and click on **Finish**.

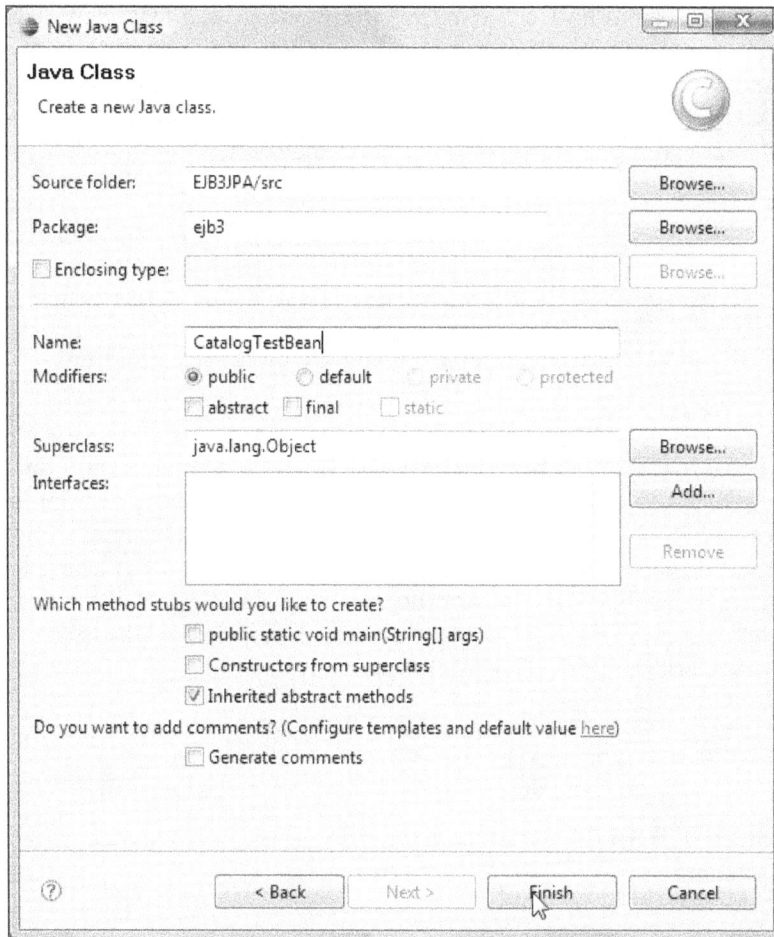

Similarly, create a `CatalogTestBeanRemote` interface by selecting **Java | Interface** in the **New** window. The session bean class and the remote interface get added to the **EJB3JPA** project.

The session bean class

The stateless session bean class, `CatalogTestBean` implements the `CatalogTestRemote` interface. We shall use the `EntityManager` API to create, find, query, and remove entity instances. Inject an `EntityManager` using the `@PersistenceContext` annotation. Specify `unitName` as the same as the `persistence-unit` name in the `persistence.xml` configuration file:

```
@PersistenceContext(unitName = "em")
EntityManager em;
```

Next, create a `test()` method, which we shall invoke from a test client. In the `test()` method we shall create and persist entity instances, query an entity instance, and delete an entity instance, all using an `EntityManager` object, which we had injected earlier in the session bean class. Injecting an `EntityManager` implies that an instance of `EntityManager` is made available to the session bean. Create an instance of the Entity bean class:

```
Catalog catalog = new Catalog(new Integer(1), "Oracle Magazine",
                    "Oracle Publishing", "September-October 2009",
                    "Put Your Arrays in a Bind","Mark Williams");
```

Persist the entity instance to the database using the `persist()` method:

```
em.persist(catalog);
```

Similarly, persist two more entity instances. Next, create a query using the `createQuery()` method of the `EntityManager` object. The query string may be specified as a EJB-QL query. Unlike HQL, the `SELECT` clause is not optional in EJB-QL. Execute the query and return the query result as a `List` using the `getResultList()` method. As an example, select the catalog entry corresponding to author `David Baum`. The `FROM` clause of a query is directed towards the mapped entity bean class, not the underlying database.

```
List catalogEntry =em.createQuery("SELECT c from Catalog c where
        c.author=:name").setParameter("name","David Baum").
                                                    getResultList();
```

Iterate over the result list to output the properties of the entity instance:

```
for (Iterator iter = catalogEntry.iterator(); iter.hasNext(); ) {
    Catalog element = (Catalog)iter.next();
    retValue =retValue + "<br/>" + element.getJournal() +
            "<br/>" + element.getPublisher() +"<br/>" +
            element.getDate() + "<br/>" + element.getTitle() +
            "<br/>" + element.getAuthor() +"<br/>";
}
```

The variable `retValue` is a `String` that is returned by the `test()` method. Similarly, create and run a EJB-QL query to return all titles in the `Catalog` database:

```
List allTitles =em.createQuery("SELECT c from Catalog c").
                                                    getResultList();
```

An entity instance may be removed using the `remove()` method:

```
em.remove(catalog2);
```

The corresponding database row gets deleted from the `Catalog` table. Subsequently, create and run a query to list all the entity instances mapped to the database. The session bean class, `CatalogTestBean`, is listed next:

```
package ejb3;
import java.util.Iterator;
import java.util.List;
import javax.ejb.Stateless;
import javax.persistence.EntityManager;
import javax.persistence.PersistenceContext;
/**
 * Session Bean implementation class CatalogTestBean
 */
@Stateless(mappedName = "EJB3-SessionEJB")
public class CatalogTestBean implements CatalogTestBeanRemote {
  @PersistenceContext(unitName = "em")
  EntityManager em;

  /**
   * Default constructor.
   */
  public CatalogTestBean() {
    // TODO Auto-generated constructor stub
  }

  public String test() {
  Catalog catalog = new Catalog(new Integer(1), "Oracle Magazine",
      "Oracle Publishing", "September-October 2009",
      "Put Your Arrays in a Bind","Mark Williams");
    em.persist(catalog);
    Catalog catalog2 = new Catalog(new Integer(2), "Oracle Magazine",
        "Oracle Publishing", "September-October 2009",
        "Oracle Fusion Middleware 11g: The Foundation for Innovation",
        "David Baum");
    em.persist(catalog2);
    Catalog catalog3 = new Catalog(new Integer(3), "Oracle Magazine",
        "Oracle Publishing", "September-October 2009",
        "Integrating Information","David Baum");
    em.persist(catalog3);
    String retValue = "<b>Catalog Entries: </b>";
    List catalogEntry = em.createQuery("SELECT c from Catalog c
                        where c.author=:name").setParameter("name",
                        "David Baum").getResultList();
    for (Iterator iter = catalogEntry.iterator(); iter.hasNext(); ) {
```

```
        Catalog element = (Catalog)iter.next();
        retValue = retValue + "<br/>" + element.getJournal() + "<br/>" +
                element.getPublisher() + "<br/>" + element.getDate()
                + "<br/>" + element.getTitle() + "<br/>" +
                element.getAuthor() + "<br/>";
    }
    retValue = retValue + "<b>All Titles: </b>";
    List allTitles =
            em.createQuery("SELECT c from Catalog c").getResultList();
    for (Iterator iter = allTitles.iterator(); iter.hasNext(); ) {
      Catalog element = (Catalog)iter.next();
      retValue = retValue + "<br/>" + element.getTitle() + "<br/>";
    }
    em.remove(catalog2); );
    retValue = retValue + "<b>All Entries after removing an entry:
            </b>";
    List allCatalogEntries =
                em.createQuery("SELECT c from Catalog c").
                                            getResultList();
    for (Iterator iter = allCatalogEntries.iterator(); iter.hasNext();
    ) {
      Catalog element = (Catalog)iter.next();
      retValue = retValue + "<br/>" + element + "<br/>";
    }
    return retValue;
  }
}
```

We also need to add a remote or a local interface for the session bean:

```
package ejb3;
import javax.ejb.Remote;
@Remote
public interface CatalogTestBeanRemote {
  public String test();
}
```

The session bean class and the remote interface are shown next:

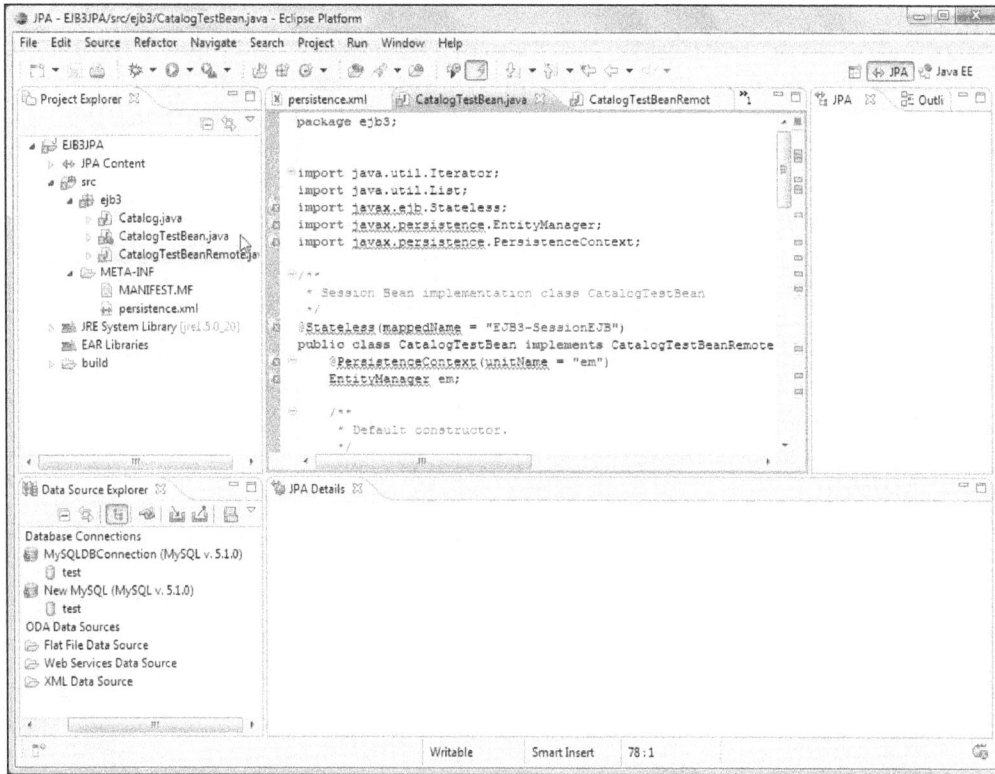

We shall be packaging the entity bean and the session bean in a EJB JAR file, and packaging the JAR file with a WAR file for the EJB 3.0 client into an EAR file as shown next:

```
EAR File
     |
     |
     |-WAR File
           |
           |-EJB 3.0 Client
     |-JAR File
           |
           |-EJB 3.0 Entity Bean
              EJB 3.0 Session Bean
```

Next, we create an `application.xml` for the EAR file. Create a `META-INF` folder for the `application.xml`. Right-click on the **EJB3JPA** project in **Project Explorer** and select **New>Folder**. In the **New Folder** window, select the **EJB3JPA** folder and specify the new **Folder name** as **META-INF**. Click on **Finish**. Right-click on the **META-INF** folder and select **New | Other**. In the **New** window, select **XML | XML** and click on **Next**. In the **New XML File** window, select the **META-INF** folder and specify **File name** as **application.xml**. Click on **Next**. Click on **Finish**.

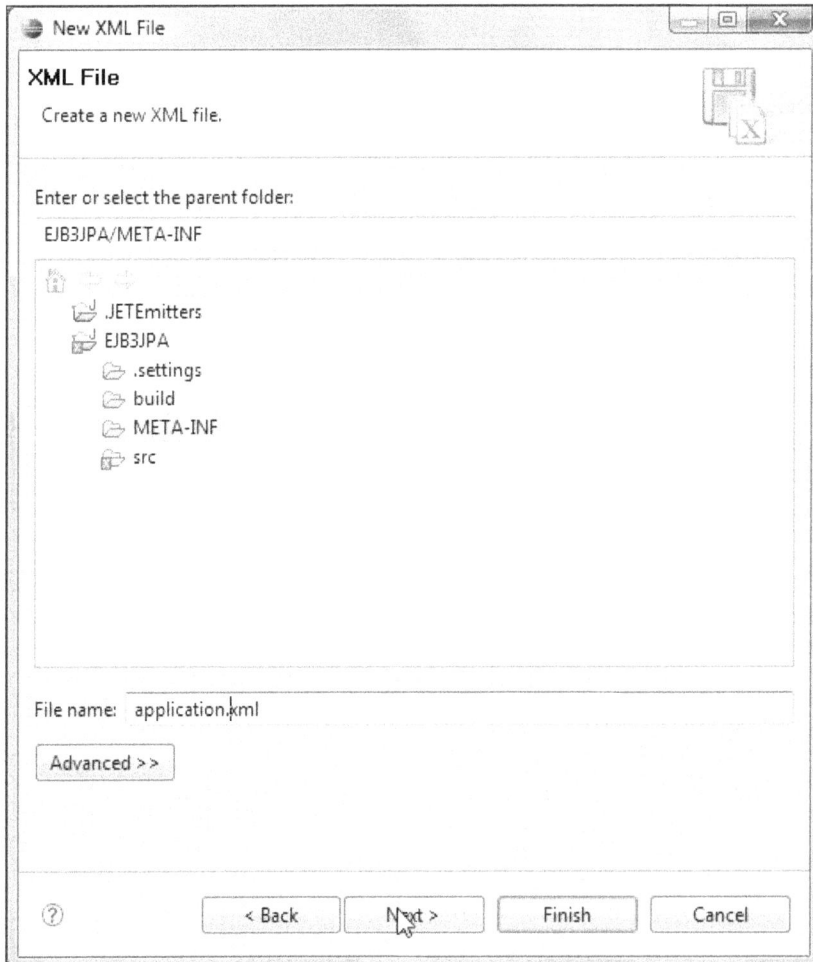

An `application.xml` file gets created. Copy the following listing to `application.xml`:

```
<?xml version = '1.0' encoding = 'windows-1252'?>
<application>
  <display-name></display-name>
  <module>
    <ejb>ejb3.jar</ejb>
  </module>
  <module>
    <web>
      <web-uri>weblogic.war</web-uri>
      <context-root>weblogic</context-root>
    </web>
  </module>
</application>
```

The **application.xml** in the **Project Explorer** is shown next:

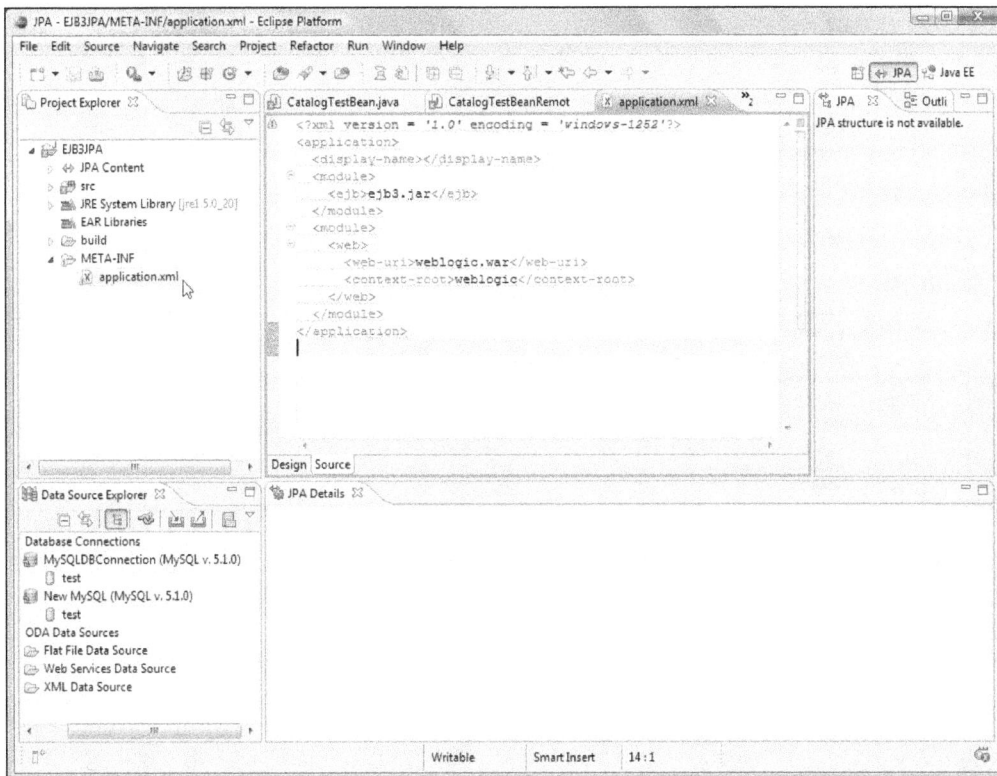

Creating a test client

We have created an entity bean that contains the business logic. We have created a session bean that is a wrapper for the entity bean. Next, we shall create a test client JSP in which we shall invoke the `test()` method of the session bean. For the web application component, we need to create a web module folder, a `WEB-INF` folder in the web module folder and a `web.xml` in the `WEB-INF` folder. To create a JSP in the `webModule` folder, right-click on the **webModule** folder and select **New | Other**.

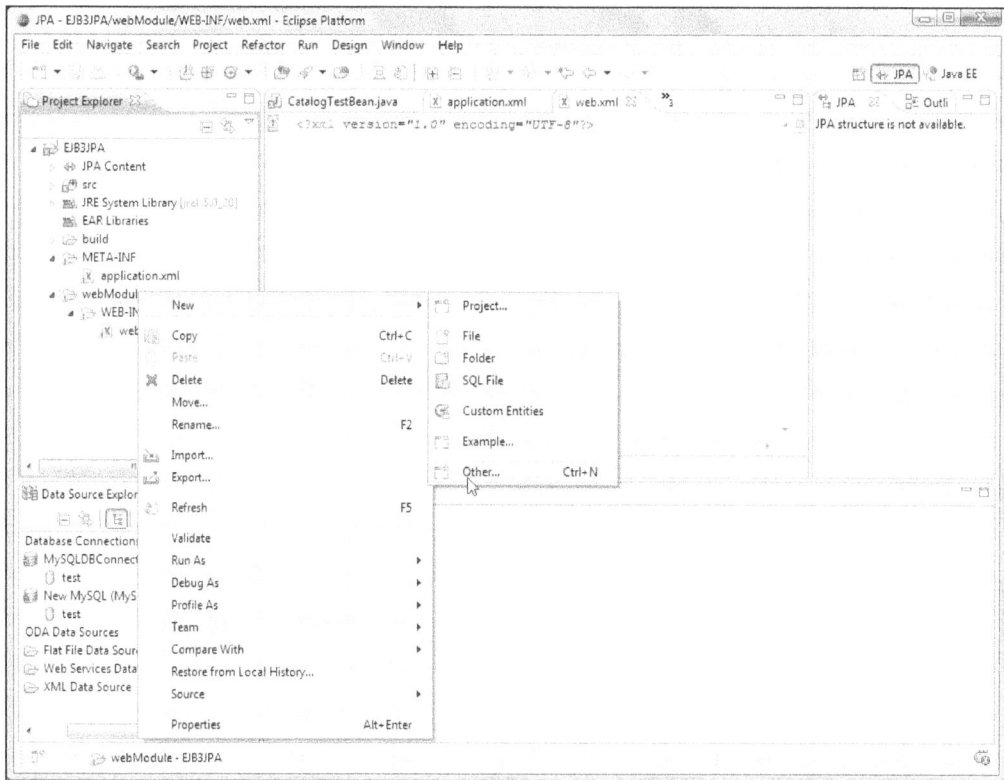

In the **New** window, select **Web | JSP** and click on **Next**.

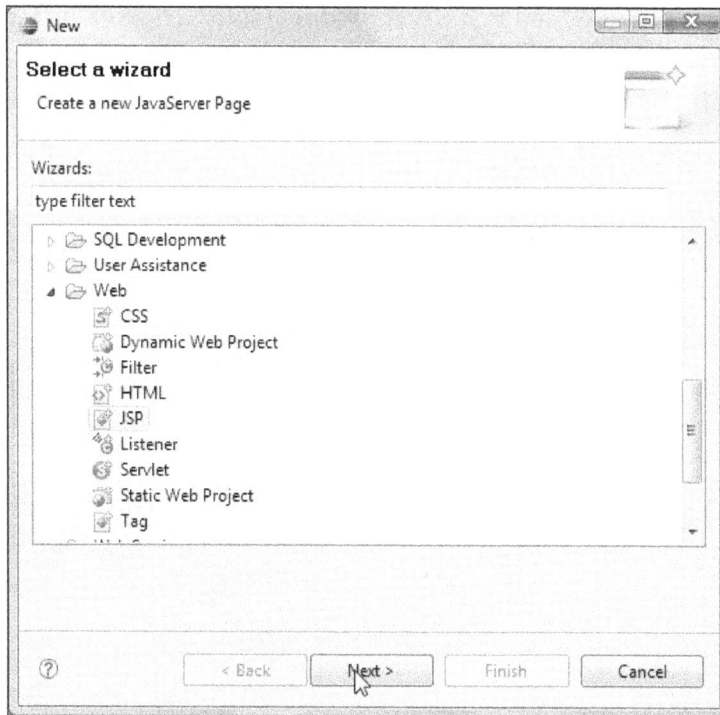

In the **New Java Server Page** window, select the **webModule** folder and specify the **JSP File name** as **catalog.jsp**. Click on **Finish**, as shown next:

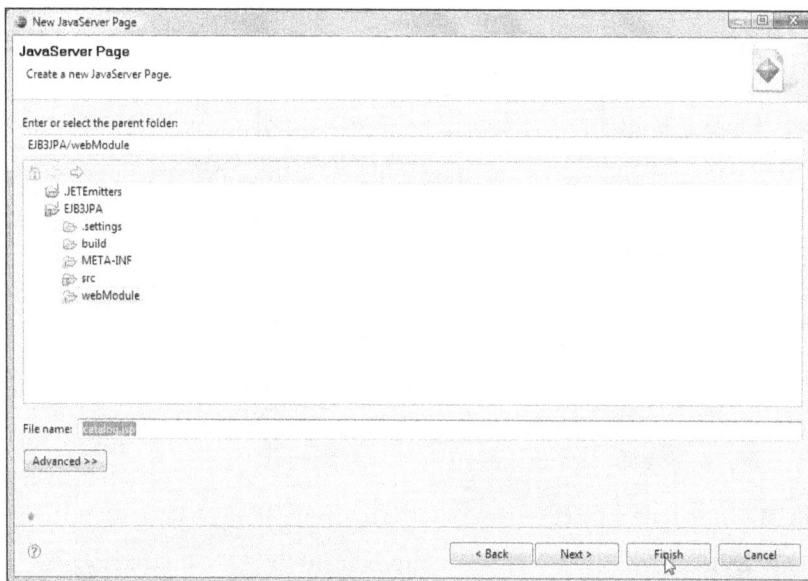

The **catalog.jsp** JSP gets added to the **webModule** folder. The **catalog.jsp** is shown below, including the JSP code, which we shall discuss next:

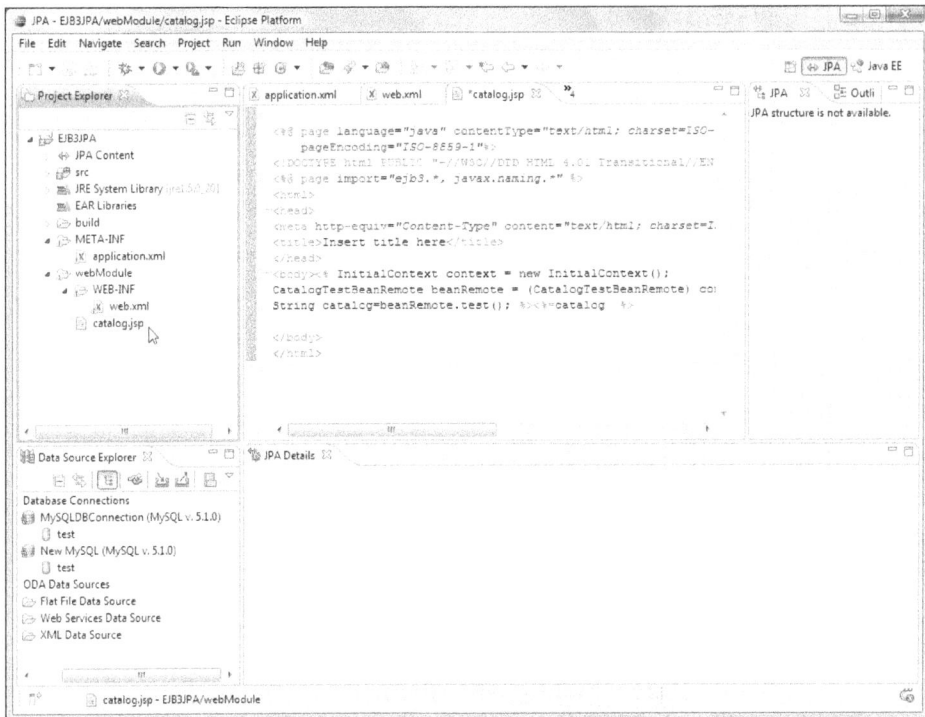

We shall create an instance of `CatalogTestRemote` using JNDI lookup for which we need to create an `IntialContext` object. We need to set the `InitialContext` environment using the environment properties:

```
InitialContext context = new InitialContext();
```

Obtain a `CatalogTestBeanRemote` instance using remote JNDI lookup on the session bean remote object. The JNDI name for WebLogic server is of the format `mapped_name#remote_interface_class_name`.

```
CatalogTestBeanRemote beanRemote = (CatalogTestBeanRemote) context.
lookup("EJB3-SessionEJB#ejb3.CatalogTestBeanRemote");
```

Invoke the `test()` method of the session bean and output the `String` returned, as shown next:

```
String catalog=beanRemote.test();
```

The test client JSP is listed next:

```
<%@ page language="java" contentType="text/html; charset=ISO-8859-1"
pageEncoding="ISO-8859-1"%>
```

```
<!DOCTYPE html PUBLIC "-//W3C//DTD HTML 4.01 Transitional//EN"
"http://www.w3.org/TR/html4/loose.dtd">
<%@ page import="ejb3.*, javax.naming.*" %>
<html>
  <head>
    <meta http-equiv="Content-Type" content="text/html;
                                         charset=ISO-8859-1">
      <title>Insert title here</title>
  </head>
  <body><% InitialContext context = new InitialContext();
    CatalogTestBeanRemote beanRemote = (CatalogTestBeanRemote)
            context.lookup("EJB3-SessionEJB#ejb3.
                                        CatalogTestBeanRemote");
    String catalog=beanRemote.test(); %><%=catalog %>
  </body>
</html>
```

Deploying the entity in WebLogic Server

We have created all the classes and configuration files we need to create an EJB 3.0 entity bean. Next, we shall compile the classes to create a EJB JAR file. We shall create a WAR file from the EJB 3.0 client JSP and package the WAR file with the JAR file into an EAR file. We shall use a `build.xml` script to compile the EJB classes, create an EAR file, and deploy the EAR file to WebLogic Server. Create a `build.xml` script in the JPA project with **File | New | Other** and **XML | XML** in the **New** window. The **build.xml** script is shown next:

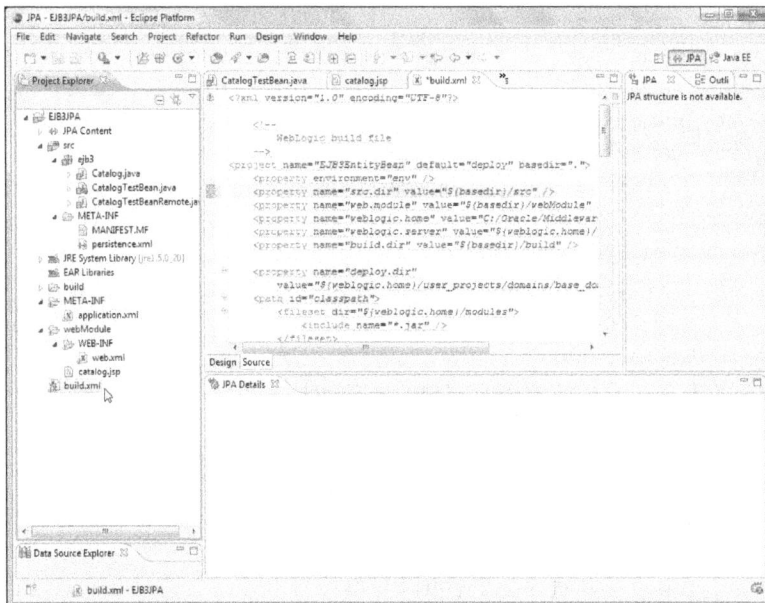

In the build script, specify properties for the various directory paths used in the script, such as the WebLogic server directory, the `build` directory, and the WebLogic Server `deploy` directory. Specify the classpath of the various JAR files required for compiling the EJB classes. Specify `targets` discussed in the following table:

Target	Description
prepare	Creates the build directory.
compile	Compiles the EJB classes.
jar	Creates an EJB JAR file.
war	Creates a WAR file.
assemble-app	Creates an EAR file.
deploy	Deploys the EAR file to WebLogic Server. The WebLogic Server deploy directory development mode is ${weblogic.home}/user_projects/domains/base_domain/autodeploy
clean	Deletes the build directory and the EJB JAR, WAR and EAR files.

The `build.xml` script is listed next:

```xml
<?xml version="1.0" encoding="UTF-8"?>
  <!--
    WebLogic build file
  -->
<project name="EJB3EntityBean" default="deploy" basedir=".">
  <property environment="env" />
  <property name="src.dir" value="${basedir}/src" />
  <property name="web.module" value="${basedir}/webModule" />
  <property name="weblogic.home" value="C:/Oracle/Middleware/wls" />
  <property name="weblogic.server"
            value="${weblogic.home}/wlserver_10.3/server" />
  <property name="build.dir" value="${basedir}/build" />
  <property name="deploy.dir"
  value="${weblogic.home}/user_projects/domains/base_domain/
                                                  autodeploy" />
  <path id="classpath">
    <fileset dir="${weblogic.home}/modules">
      <include name="*.jar" />
    </fileset>
    <fileset dir="${weblogic.server}/lib">
      <include name="*.jar" />
    </fileset>
    <pathelement location="${build.dir}" />
```

```xml
    </path>
    <property name="build.classpath" refid="classpath" />
    <target name="prepare">
      <mkdir dir="${build.dir}" />
    </target>
    <target name="compile" depends="prepare">
      <javac srcdir="${src.dir}" destdir="${build.dir}" debug="on"
             includes="**/*.java">
      <classpath refid="classpath" />
      </javac>
    </target>
    <target name="jar" depends="compile">
      <jar destfile="${build.dir}/ejb3.jar">
        <fileset dir="${build.dir}">
          <include name="**/*.class" />
        </fileset>
        <fileset dir="${src.dir}/">
          <include name="META-INF/persistence.xml" />
        </fileset>
      </jar>
    </target>
    <target name="war" depends="jar">
      <war warfile="${build.dir}/weblogic.war">
        <fileset dir="webModule">
          <include name="*.jsp" />
        </fileset>
        <fileset dir="webModule">
          <include name="WEB-INF/web.xml" />
        </fileset>
      </war>
    </target>
    <target name="assemble-app" depends="war">
      <jar jarfile="${build.dir}/ejb3.ear">
        <metainf dir="META-INF">
          <include name="application.xml" />
        </metainf>
        <fileset dir="${build.dir}" includes="*.jar,*.war" />
      </jar>
    </target>
    <target name="deploy" depends="assemble-app">
      <copy file="${build.dir}/ejb3.ear" todir="${deploy.dir}" />
    </target>
    <target name="clean">
      <delete file="${build.dir}/ejb3.ear" />
```

```
        <delete file="${build.dir}/ejb3.jar" />
        <delete file="${build.dir}/weblogic.war" />
    </target>
</project>
```

Next, run the build script. Right-click on the `build.xml` script in the **Package Explorer** and select **Run As | Ant Build** (the second **Ant Build**), as shown in the following screenshot:

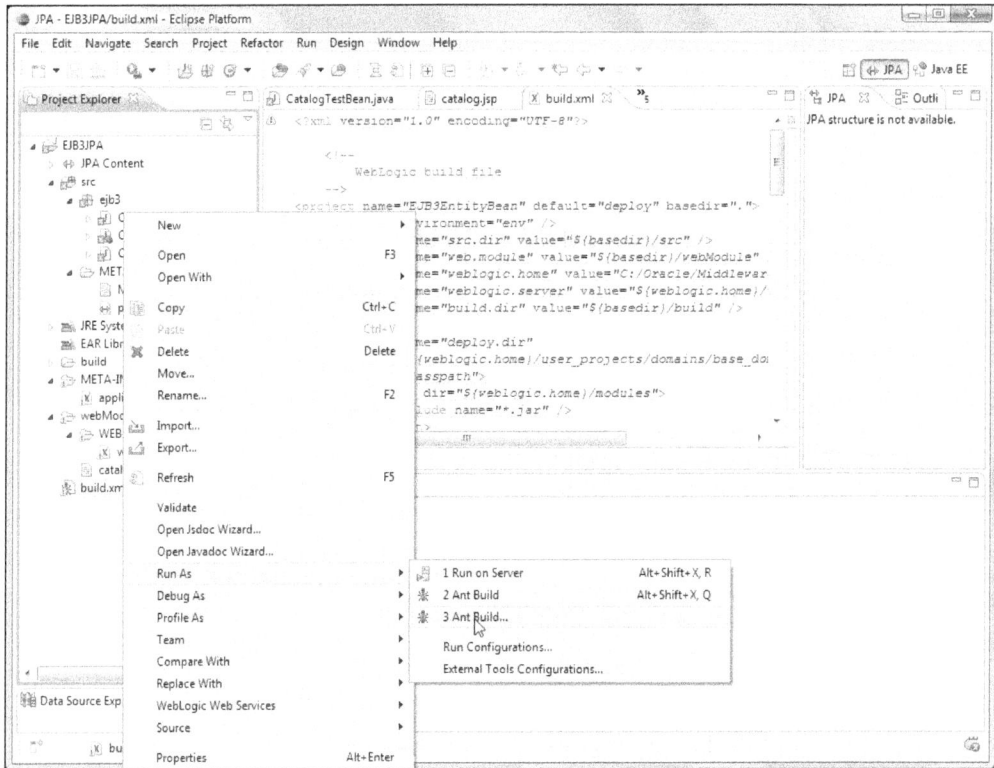

In the **Edit Configuration** window, select the target(s) to run. The default build target in the build script is **deploy** with each target having a dependence on the preceding target. The **prepare**, **compile**, **jar**, **war**, and **assemble-app** targets run when the **deploy** target is run. Select the **deploy** target and click on **Apply**. Click on **Run** to run the **deploy** target and thus deploy the EAR file to the WebLogic Server `autodeploy` directory.

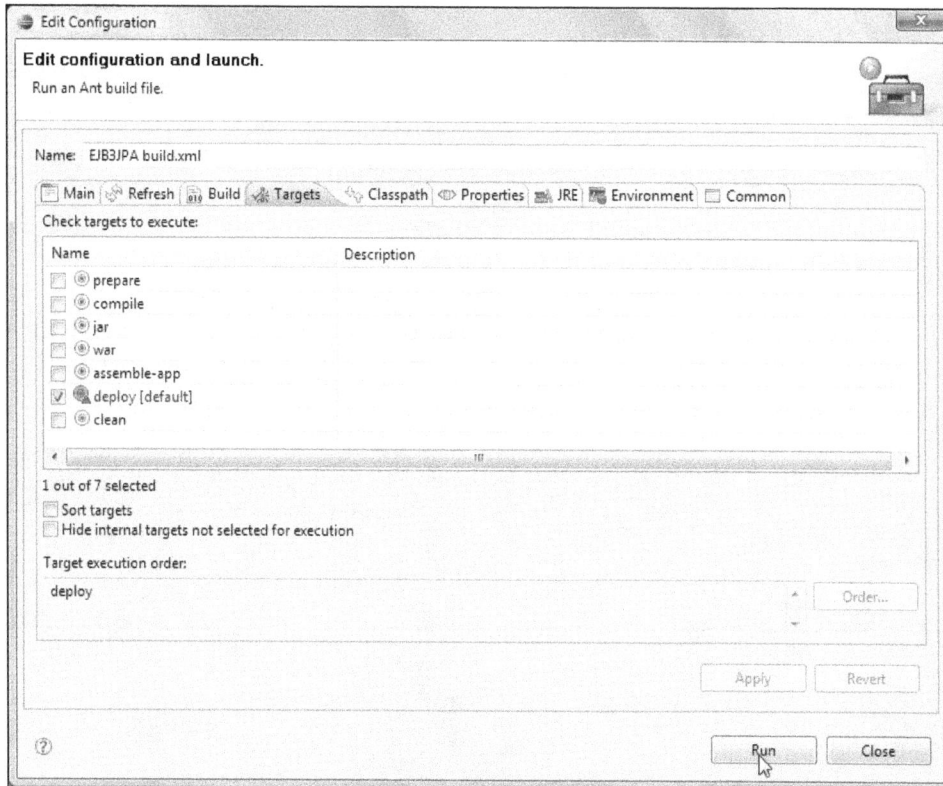

All the targets get run and the EAR file gets deployed to the WebLogic Server, as shown in the build script output:

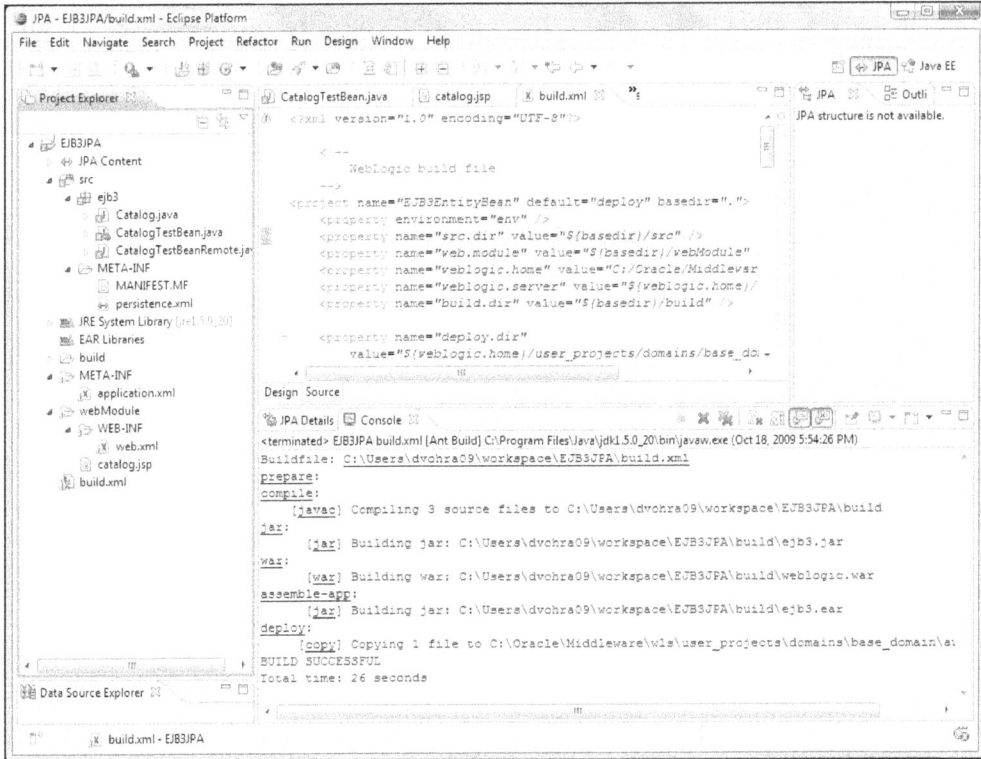

Start the WebLogic Server, if not already started, and log in to the Administration Console. Navigate to the **Deployments** node. The EAR file is shown as deployed in the **Deployments** table:

Testing the EJB 3.0 entity client

Next, run the client JSP in a browser with the URL `http://localhost:7001/weblogic/catalog.jsp`. The `test()` method of the session bean gets invoked. Three entity bean instances get created and persisted to the MySQL database. As shown in the server output, the entity bean property values for the entity instance corresponding to author `David Baum` get listed. The titles of all the three entity instances get listed. Subsequently, an entity instance gets removed, as indicated by the subsequent query to fetch all entity instances, which lists only two entity instances.

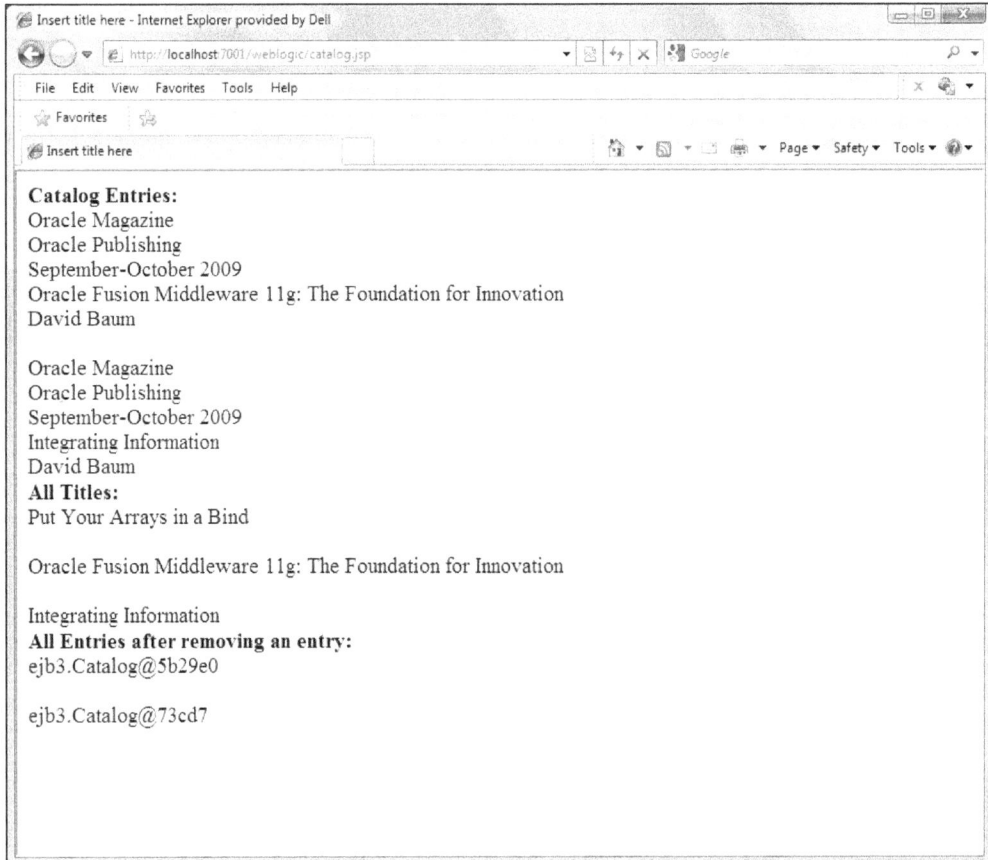

Summary

The open source combination of Eclipse-MySQL is ideally suited for developing EJB 3.0 entity beans with WebLogic Server 11*g*. An Eclipse-MySQL database is an open source alternative to a JDeveloper-Oracle database. In this chapter, we created an EJB 3.0 entity bean application including a wrapper session bean in Oracle Enterprise Pack for Eclipse, packaged the application into an EAR file, and deployed the application to WebLogic Server using a build script. Subsequently, we ran the application in WebLogic server with a MySQL database as the EJB 3.0 persistence database.

In the next chapter, we shall add an Oracle ADF Faces user interface to EJB 3.0 database persistence.

6
EJB 3.0 with ADF Faces UI

An ADF Faces client is well suited for creating/retrieving database table rows in combination with an EJB 3.0 model. In a Model-View-Controller application in which the EJB 3.0 database persistence constitutes the model, the ADF Faces framework may be used for the view and controller components. In this chapter, we shall create an EJB 3.0 entity bean with JDeveloper 11g and WebLogic Server 11g, which are components of Oracle Fusion Middleware 11g, and Oracle database. We shall demonstrate the following:

- Mapping a database table to an entity bean
- Wrapping the entity bean in a session bean
- Creating an Oracle ADF Faces client user interface
- Testing the ADF Faces client user interface

Setting the environment

Before getting started, we need to install Oracle JDeveloper 11g Studio Edition, which may be downloaded from http://www.oracle.com/technology/software/products/middleware/index.html. Oracle JDeveloper 11g is distributed as a GUI self-extractor application. Click on the **jdevstudio11110instal** application. We also need to install the Oracle database 10g or 10g XE , or 11g, which may be downloaded from http://www.oracle.com/technology/software/products/database/index.html. When installing Oracle database, also install the sample schemas.

Creating a datasource in JDeveloper

Next, we create a JDBC datasource in JDeveloper. We shall use the datasource in the EJB 3.0 entity bean for database persistence. First, we need to create a database table in some sample schema, `OE` for example. Run the following SQL script in SQL *Plus:

```
CREATE TABLE Catalog (id INTEGER PRIMARY KEY NOT NULL,
                      journal VARCHAR(100), publisher VARCHAR(100),
                      edition VARCHAR(100), title VARCHAR(100),
                      author VARCHAR(100));
```

A database table gets created in the `OE` sample schema. Next, we need to create a JDBC connection in JDeveloper with Oracle database. Open the **Database Navigator** or select the **Database Navigator** tab if already open. Right-click on the **IDE Connections** node and select **New Connection**. In the **Create Database Connection** window, specify a **Connection Name**, select **Connection Type** as **Oracle (JDBC)**, specify **Username** as OE, which is the schema in which the `Catalog` table is created, and specify the **Password** for the `OE` schema. Select **Driver** as **thin**, **Host Name** as **localhost**, **SID** as **ORCL** (If the database is **XE**, then the **SID** is **XE**), and **JDBC Port** as **1521**. Click on the **Test Connection** button to test the connection. If the connection gets established, click on **OK**:

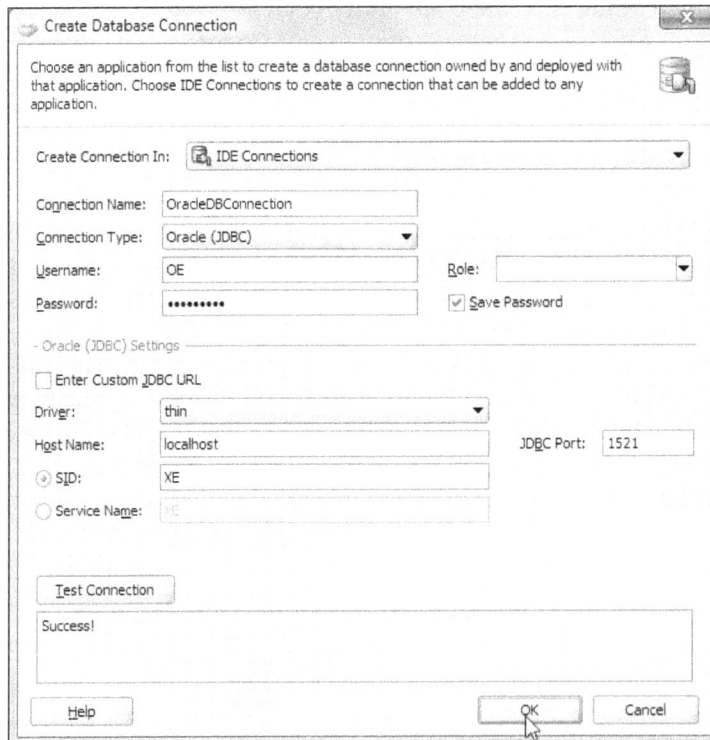

The **OracleDBConnection** gets added to the **Database Navigator** view.
The CATALOG table that we created is listed in the **Tables**.

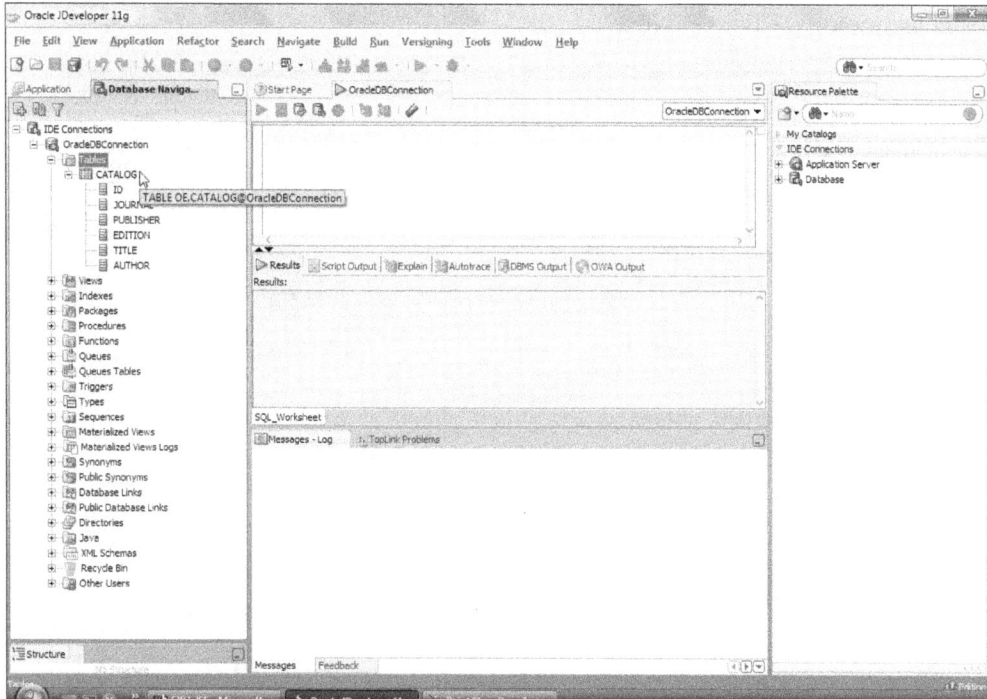

Creating an EJB 3 application

In this section, we create an EJB 3.0 application in JDeveloper. Select **New
Application** in the **Application Navigator**. Specify an **Application Name (EJB3-JSF)**,
select the **Java EE Web Application** template, which consists of a Model project and
a ViewController project, and click on **Next**.

Next, specify the **Project Name** (**JSFViewController**) for the View and Controller project. In the **Project Technologies** tab, transfer the **EJB** project technology from the **Available** list to the **Selected** list using the **>** button. Also, select the **ADF Faces** project technology. Click on **Next**.

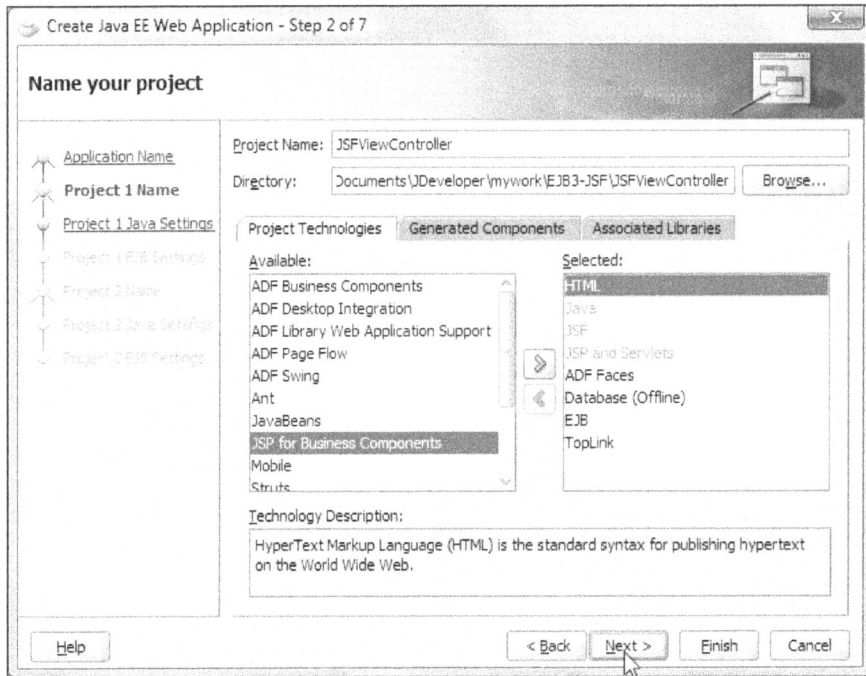

Select the default Java settings for the View project and click on **Next**. Configure the EJB Settings for the View project. Select **EJB Version** as **Enterprise JavaBeans 3.0** and select **Using Annotations**. Click on **Next**. Next, create the Model project. Specify the **Project Name** (**EJB3Model** for example), and in the **Project Technologies** tab, transfer the **EJB** project technology from the **Available** list to the **Selected** list using the **>** button. Click on **Next**.

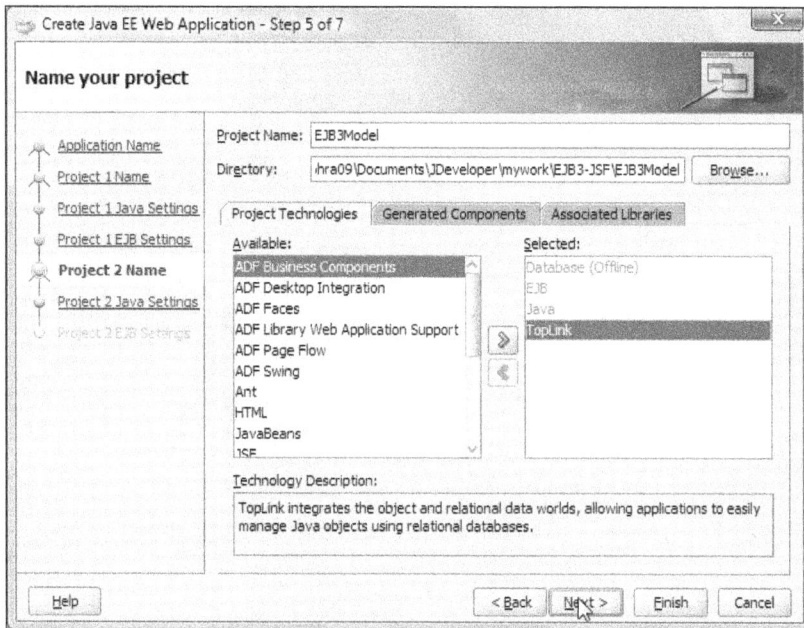

Select the default Java settings for the Model project and click on **Next**. Similar to the View project, configure the EJB settings for the Model project. Select **EJB Version** as **Enterprise JavaBeans 3.0**, select **Using annotations** and click on **Finish**.

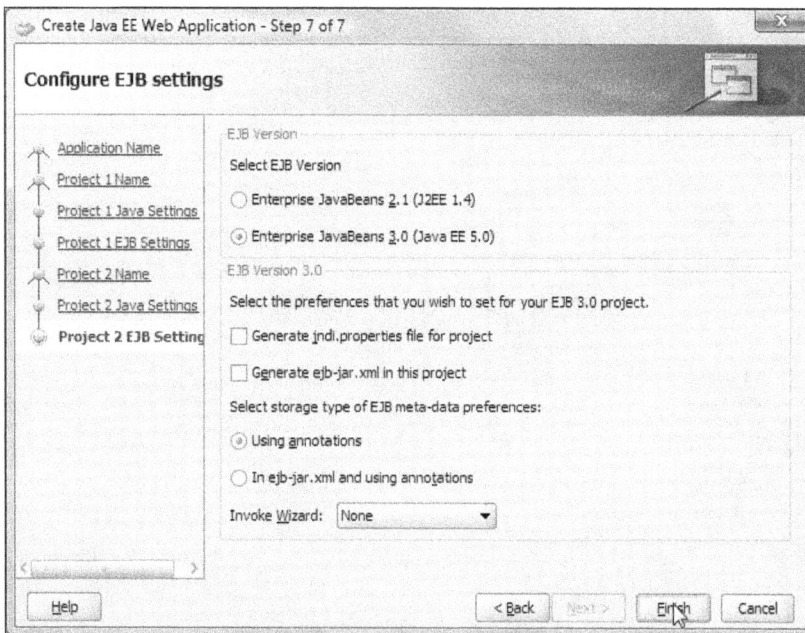

An EJB 3.0 application, which consists of a Model project and a ViewController project gets added in the **Application Navigator**.

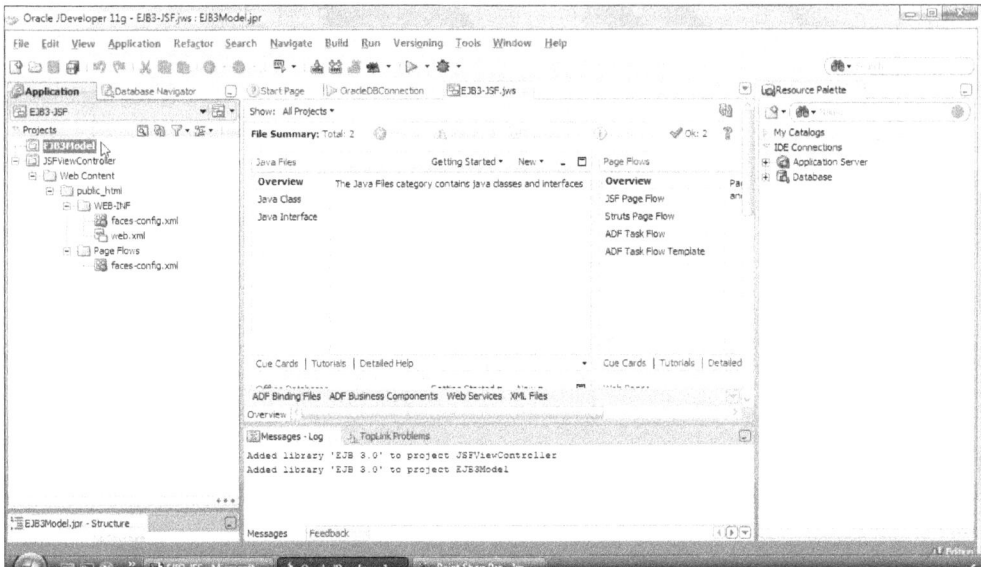

Select the **EJB3Model** project in the **Application Navigator** and select **Tools | Project Properties**. In the **Project Properties** window, select the **Libraries and Classpath** node. The **EJB 3.0** and **TopLink** libraries should be in the **Classpath Entries**.

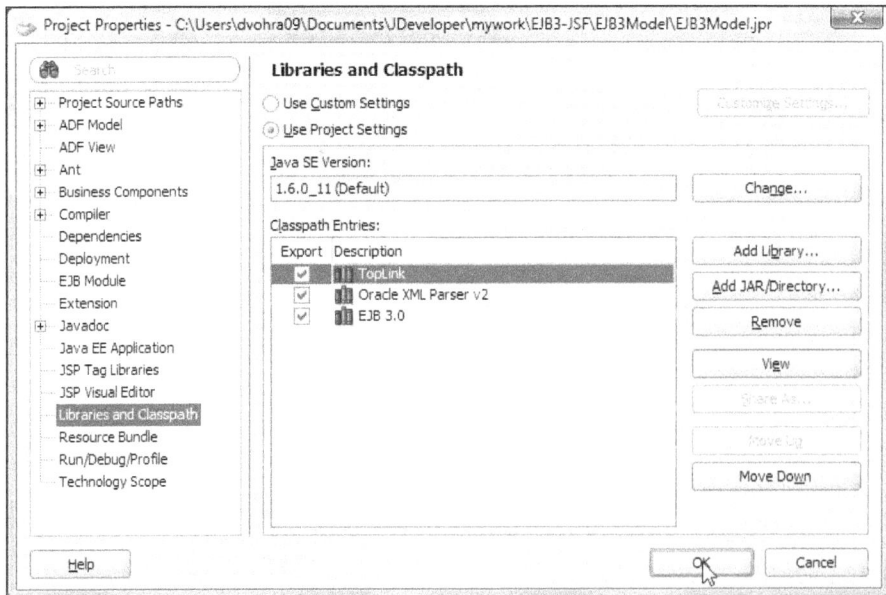

Select the **EJB Module** node and search for the **OracleDBConnection** connection. In the **Select IDE Database Connection** window, select the **OracleDBConnection** and click on **Copy Connection**.

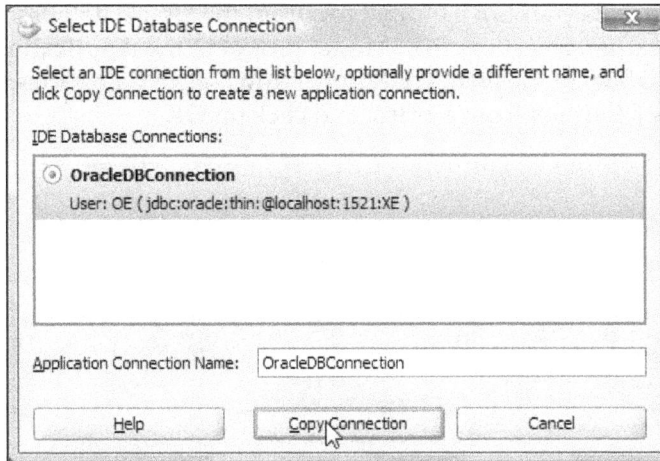

The datasource corresponding to the `OracleDBConnection` is `jdbc/OracleDBConnectionDS`. The **Annotated EJB 3.0 Bean Classes** will list the annotated entity bean after we have created the entity class in the next section. As we won't be using an `ejb-jar.xml` deployment descriptor, because the deployment descriptor is optional in EJB 3.0, the `ejb-jar.xml` option won't be used.

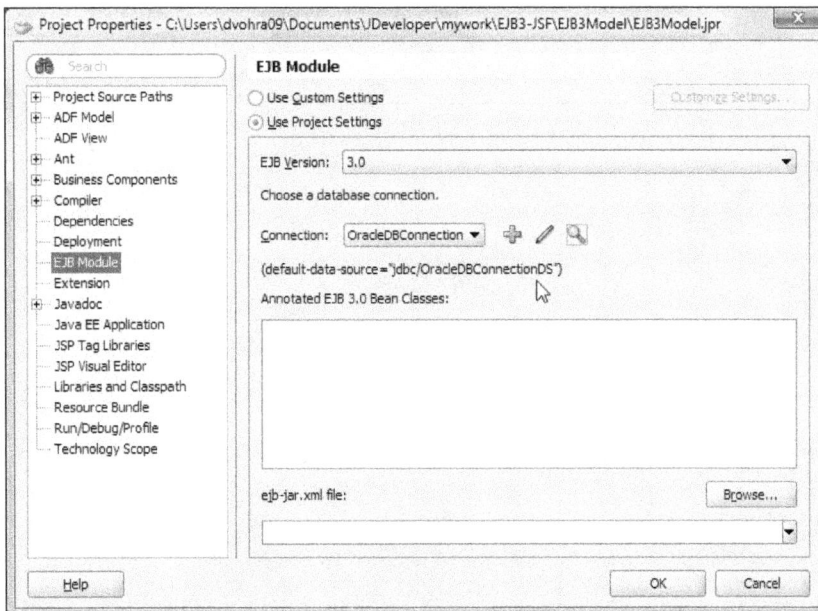

Creating an EJB 3 entity bean from Oracle database

In this section, we create an EJB 3 entity bean from the Oracle database table `CATALOG` that we created earlier. Select the **EJB3Model** project in the **Application Navigator** and select **File | New**. In the **New Gallery** window, select **Categories:Business Tier | EJB** and **Items | Entities from Tables** and click on **OK**.

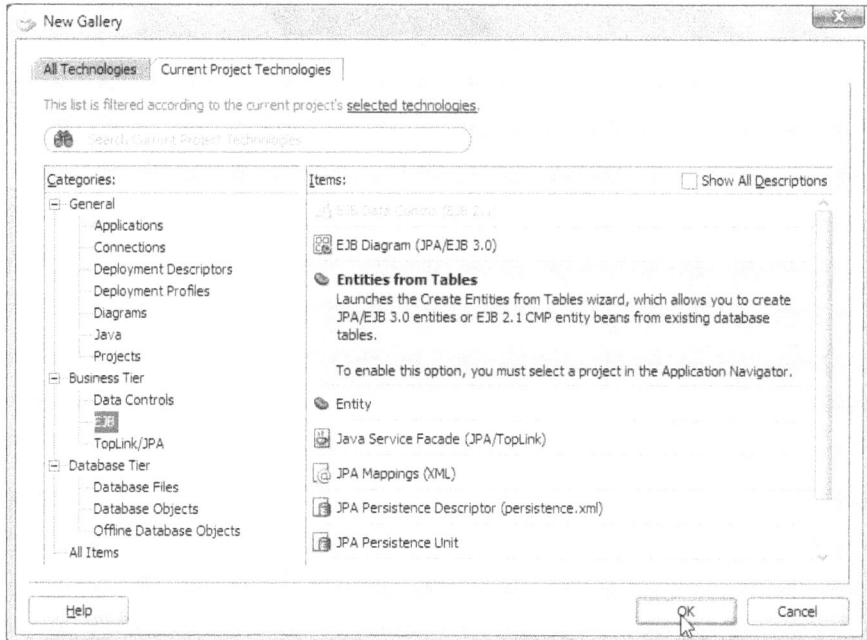

In the **Persistence Unit** window, select **New** to create a new persistence unit. In the **New Persistence Unit** window, specify a Persistence Unit name (**em**). Specify **JTA DataSource Name** as **jdbc/OracleDBConnectionDS**, which is the datasource name corresponding to the **OracleDBConnection** connection. Select the settings for **Toplink; Database Platform** as **Oracle** and **Server Platform** as **WebLogic 10** and then click on **OK**.

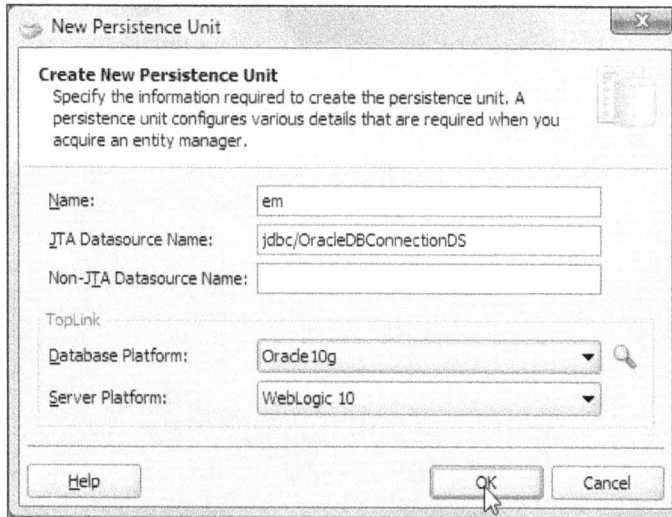

The **em** Persistence Unit gets created. Click on **OK** in the **Persistence Unit** window.

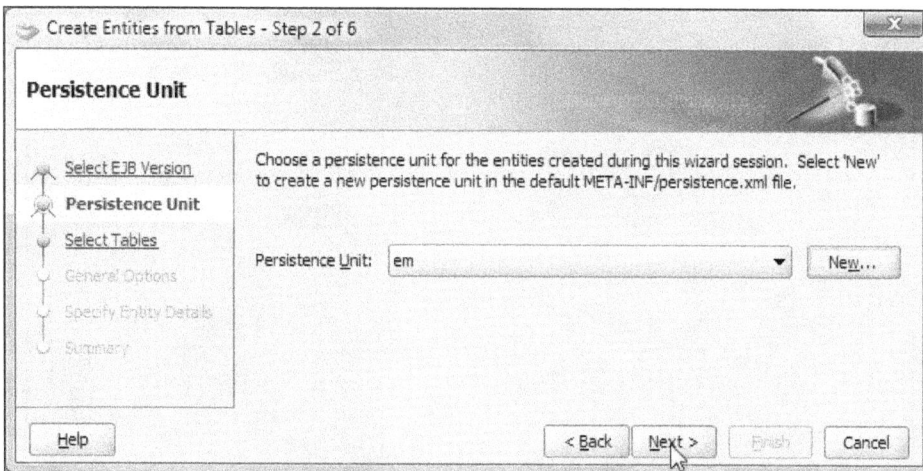

Select **Type of Connection** as **Online Database Connection** and click on **Next**. In the **Database Connection Details** window, select the **OracleDBConnection** and click on **Next**:

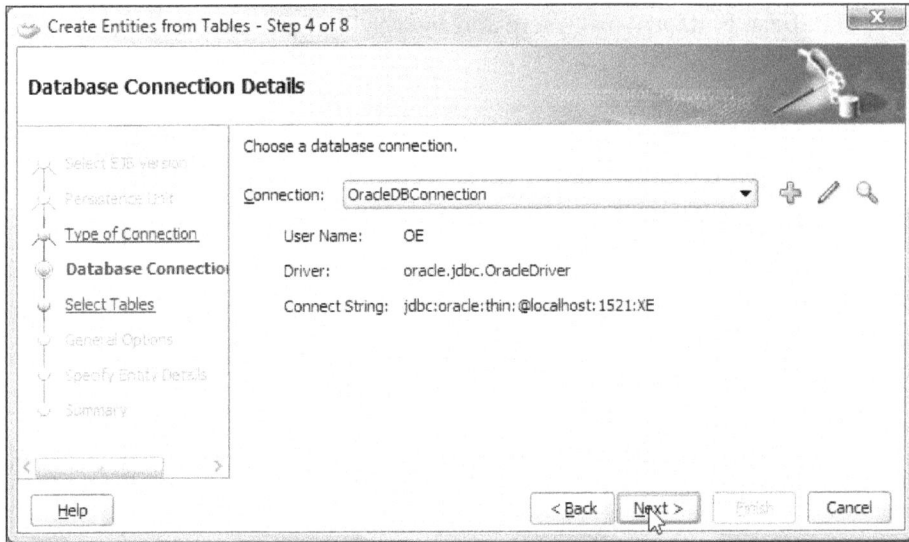

In the **Select Tables** window, select **Schema** as **OE**, **Name Filter** as %, and check the **Auto Query** checkbox. Select the **CATALOG** table and click on **Next**.

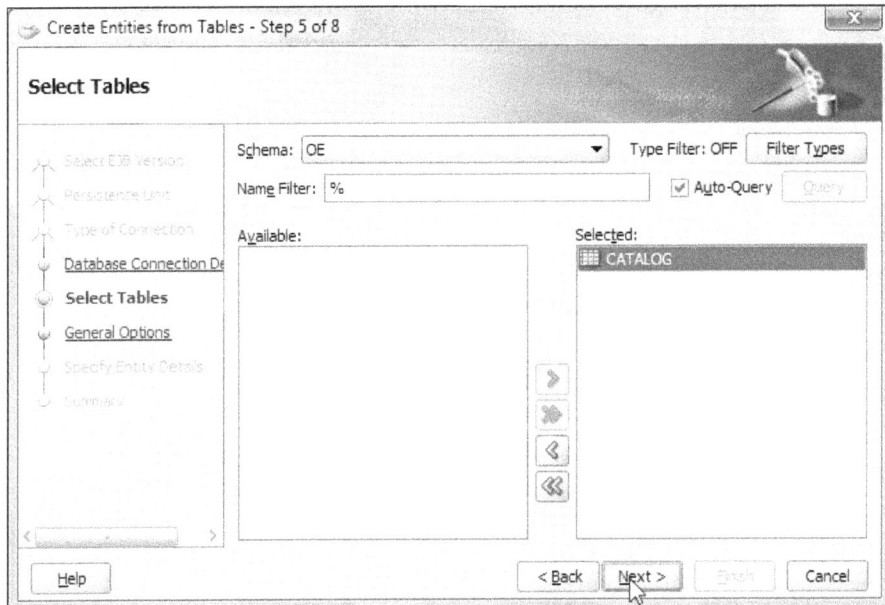

Select the default settings in the **General Options** window. The default **Package Name** is **model**. In the **Entity Class Options** select **Place member-level annotations on Fields**, and select the **Implement java.io.Serializable** checkbox. Click on **Next**:

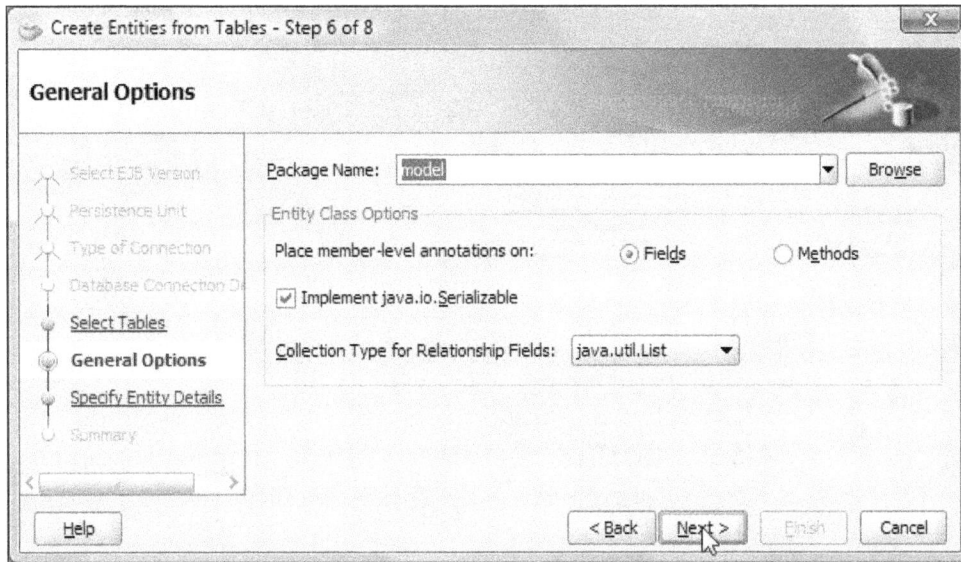

In the **Specify Entity Details** window, select **Table Name** as **OE.CATALOG**. Specify **Entity Name** as **Catalog** and **Entity Class** as **model.Catalog** and then click on **Next**.

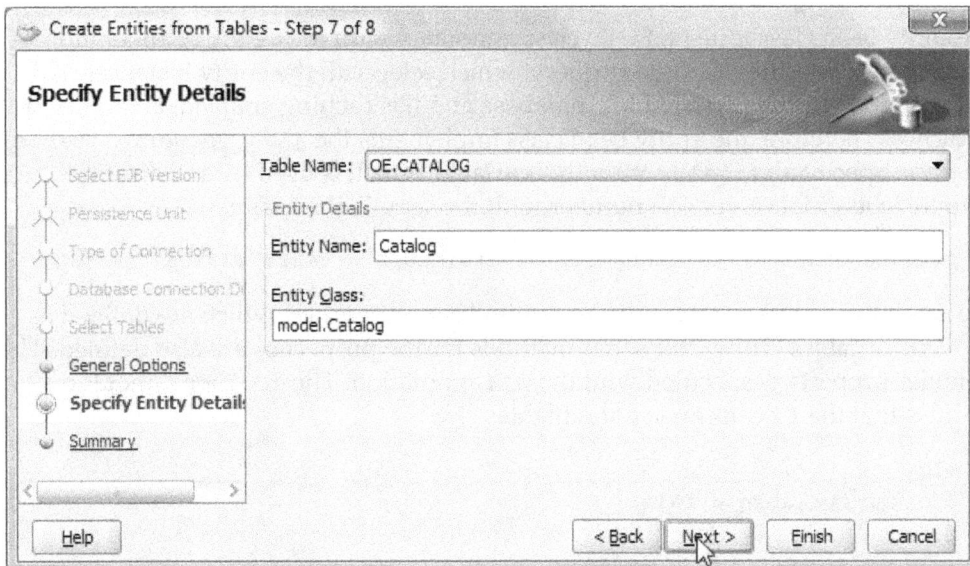

In the **Summary Page** click on **Finish**. The entity bean class `model.Catalog` gets created. The `persistence.xml` deployment descriptor gets created in the `META-INF` directory.

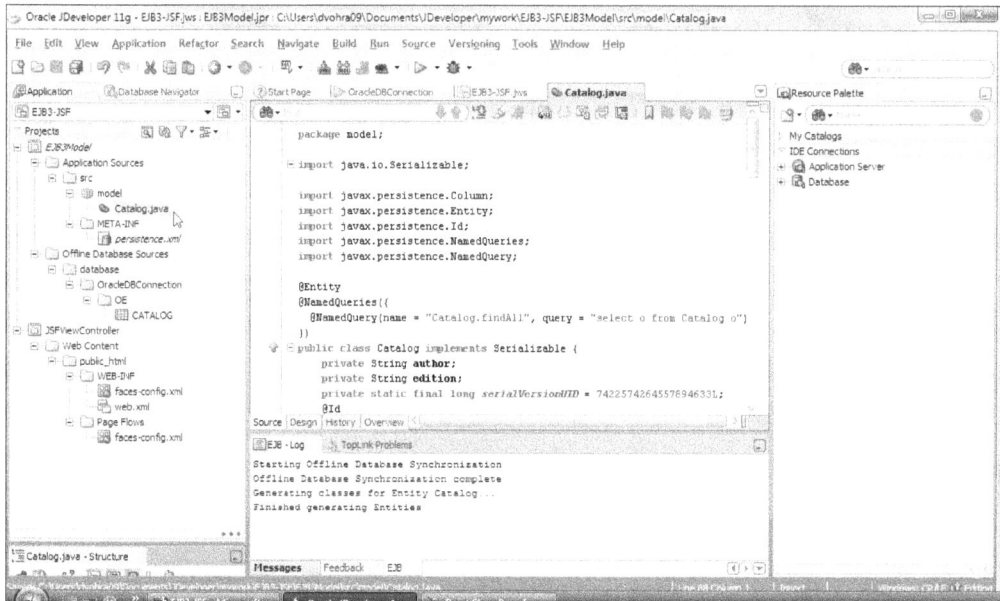

The Entity class

The entity bean class is just a POJO class annotated with the `@Entity` annotation. A `@NamedQuery` specifies a `findAll` query, which selects all the entity instances. An entity bean, which is persisted to a database and has caching enabled, is serialized by caches. Therefore, the entity bean class implements the `java.io.Serializable` interface. Specify a `serialVersionUID` variable, which is used by serialization runtime to associate a version number with the serializable class:

```
private static final long serialVersionUID = 7422574264557894633L;
```

The database columns are mapped to entity bean properties, which are defined as `private` variables. The getter setter methods for the properties are also defined. The identifier property is specified with the `@Id` annotation. The `@Column` annotation specifies that the `id` column is not nullable:

```
@Id
@Column(nullable = false)
private long id;
```

By default, the `id` column of type `INTEGER` is mapped to a field of type `long`. Modify the `id` field to type `long`, as IDs are usually a Java primitive data type. The entity bean class is listed next:

```
package model;
import java.io.Serializable;
import javax.persistence.Column;
import javax.persistence.Entity;
import javax.persistence.Id;
import javax.persistence.NamedQueries;
import javax.persistence.NamedQuery;

@Entity
@NamedQueries({
  @NamedQuery(name = "Catalog.findAll",
              query = "select o from Catalog o")
})
public class Catalog implements Serializable {
  private String author;
  private String edition;
  private static final long serialVersionUID = 7422574264557894633L;
  @Id
  @Column(nullable = false)
  private long id;
  private String journal;
  private String publisher;
  private String title;

  public Catalog() {super();
  }
  public Catalog(String author, String edition, long id,
                 String journal, String publisher, String title) {
    super();
    this.author = author;
    this.edition = edition;
    this.id = id;
    this.journal = journal;
    this.publisher = publisher;
    this.title = title;
  }
  public String getAuthor() {
    return author;
  }
  public void setAuthor(String author) {
```

```java
      this.author = author;
  }
  public String getEdition() {
    return edition;
  }
  public void setEdition(String edition) {
    this.edition = edition;
  }
  public long getId() {
    return id;
  }
  public void setId(long id) {
    this.id = id;
  }
  public String getJournal() {
    return journal;
  }
  public void setJournal(String journal) {
    this.journal = journal;
  }
  public String getPublisher() {
    return publisher;
  }
  public void setPublisher(String publisher) {
    this.publisher = publisher;
  }
  public String getTitle() {
    return title;
  }
  public void setTitle(String title) {
    this.title = title;
  }
}
```

The persistence configuration file

The persistence.xml file is used to define the persistence unit(s), which includes a JTA data source that is used for database persistence.

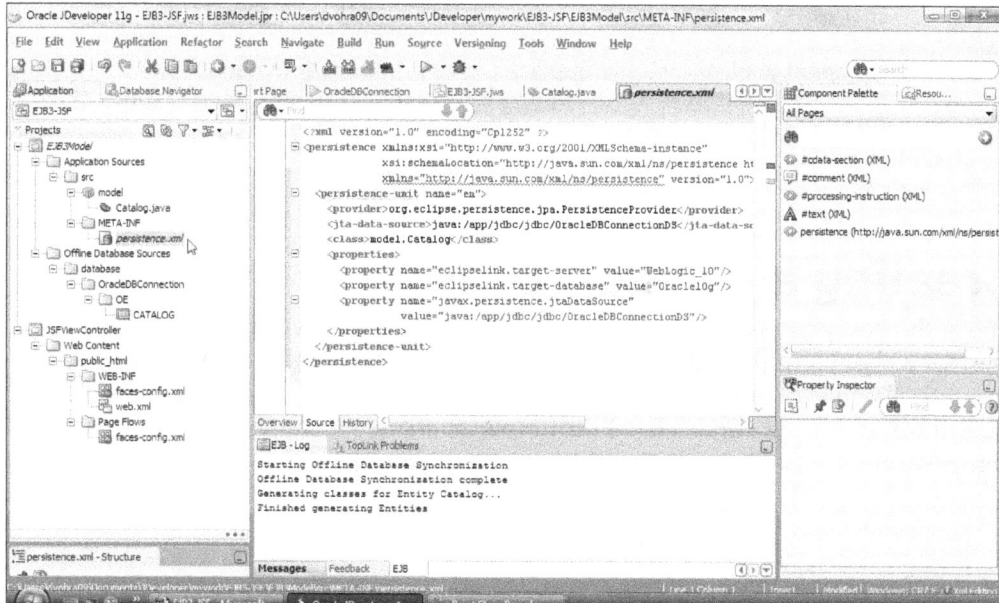

The persistence provider is specified as `org.eclipse.persistence.jpa.`
`PersistenceProvider`. The `jta-data-source` is mapped as `java:/app/jdbc/`
`jdbc/OracleDBConnectionDS`, which is a mapping performed by JDeveloper The
`java:/app/jdbc` prefix gets added in mapping a data source name to the JTA
Data Source name when creating the persistence unit. The `jdbc/` prefix and the
`DS` suffix get added in mapping a connection name to a data source name. The
`eclipselink.target-server` property is specified as `WebLogic_10`. The `javax.`
`persistence.jtaDataSource` property is specified as `java:/app/jdbc/jdbc/`
`OracleDBConnectionDS`. The `persistence.xml` configuration file is listed next:

```
<?xml version="1.0" encoding="Cp1252" ?>
<persistence xmlns:xsi="http://www.w3.org/2001/XMLSchema-instance"
  xsi:schemaLocation="http://java.sun.com/xml/ns/persistence
      http://java.sun.com/xml/ns/persistence/persistence_1_0.xsd"
  xmlns="http://java.sun.com/xml/ns/persistence" version="1.0">
  <persistence-unit name="em">
    <provider>org.eclipse.persistence.jpa.PersistenceProvider
    </provider>
    <jta-data-source>java:/app/jdbc/jdbc/OracleDBConnectionDS
    </jta-data-source>
    <class>model.Catalog</class>
    <properties>
      <property name="eclipselink.target-server"
              value="WebLogic_10" />
```

```
        <property name="eclipselink.target-database"
                 value="Oracle10g" />
        <property name="javax.persistence.jtaDataSource"
                 value="java:/app/jdbc/jdbc/OracleDBConnectionDS" />
      </properties>
    </persistence-unit>
  </persistence>
```

Creating a session bean

One of the best practices of developing an entity bean is to wrap it in a session bean for a client to reduce the number of remote calls as we discussed in *Chapter 5* The entity bean is not directly accessed by a client. To create a session bean, select the **EJB3Model** project and select **File** | **New**. In the **New Gallery** window, select **Categories:Business Tier** | **EJB** and **Items** | **Session EJB**. Click on **OK**:

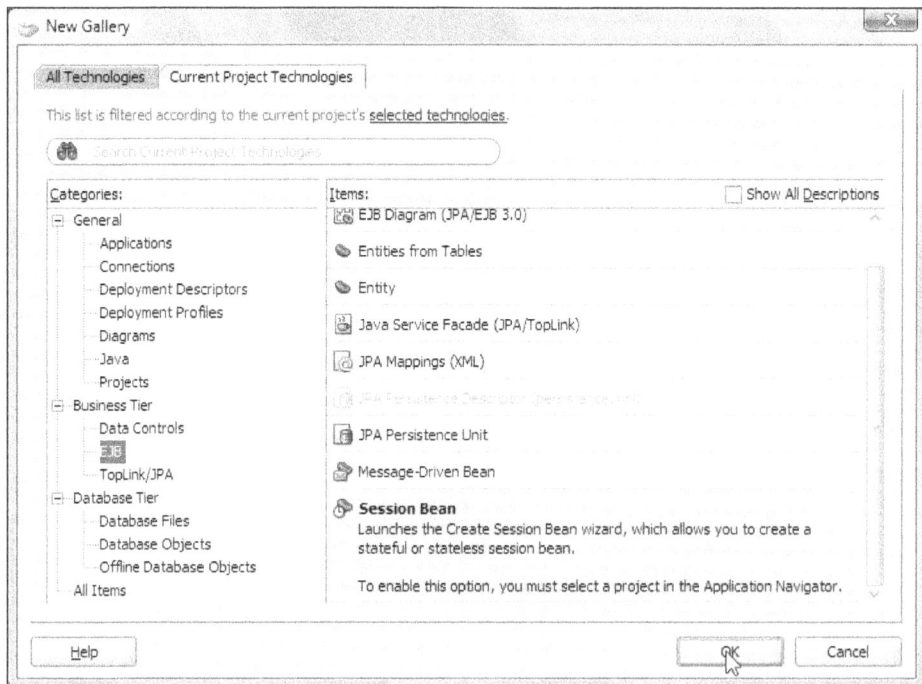

Specify the **EJB Name** as **CatalogSessionEJB**. Select **Session Type** as **Stateless** and **Transaction Type** as **Container**. A Stateless session bean does not incur the overhead of keeping the state of a unique client-bean session that a Stateful session bean does. Select the default mapped name (**EJB3-JSF-EJB3Model-CatalogSessionEJB**). The **Generate Session Façade Methods** checkbox is selected by default. The **Entity implementation** is **JPA Entities** by default. The persistence unit is **em**. Click on **Next**.

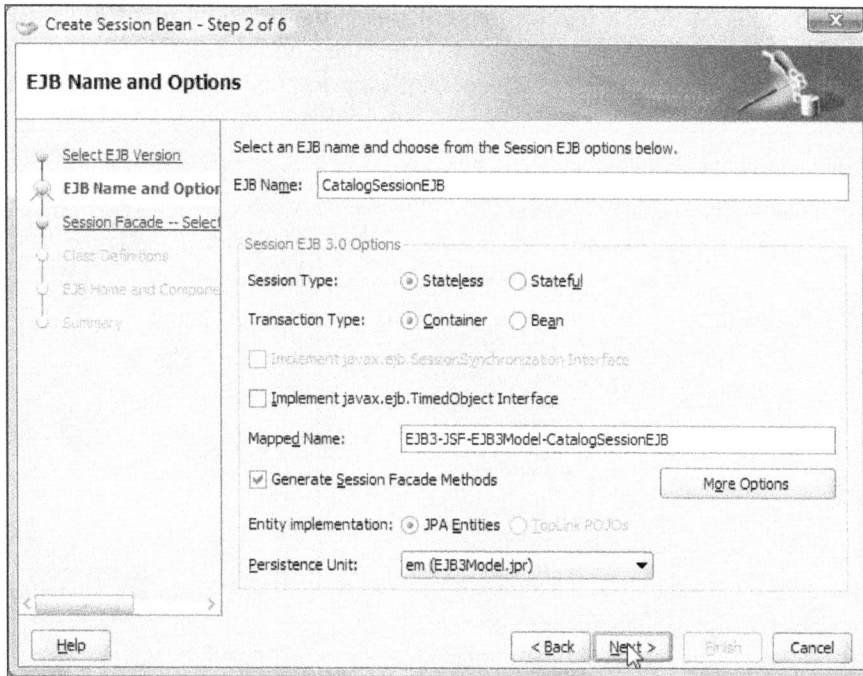

Select the default JPA Entity Methods to create and click on **Next**. Specify the **Bean Class** (**model. CatalogSessionEJBBean**) and click on **Next**.

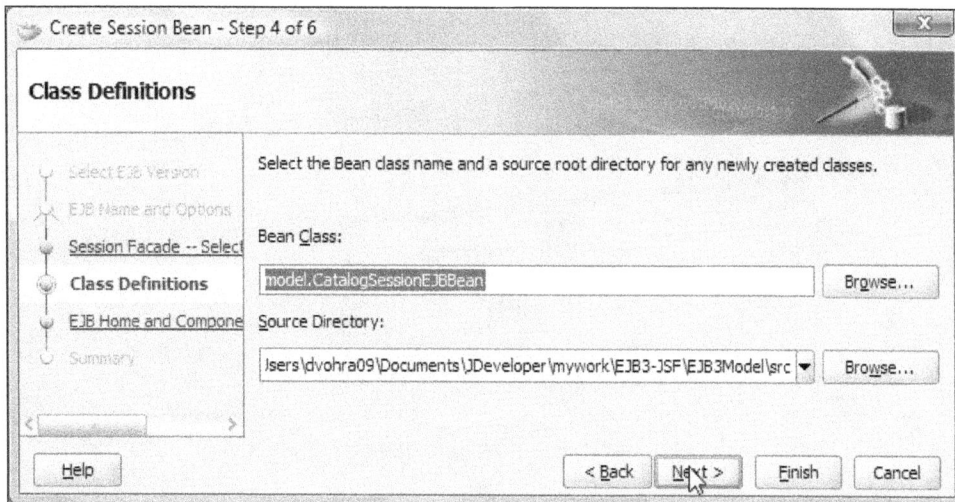

Select the EJB business interface to implement. Select the **Implement a Remote Interface** checkbox, and specify the **Remote interface (model. CatalogSessionEJB)**. If a distributed environment is not used, select **Implement a Local Interface**. Click on **Next**.

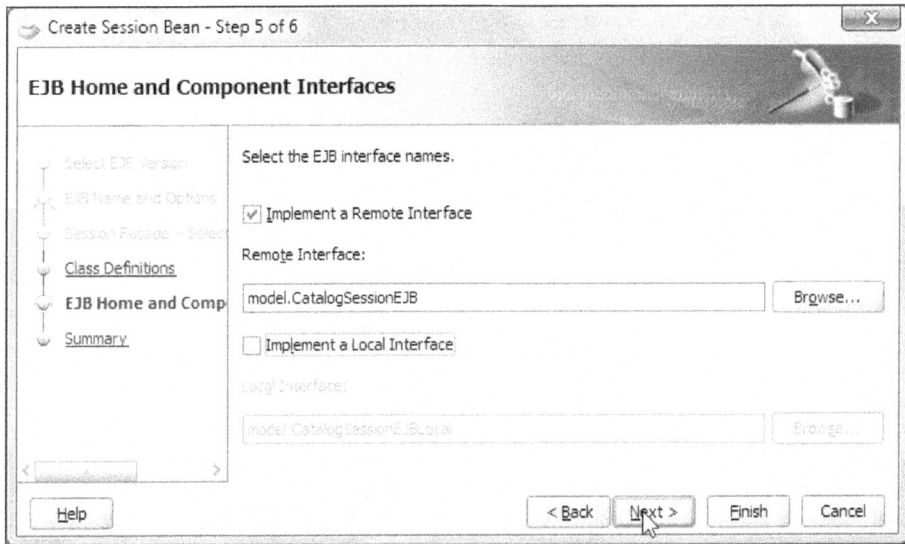

In the **Summary** window, click on **Finish**. A session bean class `CatalogSessionEJBBean` gets added to the entity bean model project. The remote business interface for the session bean, `CatalogSessionEJB`, also gets created.

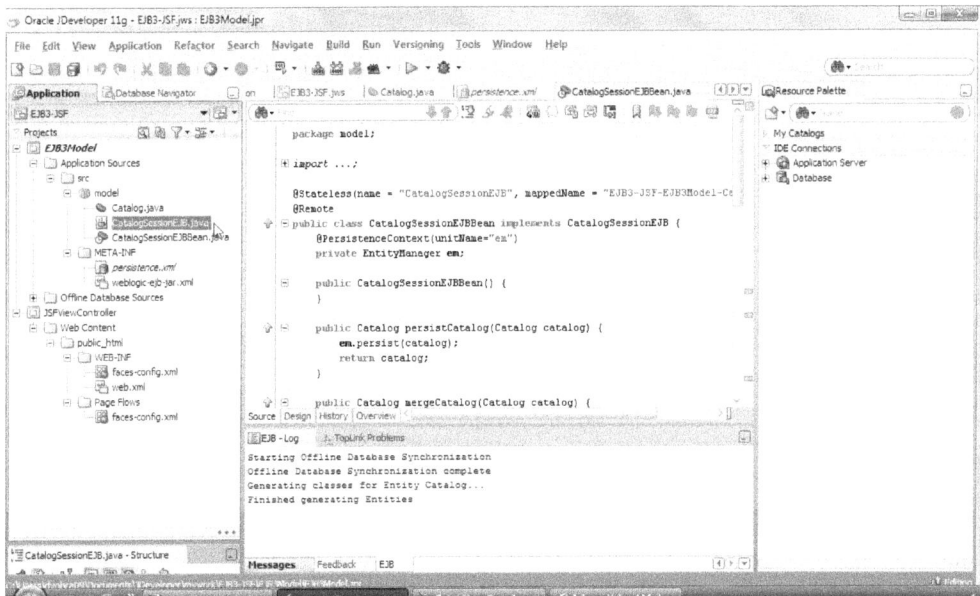

The session bean class

The `CatalogSessionEJBBean` class is annotated with the annotation `@Stateless`. The `mappedName` attribute specifies the global JNDI for the session bean. We will use the mapped name in the test client to lookup the session bean and invoke method(s) on it. The `@Remote` annotation indicates that the session bean is a remote interface.

```
@Stateless(name = "CatalogSessionEJB", mappedName = "EJB3-JSF-
EJB3Model-CatalogSessionEJB")
@Remote
public class CatalogSessionEJBBean implements CatalogSessionEJB { }
```

In the session bean an `EntityManager` is injected using the `@PersistenceContext` annotation. The `unitName` is specified, but not required, as the `EntityManager` variable name is the same as the persistence unit name:

```
@PersistenceContext(unitName = "em")
    private EntityManager em;
```

Add a method `persistEntity()` and a method `findEntity()` to the session bean and the remote interface. A method may be added to a session bean by selecting the session bean node in the **Application Navigator**, and in the **Structure** view, right-click on the session bean node and select **EJB (N) | New Method**. Similarly, a session bean field may be added by selecting **EJB(N) | New Field**. The `persistEntity()` method defines parameters for attributes of the `Catalog` entity class and persists an entity instance to the database. The `findEntity()` method finds an entity instance. In the `persistEntity()` method, create an `Catalog` entity instance:

```
Catalog catalog =new Catalog(author, edition, new Integer(catalogId),
                                      journal,publisher, title);
```

Invoke the `persist(Object)` method of `EntityManager` to persist the entity bean instance:

```
em.persist(catalog);
```

The `find()` method defines a `catalogId` parameter and finds an entity instance. In the `find()` method, create an instance of the `Query` object using the `createQuery()` method to run a Java persistence query language statement. Bind the `catalogId` to a named parameter `id` using the `setParameter()` method of the `Query` object and run the Java persistence query statement using the `getResultList()` method, which returns a `List`:

```
List catalogEntry =em.createQuery(
                "SELECT c from Catalog c
                 where c.id=:id").setParameter("id",catalogId).
                                            getResultList();
```

Iterate over the `List`, which is actually just one catalog entry, to retrieve the `Catalog` entity instance:

```
for (Iterator iter = catalogEntry.iterator(); iter.hasNext(); ) {
  entityInstance = (Catalog)iter.next();
}
```

The `find()` method returns the `Catalog` entity instance retrieved. The session bean class `CatalogSessionEJBBean` is listed next:

```
package model;

import java.util.Iterator;
import java.util.List;
import javax.ejb.Remote;
import javax.ejb.Stateless;
import javax.persistence.EntityManager;
import javax.persistence.PersistenceContext;
import javax.persistence.Query;

@Stateless(name = "CatalogSessionEJB", mappedName = "EJB3-JSF-
EJB3Model-CatalogSessionEJB")
@Remote
public class CatalogSessionEJBBean implements CatalogSessionEJB {
  @PersistenceContext(unitName = "em")
  private EntityManager em;

  public CatalogSessionEJBBean() {
  }

  public Object mergeEntity(Object entity) {
     return em.merge(entity);
  }

  public void persistEntity(int catalogId, String journal,
                            String publisher,
                            String edition, String title,
                            String author) {

    Catalog catalog =
                new Catalog(author, edition, new Integer(catalogId),
                            journal, publisher, title);
    em.persist(catalog);
```

```
  }
  public Catalog findEntity(int catalogId) {
    Catalog entityInstance =null;
    List catalogEntry = em.createQuery(
                      "SELECT c from Catalog c
                      where c.id=:id").setParameter("id",catalogId).
                                                        getResultList();
    for (Iterator iter = catalogEntry.iterator(); iter.hasNext(); ) {
        entityInstance = (Catalog)iter.next();


    }
    return entityInstance;

  }
  /** <code>select o from Catalog o</code> */
  public List<Catalog> queryCatalogFindAll() {
    return em.createNamedQuery("Catalog.findAll").getResultList();
  }
  /** <code>select o from Catalog o</code> */
  public List<Catalog> queryCatalogFindAllByRange(int firstResult,
                                                  int maxResults) {
    Query query = em.createNamedQuery("Catalog.findAll");
    if (firstResult > 0) {
      query = query.setFirstResult(firstResult);
    }
    if (maxResults > 0) {
      query = query.setMaxResults(maxResults);
    }
    return query.getResultList();
  }
  public void removeCatalog(Catalog catalog) {
    catalog = em.find(Catalog.class, catalog.getId());
    em.remove(catalog);
  }
}
```

The remote business interface `CatalogSessionEJB` is listed next:

```
package model;

import java.util.List;
import javax.ejb.Remote;

@Remote
public interface CatalogSessionEJB {
```

```
Object mergeEntity(Object entity);

public void persistEntity(int catalogId, String journal,
                          String publisher, String edition,
                          String title, String author);

public Catalog findEntity(int catalogId);

List<Catalog> queryCatalogFindAll();

List<Catalog> queryCatalogFindAllByRange(int firstResult,
                                         int maxResults);

void removeCatalog(Catalog catalog);
}
```

Creating an Oracle ADF Faces client user interface

In this section, we create an Oracle ADF Faces client to test the entity bean using the wrapper session bean. The ADF Faces library is required in the classpath of the ViewController project. If the ADF Faces library was not added when creating the EJB 3 application, right-click on **JSFViewController,** and select **Project Properties**. Transfer **ADF Faces** from the **Available** to the **Selected** column:

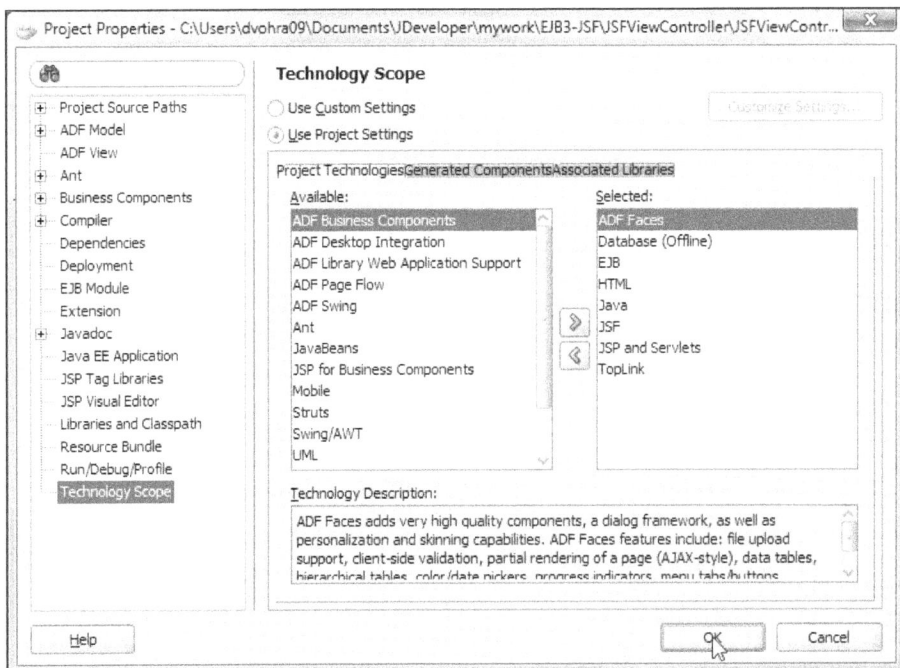

As we will be invoking the entity bean (which is in the model project) from a JSF page (which is in the view-controller project) we need to add a dependency in the **JSFViewController** project on the **EJB3Model** project. Select the **JSFViewController** project and select **Tools | Project Properties** and select **Dependencies**. Click on the **Edit Dependencies** button. In the **Edit Dependencies** window, select the **EJB3Model | Build Output** and click on **OK**.

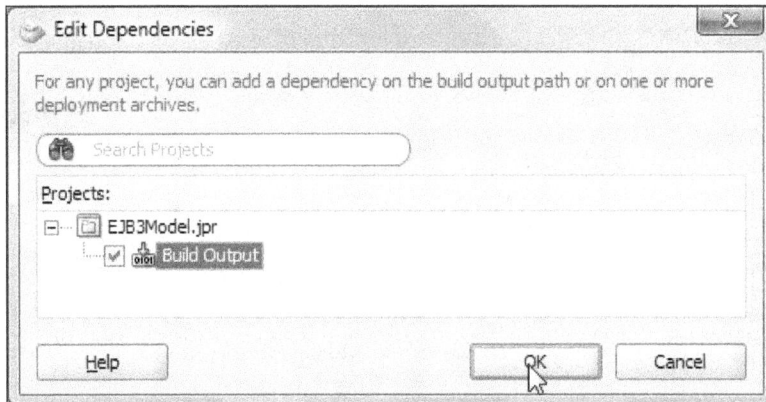

The **EJB3Model** project gets added to the **Dependencies**. Click on **OK**.

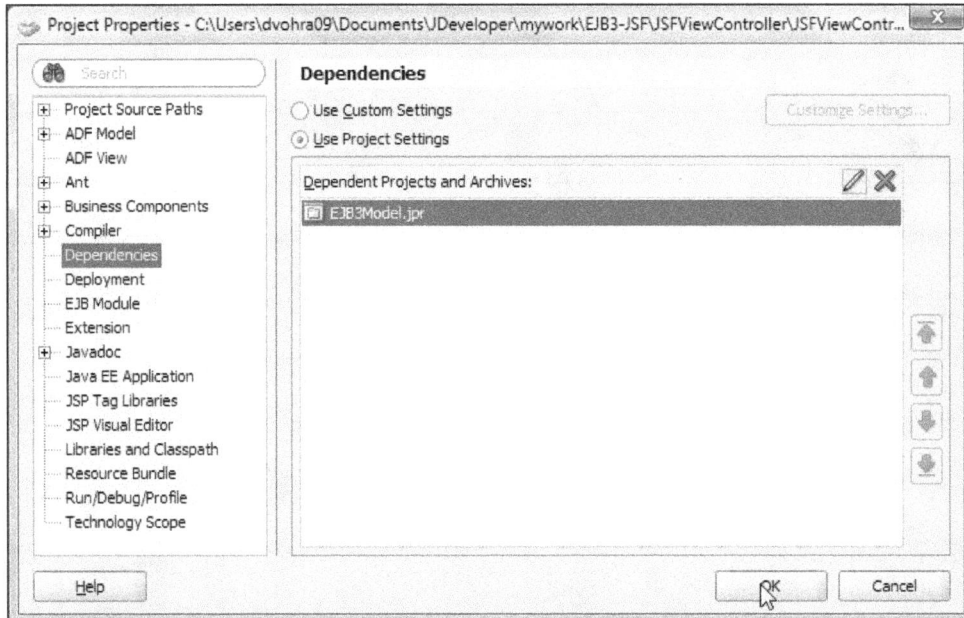

Creating a JSF page

Next, we need to create a JSF page. A JSPX page may also be used. Select the **JSFViewController** project and select **File | New**. In the **New Gallery** window, select **Categories:Web Tier | JSF** and **Items | JSF Page**. Click on **OK**.

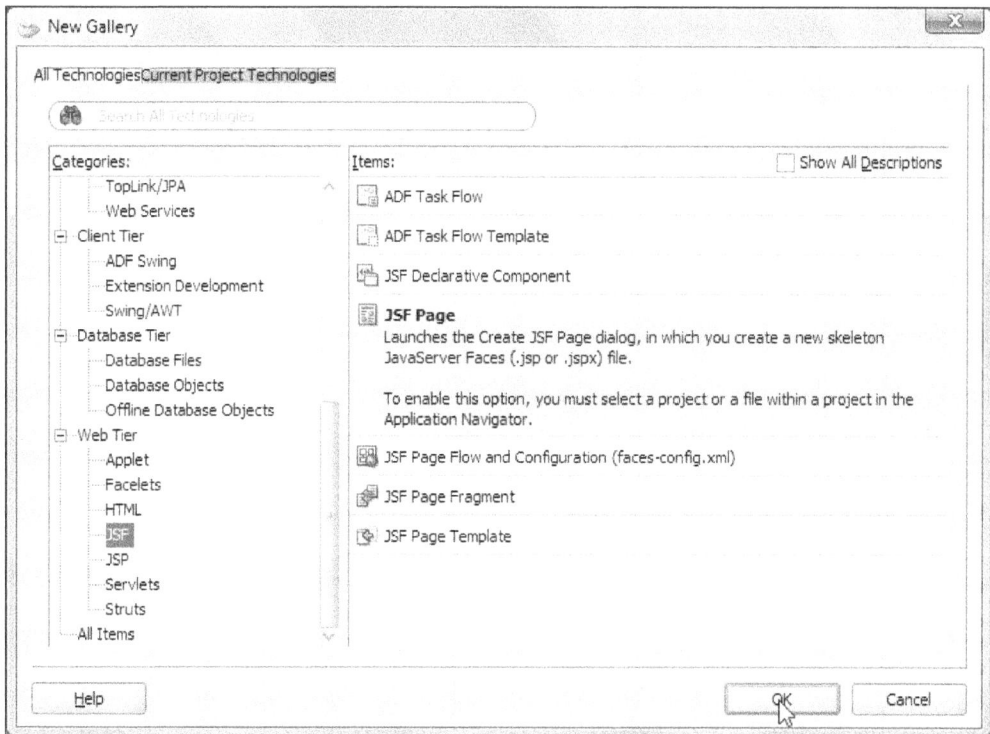

In the **Create JSF Page** window, specify a **File Name** (`create.jsp`). Expand the **Page Implementation** and select **Automatically Expose UI Components in a New Managed Bean**. The managed bean name, class, and package get specified. Click on **OK**.

Create JSF Page

Enter the name, directory, and choose a type for the JSF Page. Optionally reference a Page Template to include its content in this page, or apply a Quick Start Layout to add and configure an initial set of layout components.

File Name: create.jsp

Directory: C:\Users\dvohra09\Documents\JDeveloper\mywork\EJB3-JSF\JSFViewController\public_html   Browse...

☐ Create as XML Document (*.jspx)

☐ Render in Mobile Device

Initial Page Layout and Content

◉ Blank Page

○ Page Template   Oracle Three Column Layout ▼

○ Quick Start Layout

One Column (Stretched)

Browse...

⊟ Page Implementation

Automatically binding UI components to managed beans provides programmatic access to them.

○ Do Not Automatically Expose UI Components in a Managed Bean

◉ Automatically Expose UI Components in a New Managed Bean

Name: backing_create

Class: Create

Package: view.backing   Browse...

○ Automatically Expose UI Components in an Existing Managed Bean

Managed Bean:

Help   OK   Cancel

The `create.jsp` JSF page gets added and the JSF configuration file gets updated with the managed bean. The backing bean class `view.backing.Create.java` also gets added. Similarly, add JSF pages `index.jsp`, `find.jsp`, `catalogentry.jsp`, and `error.jsp`, but when adding these JSF pages select **Do Not Automatically Expose UI Components in a Manage Bean**. The directory structure of the EJB3-JSF application is shown in the following screenshot:

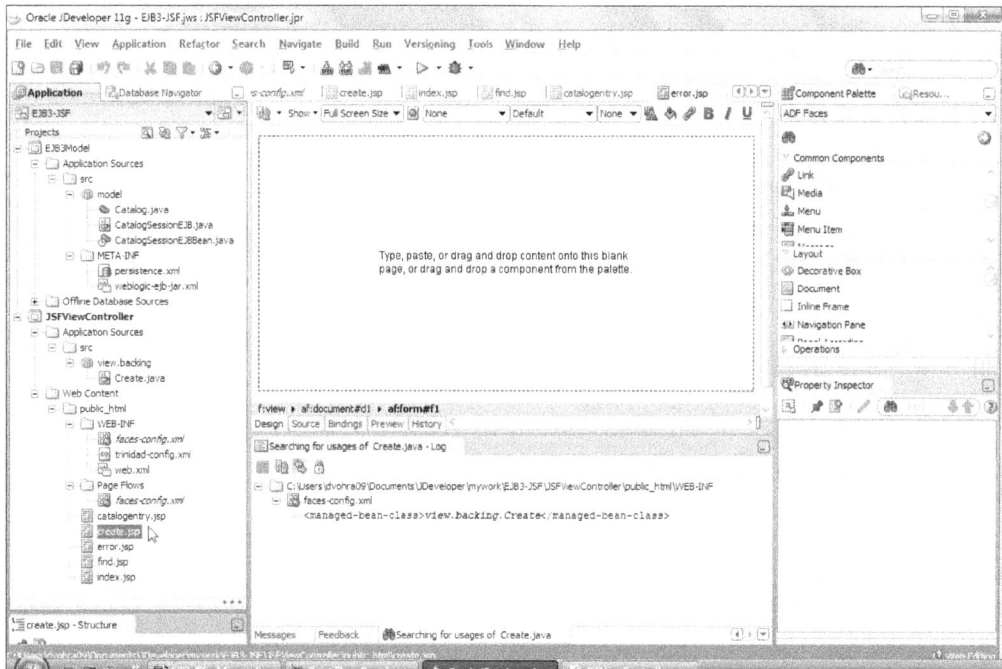

Adding ADF Faces components

We will be adding ADF Faces components to four different JSF pages: the index page, the page to create an entity instance, the page to find an entity instance, and the page to display a catalog entry.

The index JSF page

In the `index.jsp` JSF page, add a **Command Link** to a JSF page that may be used for user input to create an entity instance and persist it to the database. Add another link for user input to retrieve an entity instance with a catalog ID. First, add a **Heading 1** to `index.jsp` and apply style(s) to the heading. A **Command Link** in ADF Faces is added with the `af:commandLink` component. Position the cursor below the heading, select **ADF Faces** in the **Component Palette**, and select **Link**. An ADF Faces **Command Link** gets added to `index.jsp`.

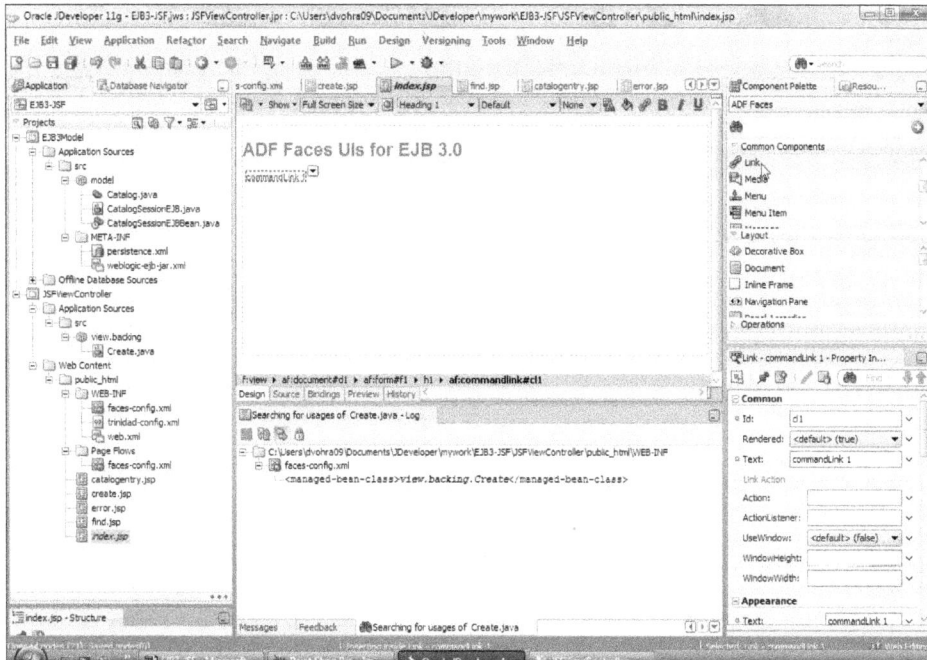

Set the **Text** for the **Command Link** in the **Property Inspector** and similarly add another **Command Link** for finding a catalog entry.

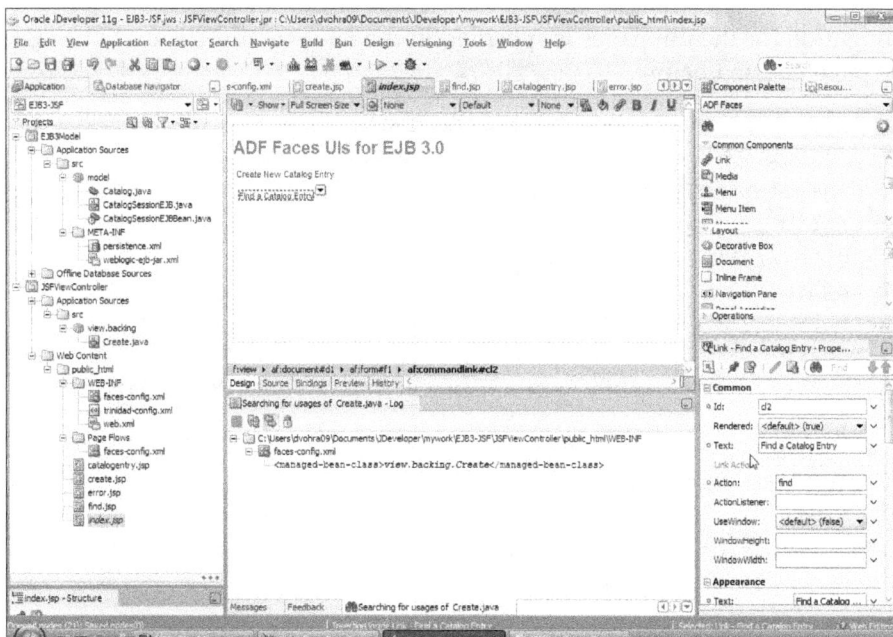

Specify the action methods for the **Command Link**s with the `action` attribute.

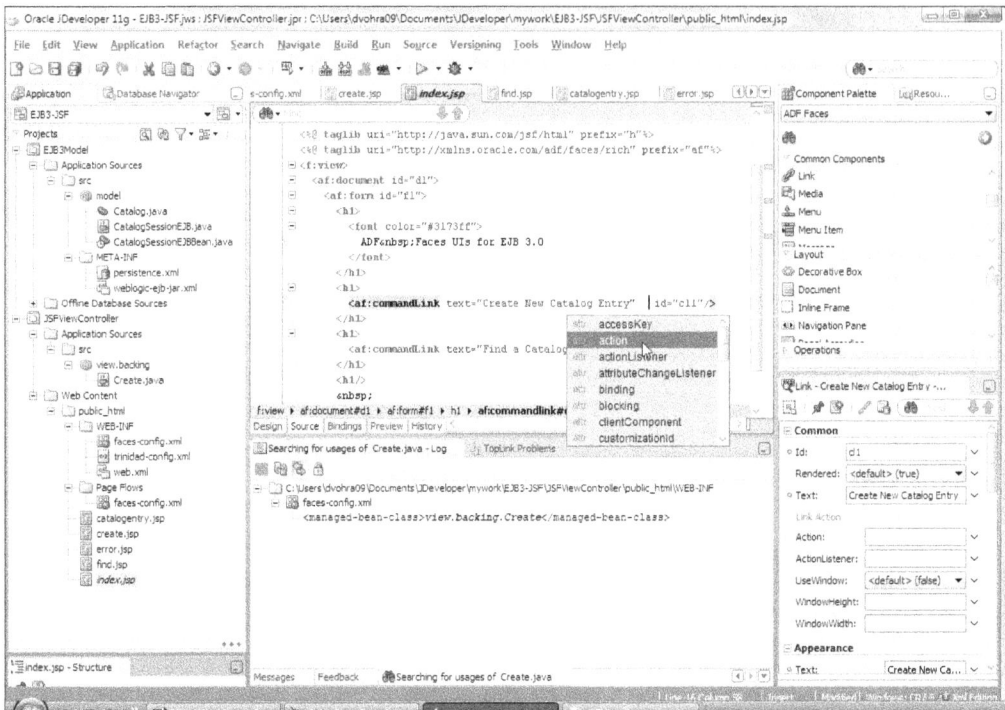

The navigation for the JSF pages is specified in the `faces-config.xml`. The `index.jsp` JSF page is listed below.

```
<!DOCTYPE HTML PUBLIC "-//W3C//DTD HTML 4.01 Transitional//EN"
"http://www.w3.org/TR/html4/loose.dtd">
<%@ page contentType="text/html;charset=windows-1252"%>
<%@ taglib
uri="http://java.sun.com/jsf/core" prefix="f"%>
<%@ taglib
uri="http://java.sun.com/jsf/html" prefix="h"%>
<%@ taglib
uri="http://xmlns.oracle.com/adf/faces/rich" prefix="af"%>
<f:view>
  <af:document id="d1">
    <af:form id="f1">
      <h1>
        <font color="#3173ff">
          JSF UIs for EJB 3.0
        </font>
```

```
    </h1>
    <h1>
       <af:commandLink text="Create New Catalog Entry"
                       action="create" id="cl1" />
    </h1>
     
    <af:commandLink text="Find a Catalog Entry" action="find"
                    id="cl2" />
    </af:form>
   </af:document>
 </f:view>
```

The ADF Faces components in the JSF pages `create.jsp`, `find.jsp`, and `catalogentry.jsp` have bindings specified with UI components in the backing bean.

The JSF page to create an Entity

Next, we add ADF Faces components to the `create.jsp` JSF page. Add a heading to `create.jsp` and set the headings font and color. The `create.jsp` has input text fields for adding Catalog ID, Journal, Publisher, Edition, Title, and Author. We shall lay out the components in a **Panel Form Layout** layout. Position the cursor in the JSF page in the **Design** view and select **Panel Form Layout** in the **Component Palette**.

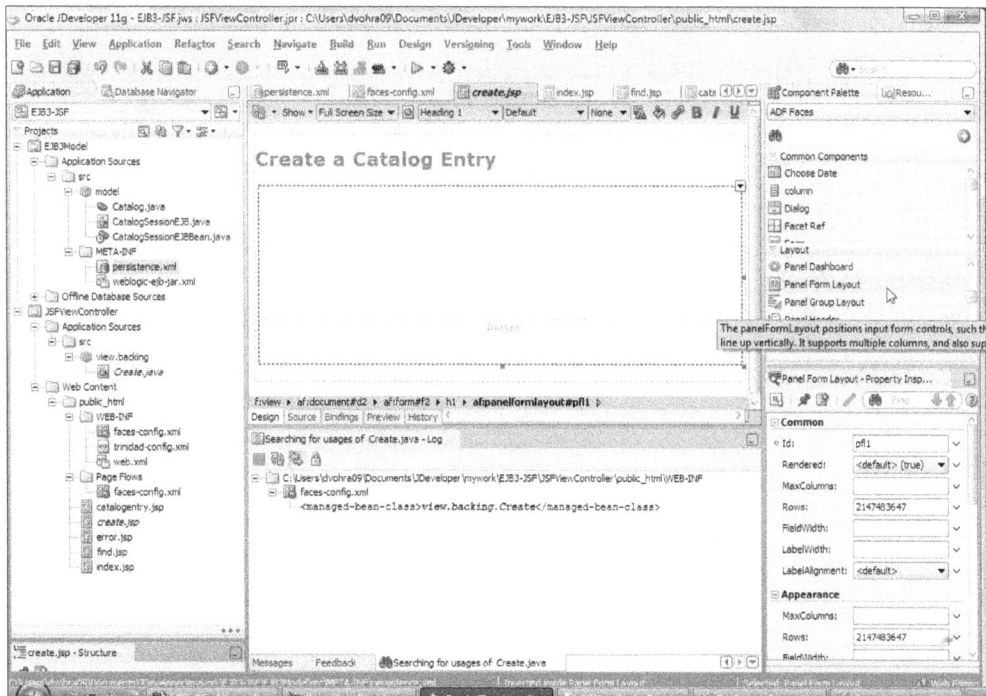

Position the cursor in the **Panel Form Layout** and select **Input Text** in the **Component Palette**. A label and an input text get added.

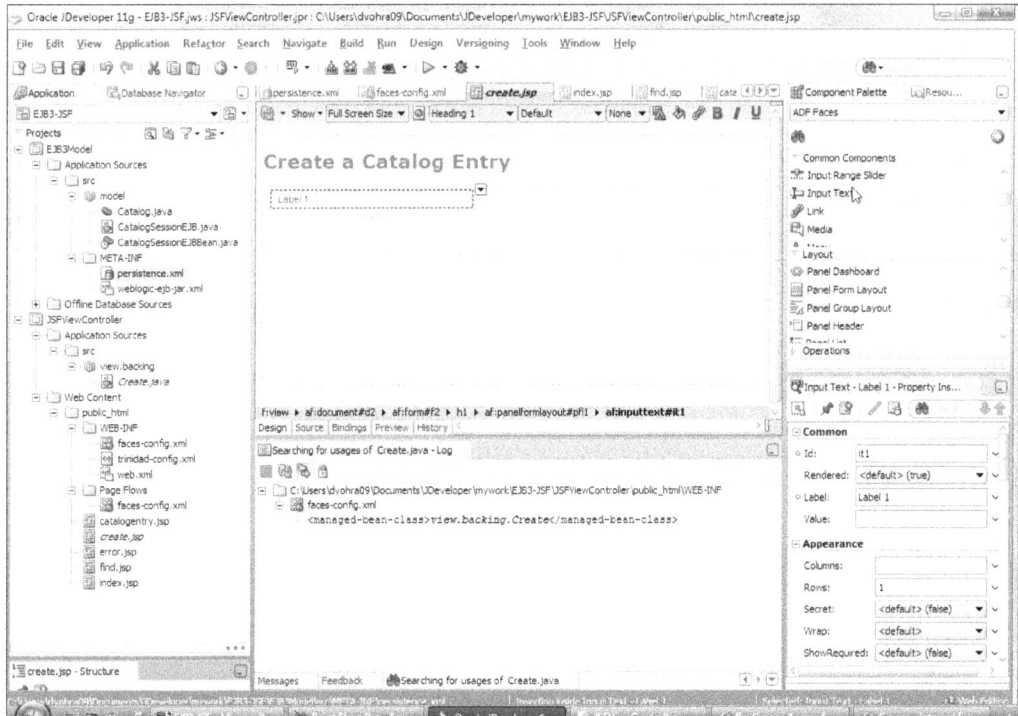

Set the label's text in the **Property Inspector**. Similarly, add **Input Text** fields for Journal, Publisher, Edition, Title, and Author. We also need to add a **Command Button** to submit the input form, invoke a method in the managed bean. Position the cursor below the **Input Text** and select **Button** in the **ADF Faces'** **Component Palette**.

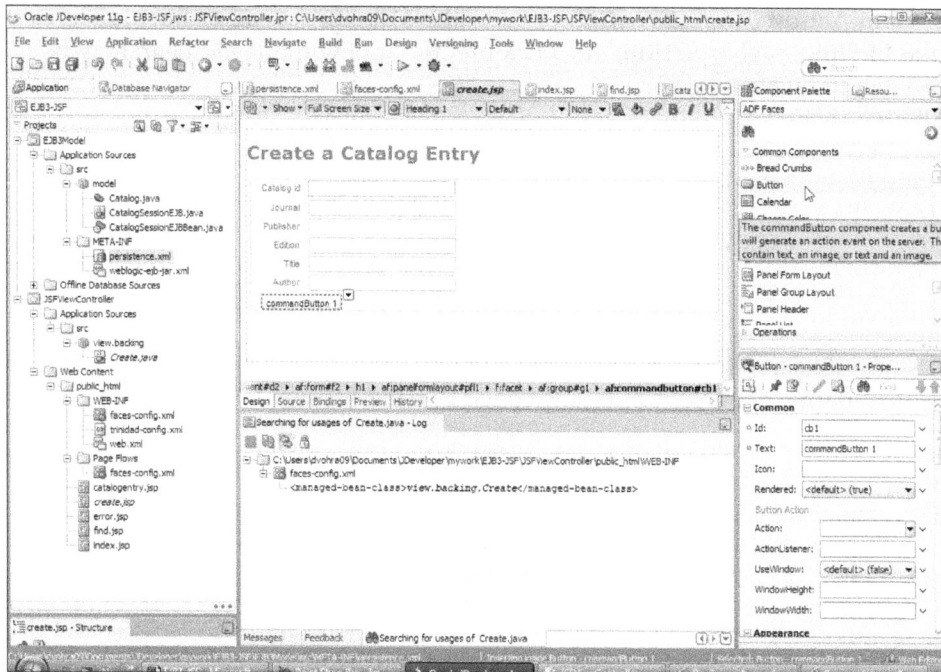

Set the button's text in the **Property Inspector**. Next, bind the button to a managed bean method. Double-click on the button in the **Design** view.

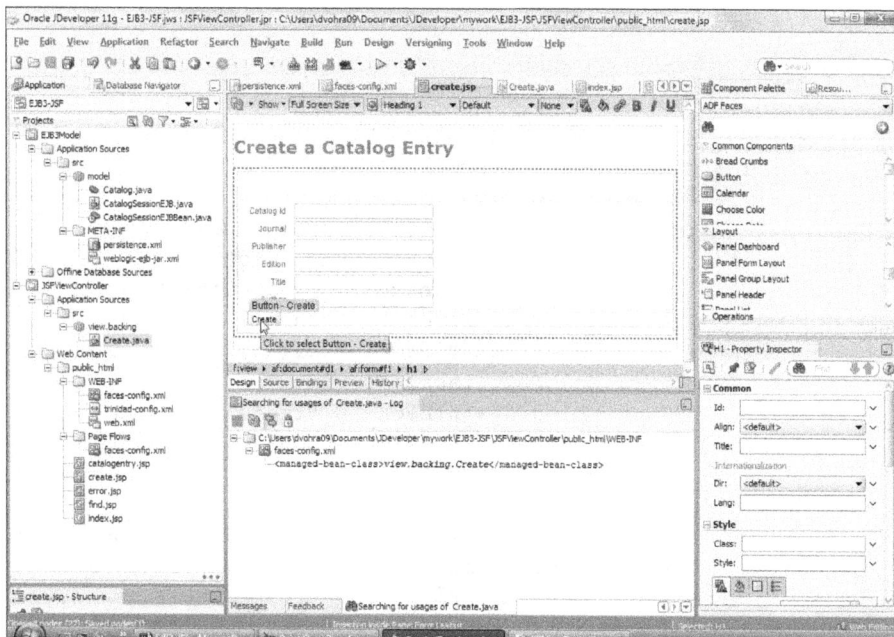

In the **Bind Action Property** window, select the **Managed Bean** as **backing_create** and the **Method** as **cb1_Action**, and click on **OK**. A new managed bean may be created using the **New** button.

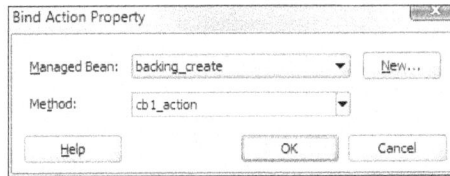

The `cb1_action` method gets added. The method name may be modified to a more descriptive name. The `create.jsp` JSF page is listed below:

```
<!DOCTYPE HTML PUBLIC "-//W3C//DTD HTML 4.01 Transitional//EN"
"http://www.w3.org/TR/html4/loose.dtd">
<%@ page contentType="text/html;charset=windows-1252"%>
<%@ taglib uri="http://java.sun.com/jsf/core" prefix="f"%>
<%@ taglib uri="http://java.sun.com/jsf/html" prefix="h"%>
<%@ taglib uri="http://xmlns.oracle.com/adf/faces/rich" prefix="af"%>
<f:view>
  <af:document id="d1" binding="#{backing_create.d1}">
    <af:form id="f1" binding="#{backing_create.f1}">
      <h1>
        <font color="#6363ff" face="Verdana">
          Create a Catalog Entry
        </font>
         
      </h1>
      <h1>
        <af:panelFormLayout binding="#{backing_create.pfl1}"
            id="pfl1">
          <f:facet name="footer">
            <af:group binding="#{backing_create.g1}" id="g1">
                <af:inputText label="Catalog Id"
                      binding="#{backing_create.it1}" id="it1"/>
                <af:inputText label="Journal"
                      binding="#{backing_create.it2}" id="it2"/>
                <af:inputText label="Publisher"
                      binding="#{backing_create.it3}" id="it3"/>
                <af:inputText label="Edition"
                      binding="#{backing_create.it4}" id="it4"/>
                <af:inputText label="Title"
                      binding="#{backing_create.it5}" id="it5"/>
                <af:inputText label="Author"
                      binding="#{backing_create.it6}" id="it6"/>
              <af:commandButton text="Create"
```

```
                      binding="#{backing_create.cb1}" id="cb1"
                      action="#{backing_create.cb1_action}"/>
           </af:group>
         </f:facet>

       </af:panelFormLayout>
     </h1>
   </af:form>
 </af:document>
</f:view>
<%-- oracle-jdev-comment:auto-binding-backing-bean-name:backing_
create--%>
```

The `Create.java` managed bean has `RichInputText` components corresponding
to each of the properties of the entity instance `Catalog`. The managed bean also
has methods `cb1_action()` and `find()` (custom added) to persist and find entity
instances respectively. The `create.jsp` JSF page has `af:inputText` components
for each of the `Catalog` entity properties. Each of the ADF Faces components in the
`create.jsp` page has a binding with ADF Faces UI components in the managed
bean. The `create.jsp` also has an `af:commandButton` button component that has
its `action` attribute's binding to the `cb1_action` method in the backing bean. In the
`cb1_action()` method in the backing bean, we lookup the session bean and invoke
the `persistEntity()` method on it, which returns a `String`. First, we create
an `InitialContext`:

```
InitialContext context = new InitialContext();
```

Two methods are available to lookup a session bean using the remote
business interface:

1. Lookup the session bean remote interface using the mapped name. The
   global JNDI name for a session bean remote business interface is derived
   from the remote business interface name. The format of the global JNDI
   name is `mappedName#qualified_name_of_businessInterface`.

2. Create a `weblogic-ejb-jar.xml` deployment descriptor and specify the
   business interface JNDI name in the `weblogic-ejb-jar.xml` deployment
   descriptor. The global JNDI name is specified as follows:

```
<weblogic-enterprise-bean>
  <ejb-name>CatalogTestSessionEJBBean</ejb-name>
```

```
<stateless-session-descriptor>
  <business-interface-jndi-name-map>
    <business-remote>CatalogTestSessionEJB
    </business-remote>
    <jndi-name>EJB3-SessionEJB</jndi-name>
  </business-interface-jndi-name-map>
</stateless-session-descriptor>
</weblogic-enterprise-bean>
```

We will use the first method to create a remote business interface instance using lookup with the mapped name.

```
CatalogSessionEJB catalogSessionEJB = (CatalogSessionEJB)
    context.lookup("EJB3-JSF-EJB3Model-CatalogSessionEJB#model.
                   CatalogSessionEJB");
```

Retrieve the input text values using the `getValue()` method on the UI components that have a binding with the JSF page components. For example, the `journal` input text's value is retrieved as follows:

```
String journal = (String)it2.getValue();
```

Invoke the `persistEntity()` method of the session bean to persist an entity instance created from the input text values:

```
catalogSessionEJB.persistEntity(id, journalField,
                                publisherField,editionField,
                                titleField,authorField);
```

The `cb1_action` method returns a `String` "persisted" that navigates back to the `index.jsp` page.

The JSF page to find an Entity

The `find.jsp` JSF page is used to find a catalog entry for a catalog ID. The `find.jsp` has a `af:inputText` component to specify a catalog ID. Add a **Heading 1** and a **Panel Form Layout** to `find.jsp`. To the **Panel Form Layout**, add an **Input Text** from the **ADF Faces' Component Palette**. Add a **Command Button** below the **Input Text** field.

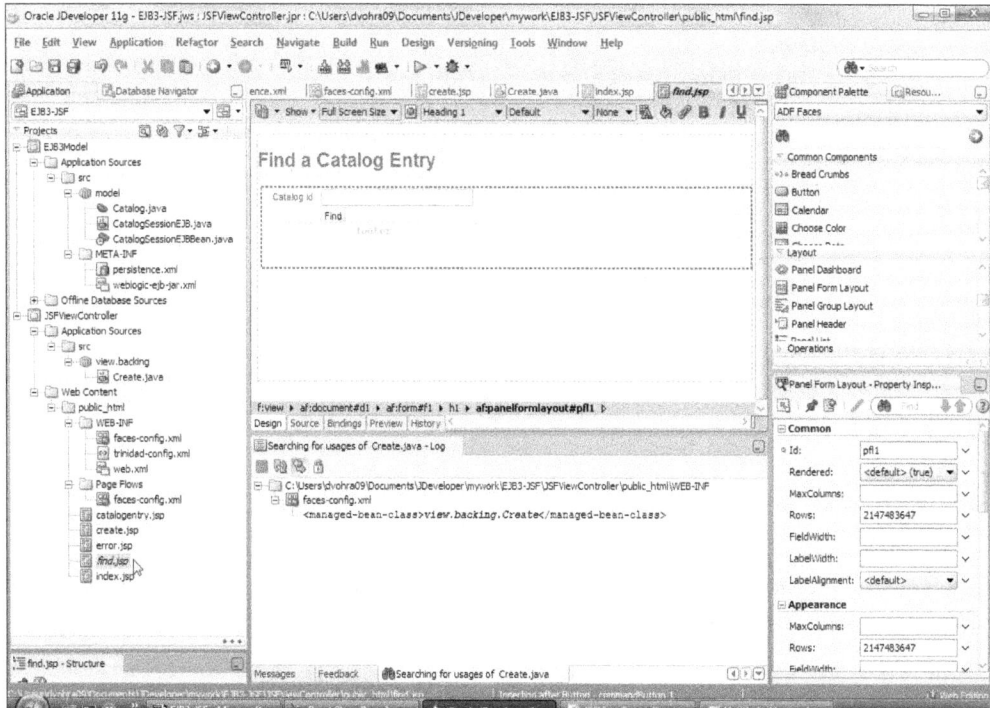

A button of type `af:commandButton` gets added. The `action` property of the button may be set with the **Bind Action Property** window, which is invoked by double-clicking on a button. Set the `action` attribute to `backing_create.cb2_action1`. The `find.jsp` JSF page is listed below:

```
<!DOCTYPE HTML PUBLIC "-//W3C//DTD HTML 4.01 Transitional//EN"
"http://www.w3.org/TR/html4/loose.dtd">
<%@ page contentType="text/html;charset=windows-1252"%>
<%@ taglib
uri="http://java.sun.com/jsf/core" prefix="f"%>
<%@ taglib
uri="http://java.sun.com/jsf/html" prefix="h"%>
<%@ taglib
uri="http://xmlns.oracle.com/adf/faces/rich" prefix="af"%>
<f:view>
    <af:document title="find" id="d1">
        <af:form id="f1">
            <h1>
                <font color="#5252ff">
                    Find a Catalog Entry
            </font>
```

```
        </h1>
        <h1>
            <af:panelFormLayout id="pfl1">
                <f:facet name="footer" />
                <af:inputText label="Catalog Id" id="it7"
                    binding="#{backing_create.it7}" />
                <af:commandButton text="Find" id="cb2"
                        binding="#{backing_create.cb2}" action="#{backing_
                        create.cb2_action1}" />
            </af:panelFormLayout>
        </h1>
    </af:form>
  </af:document>
</f:view>
<%--
oracle-jdev-comment:preferred-managed-bean-name:backing_create
--%>
```

In the `find()` method in the managed bean, retrieve the catalog id using the `getValue()` method for the UI component:

```
int id = Integer.parseInt((String)it7.getValue());
```

Create an `InitialContext` object and lookup the remote interface of the session bean using the mapped name for the session bean:

```
CatalogSessionEJB catalogSessionEJB = (CatalogSessionEJB)
    context.lookup("EJB3-JSF-EJB3Model-CatalogSessionEJB#model.
                CatalogSessionEJB");
```

Invoke the `findEntity()` method of the session bean. The `findEntity()` method returns a `Catalog` entity instance. Set the value of a managed bean's variable of type `Catalog` to the entity instance retrieved:

```
catalog = catalogSessionEJB.findEntity(id);
```

The `find()` method returns a `String` "catalogentry", which has navigation set to the `catalogentry.jsp` JSF page.

The catalog entry JSF page

The `catalogentry.jsp` has `af:outputLabel` components corresponding to a catalog entry's properties. Next, add ADF Faces components to `catalogentry.jsp`. Add a **Heading 1** and set its style and text. Add a **Panel Form Layout** to `catalogentry.jsp`.

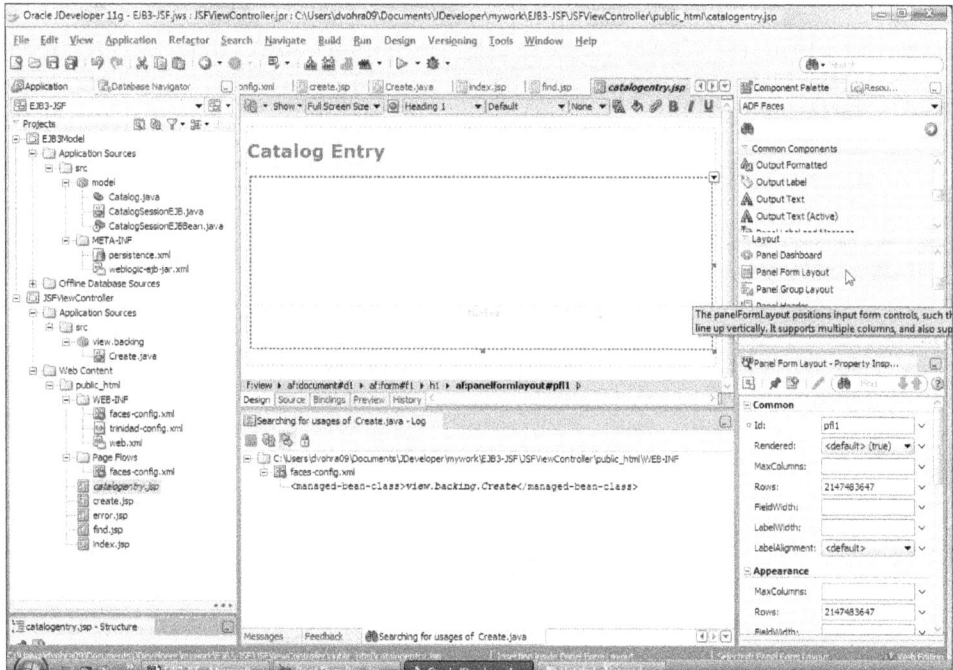

We will add two columns of **Output Label** to the **Panel Form Layout**, one for the catalog entry's property names and the other for the catalog entry's property values.

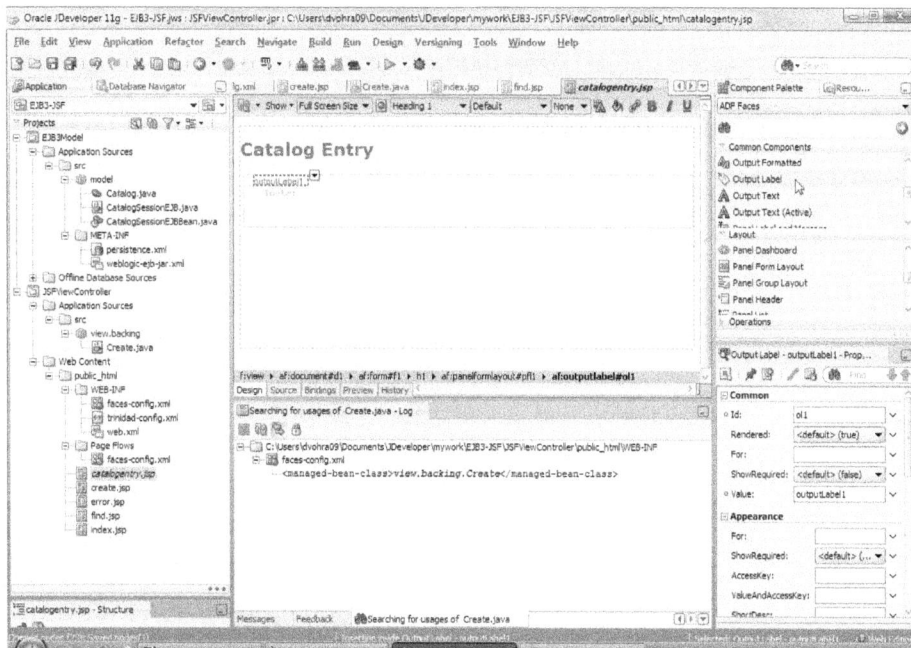

By default, the ADF Faces components get added in a single column. Set the `maxColumns` attribute of the `af:panelFormLayout` to 2 and set the rows attribute to 5, which implies that after every five rows a new column gets added up to a maximum of two columns.

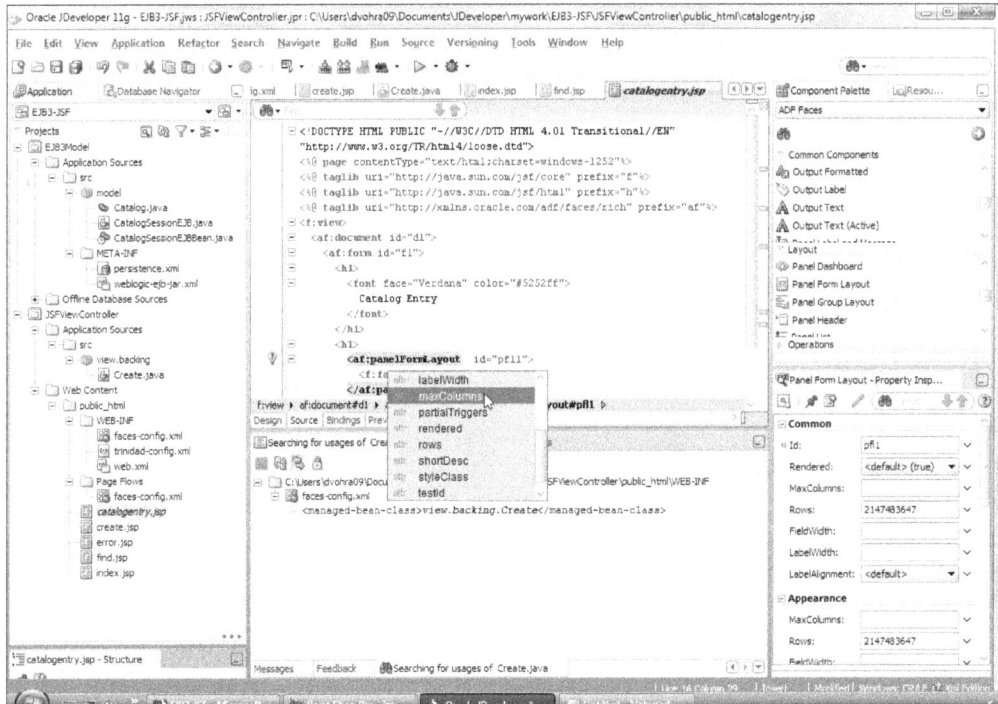

Add five **Output Label**s in the first column and set their text to **Journal, Publisher, Edition, Title, and Author**. Add five output labels in the second column for the `Catalog` entry's properties' values.

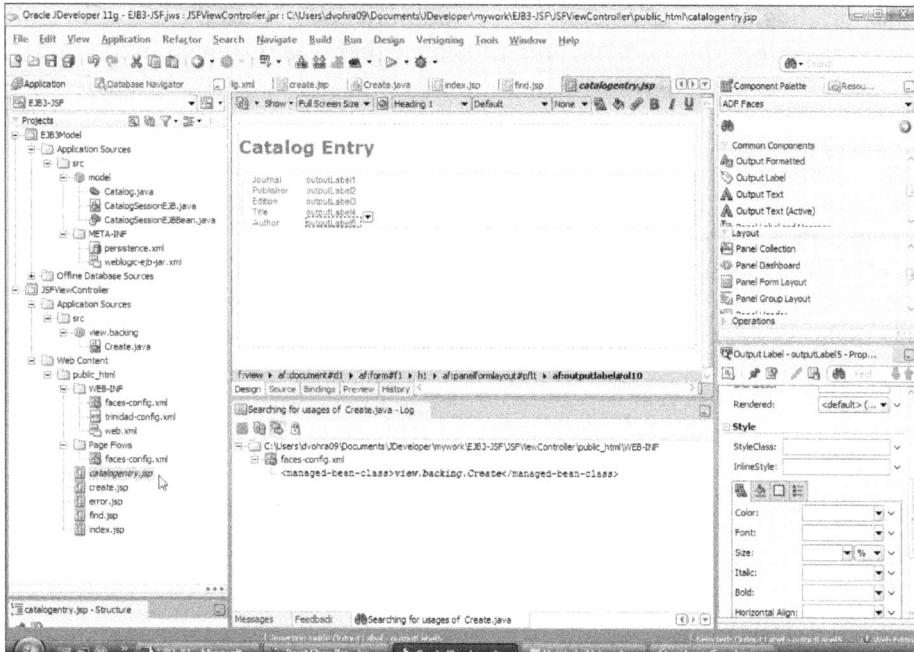

Bind the output labels for the `Catalog` entry's properties' values to the `Catalog` object's properties' values in the managed bean. The `Catalog` object is the `Catalog` entry retrieved for the specified Catalog ID.

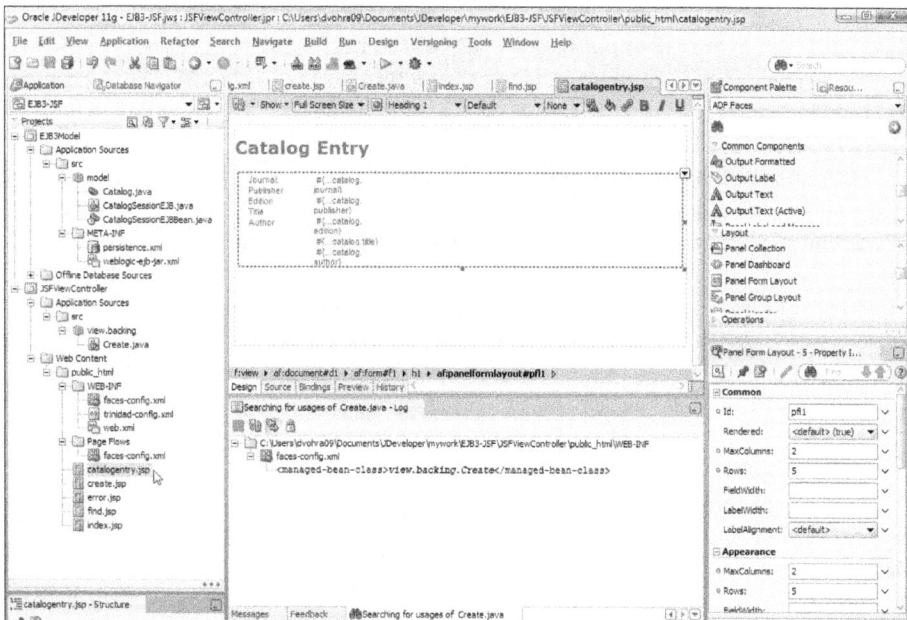

The value binding of the `af:outputLabel` components is set to the `Catalog` entity instance's properties, the `Catalog` entity instance that was retrieved in the `find()` method with the catalog id input. The `catalogentry.jsp` is listed below:

```
<!DOCTYPE HTML PUBLIC "-//W3C//DTD HTML 4.01 Transitional//EN"
"http://www.w3.org/TR/html4/loose.dtd">
<%@ page contentType="text/html;charset=windows-1252"%>
<%@ taglib
uri="http://java.sun.com/jsf/core" prefix="f"%>
<%@ taglib
uri="http://java.sun.com/jsf/html" prefix="h"%>
<%@ taglib
uri="http://xmlns.oracle.com/adf/faces/rich" prefix="af"%>
<f:view>
    <af:document title="catalogntry" id="d1">
        <af:form id="f1">
            <h1>
                <font face="Verdana" color="#5252ff">
                    Catalog Entry
        </font>
            </h1>
            <h1>
<af:panelFormLayout rows="5" maxColumns="2" id="pfl1">
<af:outputLabel value="Journal:" id="ol1" />
<af:outputLabel value="Publisher" id="ol2" />
                <af:outputLabel value="Edition" id="ol3" />
                <af:outputLabel value="Title" id="ol4" />
                <af:outputLabel value="Author" id="ol5" />
<af:outputLabel value="#{backing_create.catalog.journal}"
                id="ol6" />
<af:outputLabel value="#{backing_create.catalog.publisher}"
                id="ol7" />
<af:outputLabel value="#{backing_create.catalog.edition}"
                id="ol8" />
<af:outputLabel value="#{backing_create.catalog.title}"
                id="ol9" />
<af:outputLabel value="#{backing_create.catalog.author}"
                id="ol10" />
            </af:panelFormLayout>
        </h1>
        </af:form>
    </af:document>
</f:view>
```

The managed bean

The managed bean class `Create.java` that defines UI components backing the ADF Faces components in the JSF pages is listed below:

```java
package view.backing;

import javax.naming.InitialContext;
import javax.naming.NamingException;
import model.*;
import oracle.adf.view.rich.component.rich.RichDocument;
import oracle.adf.view.rich.component.rich.RichForm;
import oracle.adf.view.rich.component.rich.input.RichInputText;
import oracle.adf.view.rich.component.rich.layout.RichPanelFormLayout;
import oracle.adf.view.rich.component.rich.nav.RichCommandButton;
import org.apache.myfaces.trinidad.component.UIXGroup;

public class Create {
    private RichForm f1;
    private RichDocument d1;
    private RichPanelFormLayout pfl1;
    private RichInputText it1;
    private RichInputText it2;
    private UIXGroup g1;
    private RichInputText it3;
    private RichInputText it4;
    private RichInputText it5;
    private RichInputText it6;
    private RichInputText it7;
    private RichCommandButton cb1;
    private RichCommandButton cb2;
    private Catalog catalog;

    public Catalog getCatalog() {
        return catalog;
    }

    public void setCatalog(Catalog catalog) {
        this.catalog = catalog;
    }

    public void setF1(RichForm f1) {
        this.f1 = f1;
    }

    public RichForm getF1() {
        return f1;
    }
```

```
public void setD1(RichDocument d1) {
    this.d1 = d1;
}

public RichDocument getD1() {
    return d1;
}

public void setPfl1(RichPanelFormLayout pfl1) {
    this.pfl1 = pfl1;
}

public RichPanelFormLayout getPfl1() {
    return pfl1;
}

public void setIt1(RichInputText it1) {
    this.it1 = it1;
}

public RichInputText getIt1() {
    return it1;
}

public void setIt2(RichInputText it2) {
    this.it2 = it2;
}

public RichInputText getIt2() {
    return it2;
}

public void setG1(UIXGroup g1) {
    this.g1 = g1;
}

public UIXGroup getG1() {
    return g1;
}

public void setIt3(RichInputText it3) {
    this.it3 = it3;
}

public RichInputText getIt3() {
    return it3;
}

public void setIt4(RichInputText it4) {
    this.it4 = it4;
}

public RichInputText getIt4() {
```

```
        return it4;
    }
    public void setIt5(RichInputText it5) {
        this.it5 = it5;
    }
    public RichInputText getIt5() {
        return it5;
    }
    public void setIt6(RichInputText it6) {
        this.it6 = it6;
    }
    public RichInputText getIt6() {
        return it6;
    }
    public void setIt7(RichInputText it7) {
        this.it7 = it7;
    }
    public RichInputText getIt7() {
        return it7;
    }
    public void setCb1(RichCommandButton cb1) {
        this.cb1 = cb1;
    }
    public RichCommandButton getCb1() {
        return cb1;
    }
    public void setCb2(RichCommandButton cb2) {
        this.cb2 = cb2;
    }
    public RichCommandButton getCb2() {
        return cb2;
    }
    public String cb1_action() {
        try {
            InitialContext context = new InitialContext();
            int id = Integer.parseInt((String) it1.getValue());
            CatalogSessionEJB catalogSessionEJB = (CatalogSessionEJB)
              context.lookup("EJB3-JSF-EJB3Model-CatalogSessionEJB#model.
                        CatalogSessionEJB");
```

```
            String journal = (String) it2.getValue();

            String publisher = (String) it3.getValue();

            String edition = (String) it4.getValue();

            String title = (String) (it5.getValue());

            String author = (String) (it6.getValue());
        catalogSessionEJB.persistEntity(id, journal, publisher, edition,
                                 title, author);
        } catch (NamingException e) {
            System.err.println(e.getMessage());
            return "notpersisted";
        }

        return "persisted";
    }

    public String cb2_action1() {
        // Add event code here...
        try {
            InitialContext context = new InitialContext();

            int id = Integer.parseInt((String) it7.getValue());

          CatalogSessionEJB catalogSessionEJB = (CatalogSessionEJB)
            context.lookup("EJB3-JSF-EJB3Model-CatalogSessionEJB#model.
                          CatalogSessionEJB");

            catalog = catalogSessionEJB.findEntity(id);

        } catch (NamingException e) {
            System.err.println(e.getMessage());
            return "error";
        }
        return "catalogentry";
    }
}
```

The JSF configuration file

The `faces-config.xml` that has the managed bean specified and the navigation rules specified is listed below:

```
<?xml version="1.0" encoding="windows-1252"?>
<faces-config version="1.2" xmlns="http://java.sun.com/xml/ns/javaee">
    <application>
        <default-render-kit-id>oracle.adf.rich
        </default-render-kit-id>
```

```
    </application>
    <managed-bean>
        <managed-bean-name>backing_create</managed-bean-name>
        <managed-bean-class>view.backing.Create
        </managed-bean-class>
        <managed-bean-scope>request</managed-bean-scope>
        <!--oracle-jdev-comment:managed-bean-jsp-link:1create.jsp-->
    </managed-bean>
    <navigation-rule>
        <navigation-case>
            <from-outcome>create</from-outcome>
            <to-view-id>/create.jsp</to-view-id>
        </navigation-case>
    </navigation-rule>
    <navigation-rule>
        <navigation-case>
            <from-outcome>catalogentry</from-outcome>
            <to-view-id>/catalogentry.jsp</to-view-id>
        </navigation-case>
    </navigation-rule>
    <navigation-rule>
        <navigation-case>
            <from-outcome>persisted</from-outcome>
            <to-view-id>/index.jsp</to-view-id>
        </navigation-case>
    </navigation-rule>
    <navigation-rule>
        <navigation-case>
            <from-outcome>error</from-outcome>
            <to-view-id>/error.jsp</to-view-id>
        </navigation-case>
    </navigation-rule>
    <navigation-rule>
        <navigation-case>
            <from-outcome>find</from-outcome>
            <to-view-id>/find.jsp</to-view-id>
        </navigation-case>
    </navigation-rule>
</faces-config>
```

The error.jsp, which gets displayed with an error message if an error gets generated is listed as follows:

```
<!DOCTYPE HTML PUBLIC "-//W3C//DTD HTML 4.01 Transitional//EN"
"http://www.w3.org/TR/html4/loose.dtd">
```

```
<%@ page contentType="text/html;charset=windows-1252"%>
<%@ taglib
uri="http://java.sun.com/jsf/core" prefix="f"%>
<%@ taglib
uri="http://java.sun.com/jsf/html" prefix="h"%>
<%@ taglib
uri="http://xmlns.oracle.com/adf/faces/rich" prefix="af"%>
<f:view>
    <af:document id="d1">
        <af:form id="f1">
            <af:outputText value="Error Generated" id="ot1" />
        </af:form>
    </af:document>
</f:view>
```

The web application configuration file

The web.xml configuration file gets generated automatically when a JSF page is created. The context-param elements and the servlets also get added to the web.xml automatically when ADF Faces components are added. In the web.xml deployment descriptor the Faces Servlet and the URL pattern mapping for the Faces Servlet should get specified automatically. The Faces Servlet is mapped to URL pattern / faces/*. Similarly, map the ADF Face Servlet class to a URL pattern. The web.xml is listed below:

```
<?xml version = '1.0' encoding = 'windows-1252'?>
<web-app xmlns:xsi="http://www.w3.org/2001/XMLSchema-instance"
   xsi:schemaLocation="http://java.sun.com/xml/ns/javaee
   http://java.sun.com/xml/ns/javaee/web-app_2_5.xsd"
   version="2.5" xmlns="http://java.sun.com/xml/ns/javaee">
   <context-param>
      <param-name>javax.faces.STATE_SAVING_METHOD</param-name>
      <param-value>client</param-value>
   </context-param>
   <context-param>
      <param-name>
         org.apache.myfaces.trinidad.CHECK_FILE_MODIFICATION
      </param-name>
      <param-value>false</param-value>
   </context-param>
   <context-param>
      <description>
         Whether the 'Generated by...' comment at the bottom of ADF
         Faces HTML pages should contain version number information.
      </description>
```

```
      <param-name>oracle.adf.view.rich.versionString.HIDDEN
      </param-name>
      <param-value>false</param-value>
</context-param>
<filter>
   <filter-name>JpsFilter</filter-name>
   <filter-class>oracle.security.jps.ee.http.JpsFilter
   </filter-class>
   <init-param>
      <param-name>enable.anonymous</param-name>
      <param-value>true</param-value>
   </init-param>
</filter>
<filter>
   <filter-name>trinidad</filter-name>
   <filter-class>
                  org.apache.myfaces.trinidad.webapp.TrinidadFilter
   </filter-class>
</filter>
<filter-mapping>
   <filter-name>JpsFilter</filter-name>
   <servlet-name>Faces Servlet</servlet-name>
   <dispatcher>FORWARD</dispatcher>
   <dispatcher>REQUEST</dispatcher>
   <dispatcher>INCLUDE</dispatcher>
</filter-mapping>
<filter-mapping>
   <filter-name>trinidad</filter-name>
   <servlet-name>Faces Servlet</servlet-name>
   <dispatcher>FORWARD</dispatcher>
   <dispatcher>REQUEST</dispatcher>
</filter-mapping>
<servlet>
   <servlet-name>Faces Servlet</servlet-name>
   <servlet-class>javax.faces.webapp.FacesServlet</servlet-class>
   <load-on-startup>1</load-on-startup>
</servlet>
<servlet>
   <servlet-name>resources</servlet-name>
   <servlet-class>org.apache.myfaces.trinidad.webapp.
                                              ResourceServlet
   </servlet-class>
</servlet>
<servlet-mapping>
   <servlet-name>Faces Servlet</servlet-name>
   <url-pattern>/faces/*</url-pattern>
```

```
        </servlet-mapping>
        <servlet-mapping>
            <servlet-name>resources</servlet-name>
            <url-pattern>/adf/*</url-pattern>
        </servlet-mapping>
        <servlet-mapping>
            <servlet-name>resources</servlet-name>
            <url-pattern>/afr/*</url-pattern>
        </servlet-mapping>
    </web-app>
```

Testing the Oracle ADF Faces user interface

Next, we shall test the ADF Faces client user interface. We shall create a catalog entry and subsequently retrieve the catalog entry. Right-click on `index.jsp` and select **Run**.

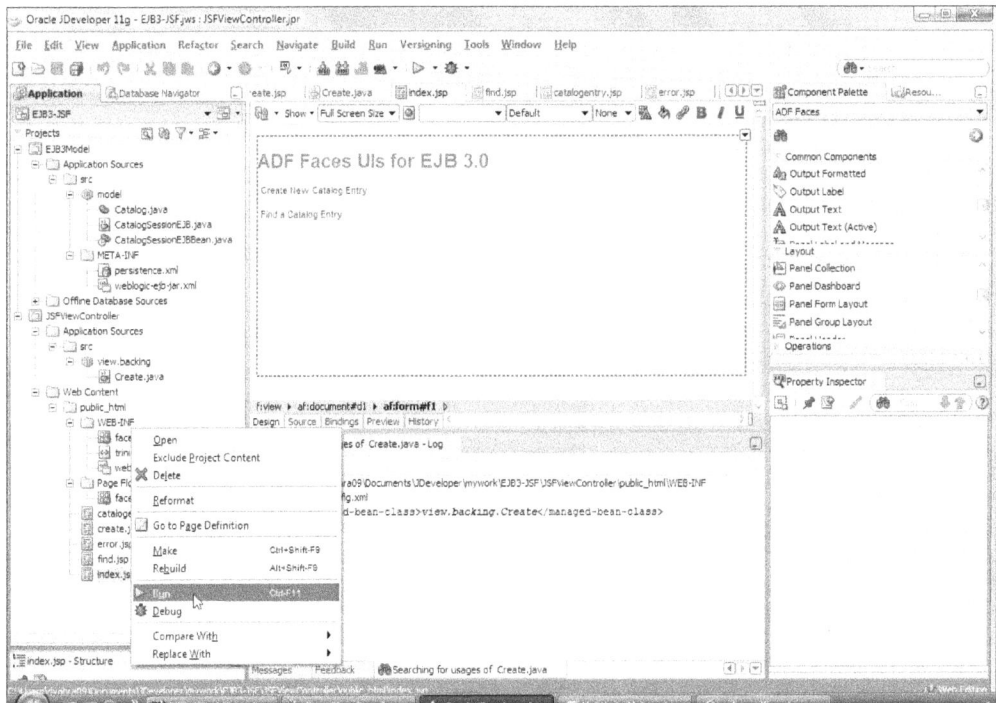

Creating an Entity instance

In the `index.jsp` JSF page, select **Create New Catalog Entry**.

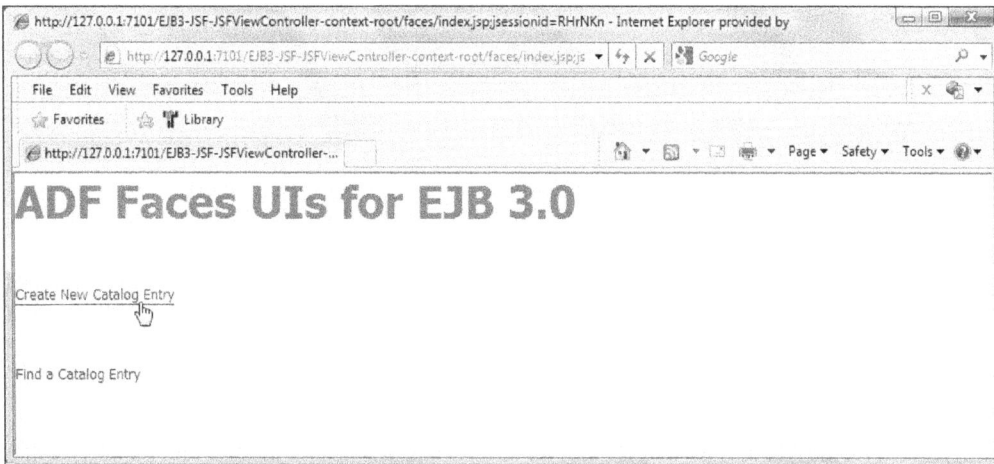

In the `create.jsp` JSF page, specify input text field values for a catalog entry and click on **Create**.

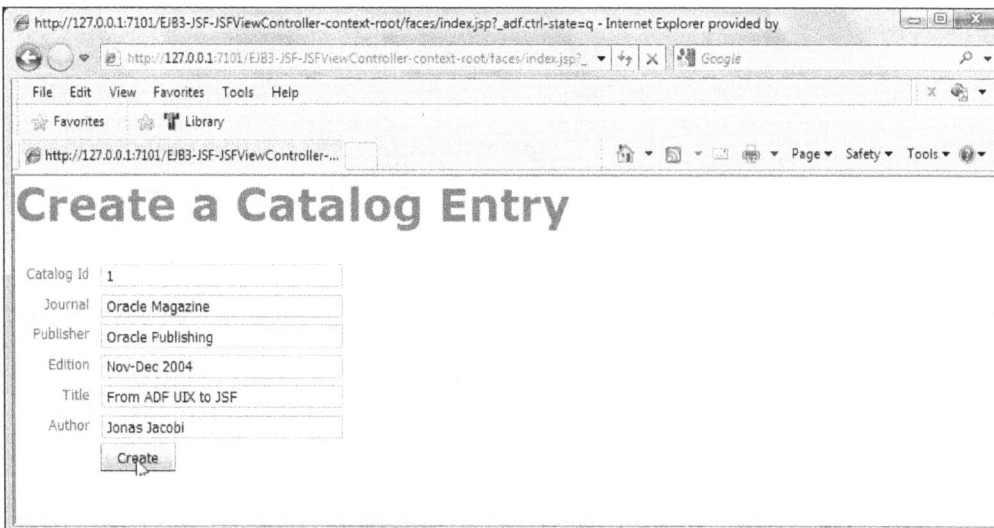

A catalog entry gets created.

Finding an Entity instance

Next, we shall find the catalog entry created. Click on **Find a Catalog Entry**.

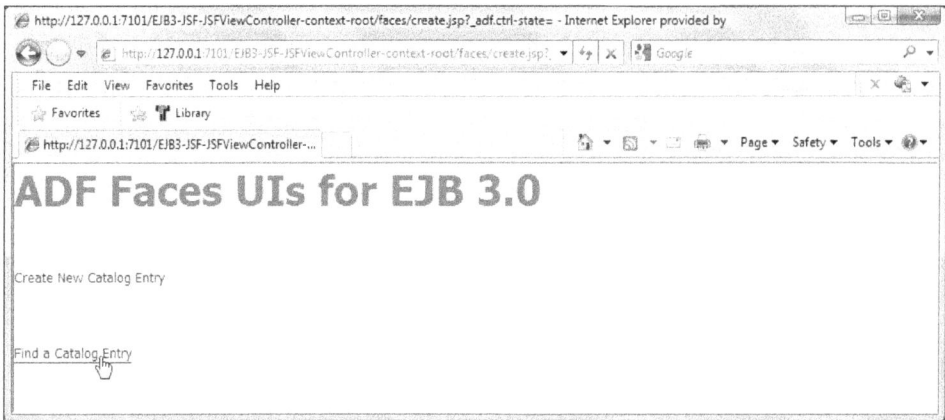

In the find.jsp JSF page, specify a catalog ID and click on **Find**.

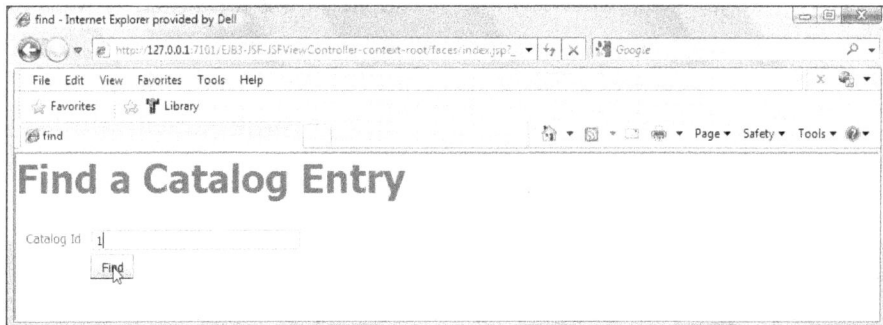

In the catalogentry.jsp JSF page the catalog entry gets listed.

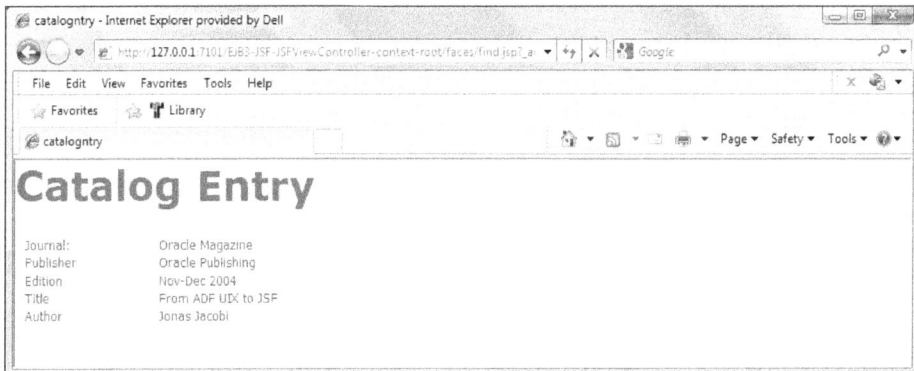

Summary

In this chapter, we created an EJB 3.0 entity bean in JDeveloper 11*g* from an Oracle database table. The Catalog entity bean is automatically created from a database table CATALOG; the database table columns are mapped to entity bean properties. We created a wrapper session bean for the entity bean including a remote business interface. We added a test method to the session bean for creating and persisting entity instances, querying entity instances, and removing an entity instance. We created an ADF Faces test client to test the entity bean. We looked up the session bean remote interface using the mapped name for the session bean and persist, and found entity instances. In the next chapter, we will discuss creating EJB 3.0 entity relationships.

7
Creating EJB 3.0 Entity Relationships

So far, we have discussed only the simple-case entity beans in which a single entity bean is mapped to a single database table. No book on EJB 3.0 is complete without a discussion of relationships between multiple entity beans with each bean mapped to a different database table. Multiple entity beans and multiple database tables become essential when it is not feasible to define all the entities in a single entity bean and a single database table. In this chapter, we shall discuss an example of multiple entity beans with relationships between them. We shall learn the following:

- Creating database tables
- Mapping the database tables to entity classes
- Creating a wrapper session bean
- Creating a client JSP for the entity bean application
- Testing the client
- Demonstrating the effect of modifying the fetch strategy

But, first we shall review the different metadata annotations provided for EJB 3.0 entity relationships.

EJB 3.0 entity relationship annotations

The Java Persistence API provides metadata annotations for EJB 3.0 entity relationships. The different types of EJB 3.0 relationships that may be defined are discussed in the following table:

Annotation	Description	Annotation Elements
@OneToOne	Defines a single-valued association to another entity. The association has one-to-one multiplicity.	targetEntity (optional): This is the entity class that is the target of the association.
		cascade(optional): The operations that must be cascaded to the target of the association. By default, no operations are cascaded.
		fetch(optional): This specifies whether the association should be lazily loaded or eagerly fetched. The default is EAGER.
		mappedBy(optional): This is the field that owns the relationship. The mappedBy element is specified on the non-owning side of the relationship.
		optional(optional): This specifies if the relationship is optional. If set to false, non-null relationships must always exist. By default, it is true.
@OneToMany	Defines a many-valued association with one-to-many multiplicity.	targetEntity (optional): The entity class that is the target of the association.
		cascade (optional): This specifies the operations that must be cascaded to the target of the association. By default, no operations are cascaded.
		fetch(optional): This specifies the fetch strategy. By default, it is LAZY.
		mappedBy: Specifies the field that owns the relationship. It isn't required unless the relationship is unidirectional. In a unidirectional relationship, only one entity has a reference to the other. In a bidirectional relationship, both entities have references to each other.

Annotation	Description	Annotation Elements
@ManyToOne	Defines a single-valued association to another entity class that has many-to-one multiplicity.	targetEntity (optional): This is the entity class that is the target of the association. cascade (optional): These are the operations that must be cascaded to the target of the association. By default no operations are cascaded. fetch (optional): The fetch strategy. By default, the value is EAGER. optional (optional): Specifies whether the association is optional. By default, the value is true.
@ManyToMany	Defines a many-valued association with many-to-many multiplicity.	targetEntity (optional): This is the entity class that is the target of the association. If the collection is defined using generics the target entity is not required to be specified. cascade (optional): These are the operations that must be cascaded to the target entity. By default, no operations are cascaded. fetch (optional): This is the fetch strategy. By default, it is LAZY. mappedBy (optional): Specified on the non-owning side, the field that owns the relationship. Required unless the relationship is unidirectional.

The Java Persistence API defines some other relationship annotations for mapping EJB 3.0 entity relationships. These annotations are discussed in the following table:

Annotation	Description	Annotation Elements
@JoinTable	This specifies the join table for mapping of associations. The default join table name is the table names of the associated primary tables concatenated together (owning-side first) using an underscore. Specified on the owning side of a many-to-many association or in a unidirectional one-to-many association.	name(optional): The name of the join table. catalog(optional): The catalog of the table. schema(optional): The schema of the table. joinColumns(optional): The foreign key columns of the join table that reference the primary table of the entity owning the association. inverseJoinColumns (optional): The foreign key columns of the join table that reference the primary table of the non-owning entity. uniqueConstraints (optional): Unique constraints on the table.
@JoinColumns	This defines composite foreign keys. Groups @ JoinColumn annotations for a relationship. The name and referencedColumnName elements must be specified for each of the @ JoinColumn.	value(optional): This specifies an array of JoinColumn .

Annotation	Description	Annotation Elements
`@JoinColumn`	Specifies a mapped column for joining an association.	`name`(optional): The name of the foreign key column. If the join is for OneToOne or ManyToOne, the foreign key column is in the source entity. If the join is for a ManyToMany, the foreign key is in the join table.
		`referencedColumnName` (optional): The name of the column referenced by the foreign key column.
		`unique` (optional): Specifies if the property is a unique key. Default value is false.
		`nullable` (optional): Specifies if the foreign key column is nullable. Default value is true.
		`insertable` (optional): Specifies if the column is included in the SQL INSERT statements generated by the persistence provider. Default is true.
		`updatable` (optional): Specifies if the column is included in the SQL UPDATE statements generated by the persistence provider. Default is true.
		`columnDefinition` (optional): The SQL fragment used to generate the DDL for the column.
		`table` (optional): The name of the table that contains the column. Default is the primary table of the applicable entity.

Annotation	Description	Annotation Elements
`@MapKey`	Defines the map key for associations of type java. util.Map.	`name` (optional): The name of the persistent field or property of the associated entity that is used as the map key.
`@PrimaryKey JoinColumns`	Defines composite foreign keys.	`value` (optional): Specifies one or more `PrimaryKeyJoinColumn` annotations.
@PrimaryKeyJoinColumn	Specifies a primary key column that is used as a foreign key column to join to another table.	`name` (optional): The name of the primary key column of the current table.
		`referencedColumnName` (optional): This is the name of the primary key column of the table being joined to.
		`columnDefinition` (optional): The SQL fragment used to generate the DDL for the column.

Setting the environment

We shall be using the WebLogic server integrated with JDeveloper 11*g*. Download and install JDeveloper 11*g* Studio edition (`http://www.oracle.com/technology/software/products/middleware/index.html`). We also need to download and install Oracle database (`http://www.oracle.com/technology/software/products/database/index.html`). Include the sample schemas when installing Oracle database. As we are using multiple entity beans, we need to create some database tables to which the entity beans are mapped.

Creating database tables

Create tables `CATALOG`, `EDITION`, `SECTION`, and `ARTICLE` with the following SQL scripts:

```
CREATE TABLE CATALOG (id INTEGER PRIMARY KEY NOT NULL,
  journal VARCHAR(100));
CREATE TABLE EDITION (id INTEGER PRIMARY KEY NOT NULL,
  edition VARCHAR(100));
CREATE TABLE SECTION (id VARCHAR(100) PRIMARY KEY NOT NULL,
  sectionName VARCHAR(100));
CREATE TABLE ARTICLE(id INTEGER PRIMARY KEY NOT NULL,
  title VARCHAR(100));
```

Creating an EJB project

First, we need to create an EJB project in JDeveloper 11*g*. Click on **New Application**. In the **Create Java EE Web Application** window, specify an **Application Name** (**EJB3Rels**), select the **Java EE Web Application** template, and click on **Next**.

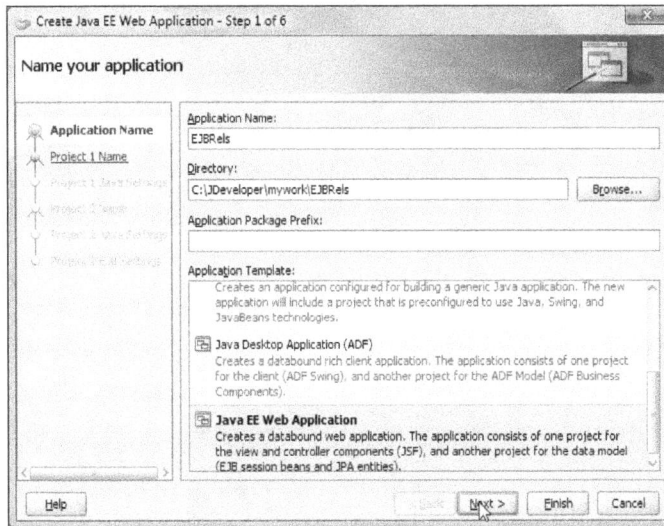

In the **Name your View and Controller Project window,** specify a **Project Name** (**JSPViewController**), select the **EJB** project technology, and click on **Next**.

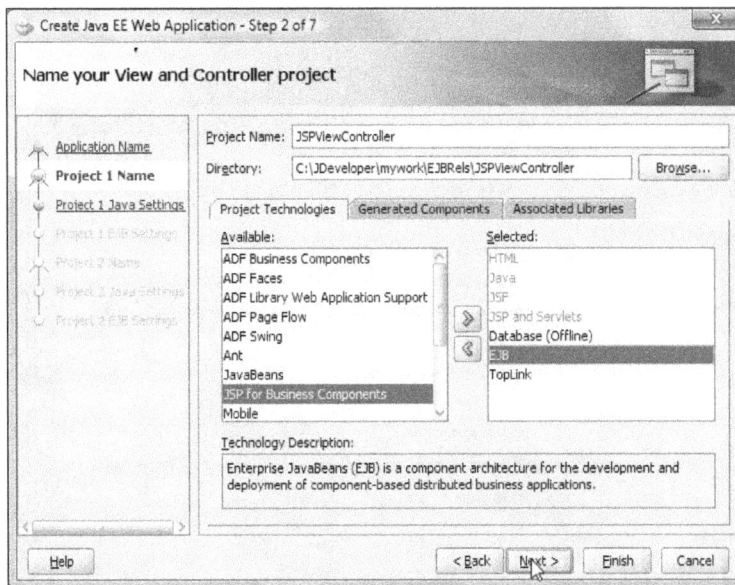

Select the default settings in the **Configure Java Settings for the View** window and click on **Next**. Select the default EJB Settings for the View and click on **Next**. In the **Name your Model Project** window, specify a model project name (**EJB3Model**) and click on **Next**.

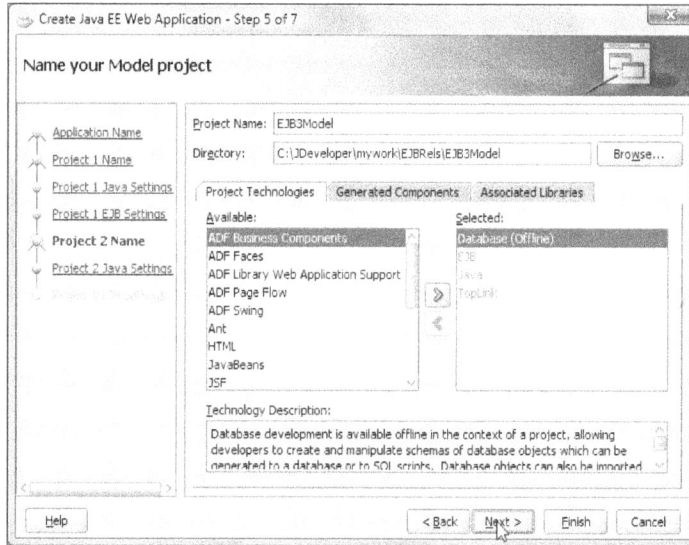

Select the default settings in the **Configure Java Settings for the Model** window and click on **Next**. In the **Configure EJB Settings for the Model window**, select EJB **Version** as EJB 3.0, select **Using Annotations,** and click on **Finish**.

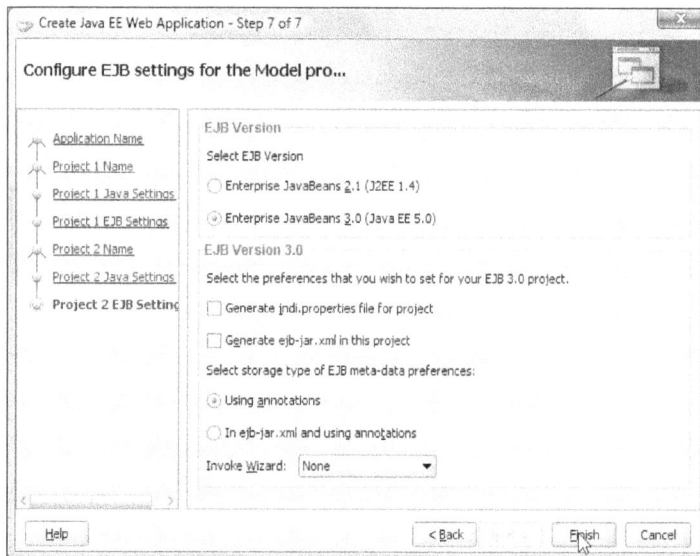

An EJB3 project gets added to the **Application** navigator tab in JDeveloper, as shown next:

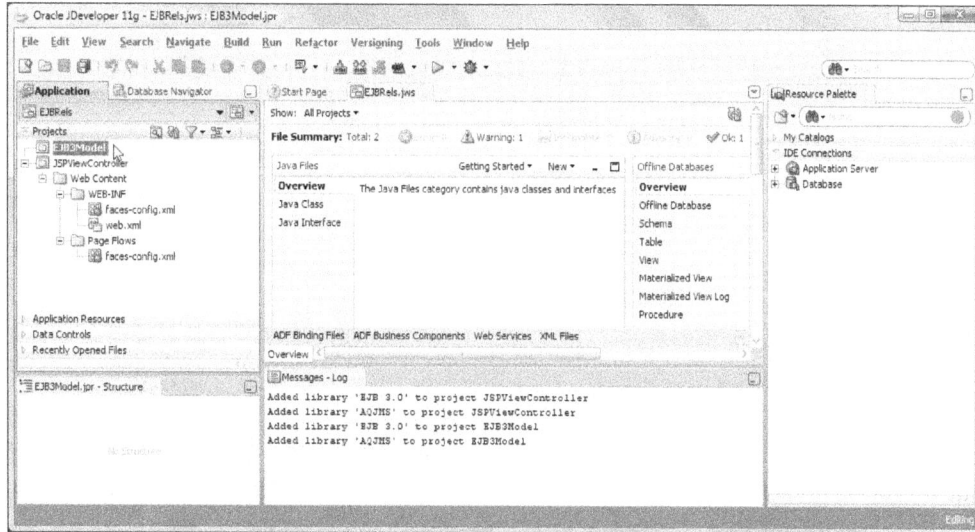

Creating the entity beans

Next, we shall map the database tables that we created to the entity beans. But, before we may generate the entity beans from tables, we need a database connection. Using the procedure explained in some of the earlier chapters, create a database connection (**OracleDBConnection**) to an Oracle database.

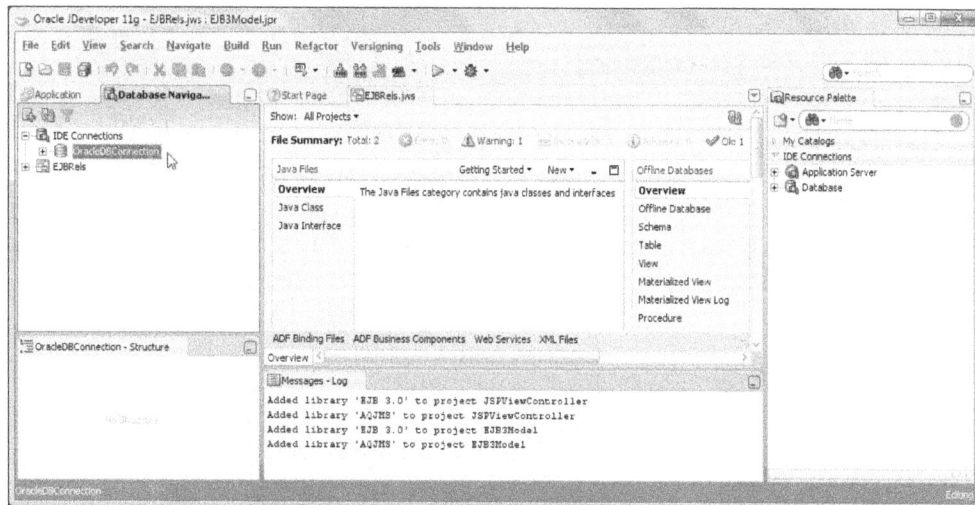

Select the project properties for the **EJB3Model** project and select the **EJB Module** node. The data source name corresponding to the **OracleDBConnection** is **jdbc/ OracleDBConnectionDS**.

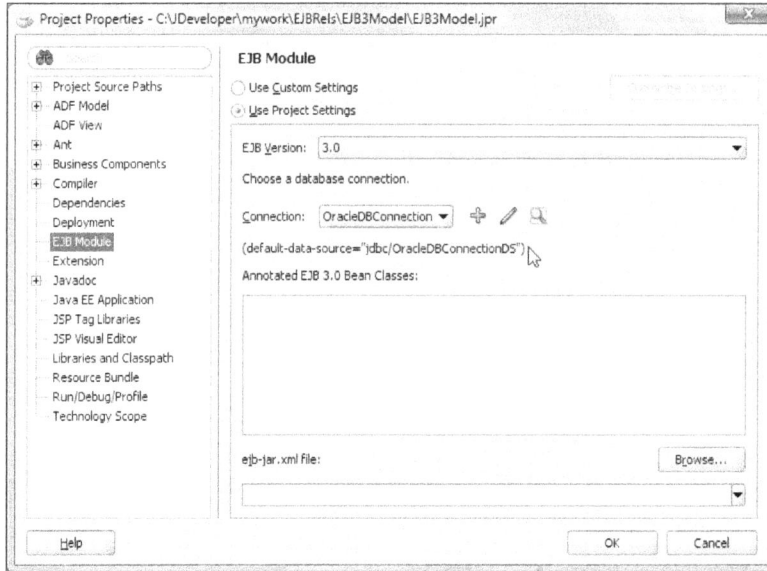

To create the entity beans from tables select **File | New**, and in the **New Gallery** window, select **Business Tier | EJB** in **Categories** and **Entities from Tables** in the **Items** header, as shown in the following screenshot. Click on **OK**.

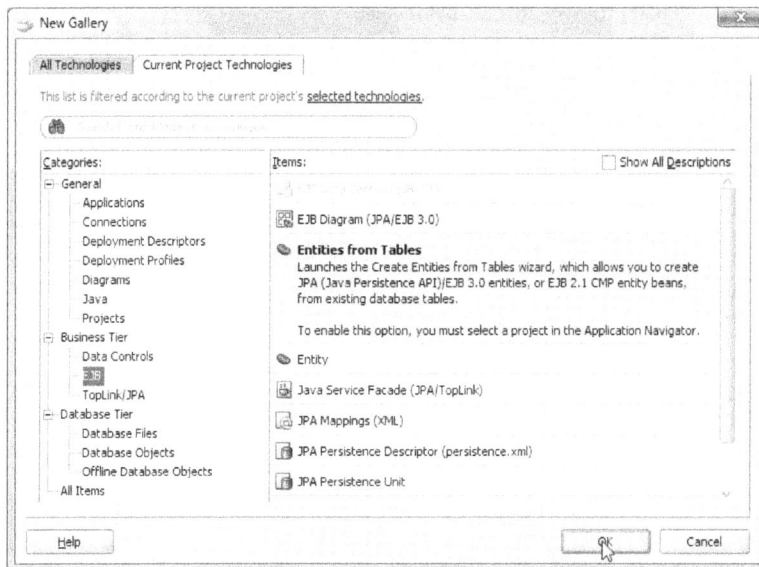

Click on **New** in the **Persistence Unit** window. In the **New Persistence Unit** window, specify a persistence unit name (**em**), and specify a **JTA Datasource Name**, which is the datasource we created earlier. When we use a JTA datasource with transaction type JTA (the default), the transactions are managed by the EJB container.

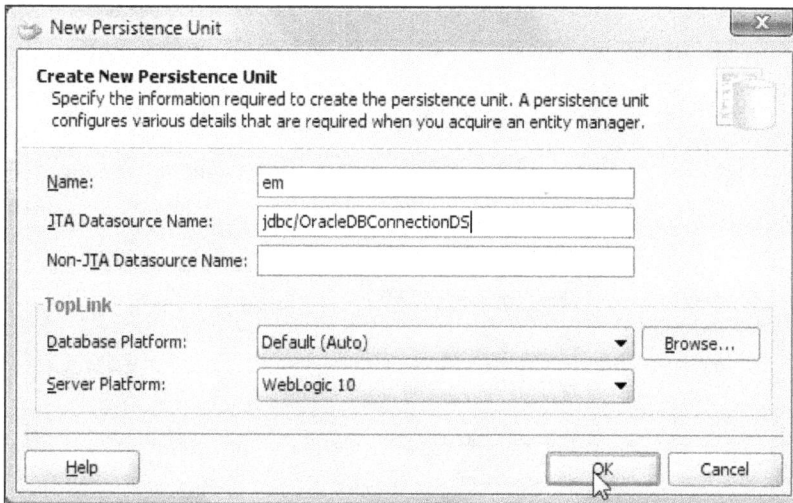

The **em** persistence unit gets added to the **Persistence Unit** window. Click on **Next**.

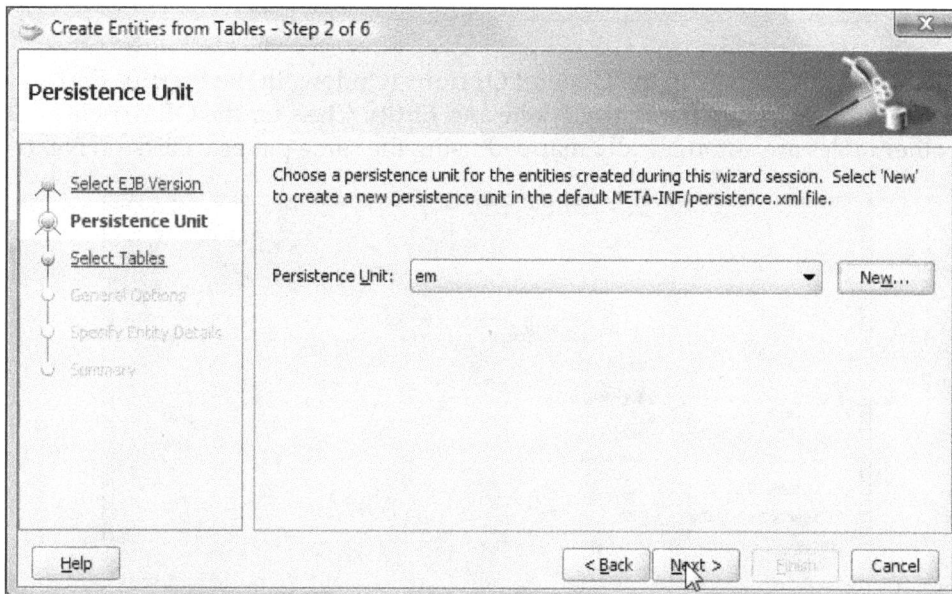

In the **Type of Connection** window, select **Online Database Connection** and click on **Next**. In the **Database Connection Details** window, select the **OracleDBConnection** and click on **Next**. In the **Select Tables** window, select the **OE** Schema and check the **Auto Query** checkbox. From the tables listed, select the **CATALOG**, **EDITION**, **SECTION**, and **ARTICLE** tables. Click on **Next**.

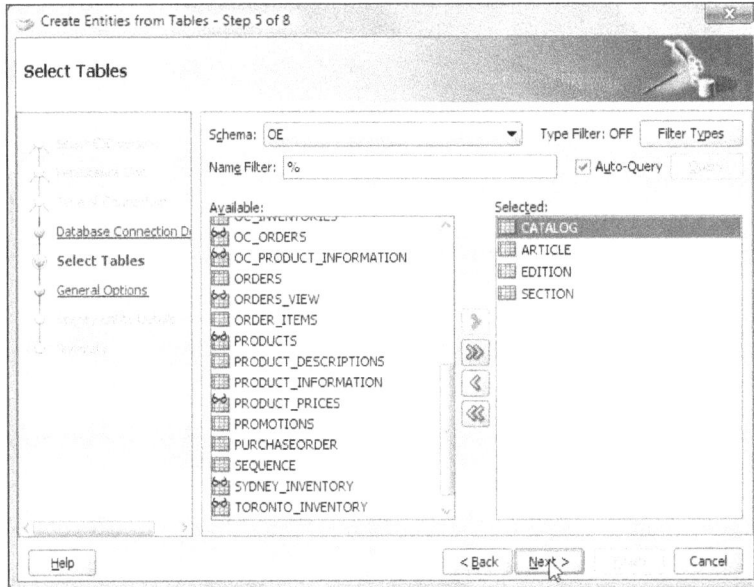

Select the default settings in the **General Options** window. In the **Specify Entity Details** window, specify the **Entity Name** and **Entity Class** for the **OE.Article** table. The other tables are automatically mapped using the same pattern. Click on **Next**.

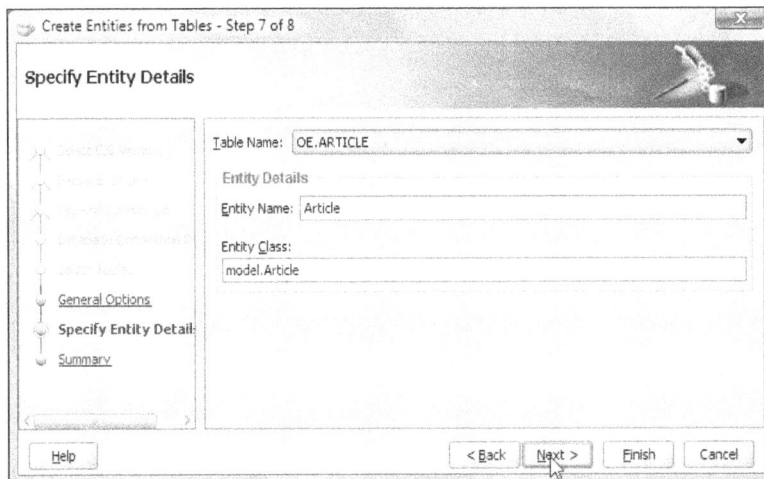

The **Summary** page displays the entity beans that will be created from the database tables. Click on **Finish**.

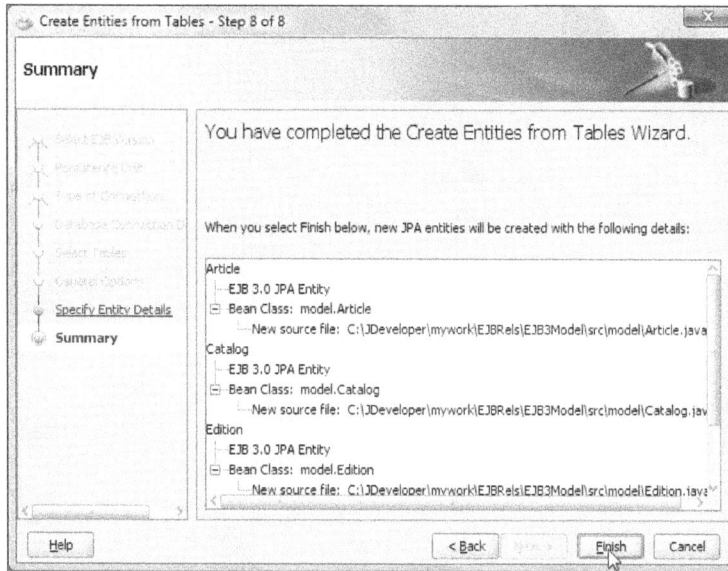

The entity beans **Article**, **Section**, **Edition**, and **Catalog** get created in the **EJB3Model** project.

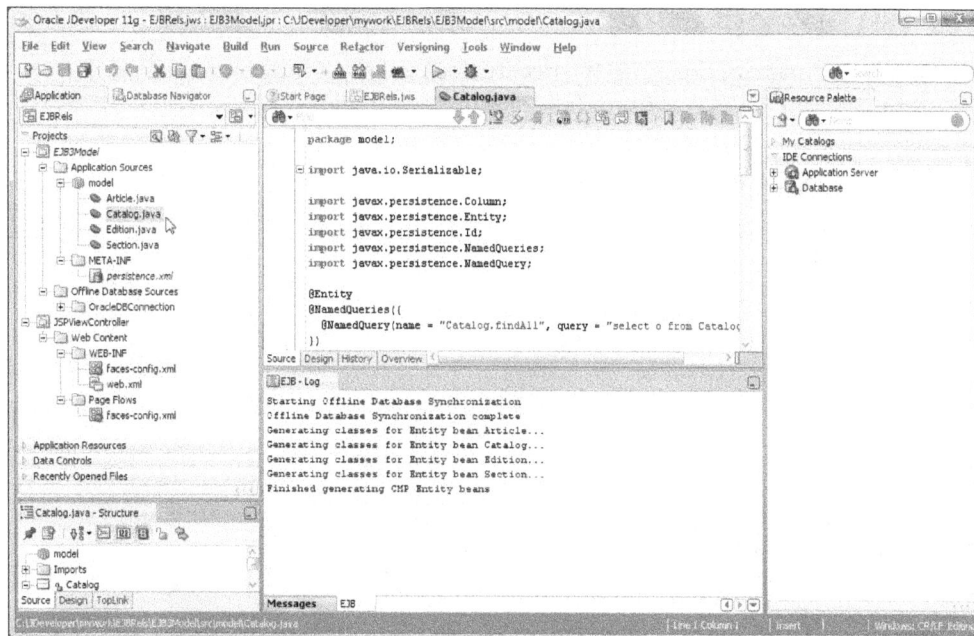

Select the **EJB3Model** project node and select **Tools | Project Properties**. Select the **Libraries and Classpath** node. The **EJB 3.0** library should be in the classpath.

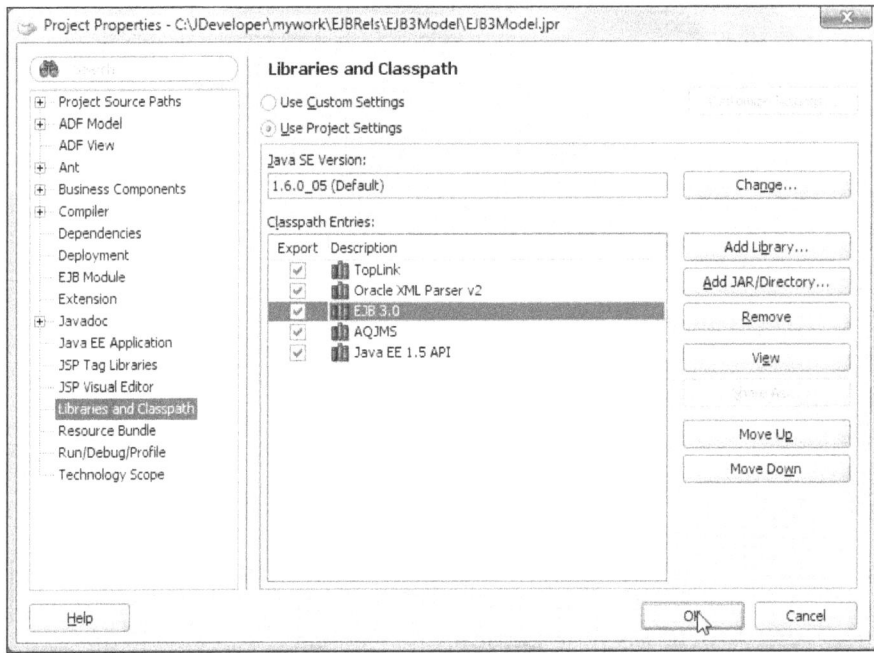

The Entity classes

Next, we shall construct the entity beans created; we shall add the required `NamedQueries` and EJB 3.0 entity relationship mappings.

The Catalog entity class

The `Catalog` entity bean has properties `id` and `journal`, as shown below:

```
private int id;
private String journal;
```

In the `Catalog` entity add `NamedQueries` `findCatalogAll()`, which selects all the `Catalog` entity instances and `findCatalogByJournal()`, which selects a `Catalog` entity by journal name.

```
@NamedQueries({
  @NamedQuery(name="findCatalogAll", query="SELECT c FROM Catalog c"),
  @NamedQuery(name="findCatalogByJournal",
          query="SELECT c FROM Catalog c
          WHERE c.journal = :journal")
})
```

The `Catalog` entity has a many-to-many relationship with the `Edition` entity. We shall make the `Catalog` entity the owning-side of the relationship. The join table is defined on the owning side and cascade operations may be initiated only from the owning side. Specify the `@ManyToMany` annotation in the `Catalog` entity with `cascade` element set to `ALL`, as we want to cascade all changes to the associated `Edition` entities when a `Catalog` entity is deleted. Setting cascading to `ALL` does degrade performance slightly, as extra queries are required to be created, but cascading propagates modifications to the associated entities.

```
@ManyToMany(cascade=CascadeType.ALL)
  @JoinTable(name="CATALOGEDITIONS",
        joinColumns=@JoinColumn(
          name="catalogId", referencedColumnName="ID"),
        inverseJoinColumns=
          @JoinColumn(name="editionId", referencedColumnName="ID"))
```

The join table, `CATALOGEDITIONS`, is generated by the EJB container when the EJB is deployed to the server; therefore, we don't need to generate the join table. The join column `catalogId` references the primary key id of the `CATALOG` table, and the inverse join column `editionId` references the primary key id of the `EDITION` table. The `cascade` element is set to `ALL`, which implies that all operations are cascaded. The `Catalog` entity bean class is listed next:

```
package model;

import java.io.Serializable;
import javax.persistence.*;
import java.util.*;
@Entity
@NamedQueries({
  @NamedQuery(name="findCatalogAll", query="SELECT c FROM Catalog c"),
  @NamedQuery(name="findCatalogByJournal",
            query="SELECT c FROM Catalog c
            WHERE c.journal = :journal")
})
public class Catalog implements Serializable {
  static final long serialVersionUID = 1;

  private int id;
  private String journal;
  private List<Edition> editions;

  @Id
  @GeneratedValue
```

```
public int getId() {
  return id;
}

public void setId(int id) {
  this.id = id;
}

public String getJournal() {
  return journal;
}

public void setJournal(String journal) {
  this.journal = journal;
}

@ManyToMany(cascade=CascadeType.ALL)
@JoinTable(name="CATALOGEDITIONS",
  joinColumns=@JoinColumn(
    name="catalogId", referencedColumnName="ID"),
  inverseJoinColumns=@JoinColumn(
    name="editionId", referencedColumnName="ID")
    )
public List<Edition> getEditions() {
  return editions;
}

public void setEditions(List<Edition> editions) {
  this.editions = editions;
}

public void addEdition(Edition edition) {
  this.getEditions().add(edition);
}

public void removeEdition(Edition edition) {
  this.getEditions().remove(edition);
}
}
```

The Edition entity class

The `Edition` entity bean has the properties `id` and `edition`:

```
private int id;
private String edition;
```

The `Edition` entity defines a `NamedQueries` `findEditionAll()` (which finds all the `Edition` instances) and `findEditionByEdition()` (which finds an `Edition` by the `edition` date):

```
@NamedQueries( { @NamedQuery(name = "findEditionAll",
                            query = "SELECT e FROM Edition e"),
@NamedQuery(name = "findEditionByEdition",
          query = "SELECT e from Edition e
          WHERE e.edition = :edition")
        } )
```

The `Edition` entity is on the non-owning side of a bidirectional many-to-many relationship with the `Catalog` entity. Therefore, we specify the `@ManyToMany` annotation with the `mappedBy` element. We don't need to specify a join table, as `Edition` entity is the non-owning side. The `cascade` element is set to cascade `MERGE`, `PERSIST`, and `REFRESH` operations:

```
@ManyToMany(cascade =
  { CascadeType.MERGE, CascadeType.PERSIST,
    CascadeType.REFRESH },
  mappedBy = "editions")
  protected List<Catalog> getCatalogs() {
    return catalogs;
  }
```

The `editions` field is defied in the `Catalog` entity, which is the owning side of the relationship. The `Edition` entity also has a one-to-many relationship with the `SECTION` entity. In a one-to-many relationship the many side is made the owning side; therefore, the many side has the join table. But, a join table may be added on the one side also to initiate cascade operations from the one side. Therefore, we have added a join table on the one side (`Edition` entity) also:

```
@OneToMany(cascade = CascadeType.ALL, mappedBy = "edition")
  @JoinTable(name = "EditionSection",
    joinColumns = { @JoinColumn(
      name = "editionId", referencedColumnName = "ID") },
    inverseJoinColumns = { @JoinColumn(
      name = "sectionId", referencedColumnName ="ID") } )
```

```
        public List<Section> getSections() {
            return sections;
        }
```

The Edition entity class is listed next:

```
package model;

import java.io.Serializable;
import javax.persistence.*;
import java.util.*;

@Entity
@NamedQueries( { @NamedQuery(name = "findEditionAll",
                            query = "SELECT e FROM Edition e")
        ,
@NamedQuery(name = "findEditionByEdition",
  query = "SELECT e from Edition e
  WHERE e.edition = :edition")
        } )
public class Edition implements Serializable {
    static final long serialVersionUID = 2;
    private String edition;
    private int id;
    private List<Catalog> catalogs;
    private List<Section> sections;
    @ManyToMany(cascade = {
      CascadeType.MERGE, CascadeType.PERSIST, CascadeType.REFRESH },
      mappedBy = "editions")
    protected List<Catalog> getCatalogs() {
        return catalogs;
    }
    protected void setCatalogs(List<Catalog> catalogs) {
        this.catalogs = catalogs;
    }
    @OneToMany(cascade = CascadeType.ALL, mappedBy = "edition",
              fetch = FetchType.EAGER)
    @JoinTable(name = "EditionSection",
    joinColumns = { @JoinColumn(
      name = "editionId", referencedColumnName = "ID") },
    inverseJoinColumns = { @JoinColumn(
      name = "sectionId", referencedColumnName = "ID")
} )
    public List<Section> getSections() {
```

```
            return sections;
    }
    public void setSections(List<Section> sections) {
        this.sections = sections;
    }
    public void addSection(Section section) {
        this.getSections().add(section);
        section.setEdition(this);
    }
    @Id
    @GeneratedValue
    public int getId() {
        return id;
    }
    public void setId(int id) {
        this.id = id;
    }
    public String getEdition() {
        return edition;
    }
    public void setEdition(String edition) {
        this.edition = edition;
    }
    public void removeSection(Section section) {
        this.getSections().remove(section);
    }
}
```

The Section entity class

The Section entity has properties id and sectionName:

```
private String id;
private String sectionName;
```

The Section entity defines NamedQueries findSectionAll, which finds all the Section entities, and findSectionBySectionName, which finds a Section entity by section name:

```
@NamedQueries({
@NamedQuery(name="findSectionAll", query="SELECT s FROM Section s"),
@NamedQuery(name="findSectionBySectionName",
  query="SELECT s from Section s WHERE s.sectionName = :section")
})
```

The Section entity is on the owning side (many side) of a many-to-one relationship with the Edition entity. Specify a @ManyToOne annotation with a @JoinTable annotation. The cascade element is set to cascade MERGE, PERSIST, and REFRESH operations:

```
@ManyToOne(cascade={CascadeType.MERGE,
  CascadeType.PERSIST, CascadeType.REFRESH})
@JoinTable(name = "SectionEdition",
  joinColumns = { @JoinColumn(
    name = "sectionId",referencedColumnName = "ID") } ,
  inverseJoinColumns = { @JoinColumn(
    name = "editionId", referencedColumnName ="ID") } )
public Edition getEdition() {
      return edition;
   }
```

The Section entity also has a one-to-many relationship with the Article entity. The Section entity is the non-owning side of the one-to-many relationship, but to be able to initiate cascade operations from the Section entity, we shall add a join table on the Section entity side. The section field specified in the mappedBy element is defined in the Article entity class:

```
@OneToMany(cascade={CascadeType.ALL},mappedBy = "section")
@JoinTable(name = «SectionArticle», joinColumns = {
  @JoinColumn(name=»sectionId», referencedColumnName=»ID»)},
  inverseJoinColumns = { @JoinColumn(
    name=»articleId», referencedColumnName=»ID»)})
    public List<Article> getArticles() {
        return articles;
   }
```

The Section entity is listed next:

```
package model;

import java.io.Serializable;
import java.util.List;
import javax.persistence.*;
@Entity
@NamedQueries({
  @NamedQuery(name="findSectionAll", query="SELECT s FROM Section s"),
  @NamedQuery(
    name="findSectionBySectionName",
```

```
        query="SELECT s from Section s WHERE s.sectionName = :section")
})
public class Section implements Serializable {
  static final long serialVersionUID = 1;

  private String id;
  private String sectionName;
  private List<Article> articles;
  private Edition edition;

  @Id
  public String getId() {
    return id;
  }

  public void setId(String id) {
    this.id = id;
  }
  public String getSectionName() {
    return sectionName;
  }

  public void setSectionName(String sectionName) {
    this.sectionName = sectionName;
  }

  @OneToMany(cascade={CascadeType.ALL},
            mappedBy = "section",fetch=FetchType.EAGER)
  @JoinTable(name = "SectionArticle", joinColumns = {
    @JoinColumn(name="sectionId", referencedColumnName="ID")},
    inverseJoinColumns = { @JoinColumn(
      name="articleId", referencedColumnName="ID")})
  public List<Article> getArticles() {
    return articles;
  }

  public void setArticles(List<Article> articles) {
    this.articles = articles;
  }

  public void addArticle(Article article) {
    this.getArticles().add(article);
    article.setSection(this);
  }

  @ManyToOne(cascade={CascadeType.MERGE, CascadeType.PERSIST,
                      CascadeType.REFRESH},
            fetch=FetchType.EAGER)
```

```
@JoinTable(name = "SectionEdition", joinColumns = {
  @JoinColumn(name = "sectionId", referencedColumnName = "ID")} ,
  inverseJoinColumns = { @JoinColumn(
    name = "editionId", referencedColumnName ="ID") } )
public Edition getEdition() {
  return edition;
}

public void setEdition(Edition edition) {
  this.edition = edition;
}

public void removeArticle(Article article) {
  this.getArticles().remove(article);
}
}
```

The Article entity class

The Article entity has properties id and title, as shown next:

```
private int id;
private String title;
```

The Article entity defines NamedQueries findArticleAll, which finds all the Article entity instances, and findArticleByTitle, which finds an article by title:

```
@NamedQueries({
  @NamedQuery(name="findArticleAll", query="SELECT a FROM Article a"),
  @NamedQuery(
          name="findArticleByTitle",
          query="SELECT a from Article a WHERE a.title = :title")
})
```

The Article entity is on the many side (the owning side) of a many-to-one relationship with the Section entity. Once again, a @JoinTable is required on the owning side. Therefore, add a @ManyToOne annotation with a @JoinTable annotation. The cascade element is set to cascade MERGE, PERSIST, and REFRESH operations:

```
@ManyToOne(cascade={CascadeType.MERGE,
                    CascadeType.PERSIST, CascadeType.REFRESH})
@JoinTable(name = "ArticleSection", joinColumns = {
  @JoinColumn(name="articleId", referencedColumnName="ID")},
  inverseJoinColumns = { @JoinColumn(
  name="sectionId", referencedColumnName="ID")})
public Section getSection() {
```

```
      return section;
  }
```

The `Article` entity class is listed next:

```
package model;

import java.io.Serializable;
import javax.persistence.*;

@Entity
@NamedQueries({
  @NamedQuery(name="findArticleAll", query="SELECT a FROM Article a"),
  @NamedQuery(
            name="findArticleByTitle",
            query="SELECT a from Article a WHERE a.title = :title")
})
public class Article implements Serializable {
  static final long serialVersionUID = 1;

  private int id;
  private String title;
  private Section section;
  public Article() {

  }

  public Article(Section section) {
    this.section = section;
  }
  @Id
  @GeneratedValue
  public int getId() {
    return id;
  }

  public void setId(int id) {
    this.id = id;
  }
```

```
@ManyToOne(cascade={CascadeType.MERGE,
                    CascadeType.PERSIST, CascadeType.REFRESH},
       fetch=FetchType.EAGER)
@JoinTable(name = "ArticleSection",
      joinColumns = {
          @JoinColumn(name="articleId", referencedColumnName="ID")},
          inverseJoinColumns = { @JoinColumn(name="sectionId",

referencedColumnName="ID")})
  public Section getSection() {
    return section;
  }

  public void setSection(Section section) {
    this.section = section;
  }
  public String getTitle() {
    return title;
  }

  public void setTitle(String title) {
    this.title = title;
  }

}
```

Creating a session bean

In this section, we shall create a wrapper session bean for the entity bean. In the session bean, we shall add query methods corresponding to the named queries defined in the entity beans. We shall add a method to create test data, and a method to delete data. Also, we shall add remove methods to remove Catalog, Edition, Section, and Article entity instances. To create a session bean, select **File | New**, and in the **New Gallery** window, select **Business Tier | EJB** in **Categories** and **Session Bean** in **Items**. Click on **OK**:

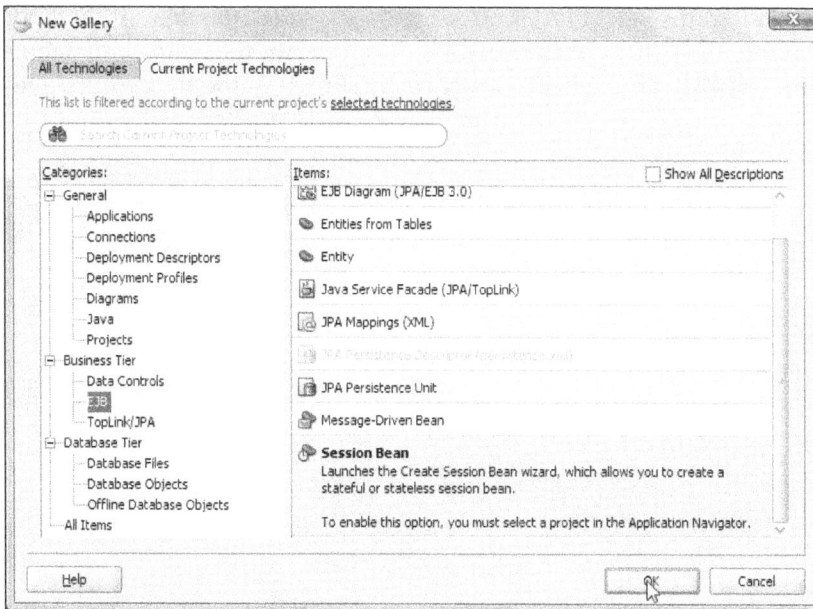

In the **EJB Name** and **Options** window, specify an **EJB Name (CatalogSessionEJB)**, and a **Mapped Name (EJB3-SessionEJB)**, which is the global JNDI name for the session bean. Click on **Next,** as shown:

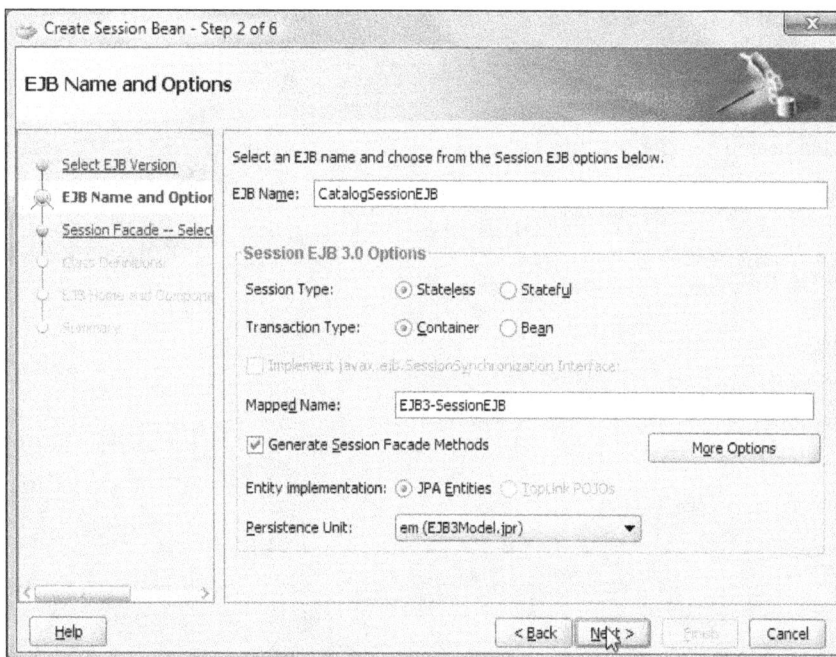

In the **Session Façade-Select JPA Entity Methods**, select the default methods and click on **Next**. In the **Class Definitions** window, specify the bean class name (**model. CatalogSessionEJBBean**) and click on **Next**, as shown in the following screenshot:

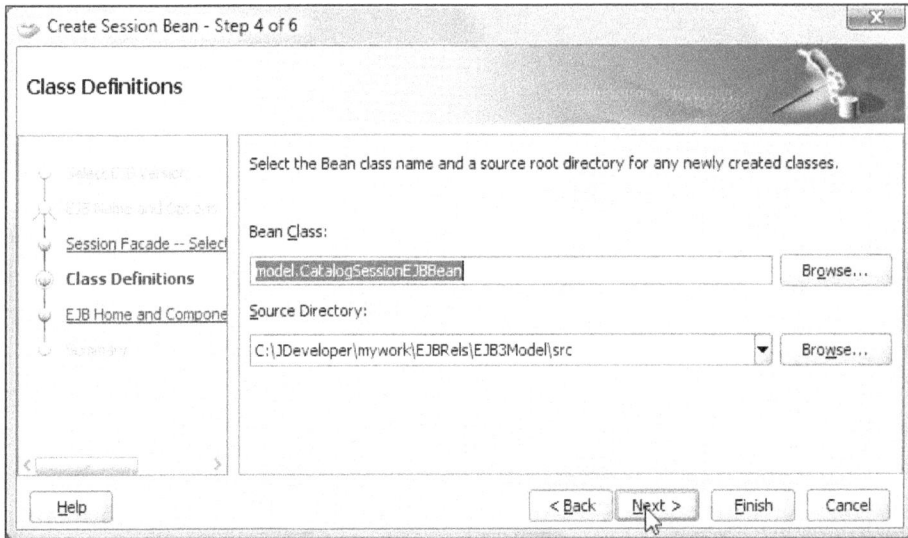

In the **EJB Home and Component Interfaces** window, check **Implement a Remote Interface**, specify the **Remote Interface** name (**model.CatalogSessionEJBRemote**), and click on **Next**, as shown next:

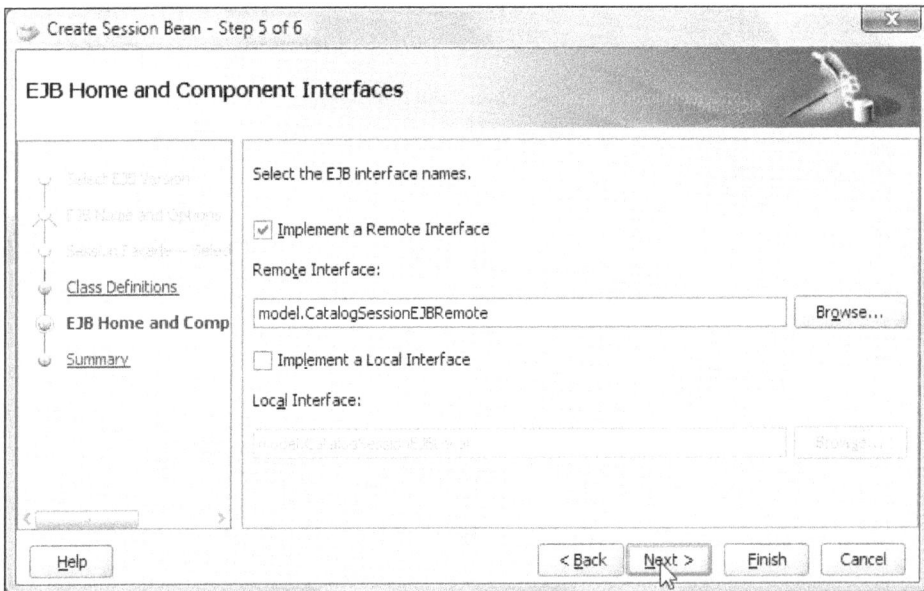

The **Summary** page lists the session bean and the remote interface that will be created. Click on **Finish**. A session bean and a remote business interface get created.

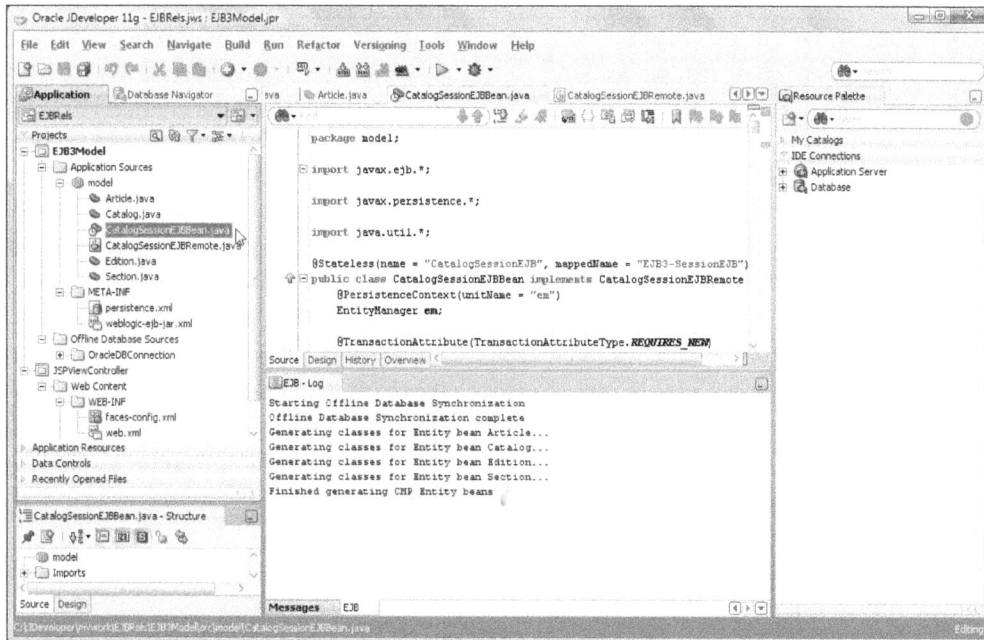

The Session Bean class

The session bean is a `Stateless` session bean. The global JNDI name is specified with the `mappedName` element:

```
@Stateless(name = "CatalogSessionEJB", mappedName = "EJB3-SessionEJB")
public class CatalogSessionEJBBean implements CatalogSessionEJBRemote
{
}
```

Inject an `EntityManager` into the session bean using the dependency injection.

```
@PersistenceContext(unitName = "em")
    EntityManager em;
```

To the session bean, add the methods discussed in the following table:

Method	Description
List<Edition> getAllEditions()	It gets a List of all the defined Edition entity instances.
List<Section> getAllSections()	It gets a List of all the defined Session entity instances.
List<Article> getAllArticles()	It gets a List of all the defined Article entity instances.
List<Catalog> getAllCatalogs()	It gets a List of all the defined Catalog entity instances.
List<Catalog> getEditionCatalogs(Edition edition)	It gets all the Catalog entities for an Edition entity.
List<Edition> getCatalogEditions(Catalog catalog)	It gets all the Edition entities for a Catalog entity.
List<Section> getEditionSections(Edition edition)	It gets all the Section entities for an Edition entity.
List<Article> getSectionArticles(Section section)	It gets all the Article entities for a Section entity.
void createTestData()	It creates test data.
void deleteSomeData()	It deletes data.
void removeEdition(Edition edition)	It removes an Edition entity.
void removeSection(Section section)	It removes a Section entity.
void removeArticle(Article article)	It removes an Article entity.

The createTestData() method is used to create some test data. In the method magazine, catalogs are created using the Catalog entity. Set the catalog journal with the setJournal() method. Persist the entity using the persist() method and flush the entity using the flush() method, as shown in the following code snippet. The flush() method synchronizes the entity with the database.

```
Catalog catalog1 = new Catalog();
        catalog1.setJournal("Oracle Magazine");
        em.persist(catalog1);
        em.flush();
```

Magazine editions are added to a catalog using the `Edition` entity in which the `Edition` id is set using the `setId()` method and the `Edition` date is set using the `setEdition()` method. An `Edition` entity is persisted using the `persist()` method and an `Edition` entity instance is flushed to the database using the `flush()` method. Before we may add the `Edition` entity to the `Catalog` entity, we need to merge the `Catalog` entity with the persistence context using the `merge()` method. Subsequently, add the `Edition` entity to the `Catalog` entity with the `addEntity()` method.

```
Edition edition = new Edition();
        edition.setId(1022009);
        edition.setEdition("January/February 2009");
        em.persist(edition);
        em.flush();
        em.merge(catalog1);
        catalog1.addEdition(edition);
```

A magazine edition has sections. Sections are created using the `Section` entity. Section ID is set using the `setId()` method, and the section name is set using the `setSectionName()` method. A `Section` entity is persisted using the `persist()` method and an `Edition` entity is merged with the persistence context using the `merge()` method. A `Section` entity is added to an `Edition` entity using the `addSection()` method.

```
Section features = new Section();
        features.setId("Oracle_Mag_Features_022009");
        features.setSectionName("FEATURES");
        em.persist(features);
        em.merge(edition);
        edition.addSection(features);
```

Create an `Article` entity using the `new` operator. Set the article ID using the `setId()` method. Set the article title using the `setTitle()` method. Persist the `Article` entity using the `persist()` method. Before adding an `Article` entity to a `Section` entity merge the `Section` entity using the `merge()` method. Add an `Article` entity to a `Section` entity using the `addArticle()` method. Invoke the `flush()` method to flush the additions to the database.

```
Article article = new Article(features);
        article.setId(12009);
        article.setTitle(«Launching Performance»);
        em.persist(article);
        em.merge(features);
        features.addArticle(article);
        em.flush();
```

In the `deleteSomeData()` method, we shall delete some data. For example, we shall delete the magazine catalog for `Oracle Magazine`. First we create a `Query` object to find a `Catalog` entity instance by journal name:

```
Query q = em.createNamedQuery("findCatalogByJournal");
```

Set the journal name to `Oracle Magazine` using the `setParameter()` method:

```
q.setParameter("journal", "Oracle Magazine");
```

Get a `List` of `Catalog`s for the specified query using the `getResultList()` method:

```
List list = q.getResultList();
```

Iterate over the `List` and remove the `Catalog` entities using the `remove()` method:

```
for (Object catalog : list) {
  em.remove(catalog);
}
```

The `CatalogSessionEJBBean` class is listed next:

```
package model;

import javax.ejb.*;
import javax.persistence.*;
import java.util.*;

@Stateless(name = "CatalogSessionEJB", mappedName = "EJB3-SessionEJB")
public class CatalogSessionEJBBean implements CatalogSessionEJBRemote
{
```

First, inject an `EntityManager`:

```
@PersistenceContext(unitName = "em")
EntityManager em;
```

Define the getter methods:

```
@TransactionAttribute(TransactionAttributeType.REQUIRES_NEW)
public List<Edition> getAllEditions() {
  ArrayList<Edition> editions = new ArrayList<Edition>();
  Query q = em.createNamedQuery("findEditionAll");
  for (Object ed : q.getResultList()) {
    editions.add((Edition)ed);
  }
  return editions;
}

@TransactionAttribute(TransactionAttributeType.REQUIRES_NEW)
public List<Section> getAllSections() {
```

```
    ArrayList<Section> sections = new ArrayList<Section>();
    Query q = em.createNamedQuery("findSectionAll");
    for (Object ed : q.getResultList()) {
      sections.add((Section)ed);
    }
    return sections;
  }

  @TransactionAttribute(TransactionAttributeType.REQUIRES_NEW)
  public List<Article> getAllArticles() {
    ArrayList<Article> articles = new ArrayList<Article>();
    Query q = em.createNamedQuery("findArticleAll");
    for (Object ed : q.getResultList()) {
      articles.add((Article)ed);
    }
    return articles;
  }

  @TransactionAttribute(TransactionAttributeType.REQUIRES_NEW)
  public List<Catalog> getAllCatalogs() {

    Query q = em.createNamedQuery("findCatalogAll");
    List<Catalog> catalogs = q.getResultList();
    ArrayList<Catalog> catalogList = new ArrayList<Catalog>(catalogs.
      size());
    for (Catalog catalog : catalogs) {
      catalogList.add(catalog);
    }
    return catalogList;
  }

  @TransactionAttribute(TransactionAttributeType.REQUIRES_NEW)
  public List<Catalog> getEditionCatalogs(Edition edition) {
    em.merge(edition);
    List<Catalog> catalogs = edition.getCatalogs();
    ArrayList<Catalog> catalogList = new ArrayList<Catalog>(catalogs.
      size());
    for (Catalog catalog : catalogs) {
      catalogList.add(catalog);
    }
    return catalogList;
  }
  /**
   * Client can't call getEditions() on catalog, as it's detached &
   * lazilly fetched
   */
```

```
@TransactionAttribute(TransactionAttributeType.REQUIRES_NEW)
public List<Edition> getCatalogEditions(Catalog catalog) {
  em.merge(catalog);
  List<Edition> editions = catalog.getEditions();
  ArrayList<Edition> editionList =
  new ArrayList<Edition>(editions.size());
  for (Edition edition : editions) {
    editionList.add(edition);
  }
  return editionList;
}

@TransactionAttribute(TransactionAttributeType.REQUIRES_NEW)
public List<Section> getEditionSections(Edition edition) {
  em.merge(edition);
  List<Section> sections = edition.getSections();
  ArrayList<Section> sectionList = new ArrayList<Section>(sections.
    size());
  for (Section section : sections) {
    sectionList.add(section);
  }
  return sectionList;
}

@TransactionAttribute(TransactionAttributeType.REQUIRES_NEW)
public List<Article> getSectionArticles(Section section) {
  em.merge(section);
  List<Article> articles = section.getArticles();
  ArrayList<Article> articleList =
  new ArrayList<Article>(articles.size());
  for (Article article : articles) {
    articleList.add(article);
  }
  return articleList;
}
```

Define a method to create test data:

```
public void createTestData() {
```

Create a catalog for Oracle Magazine:

```
Catalog catalog1 = new Catalog();
catalog1.setJournal("Oracle Magazine");
em.persist(catalog1);
em.flush();
Edition edition = new Edition();
```

```
edition.setId(1022009);
edition.setEdition("January/February 2009");
em.persist(edition);
em.flush();
em.merge(catalog1);
catalog1.addEdition(edition);
Section features = new Section();
features.setId("Oracle_Mag_Features_022009");
features.setSectionName("FEATURES");
em.persist(features);
em.merge(edition);
edition.addSection(features);
```

Also, create an article to the `features` section:

```
Article article = new Article(features);
article.setId(12009);
article.setTitle("Launching Performance");
em.persist(article);
em.merge(features);
features.addArticle(article);
em.flush();
article = new Article(features);
article.setId(22009);
article.setTitle("Building on a Solid Foundation");
em.persist(article);
features.addArticle(article);
em.flush();
```

Add an article to the `technology` section:

```
Section technology = new Section();
technology.setId("Oracle_Mag_Tech_022009");
technology.setSectionName("Technology");
em.persist(technology);
em.merge(edition);
edition.addSection(technology);

article = new Article(technology);
article.setId(32009);
article.setTitle("On Dynamic Sampling");
em.persist(article);

em.merge(technology);
technology.addArticle(article);
em.flush();
```

Add another article to the technology section:

```
article = new Article(technology);
article.setId(42009);
article.setTitle("Encrypting Tablespaces");
em.persist(article);
technology.addArticle(article);
em.flush();
```

Add an article to the Developer section:

```
Section developer = new Section();
developer.setId("Oracle_Mag_Dev_022009");
developer.setSectionName("Developer");
em.persist(developer);
em.merge(edition);
edition.addSection(developer);

article = new Article(developer);
article.setId(52009);
article.setTitle("Easier Interactive Data Entry");
em.persist(article);
em.merge(developer);
developer.addArticle(article);
em.flush();
```

Add another article to the developer section.

```
article = new Article(developer);
article.setId(62009);
article.setTitle("Easy Application Attachments");
em.persist(article);
developer.addArticle(article);
em.flush();

edition = new Edition();
edition.setId(3042009);
edition.setEdition("March/April 2009");
em.persist(edition);
em.merge(catalog1);
catalog1.addEdition(edition);

features = new Section();
features.setId("Oracle_Mag_Features_042009");
features.setSectionName("FEATURES");
em.persist(features);
em.merge(edition);
edition.addSection(features);
```

Add an article to the `features` section:

```
article = new Article(features);
article.setId(72009);
article.setTitle("Scale to Fit");
em.persist(article);
em.merge(features);
features.addArticle(article);
em.flush();
```

Add another article to the `features` section:

```
article = new Article(features);
article.setId(82009);
article.setTitle("Integrating Applications");
em.persist(article);
features.addArticle(article);
em.flush();

technology = new Section();
technology.setId("Oracle_Mag_Tech_042009");
technology.setSectionName("Technology");
em.persist(technology);
em.merge(edition);
edition.addSection(technology);
```

Add an article to the `technology` section:

```
article = new Article(technology);
article.setId(92009);
article.setTitle("On Wrong and Right");
em.persist(article);
em.merge(technology);
technology.addArticle(article);
em.flush();
```

Add another article to the `technology` section:

```
article = new Article(technology);
article.setId(102009);
article.setTitle("Baselines and Better Plans");
em.persist(article);
technology.addArticle(article);
em.flush();

developer = new Section();
```

```
        developer.setId("Oracle_Mag_Dev_042009");
developer.setSectionName("Developer");
em.persist(developer);
em.merge(edition);
edition.addSection(developer);
```

Add an article to the `developer` section:

```
article = new Article(developer);
article.setId(112009);
article.setTitle("The Next-Generation Data Center");
em.persist(article);
em.merge(developer);
developer.addArticle(article);
em.flush();
```

Add another article to the `developer` section:

```
article = new Article(developer);
article.setId(122009);
article.setTitle("On Avoiding Termination");
em.persist(article);
developer.addArticle(article);
em.flush();
```

Create a catalog for the MSDN Magazine:

```
Catalog catalog2 = new Catalog();
catalog2.setJournal("MSDN Magazine");
em.persist(catalog2);
em.flush();

edition = new Edition();
edition.setId(62009);
edition.setEdition("June 2009");
em.persist(edition);

Section msdn_features = new Section();
msdn_features.setId("MSDN_Mag_Features_062009");
msdn_features.setSectionName("FEATURES");
em.persist(msdn_features);
em.merge(edition);
edition.addSection(msdn_features);
```

Add an article to the `features` section:

```
article = new Article(msdn_features);
article.setId(6012009);
```

```
article.setTitle("Test-Driven Design");
em.persist(article);
em.merge(msdn_features);
msdn_features.addArticle(article);
em.flush();

article = new Article(msdn_features);
article.setId(6022009);
article.setTitle("Entity Framework");
em.persist(article);
msdn_features.addArticle(article);
em.flush();

Section columns = new Section();
columns.setId("MSDN_Mag_Columns_062009");
columns.setSectionName("COLUMNS");
em.persist(columns);
em.merge(edition);
edition.addSection(columns);
```

Add an article to the columns section:

```
article = new Article(columns);
article.setId(6032009);
article.setTitle("Windows With C++");
em.persist(article);
em.merge(columns);
columns.addArticle(article);
em.flush();
```

Add another article to the columns section:

```
article = new Article(columns);
article.setId(6042009);
article.setTitle("Patterns in Practice");
em.persist(article);
columns.addArticle(article);
em.flush();
em.merge(catalog2);

catalog2.addEdition(edition);
edition = new Edition();
edition.setId(52009);
edition.setEdition("May 2009");
em.persist(edition);

msdn_features = new Section();
msdn_features.setId("MSDN_Mag_Features_052009");
```

```
msdn_features.setSectionName("FEATURES");
em.persist(msdn_features);
em.merge(edition);
edition.addSection(msdn_features);
```

Add an article to the `features` section:

```
article = new Article(msdn_features);
article.setId(5012009);
article.setTitle("Data Services");
em.persist(article);
em.merge(msdn_features);
msdn_features.addArticle(article);
em.flush();
```

Add another article to the `features` section:

```
article = new Article(msdn_features);
article.setId(5022009);
article.setTitle("SOA Simplified");
em.persist(article);
msdn_features.addArticle(article);
em.flush();

columns = new Section();
columns.setId("MSDN_Mag_Columns_052009");
columns.setSectionName("COLUMNS");
em.persist(columns);
em.merge(edition);
edition.addSection(columns);
```

Add an article to the `columns` section:

```
article = new Article(columns);
article.setId(5032009);
article.setTitle("Extreme ASP.NET");
em.persist(article);
em.merge(columns);
columns.addArticle(article);
em.flush();
```

Add an article to the `columns` section:

```
article = new Article(columns);
article.setId(5042009);
article.setTitle("Patterns and Practices");
```

```
em.persist(article);
columns.addArticle(article);
em.flush();
em.merge(catalog2);
catalog2.addEdition(edition);
}
```

Remove a `catalog`:

```
public void deleteSomeData() {
Query q = em.createNamedQuery("findCatalogByJournal");
q.setParameter("journal", "Oracle Magazine");
List list = q.getResultList();
for (Object catalog : list) {
  em.remove(catalog);
}
}
```

Remove an `edition`:

```
public void removeEdition(Edition edition) {
  List<Catalog> catalogs = edition.getCatalogs();
  for (Catalog catalog : catalogs) {
    catalog.removeEdition(edition);
  }
  em.remove(edition);
}
```

Remove a `section`:

```
public void removeSection(Section section) {
    Edition edition = section.getEdition();
    edition.removeSection(section);
    em.remove(section);
}
```

Remove an `article`:

```
public void removeArticle(Article article) {
    Section section = article.getSection();
    section.removeArticle(article);
    em.remove(article);
  }
}
```

Creating the client

In this section, we create a JSP test client to test the entity bean via the wrapper session bean. First, create a JSP by selecting **File | New**. In the **New Gallery** window, select **Web Tier | JSP** in **Categories** and **JSP** in **Items**. Click on **OK**:

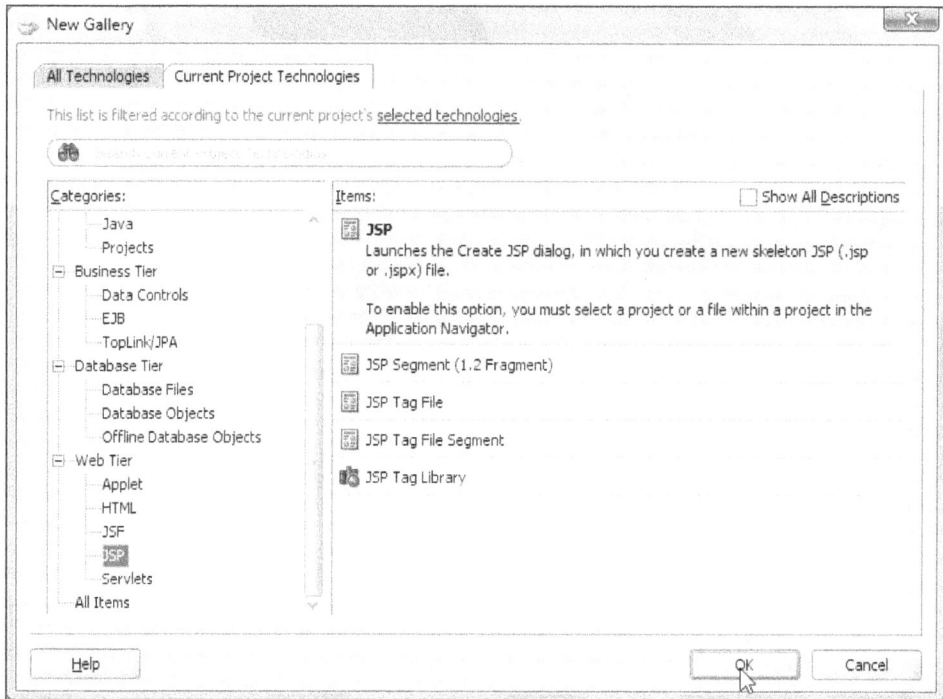

In the **Create JSP** window, specify a **File Name**, **EJB3Client.jsp**, and click on **OK**. A JSP gets added to the **JSPViewController** project. In JSP, create an `InitialContext` object and lookup the session bean using the global JNDI name:

```
InitialContext context = new InitialContext();
CatalogSessionEJBRemote beanRemote = (CatalogSessionEJBRemote)
context.lookup("EJB3-SessionEJB#model.CatalogSessionEJBRemote");
```

The `lookup()` method returns an instance of the remote business interface. Create some test data with the `createTestData()` method:

```
beanRemote.createTestData();
```

Next, list all the `Catalog`, `Edition`, `Section`, and `Article` entity instances. For example, a `List` of all the `Catalog` entity instances is obtained with the `getAllCatalogs()` method:

```
List<Catalog> catalogs=beanRemote.getAllCatalogs();
```

Iterate over the list and output the `Catalog` ids and `Catalog` journals:

```
for(Catalog catalog:catalogs){
out.println("<br/>"+"Catalog Id:");
out.println(catalog.getId()+"<br/>");
out.println("Catalog Journal:");
out.println(catalog.getJournal()+"<br/>");
```

Similarly, output all the entity instances of `Edition`, `Section`, and `Article`. Next, delete some data with the `deleteSomeData()` method:

```
beanRemote.deleteSomeData();
```

Output all the `Catalog`, `Edition`, `Section`, and `Article` instances after deleting some data. The `EJB3Client.jsp` is listed next:

```
<!DOCTYPE HTML PUBLIC "-//W3C//DTD HTML 4.01 Transitional//EN"
"http://www.w3.org/TR/html4/loose.dtd">
<%@ page import="model.*,java.util.*,javax.naming.*"%>
<%@ page contentType="text/html;charset=windows-1252"%>
<html>
<head>
<meta http-equiv="Content-Type"
  content="text/html; charset=windows-1252" />
<title>EJB3Client</title>
</head>
<body>
<%
  InitialContext context = new InitialContext();
  CatalogSessionEJBRemote beanRemote = (CatalogSessionEJBRemote)
    context.lookup("EJB3-SessionEJB#model.
      CatalogSessionEJBRemote");
  beanRemote.createTestData();
  List<Catalog> catalogs = beanRemote.getAllCatalogs();

  out.println("<br/>" + "List of Catalogs" + "<br/>");
  for (Catalog catalog : catalogs) {
    out.println("Catalog Id:");
    out.println("<br/>" + catalog.getId() + "<br/>");
    out.println("Catalog Journal:");
    out.println(catalog.getJournal() + "<br/>");
  }

    out.println("<br/>" + "List of Editions" + "<br/>");
  List<Edition> editions = beanRemote.getAllEditions();
  for (Edition edition : editions) {
```

```
out.println("Edition Id:");
out.println(edition.getId() + "<br/>");
out.println("Edition Date:");
out.println(edition.getEdition() + "<br/>");

}
out.println("<br/>" + "List of Sections" + "<br/>");
List<Section> sections = beanRemote.getAllSections();
for (Section section : sections) {
  out.println("Section Id:");
  out.println(section.getId() + "<br/>");
  out.println("Section Name:");
  out.println(section.getSectionName() + "<br/>");

}
out.println("<br/>" + "List of Articles" + "<br/>");
List<Article> articles = beanRemote.getAllArticles();
for (Article article : articles) {
  out.println("Article Id:");
  out.println(article.getId() + "<br/>");
  out.println("Article Title:");
  out.println(article.getTitle() + "<br/>");

}
out.println("Delete some Data" + "<br/>");
beanRemote.deleteSomeData();

catalogs = beanRemote.getAllCatalogs();
out.println("<br/>" + "List of Catalogs" + "<br/>");
for (Catalog catalog : catalogs) {
  out.println("Catalog Id:");
  out.println(catalog.getId() + "<br/>");
  out.println("Catalog Journal:");
  out.println(catalog.getJournal() + "<br/>");
}
out.println("<br/>" + "List of Editions" + "<br/>");
editions = beanRemote.getAllEditions();
for (Edition edition : editions) {
  out.println("Edition Id:");
  out.println(edition.getId() + "<br/>");
  out.println("Edition Date:");
  out.println(edition.getEdition() + "<br/>");

}
out.println("<br/>" + "List of Sections" + "<br/>");
sections = beanRemote.getAllSections();
for (Section section : sections) {
```

```
      out.println("Section Id:");
      out.println(section.getId() + "<br/>");
      out.println("Section Name:");
      out.println(section.getSectionName() + "<br/>");
    }
    out.println("<br/>" + "List of Articles" + "<br/>");
    articles = beanRemote.getAllArticles();
    for (Article article : articles) {
      out.println("Article Id:");
      out.println(article.getId() + "<br/>");
      out.println("Article Title:");
      out.println(article.getTitle() + "<br/>");
    }
%>
</body>
</html>
```

Testing the client

In this section, we test the client. But, before we may do so, we need to add the
`EJB3Model` project as a dependency to the `JSPViewController` project. Select
the **JSPViewController** project, and select **Tools | Project Properties**. In the
Project Properties window, select the **Dependencies** node, and select the **Edit
Dependencies** button to add a new dependency. In the **Edit Dependencies** window,
select the **EJB3Model** project and the **Build Output**. Click on **OK**.

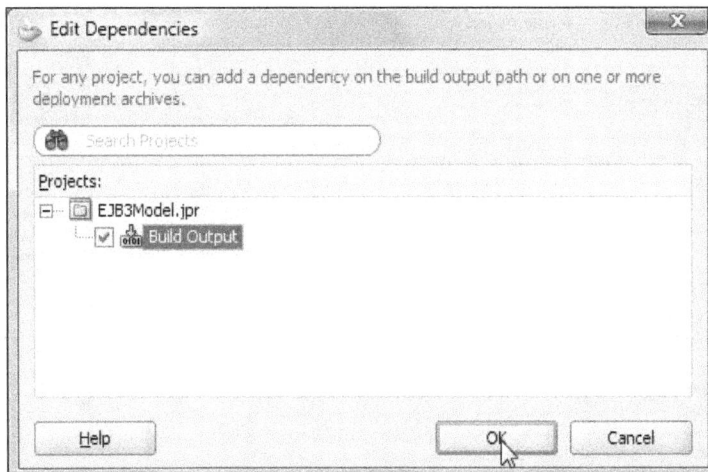

The **EJB3Model** project dependency gets added. Click on **OK**.

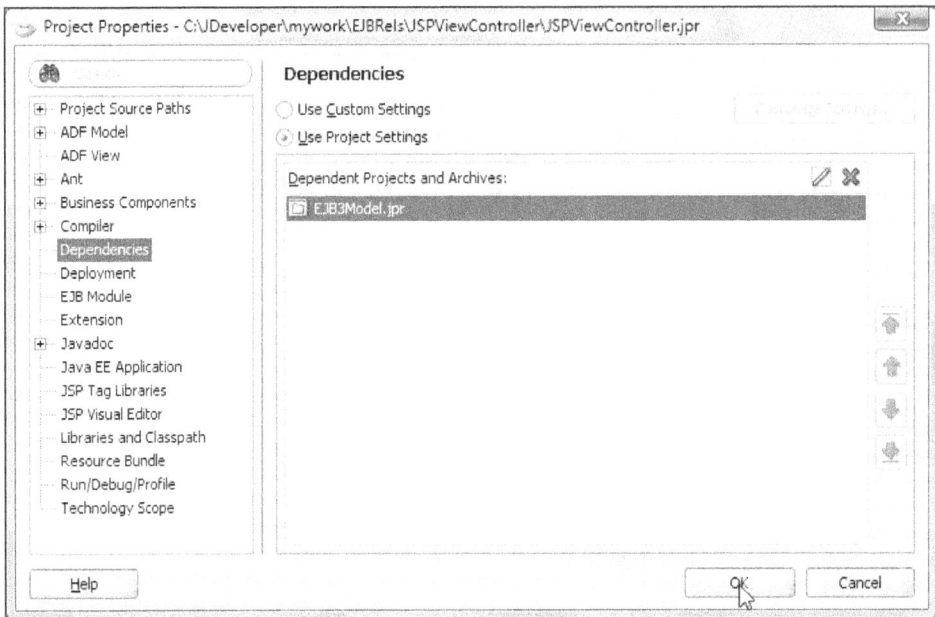

Right-click on the **EJB3Client.jsp** and select **Run**:

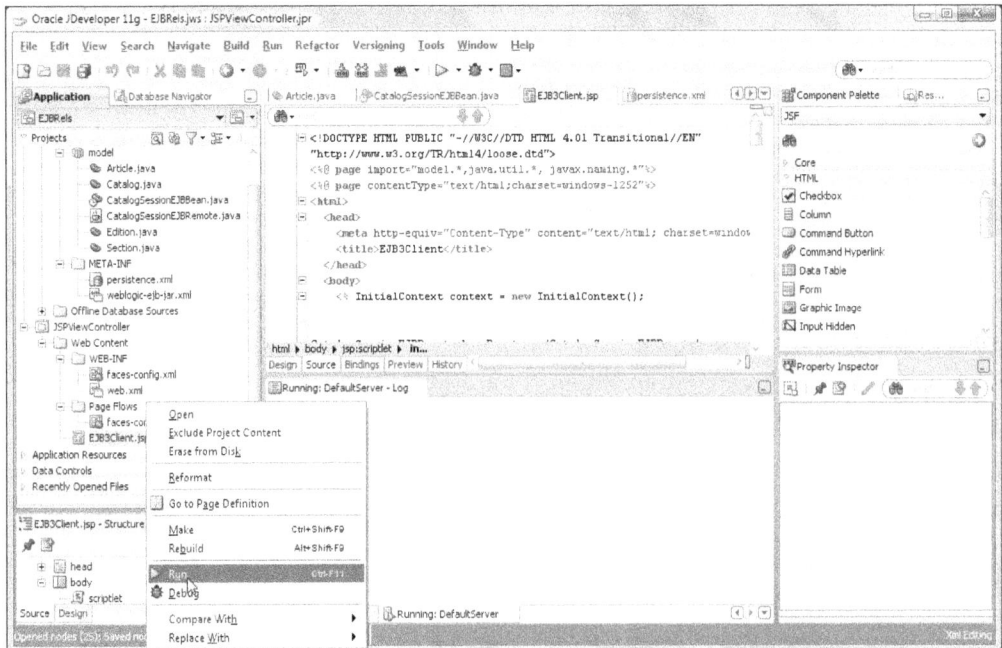

All the **Catalog**, **Edition**, **Section**, and **Article** entities and their properties get listed, as shown next:

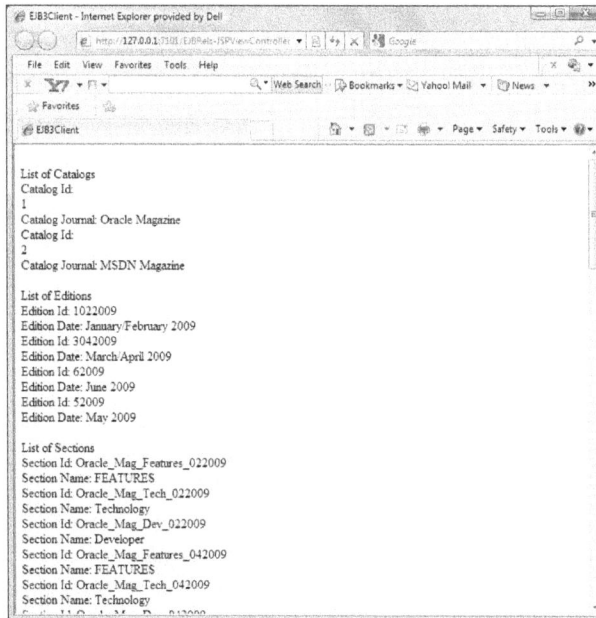

All the **Article** entities and the article titles get listed:

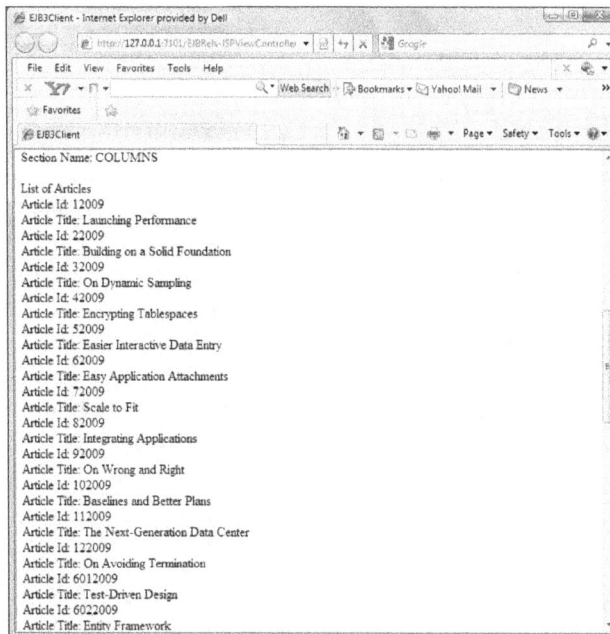

After the deletion of some data the **Oracle Magazine** catalogs do not get listed:

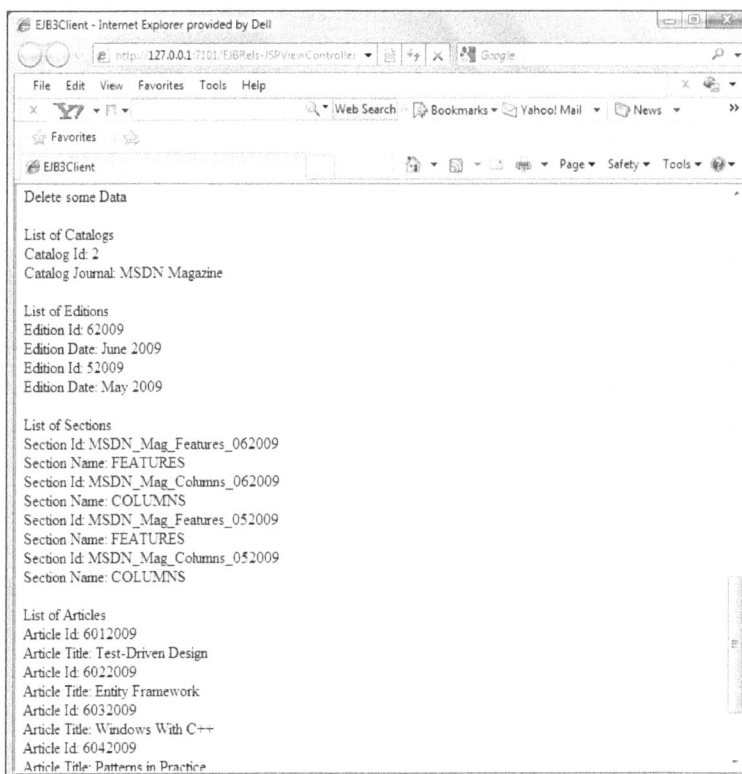

Modifying the fetch strategy

We have used the default fetch strategy in the preceding example. The default fetch strategy for `OneToMany` and `ManyToMany` relationships is `LAZY`. With `LAZY` fetching, the containing entities are not fetched when the contained entity is retrieved. Therefore, we were not able to retrieve all the editions for a catalog, all the sections in an edition, and all the articles in a section. We just listed all the catalogs, editions, sections, and articles. With `EAGER` fetching, the entities contained by an entity are immediately fetched. Next, we shall modify the fetch strategy to `EAGER` in the `@ManyToMany` and `@OneToMany` relationship mappings. The fetch strategy is set with the `fetch` element. In the `Catalog` entity replace:

```
@ManyToMany(cascade=CascadeType.ALL)
```

with:

```
@ManyToMany(cascade=CascadeType.ALL, fetch=FetchType.EAGER)
```

In the `Edition` entity replace:

```
@ManyToMany(cascade =
                { CascadeType.MERGE, CascadeType.PERSIST,
                  CascadeType.REFRESH },
            mappedBy = "editions")
```

with:

```
@ManyToMany(cascade =
                { CascadeType.MERGE, CascadeType.PERSIST,
                  CascadeType.REFRESH },
            mappedBy = "editions", fetch = FetchType.EAGER)
```

In the `Edition` entity replace:

```
@OneToMany(cascade = CascadeType.ALL, mappedBy = "edition")
```

with:

```
@OneToMany(cascade = CascadeType.ALL, mappedBy = "edition",
            fetch = FetchType.EAGER)
```

In the `Section` entity replace:

```
@OneToMany(cascade={CascadeType.ALL},mappedBy = "section")
```

with:

```
@OneToMany(cascade={CascadeType.ALL},
            mappedBy = "section",fetch=FetchType.EAGER)
```

Also, modify the `EJB3Client.jsp`. Instead of just listing all the entities, list the contained entities. For example, retrieve all the editions in a catalog with the `getCatalogEditions()` method:

```
List<Edition> editions=beanRemote.getCatalogEditions(catalog);
```

Similarly, retrieve all the sections in an edition with the `EditionSections` method and all the articles in a section with the `getSectionArticles()` method. The modified `EJB3Client.jsp` is listed next:

```
<!DOCTYPE HTML PUBLIC "-//W3C//DTD HTML 4.01 Transitional//EN"
"http://www.w3.org/TR/html4/loose.dtd">
<%@ page import="model.*,java.util.*,javax.naming.*"%>
<%@ page contentType="text/html;charset=windows-1252"%>
<html>
<head>
<meta http-equiv="Content-Type"
```

```
      content="text/html; charset=windows-1252" />
      <title>EJB3Client</title>
</head>
<body>
<%
   InitialContext context = new InitialContext();

   CatalogSessionEJBRemote beanRemote = (CatalogSessionEJBRemote)
      context.lookup("EJB3-SessionEJB#model.CatalogSessionEJBRemote");
   beanRemote.createTestData();
   List<Catalog> catalogs = beanRemote.getAllCatalogs();
   out.println("<br/>" + "List of Catalogs" + "<br/>");
   for (Catalog catalog : catalogs) {
      out.println("<br/>" + "Catalog Id:");
      out.println(catalog.getId() + "<br/>");
      out.println("Catalog Journal:");
      out.println(catalog.getJournal() + "<br/>");
      out.println("<br/>" + "List of Editions in a Catalog" + "<br/>");
   List<Edition> editions = beanRemote.getCatalogEditions(catalog);
      for (Edition edition : editions) {
         out.println("Edition Id:");
         out.println(edition.getId() + "<br/>");
         out.println("Edition Date:");
         out.println(edition.getEdition() + "<br/>");

         out.println("<br/>" + "List of Sections in a Edition" +
            "<br/>");
         List<Section> sections = beanRemote.getEditionSections(edition);
         for (Section section : sections) {
            out.println("<br/>" + "Section Id:");
            out.println(section.getId() + "<br/>");
            out.println("Section Name:");
            out.println(section.getSectionName() + "<br/>");
            out.println("<br/>" + "List of Articles in a Section" +
               "<br/>");
            List<Article> articles = beanRemote
                                    .getSectionArticles(section);
                  for (Article article : articles) {
                        out.println("Article Id:");
                        out.println(article.getId() + "<br/>");
                        out.println("Article Title:");
                        out.println(article.getTitle() +
                           "<br/>");
                  }
            }
```

```
            }
    }
    out.println("<br/>" + "Delete some Data" + "<br/>");
    beanRemote.deleteSomeData();
    catalogs = beanRemote.getAllCatalogs();
    out.println("<br/>" + "List of Catalogs" + "<br/>");
    for (Catalog catalog : catalogs) {
            out.println("<br/>" + "Catalog Id:");
            out.println(catalog.getId() + "<br/>");
            out.println("Catalog Journal:");
            out.println(catalog.getJournal() + "<br/>");

            out.println("<br/>" + "List of Editions in a Catalog"
                                + "<br/>");
List<Edition> editions = beanRemote.getCatalogEditions(catalog);
            for (Edition edition : editions) {
                    out.println("Edition Id:");
                    out.println(edition.getId() + "<br/>");
                    out.println("Edition Date:");
                    out.println(edition.getEdition() + "<br/>");

                    out.println("<br/>" + "List of Sections in a Edition"
                                + "<br/>");
                    List<Section> sections = beanRemote
                                .getEditionSections(edition);
                    for (Section section : sections) {
                            out.println("<br/>" + "Section Id:");
                            out.println(section.getId() + "<br/>");
                            out.println("Section Name:");
                            out.println(section.getSectionName() +
                              "<br/>");
out.println("<br/>" + "List of Articles in a Section"
                                + "<br/>");
                            List<Article> articles = beanRemote
                                .getSectionArticles(section);
                            for (Article article : articles) {
                                    out.println("Article Id:");
                                    out.println(article.getId() + "<br/>");
                                    out.println("Article Title:");
                                    out.println(article.getTitle() +
                                      "<br/>");
                            }
                    }
            }
    }
%>
</body>
</html>
```

Right-click on **EJB3Client.jsp** and select **Run**.

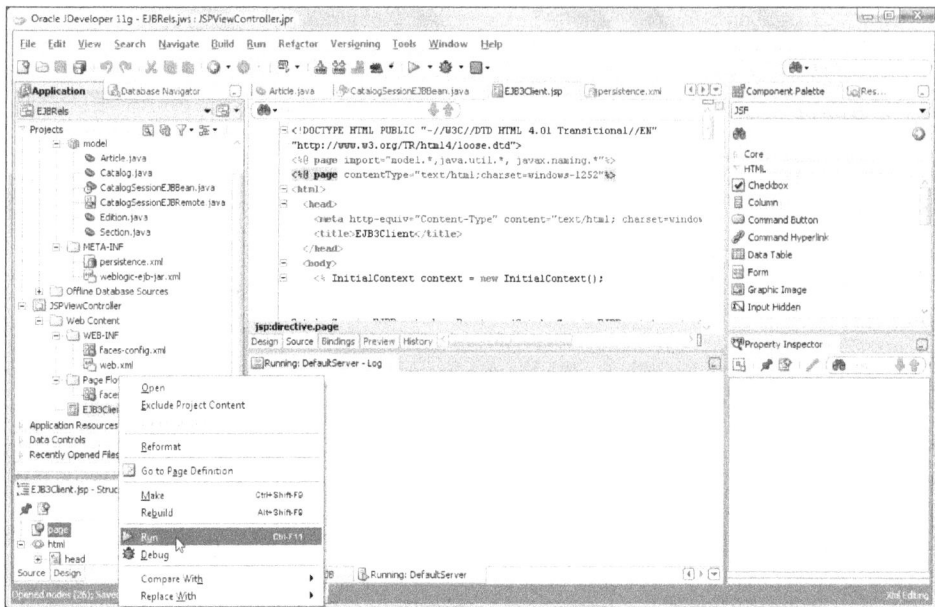

All the entities and the contained entities get listed. For example, all the editions in a catalog, all the sections in an edition , and all the articles in a section get listed.

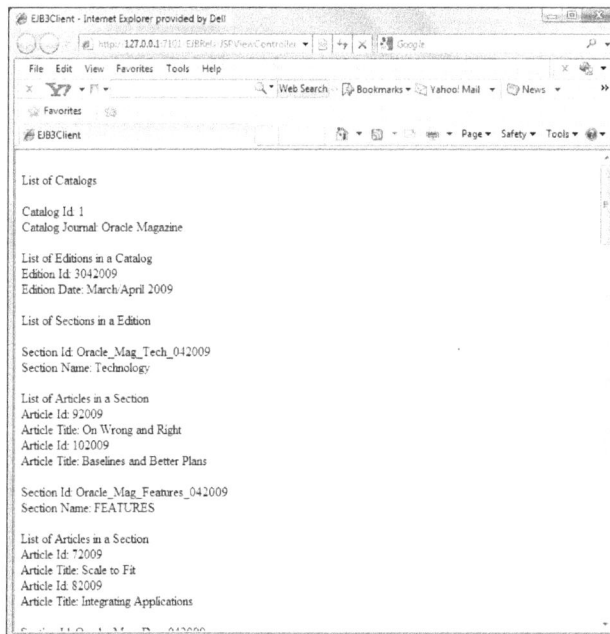

After deleting some data, the `Oracle Magazine` catalog and the contained entities do not get listed, but the other catalogs and the contained entities get listed.

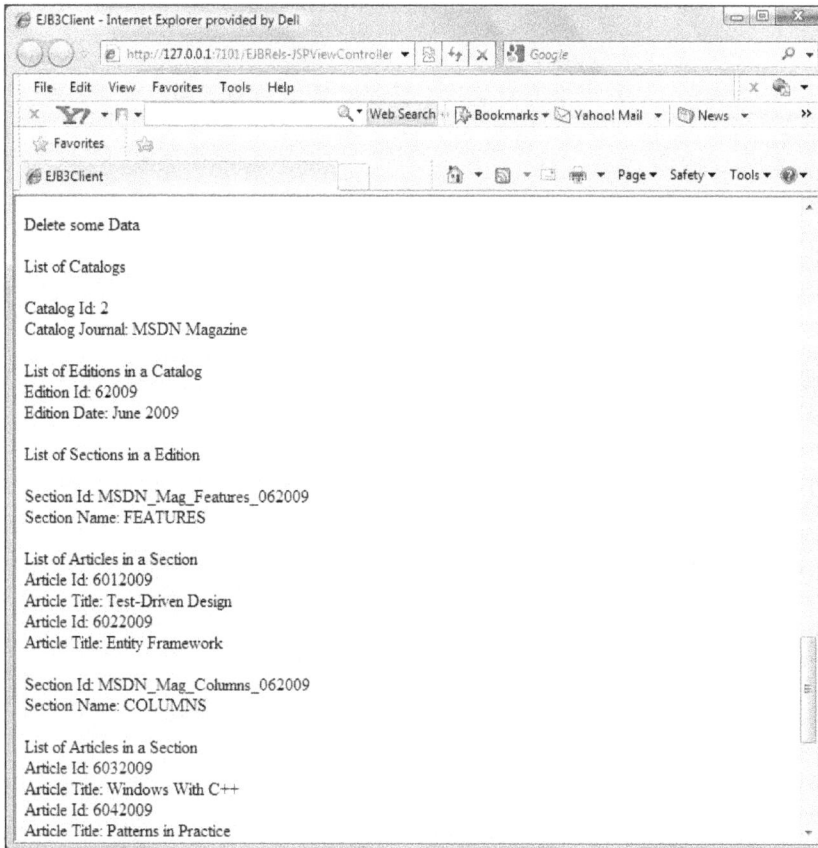

Summary

In this chapter we discussed EJB 3.0 entity relationships between entity beans. We mapped some database tables to entity beans. We added relationship mappings to the entities. We added some test data and ran a test client to retrieve the entities and the contained entities. We demonstrated the use of fetch strategy. In the next chapter we shall create an Ajax user interface for EJB 3.0 entity bean persistence.

8
EJB 3.0 Database Persistence with Ajax in the UI

While EJB 3.0 has facilitated database persistence, Ajax has simplified the user interface facet of web applications. **Asynchronous JavaScript And XML (AJAX)** is a web technique for developing asynchronous web applications using JavaScript, **Document Object Model (DOM)** and `XMLHttpRequest` technologies. AJAX provides dynamic interaction between a client and a server. In this chapter, we discuss the following:

- The `XMLHttpRequest` object
- Creating an EJB 3.0 application
- Creating a data source in WebLogic Server
- Creating an entity bean
- Creating a wrapper session bean
- Creating a servlet client
- Creating an Ajax user interface
- Deploying the EJB 3 application to WebLogic Server
- Testing the Ajax user interface

The XMLHttpRequest Object

The XMLHttpRequest object, which is supported by most browsers, provides asynchronous communication between a web browser and an underlying server. Using the object, clients may submit XML data to a server, and retrieve it from the server, without reloading the page. XML data may be converted to HTML on the client side, using the DOM API and **Extensible Stylesheet Transformations** (**XSLT**). The implementations of XMLHttpRequest may vary across browsers. For example, an instance of an XMLHttpRequest object is created in IE 6 as follows:

```
var req = new ActiveXObject("Microsoft.XMLHTTP");
```

In Internet Explorer 7, XMLHttpRequest is available as a window object property. An instance of an XMLHttpRequest object in IE 7 is created as follows:

```
var req = new XMLHttpRequest();
```

W3C has introduced an XMLHttpRequest object specification (http://www.w3.org/TR/XMLHttpRequest/) to standardize implementations of the XMLHttpRequest object. The XMLHttpRequest object has various attributes/properties, which are discussed in the following table, to provide HTTP client functionality.

Property	Description
onreadystatechange	Sets the callback method for asynchronous requests.
readyState	Retrieves the current state of a request.
	0 – XMLHttpRequest object has been created.
	1 – The object has been created and open() method has been invoked.
	2 – The send() method has been called, but the response has not been received.
	3 – Some data has been received that is available in the responseText property. responseXML produces null and response headers and status are not completely available.
	4 – Response has been received.
responseText	Retrieves the text of response from server.
responseXML	Retrieves the XML DOM of response from server.
status	Retrieves the HTTP status code of request.
statusText	Retrieves the status text of the HTTP request.

XMLHttpRequest object methods, which are discussed in the following table, are used to open an HTTP request, send the request, and receive the response.

Method	Description
`abort()`	Aborts the current HTTP request.
`getAllResponseHeaders()`	Gets all the response headers.
`getResponseHeader(string header)`	Gets a specified response header.
`open(string method, string url, boolean asynch, string username, string password)`	Opens a HTTP request. Does not send a request. Boolean parameter asynch specifies if HTTP request is asynchronous; default value is true. Username and password are optional.
`send(data)`	Sends a HTTP request to the server, including data. The `send()` method is synchronous or asynchronous corresponding to the value of the asynch argument in the open() method. If synchronous, the method does not return until the request is completely loaded and the entire response has been received. If asynchronous, method returns immediately.
`setRequestHeader(string headerName, string headerValue)`	Sets HTTP request headers.

In this chapter, we create an EJB 3.0 Ajax application in which an input form is validated using Ajax and persisted using EJB 3.0. The following procedure is used for a catalog entry form validation and submission:

1. A user inputs a catalog ID in a catalog entry form.

2. The catalog id value is sent to a servlet `doGet` method. The servlet looks up the remote component interface of a session bean and invokes a `validate()` method that returns a `Catalog` entity instance to validate the catalog id.

3. The session bean `validate()` method runs a Java persistence language query using the catalog id value. If the query returns an empty list, the `validate()` method returns `null`, else it returns a list with a `Catalog` entity instance; the `validate()` method returns the `Catalog` entity instance.

4. In the servlet, if the `validate()` method returns null, the servlet constructs a `String` consisting of an XML element `<valid>true</valid>`, which is returned to the browser that sent the catalog id value via Ajax.

5. In the catalog entry form, the XML is parsed and if the valid element value is `true`, a validation message that the catalog ID specified is valid gets displayed. A user may continue to fill the form and submit it to create a new catalog entry.

6. If the `validate()` method returns a `Catalog` entity instance, the servlet constructs a `String` that consists of an element valid with text set to `false` and also consists of elements corresponding to the `Catalog` bean properties `journal`, `publisher`, `edition`, `title`, and `author`. The `String` is returned to the browser, which parses the `String` and finding a `false` value for the valid element displays a validation message that the catalog id value specified is false. The JavaScript in the Catalog entry form JSP also fills the form fields with the values returned in the `String` and disables the **Submit** button.

7. If the catalog id is valid, a user may fill out the form and submit it, which invokes the `doPost` method. In the `doPost` method of the servlet, the input field values are retrieved and the remote business interface of the session bean is looked up. The `persist()` method of the session bean is invoked with the input form field values.

8. In the `persist()` method of the session bean, a new `Catalog` entity instance is created from the input field values and the `persist()` method of the `EntityManager` is invoked to persist the entity instance to the database. Thus, a user did not have to fill out the form only to find later that a catalog id is not valid. Ajax validates the catalog id value and displays a validation message.

Setting the environment

We need to install Oracle Fusion Middleware 11*g* (`http://www.oracle.com/technology/software/products/middleware/index.html`). We need to download the following two components from the **For Development** section.

*   Oracle WebLogic Server 11*g* Rel 1 (10.3.2) Net Installer
*   Oracle JDeveloper 11*g* Rel 1 (11.1.1.2.0) (JDeveloper + ADF)

First, install JDeveloper 11*g* Studio Edition. Also install Oracle database 10*g*/11*g*/ XE (including the sample schemas). We shall be using the XE version in this chapter. Create an Oracle database table CATALOG with the following SQL script:

```
CREATE TABLE Catalog(CatalogId VARCHAR(255), Journal VARCHAR(255),
Publisher Varchar(255), Edition VARCHAR(255), Title Varchar(255),
Author Varchar(255));

INSERT INTO Catalog VALUES('catalog1', 'Oracle Magazine', 'Oracle
Publishing', 'September-October 2009','Oracle Fusion Middleware 11g:
The Foundation for Innovation', 'David Baum');

INSERT INTO Catalog VALUES('catalog2',  'Oracle Magazine', 'Oracle
Publishing', 'September-October 2009', 'Put Your Arrays in a Bind',
'Mark Williams');
```

Installing WebLogic Server

Next, install WebLogic Server 11*g*. Subsequently, create a WebLogic server domain. A domain is an administration unit for WebLogic Server instances. Start the Fusion Middleware Configuration Wizard. Select **Create a new WebLogic domain** and click on **Next**:

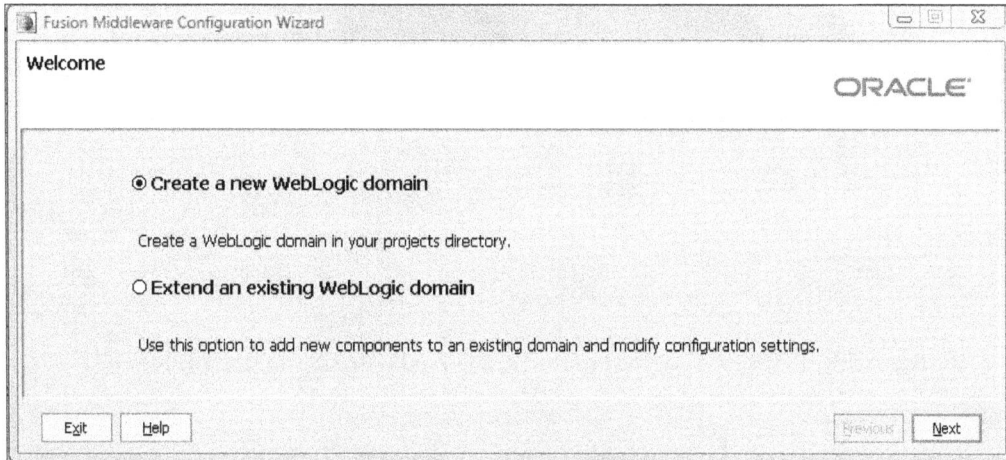

In the **Domain Source** window select **Basic WebLogic Server Domain** as the domain to generate. Click on **Next**:

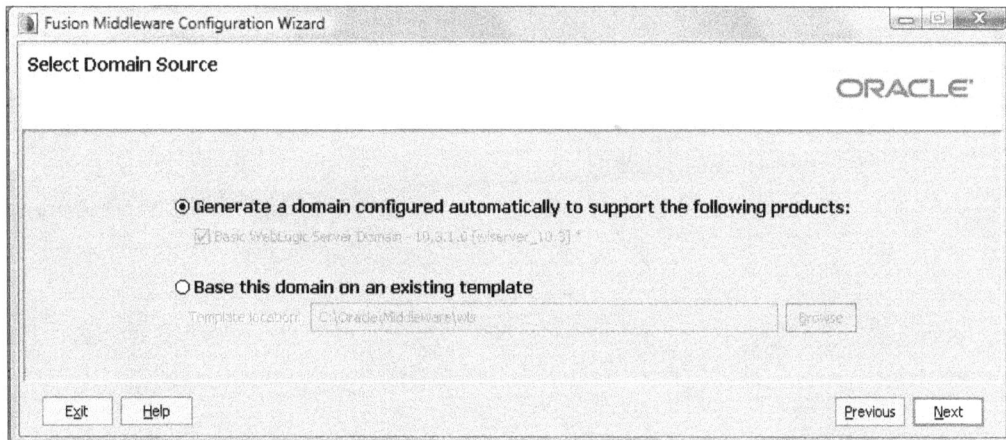

Specify **Domain name** as **base_domain** and select the default **Domain location**. Click on **Next**:

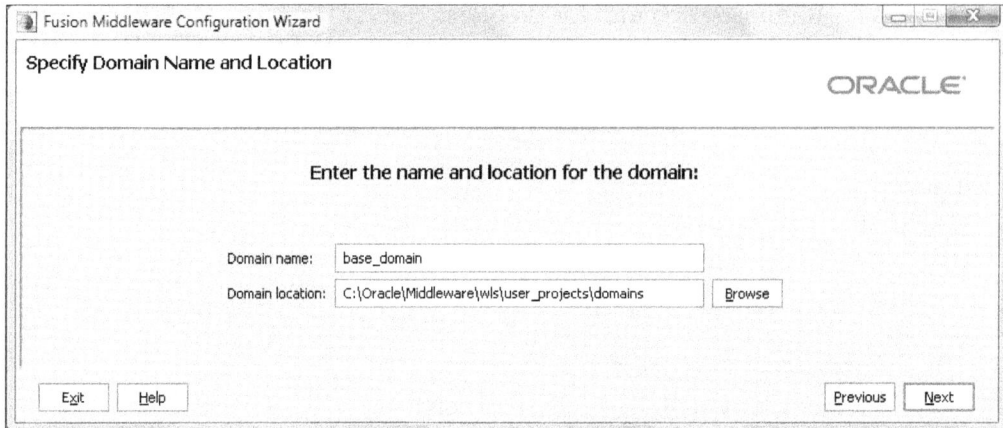

Specify the Administrator **User name** and **User password** and click on **Next**:

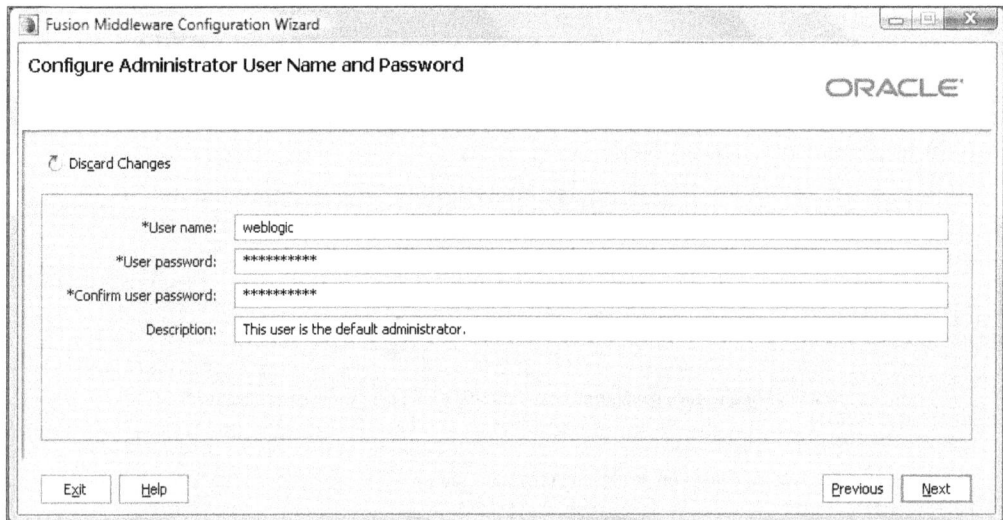

Select **WebLogic Domain Startup Mode** as **Development Mode**, which is for developing applications. The development mode supports auto deployment of applications. Select **JDK** as **Sun JDK 1.6** and click on **Next**:

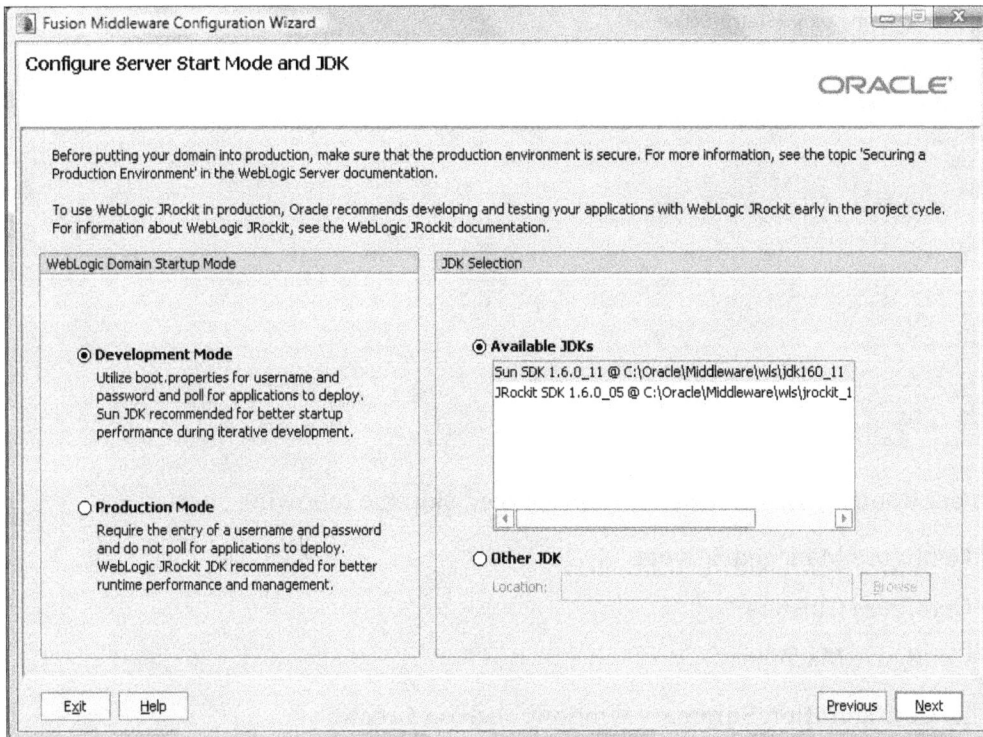

In the **Select Optional Configuration** window, select at least the **Administration Server** option and click on **Next**:

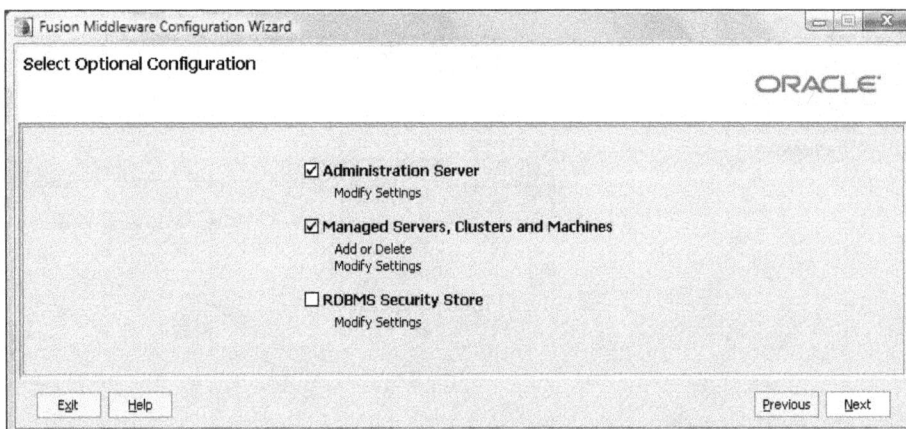

In the **Configure the Administration Server** window, select the default settings for server **Name**, **Listen address**, and **Listen port** (7001), and click on **Next**:

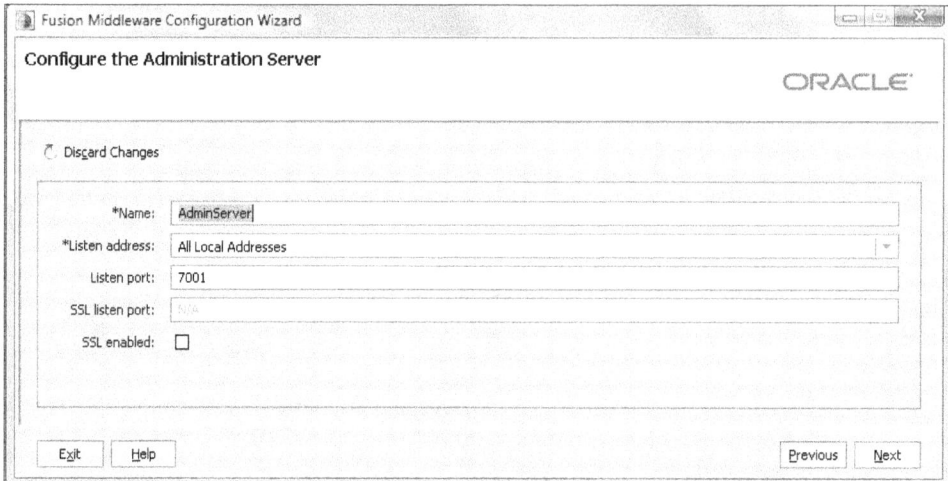

As our domain will only have a single server, skip the following steps :

=> Configure Managed Servers

=> Configure Clusters

=> Configure Machines

In the **Configuration Summary** window, click on **Create**:

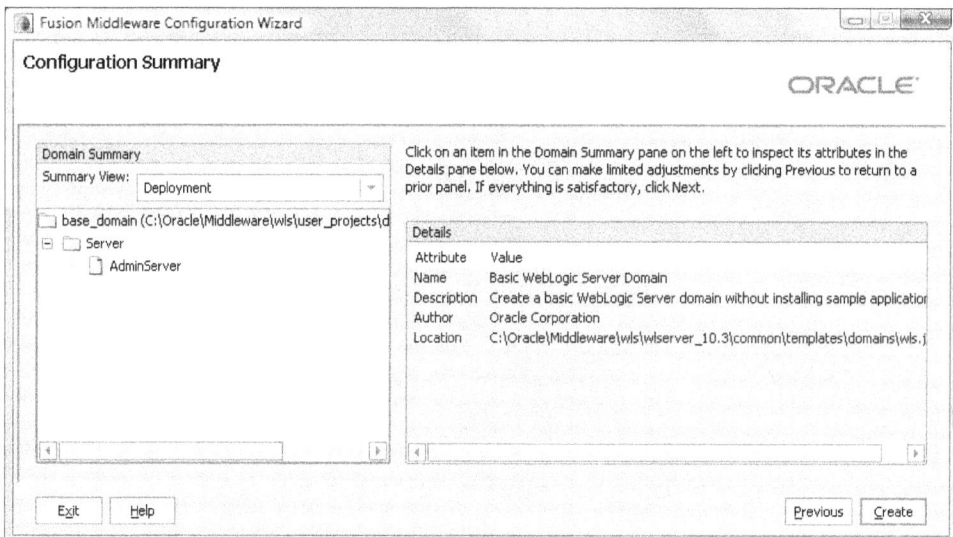

A WebLogic Server domain gets created. Click on **Done**:

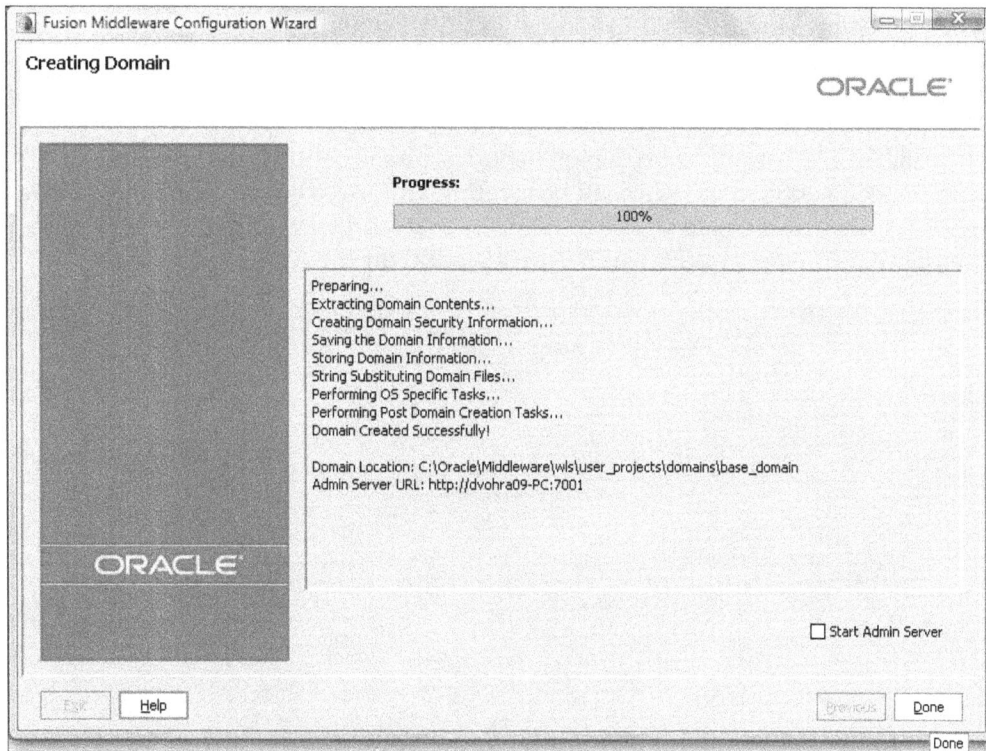

Creating an EJB 3.0 application in JDeveloper

In this section, we create an EJB 3 application and project in JDeveloper 11*g*. Select **New Application** in JDeveloper 11*g*. Specify an **Application Name** and select **Java EE Web Application** as the **Application Template**. Click on **Next**. Specify a **Project Name** for the view controller project, the default being **ViewController**. Select **EJB** in the **Available** list and add to the **Selected** list of **Project Technologies**. Click on **Next**. Select the default Java settings for the view controller project, which include the package name, source path, and output directory, and click on **Next**.

Select the default EJB settings; select **EJB Version** as **EJB 3.0**, and select the **Using annotations** feature. Click on **Next**. Specify a **Project Name** for the model project, the default being **Model**. Select **EJB** in the **Project Technologies**. Click on **Next**. Select the default Java settings for the model project, which include the package name, **Java Source Path**, and the **Output Directory**. Click on **Next**. Select the default EJB settings; set **EJB Version** as **3.0** and select the **Using annotations** feature. Click on **Finish**. An EJB 3 application, which includes a view controller project and a model project, gets created. We shall be creating an EJB 3.0 entity bean in the Model project. We shall also create an EJB 3.0 session bean and servlet in the Model project. In the ViewController project, we shall create a JSP for the Ajax user interface.

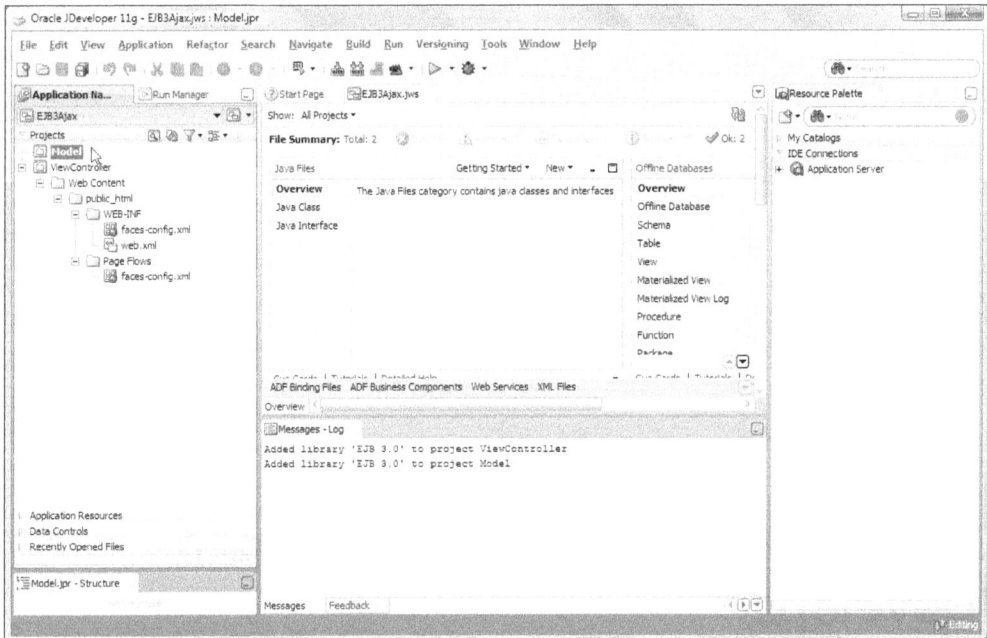

Creating a database connection

We need to create a database connection to the Oracle database for generating an EJB 3.0 entity bean from the CATALOG table, which we created in the *Setting the environment* section. In the **Database Navigator,** right-click on **EJB3Ajax** and select **New Connection**. In the **Create Database Connection**, specify a **Connection Name**, and select **Connection Type** as **Oracle (JDBC)**. Specify **Username** as **OE** and the **Password** for the **OE** schema. Select **Driver Type** as **thin, Host Name** as **localhost**, and **SID** as **XE**. Click on **Test Connection** to test the connection. If a connection gets established, click on **OK**.

A JDBC connection gets added to the **Database Navigator**.

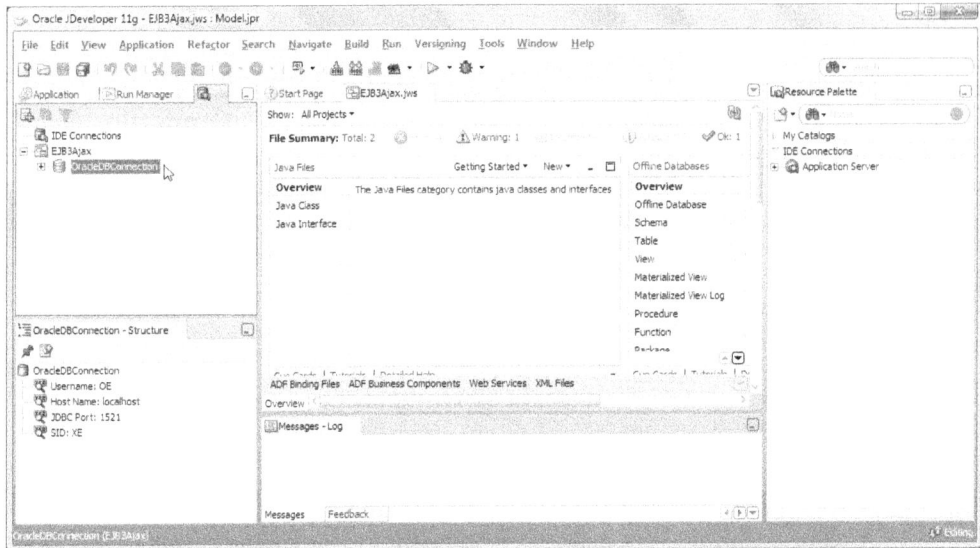

An `OracleDBConnection-jdbc.xml` configuration file gets created in the `src/META-INF` directory. The configuration file specifies the connection settings such as the driver class and the connection URL. The configuration file also specifies a JNDI data source, `jdbc/OracleDBConnectionDS`, which gets created when the JDBC connection `OracleDBConnection` is created. The configuration file is listed next:

```
<?xml version = '1.0' encoding = 'windows-1252'?>
<jdbc-data-source xmlns:xsi="http://www.w3.org/2001/XMLSchema-
instance"
    xsi:schemaLocation="http://www.bea.com/ns/weblogic/jdbc-data-
source http://www.bea.com/ns/weblogic/jdbc-data-source/1.0/jdbc-data-
source.xsd"
    xmlns="http://www.bea.com/ns/weblogic/jdbc-data-source">
    <name>OracleDBConnection</name>
    <jdbc-driver-params>
        <url>jdbc:oracle:thin:@localhost:1521:XE</url>
        <driver-name>oracle.jdbc.OracleDriver</driver-name>
        <properties>
            <property>
                <name>user</name>
                <value>OE</value>
            </property>
            <property>
                <name>servername</name>
                <value>localhost</value>
            </property>
            <property>
```

```
                <name>portnumber</name>
                <value>1521</value>
        </property>
        <property>
                <name>sid</name>
                <value>XE</value>
        </property>
    </properties>
    <password-encrypted>46969068B219FCC29EC5B6B5A9B8F846D62D1A19
                        DF561D1E</password-encrypted>
</jdbc-driver-params>
<jdbc-connection-pool-params>
    <test-table-name>dual</test-table-name>
</jdbc-connection-pool-params>
<jdbc-data-source-params>
    <jndi-name>jdbc/OracleDBConnectionDS</jndi-name>
    <scope>Application</scope>
</jdbc-data-source-params>
</jdbc-data-source>
```

Creating a data source in WebLogic Server

As we shall be deploying the EJB 3.0 Ajax application to WebLogic Server, we need to create a data source in WebLogic Server for the Oracle database. The data source JNDI name should correspond to the data source JNDI name used in the `persistence.xml` configuration file for the entity bean, which we shall create in the next section. We shall be using a data source with JNDI name `jdbc/OracleDBConnectionDS`; therefore, create a data source with JNDI name `jdbc/OracleDBConnectionDS` in WebLogic Server. Start the WebLogic Server and log in to the Administration Console.

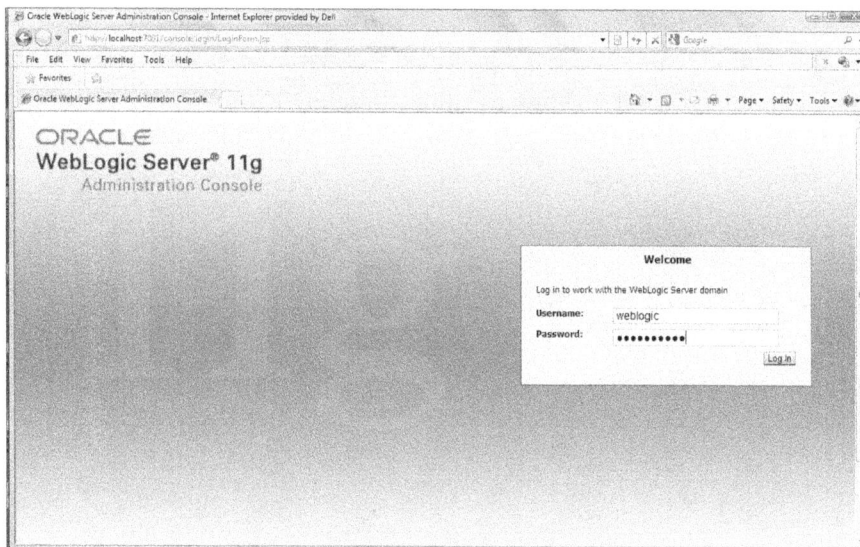

Select the **base_domain | Services | JDBC | Data Sources** node. To create a new data source, click on **New** in the **Data Sources** table as shown in the following screenshot:

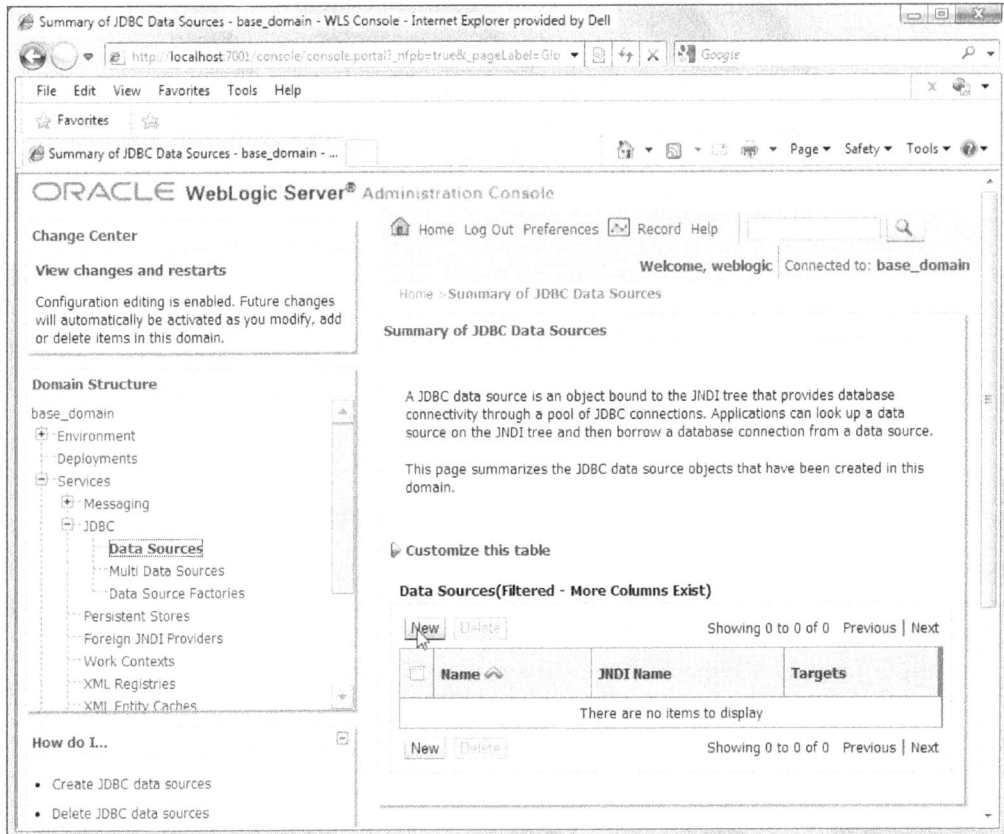

In the **Create a New JDBC Data Source** window, specify a data source **Name**, and specify **JNDI Name** for the data source as **jdbc/OracleDBConnectionDS**. Select **Database Type** as **Oracle** and select **Database Driver** as **Oracle's Driver (Thin XA)**. Click on **Next**:

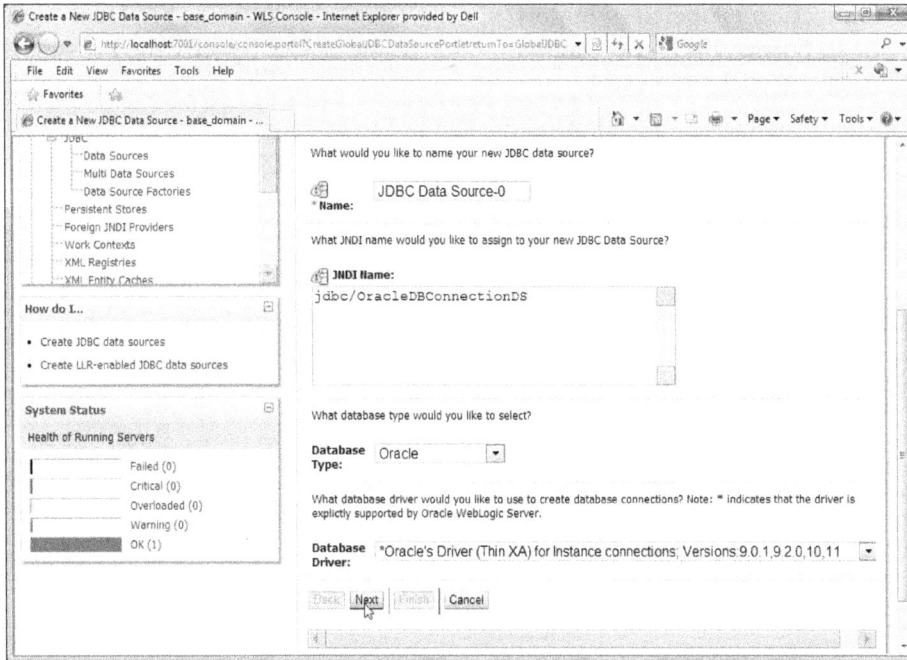

As we selected the XA JDBC driver, the driver will support global transactions and the **Two-Phase Commit** transaction protocol. Click on **Next** in **Transaction Options**:

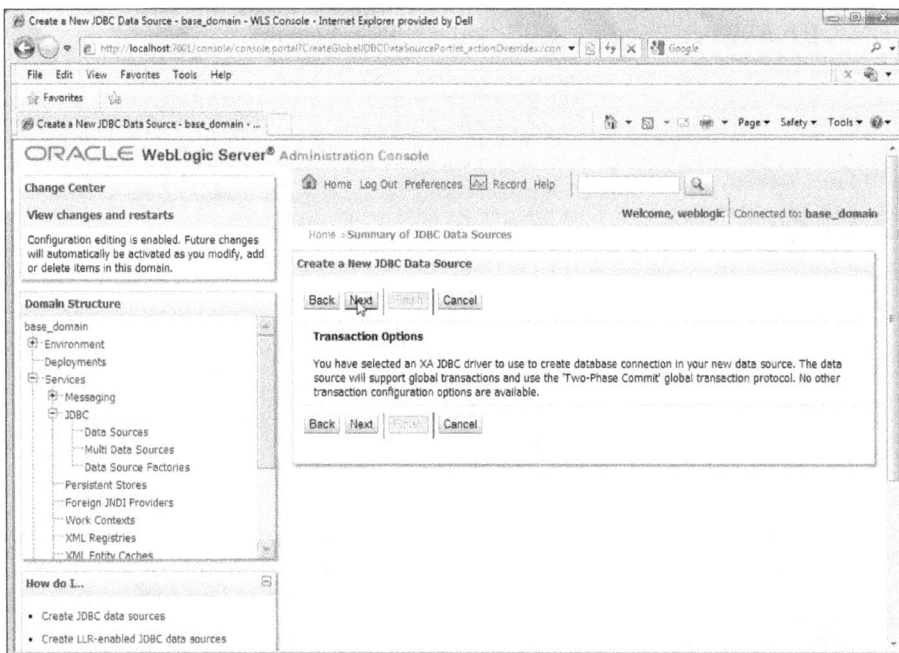

In the **Connection Properties** window, specify **Database Name** as **XE**, **Host Name** as **localhost**, **Port** as **1521**, and **Database User Name** as OE. Specify the **Password** for the **OE** user and click on **Next**:

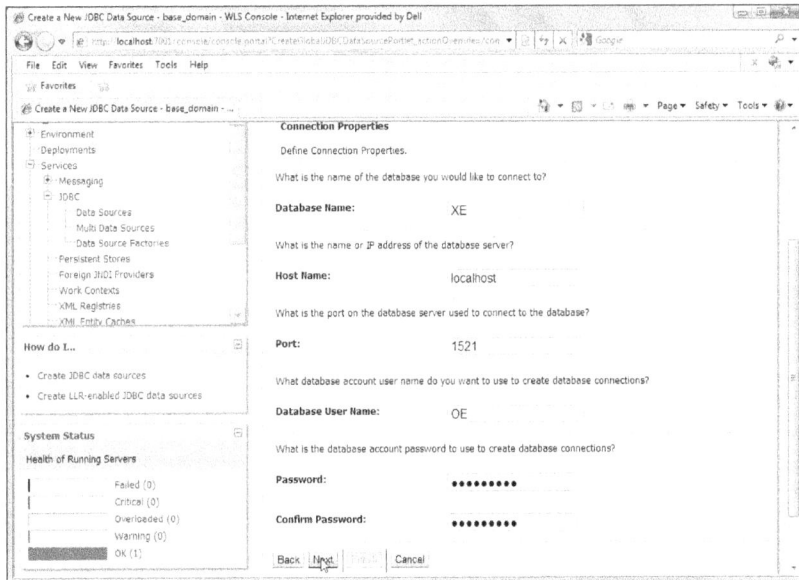

In the **Test Database Connection** window, the **Driver Class Name** and the connection **URL** are specified. Click on **Test Configuration** to test the data source connection. If a connection gets established, click on **Finish**:

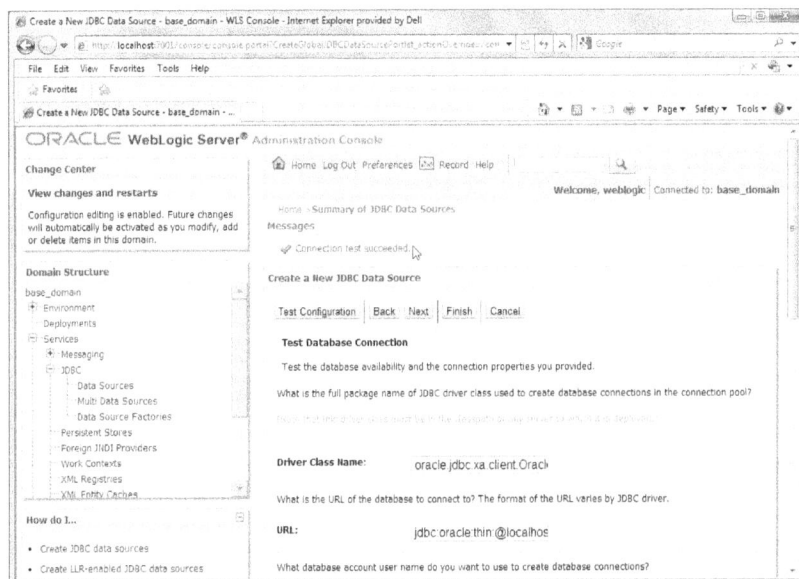

A data source with JNDI name `jdbc/OracleDBConnectionDS` gets added to the
Data Sources table.

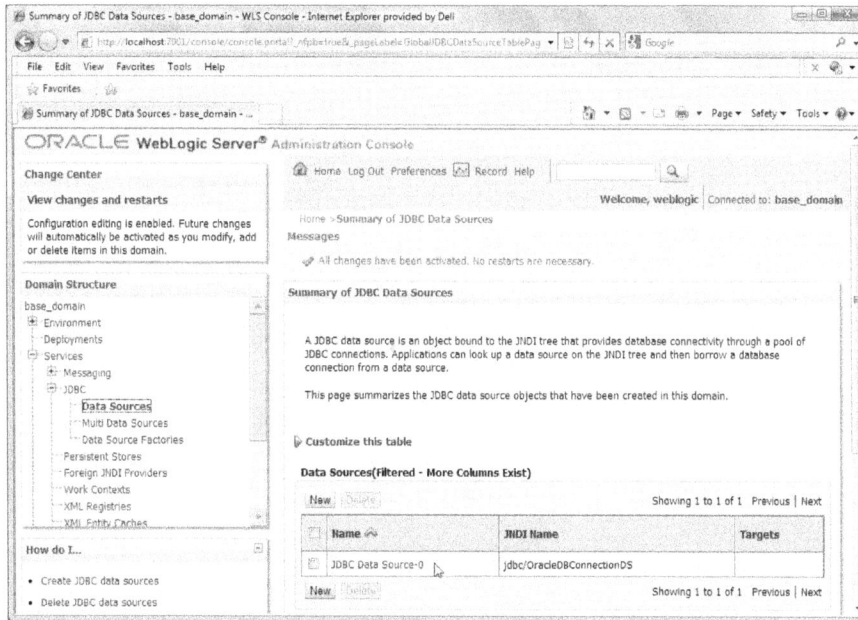

Click on the data source in the **Data Sources** table. The settings for the data source
get displayed. Select the **Targets** tab and select the **AdminServer** as the target server.
Click on **Save**. The target server settings get applied.

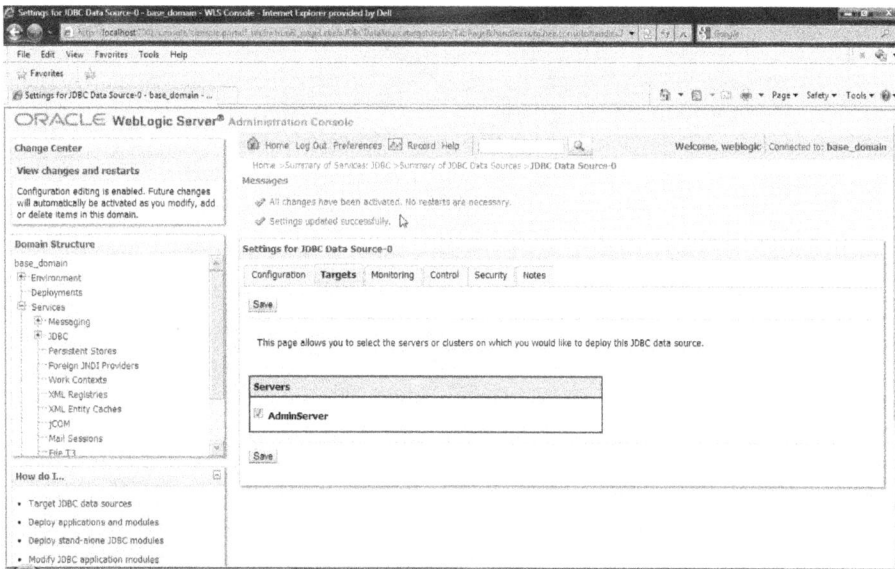

Click on the **Monitoring** tab and click on the **Testing** tab. Click on **Test Data Source**. If the test is successful, a message gets displayed as in the following screenshot:

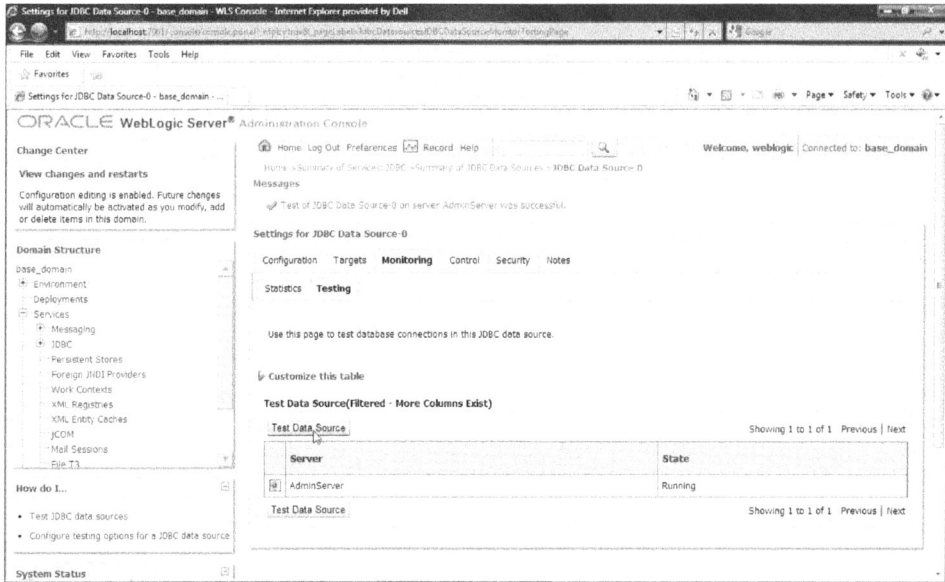

Creating an entity bean

In this section, we create an entity bean from the database table CATALOG. Select the Model project node in the **Application** navigator. Select **File | New**. In the **New Gallery** window select **Business Tier | EJB** in the **Categories** and select **Entities from Tables** in **Items**. Click on **OK**.

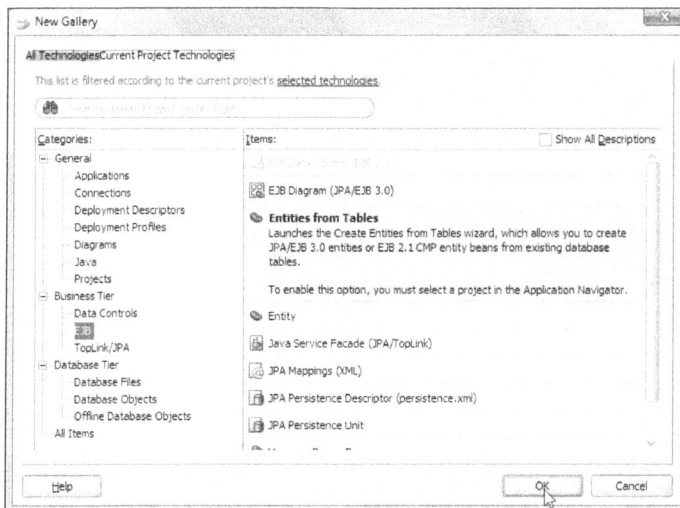

As discussed in some of the earlier chapters, in the **Persistence Unit** window, click on **New** to create a new persistence unit. Specify the persistence unit Name as **em** and specify **JTA Data Source Name** as **jdbc/OracleDBConnectionDS**. Select **WebLogic Server 10** as the **Server Platform**. Click on **OK**. Click on **Next** in the **Persistence Unit** window. In the **Type of Connection** window, select **Online Database Connection** and click on **Next**. In **Database Connection Details,** select the **OracleDBConnection** and click on **Next**. In **Select Tables,** select the OE Schema and select the **Auto Query** checkbox. Shift the **CATALOG** table from the **Available** to the **Selected** list and click on **Next**. In **General Options,** specify the **Package Name** (default being **model**), and select the default **Entity Class** options. Click on **Next**. In **Specify Entity Details,** select **Table Name** as OE.CATALOG. Specify **Entity Name** as **Catalog** and **Entity Class** as **model.Entity**. Click on **Next**. In the **Summary** page, click on **Finish**. An entity class **model.Catalog** gets created. An entity bean configuration file **persistence.xml** also gets created in the **META-INF** directory.

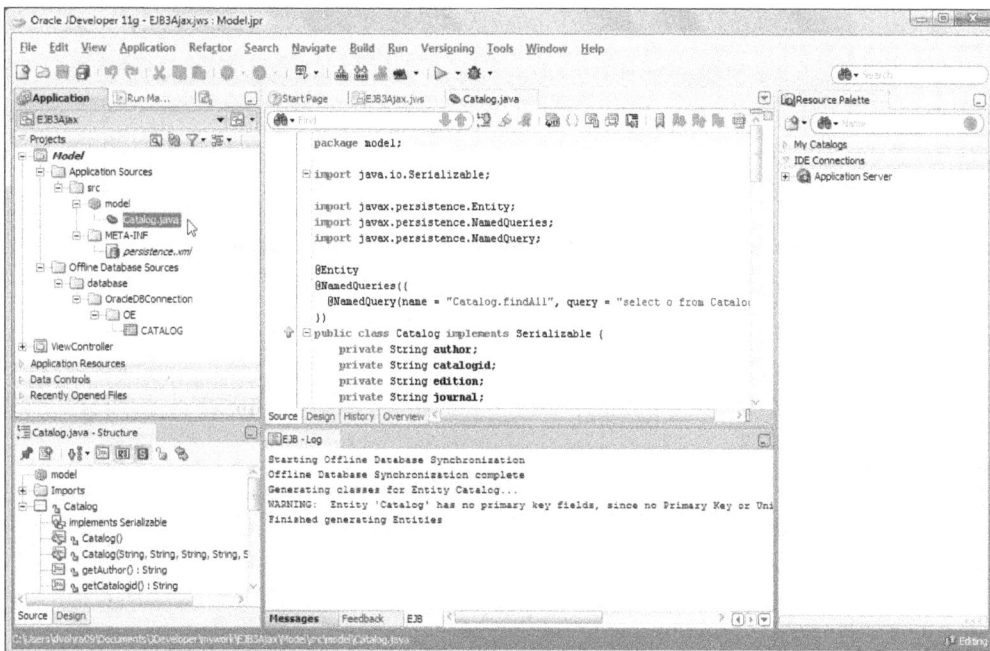

Right-click on the **Model** project and select the **Project Properties** for the **Model** project. In the **Project Properties** window, select **Libraries and Classpath**. The libraries in the EJB 3.0 project get displayed. The libraries include the **TopLink** library, as the entity bean uses the TopLink persistence provider.

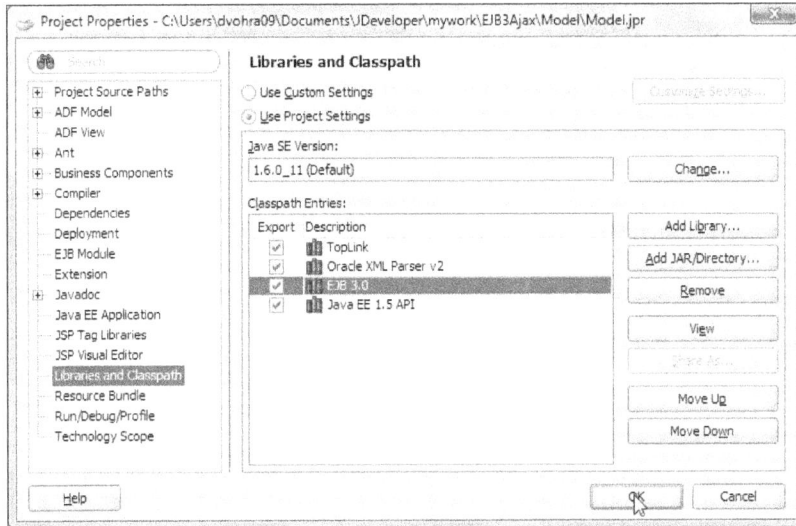

Select the **EJB Module** node. The **EJB Module** displays the default data source JNDI name, the **EJB Version**, the connection, and the annotated entity bean class. Click on **OK**:

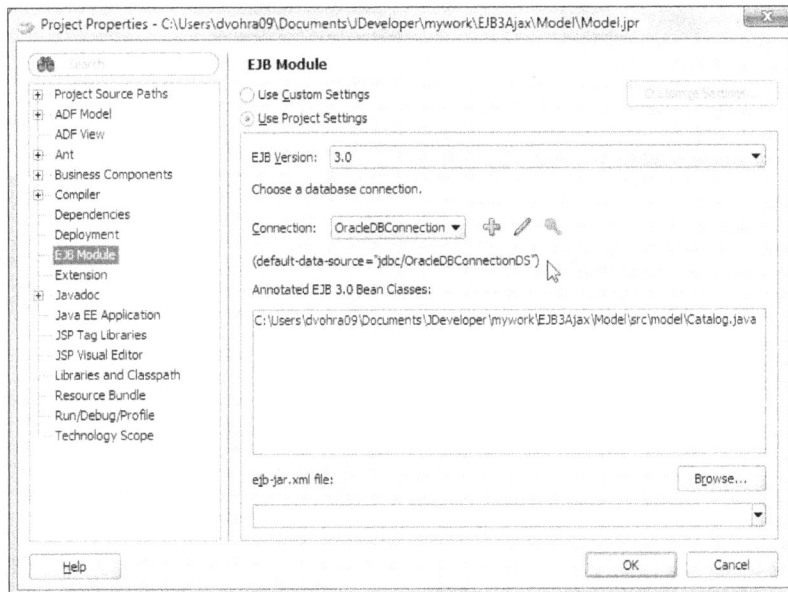

The entity bean class

An entity bean in EJB 3.0 is just a POJO (Plain Old Java Object) annotated with the `@Entity` annotation. Entity bean mappings to a relational database are defined using metadata annotations. Simply annotating a POJO class with the `@Entity` annotation makes it an entity bean. The `@Table` annotation is used to specify the database schema and table name to which the entity bean is mapped. If the `@Table` annotation is not specified, the entity bean class name is used for the default table name. The class declaration of the `Catalog` class consists of an `@Entity` annotation and an `@Table` annotation.

```
@Entity
@Table(name="Catalog")
public class Catalog implements Serializable {
...
}
```

If a cache-enabled entity bean is persisted to a database via an `EntityManager`, the entity bean is added to the cache. Similarly, if you update/remove a cache-enabled entity bean to a database via an entity manager, the entity bean is updated/removed from the cache. Therefore, an entity bean is recommended to implement the `java.io.Serializable` interface. We also need to specify the `serialVersionUID`, which is used by the serialization runtime to associate a version number with the serializable class. In the entity bean class, specify the POJO properties `catalogId`, `journal`, `publisher`, `edition`, `title`, and `author`. Add the getter and setter methods for the entity bean properties. Specify the identifier property, which is mapped to the primary key of a database table, with the `@Id` annotation. The `Catalog` class includes a constructor that creates a `Catalog` entity instance from the entity bean properties. The entity bean class `Catalog` is listed below.

```
package model;

import java.io.Serializable;
import javax.persistence.*;

@Entity
@Table(name = "Catalog")
public class Catalog implements Serializable {
    private static final long serialVersionUID = 7422574264557894633L;
    private String catalogId;
    private String journal;
    private String publisher;
    private String edition;
    private String title;
    private String author;
```

```java
public Catalog() {
      super();
}
public Catalog(String catalogId, String journal,
               String publisher, String edition,
               String title, String author) {
      super();
      this.catalogId = catalogId;
      this.journal = journal;
      this.publisher = publisher;
      this.edition = edition;
      this.title = title;
      this.author = author;
}
@Id
public String getCatalogId() {
      return catalogId;
}
public void setCatalogId(String catalogId) {
      this.catalogId = catalogId;
}
public String getJournal() {
      return journal;
}
public void setJournal(String journal) {
      this.journal = journal;
}
public String getPublisher() {
      return publisher;
}
public void setPublisher(String publisher) {
      this.publisher = publisher;
}
public String getEdition() {
      return edition;
}
public void setEdition(String edition) {
      this.edition = edition;
}
public String getTitle() {
      return title;
```

```
    }
    public void setTitle(String title) {
          this.title = title;
    }
    public String getAuthor() {
          return author;
    }
    public void setAuthor(String author) {
          this.author = author;
    }
}
```

The Entity configuration file

The `persistence.xml` configuration file specifies a persistence unit, including a `jta-data-source` for the entity bean. The entity bean is persisted to the database using the data source specified in the `persistence.xml` file. A persistence unit is associated with the `EntityManager` when an `EntityManager` is injected into a session bean, which we shall discuss in the next section. The `persistence.xml` file also specifies the JPA persistence provider as `EclipseLink`. Add a property for the target server with `WebLogic_10` as the target server. The `persistence.xml` configuration file is listed below:

```xml
<?xml version="1.0" encoding="Cp1252" ?>
<persistence xmlns:xsi="http://www.w3.org/2001/XMLSchema-instance"
    xsi:schemaLocation="http://java.sun.com/xml/ns/persistence http://
java.sun.com/xml/ns/persistence/persistence_1_0.xsd"
    xmlns="http://java.sun.com/xml/ns/persistence" version="1.0">
    <persistence-unit name="em">
          <provider>org.eclipse.persistence.jpa.PersistenceProvider</
provider>
          <jta-data-source>jdbc/OracleDBConnectionDS</jta-data-source>
          <class>model.Catalog</class>
          <properties>
                <property name="eclipselink.target-server"
value="WebLogic_10" />
                <property name="javax.persistence.jtaDataSource"
value="jdbc/OracleDBConnectionDS" />
          </properties>
    </persistence-unit>
</persistence>
```

Creating a session bean

As mentioned before, one of the best practices when developing entity beans is to wrap them in a session bean for a client. In this section we create a session bean, which will be a wrapper for the entity bean. Select the **Model** project and select **File>New**. In the **New Gallery** window, select **Business Tier>EJB** and select **Session Bean**. Click on **OK**. In the **Create Session Bean** window, specify an **EJB Name**. Select the default **EJB 3.0 Options**: **Session Type** as **Stateless** and **Transaction Type** as **Container**. The **Mapped Name** is used in the remote JNDI lookup of the session bean. Click on **Next**. In the **Session Façade** window, select the default JPA entity methods to expose. Click on **Next**. In **Class Definitions,** specify the **Bean Class** and click on **Next**. In **EJB Home and Component Interfaces** specify, which interfaces to implement and specify the interface names. Click on **Next**. The **Summary** page lists the session bean class and interfaces to be generated. Click on **Finish**. A session bean class and the remote and home interfaces get generated.

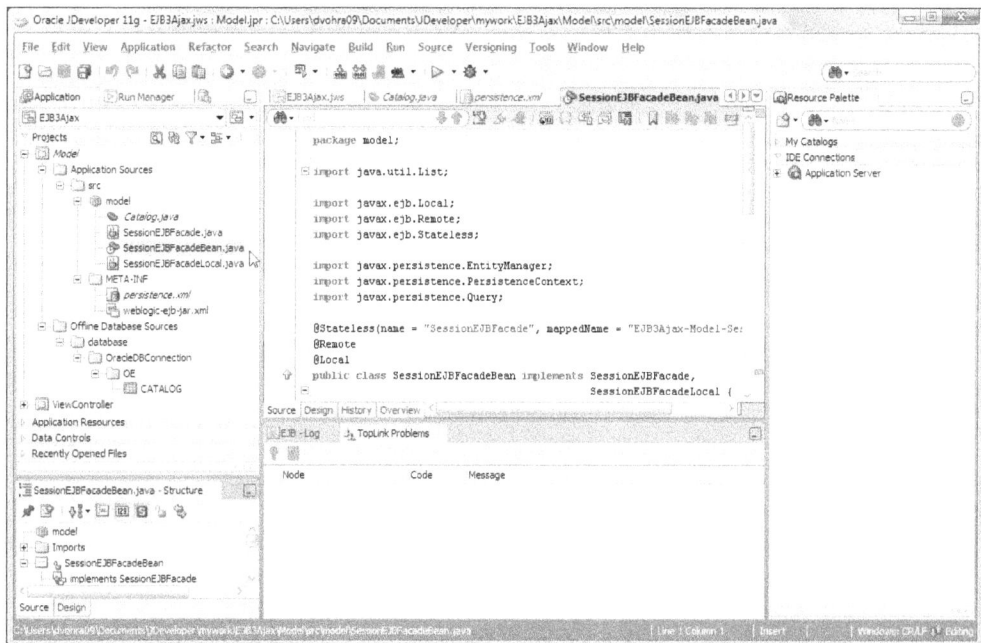

The session bean class

The session bean class is annotated with the @Stateless annotation and implements the component interfaces:

```
@Stateless(name = "SessionEJBFaçade", mappedName = "EJB3-SessionEJB")
public class SessionEJBFaçadeBean implements SessionEJBFaçade,SessionE
JBFaçadeLocal { }
```

Inject an EntityManager into the session bean using dependency injection with the @PersistenceContext annotation. An entity manager is used for persisting an entity bean to a database:

```
@PersistenceContext(unitName = "em")
private EntityManager em;
```

A session bean deployed to a JAR file and packaged with a WAR file in an EAR file has the default JNDI name of mappedName#remote_interface_name for the remote interface. For convenient access to the JNDI name from a client class, assign a public static final variable to the remote JNDI name:

```
public static final String RemoteJNDIName = "EJB3-SessionEJB#model.
SessionEJBFaçade";
```

The session bean is used to wrap the entity bean. In the Ajax application, we shall be validating an input form to create a catalog entry. In the input form, we shall specify a catalog id and the catalog id will be transferred to a servlet client via Ajax. The servlet will invoke a session bean method to validate the catalog id. A catalog id is valid if it is not already defined in the database and not valid if it is defined in the database. Add a method validate(String catalogId) that returns a Catalog object to the session bean. In the validate() method, create a Query object using a Java persistence query language statement, which includes a named parameter for catalogId:

```
Query query = em.createQuery("SELECT c from Catalog c where
c.catalogId=:catalogId");
```

Set the value of the named parameter using the setParameter() method:

```
query.setParameter("catalogId", catalogId);
```

Run the query statement using the getResultList() method:

```
List catalogEntry =query.getResultList();
```

Creating a query, setting the parameter/s, and running the query may be combined. If the catalog entry is empty, we don't need to iterate over the List returned:

```
if ((catalogEntry.isEmpty()) == true) {
            }
```

If the catalog entry is not empty, iterate over the list returned to retrieve the Catalog entity instance:

```
for (Iterator iter = catalogEntry.iterator(); iter.hasNext();) {
                    catalog = (Catalog) iter.next();
                }
```

If the catalog entry is null, return null, and if the catalog entry is not empty, return the Catalog entity instance returned. Add another method, persist(), to the session bean for storing a Catalog entity instance to the database. The persist() method specifies the Catalog entity bean properties as parameters. In the persist() method, create a Catalog entity instance from the entity bean properties and persist the entity instance to the database:

```
Catalog catalog = new Catalog(catalogId, journal,
                    publisher, edition, title, author);
        em.persist(catalog);
```

The SessionEJBFaçadeBean session bean class is listed below:

```
package model;

import java.util.Iterator;
import java.util.List;
import javax.ejb.Stateless;
import javax.persistence.EntityManager;
import javax.persistence.PersistenceContext;

@Stateless(name = "SessionEJBFaçade", mappedName = "EJB3-SessionEJB")
public class SessionEJBFaçadeBean implements SessionEJBFaçade,
        SessionEJBFaçadeLocal {
    @PersistenceContext(unitName = "em")
    private EntityManager em;
    public static final String RemoteJNDIName = "EJB3-
SessionEJB#model.SessionEJBFaçade";
    public Catalog validate(String catalogId) {


        Catalog catalog = null;
```

```
        List catalogEntry = em.createQuery("SELECT c from Catalog c
where c.catalogId=:catalogId")
                    .setParameter("catalogId", catalogId).
getResultList();

        if (!catalogEntry.isEmpty()) {

                for (Iterator iter = catalogEntry.iterator(); iter.
hasNext();) {

                    catalog = (Catalog) iter.next();

                }
        }
        return catalog;
    }
    public void persist(String catalogId, String journal, String
publisher,
                String edition, String title, String author) {
        Catalog catalog = new Catalog(catalogId, journal,
                    publisher, edition, title, author);
        em.persist(catalog);

    }

}
```

In the remote business interface, specify the method signatures of the methods defined in the session bean. The remote component interface is listed below:

```
package model;
import javax.ejb.Remote;

@Remote
public interface SessionEJBFaçade {
    Catalog validate(String catalogId);
    void persist(String catalogId, String journal, String
publisher,String edition, String title, String author);
}
```

Creating a servlet client

Next, we create a servlet client that is invoked from the input form using an Ajax request. The servlet does not differentiate between an Ajax request and a regular HTTP request. It is the Java Script in the browser that implements the Ajax. The servlet is the client to the session bean and invokes session bean methods to validate a catalog id specified in the input form, and persist a `Catalog` entity instance constructed from the input form field values if a catalog id is valid.

To create a Servlet class, select the **ViewController** project in the **Application** navigator and select **File | New** and **Web Tier | Servlets** in **New Gallery**. Select **HTTP Servlet** in **Items** and click on **OK**.

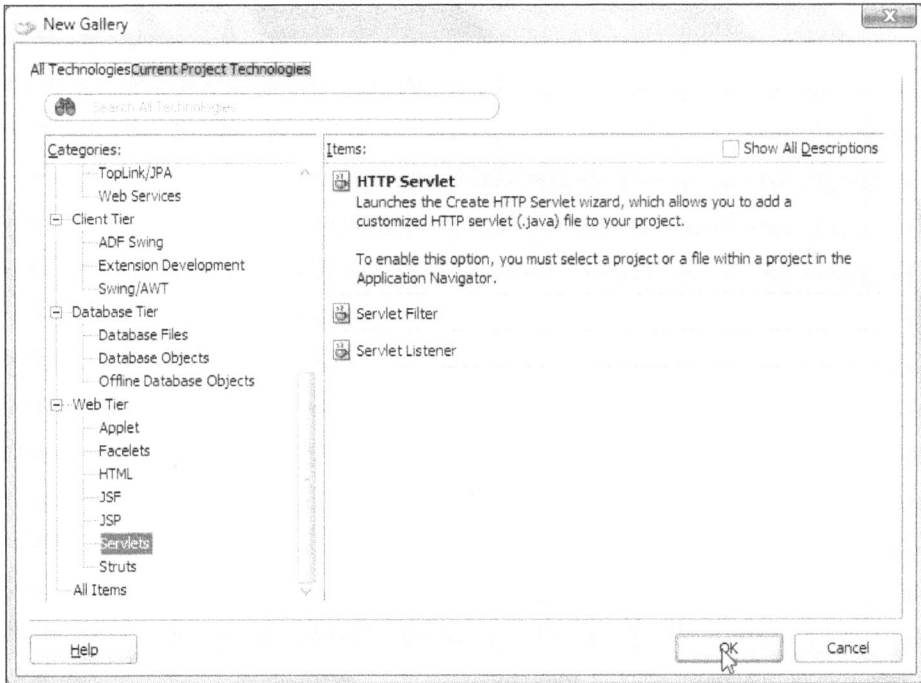

In the **Create HTTP Servlet** window, click on **Next**. Select **Web Application Version: Java EE 1.5** and click on **Next**.

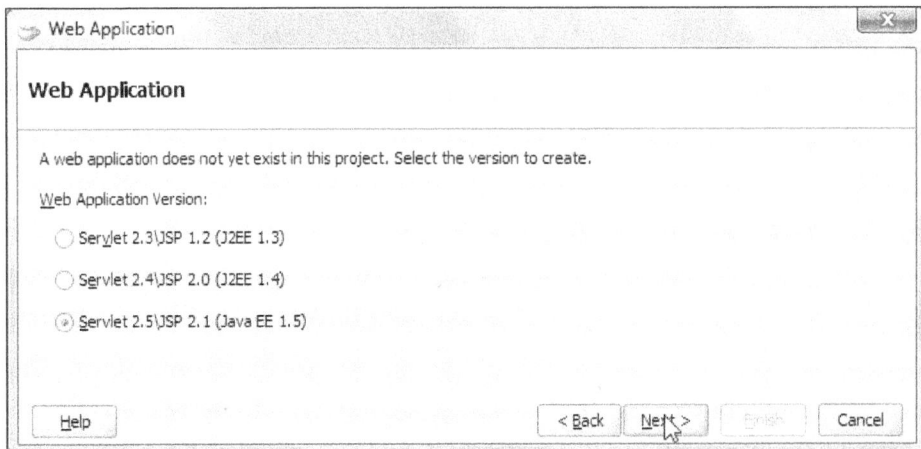

Specify **Servlet Class** as **EJB3ClientServlet**, **Package** as **model**, and **Content Type** as **HTML**. Click on **Next**.

Specify the servlet mapping **URL Pattern** and click on **Next**.

In the **Servlet Parameters** window, servlet parameters may be specified. Click on **Finish**. We shall be packaging the servlet class in a **WAR** file along with the JSP UIs for the Ajax. In the `web.xml`, the `EJB3ClientServlet` and the url pattern to invoke the servlet get specified. The `web.xml` is listed below:

```xml
<?xml version = '1.0' encoding = 'windows-1252'?>
<web-app xmlns:xsi="http://www.w3.org/2001/XMLSchema-instance"
    xsi:schemaLocation="http://java.sun.com/xml/ns/javaee http://java.
sun.com/xml/ns/javaee/web-app_2_5.xsd"
    version="2.5" xmlns="http://java.sun.com/xml/ns/javaee">
    <servlet>
            <servlet-name>EJB3ClientServlet</servlet-name>
            <servlet-class>view.EJB3ClientServlet</servlet-class>
            <load-on-startup>1</load-on-startup>
    </servlet>
    <servlet-mapping>
            <servlet-name>EJB3ClientServlet</servlet-name>
            <url-pattern>/ejb3clientservlet</url-pattern>
    </servlet-mapping>
</web-app>
```

The Servlet class

The Ajax request is sent from the input form to the `doGet()` method of the servlet. In the `doGet()` method, create an `InitialContext` object:

```java
InitialContext context = new InitialContext();
```

Lookup the remote business interface using the remote JNDI name:

```java
SessionEJBFaçade beanRemote = (SessionEJBFaçade) context.
lookup(SessionEJBFaçadeBean.RemoteJNDIName);
```

Retrieve the catalog id input field value and invoke the `validate()` method of the session bean:

```java
String catalogId =request.getParameter("catalogId");
Catalog catalog = beanRemote.validate(catalogId);
```

The servlet sends a response to the browser as an XML string; therefore, set the content type of the `HttpServletResponse` to `text/xml`, and the `cache-control` header to `no-cache`:

```java
response.setContentType("text/xml");
response.setHeader("Cache-Control", "no-cache");
```

Create a `PrintWriter` from the `response` object:

```
PrintWriter out = response.getWriter();
```

Create the response to be sent to the browser. If the `validate()` method returns
a `Catalog` entity instance, the catalog id is not valid, as a `Catalog` entity instance
for the catalog id is already defined. Create an XML string that has root element
`Catalog` and a sub-element `valid` with value set to `false`, and sub-elements
`journal`, `publisher`, `edition`, `title` and `author` with values set to the properties
of the `Catalog` entity instance. If the `validate()` method returns `null`, the catalog is
valid, as a new `Catalog` entity instance for the catalog id is not defined. Construct an
XML string that has root element `valid` with value set to `true`.

```
if (catalog != null) {
    out.println("<catalog>" + "<valid>false</valid>"+"<journal>" +
    catalog.getJournal() + "</journal>" + "<publisher>" +
    catalog.getPublisher() + "</publisher>" + "<edition>" +
    catalog.getEdition() + "</edition>" + "<title>" +
    catalog.getTitle() + "</title>" + "<author>" +
    catalog.getAuthor() + "</author>" + "</catalog>");
} else {
    out.println("<valid>true</valid>");
}
```

The `doPost()` method of the servlet is invoked when the input form is submitted
for a valid catalog id. In the `doPost()` method, create an `InitialContext` object.
Lookup the remote interface of the session bean using the remote JNDI name.
Retrieve the input form field values and invoke the `persist()` method of the session
bean to persist a new `Catalog` entity instance. The `doPost()` method is not invoked
with an Ajax request; therefore, the method does not return a response, but redirects
to a JSP that displays a message that the database has been updated with a new
catalog entry.

```
beanRemote.persist(catalogId, journal, publisher, edition, title,
                   author);
response.sendRedirect("catalog.jsp");
```

If an error is generated in updating the database, redirect the response to an error JSP
`error.jsp`. The `EJB3ClientServlet` class is listed below:

```
package view;
import model.*;
import java.io.*;
import javax.naming.*;
import javax.servlet.*;
import javax.servlet.http.*;
public class EJB3ClientServlet extends HttpServlet {
```

```
public void doGet(HttpServletRequest request,
                  HttpServletResponse response)
throws ServletException, IOException {
  try {
    // Obtain value of Catalog Id field to ve validated.
    String catalogId = request.getParameter("catalogId");
    InitialContext context = new InitialContext();
    SessionEJBFaçade beanRemote = (SessionEJBFaçade) context.
                        lookup(SessionEJBFaçadeBean.RemoteJNDIName);
    Catalog catalog = beanRemote.validate(catalogId);
    // set headers before accessing the Writer
    response.setContentType("text/xml");
    response.setHeader("Cache-Control", "no-cache");
    PrintWriter out = response.getWriter();
    // then write the response
    // If Catalog is null set valid element to true
    if (catalog != null) {
      out.println("<catalog>" + "<valid>false</valid>" +
      "<journal>" + catalog.getJournal() + "</journal>" +
      "<publisher>" + catalog.getPublisher() + "</publisher>" +
      "<edition>" + catalog.getEdition() + "</edition>" +
      "<title>" + catalog.getTitle() + "</title>" + "<author>" +
      catalog.getAuthor() + "</author>" + "</catalog>");
    } else {
      out.println("<valid>true</valid>");
    }
  } catch (javax.naming.NamingException e) {
    System.err.println(e.getMessage());
  }
}
public void doPost(HttpServletRequest request,
                   HttpServletResponse response)
throws ServletException, IOException {
  try {
    // Obtain Connection
    InitialContext context = new InitialContext();
    SessionEJBFaçade beanRemote = (SessionEJBFaçade) context.
                        lookup(SessionEJBFaçadeBean.RemoteJNDIName);
    String catalogId = request.getParameter("catalogId");
    String journal = request.getParameter("journal");
    String publisher = request.getParameter("publisher");
    String edition = request.getParameter("edition");
    String title = request.getParameter("title");
    String author = request.getParameter("author");
    beanRemote.persist(catalogId, journal, publisher, edition,
                       title,author);
    response.sendRedirect("catalog.jsp");
  } catch (javax.naming.NamingException e) {
```

```
            response.sendRedirect("error.jsp");
        }
    }
}
```

The `EJB3ClientServlet.java` servlet class is in the `ViewController` project and the EJB 3.0 classes are in the `Model` project. The servlet class has a dependency on the EJB 3.0 classes. Therefore, we need to add a dependency from the `ViewController` project on the `Model` project. Right-click on the **ViewController** project and select **Project Properties**. In the **Project Properties** window, select **Dependencies** and select **Edit Dependencies** to add a dependency on the **Model** project. In the **Edit Dependencies** window, select the **Model** project and select the checkbox **Build Output**. Click on **OK**. A dependency on the **Model** project gets added to the **ViewController** project. Click on **OK** in **Project Properties**.

Creating an Ajax user interface

In this section, we create an input form that initiates an Ajax request to the WebLogic server. The input form is a JSP, which we shall create next. Select **File>New** and in the **New Gallery** window, select **Web Tier | JSP** in **Categories** and **JSP** in **Items**, and click on **OK**. In the **Create JSP** window, specify the **File Name** as **input.jsp**. Click on **OK**. The JSP **input.jsp** gets created. Similarly, add JSPs **catalog.jsp** for redirecting to if a new catalog entry gets created and an **error.jsp** JSP for redirecting to if a catalog entry does not get created.

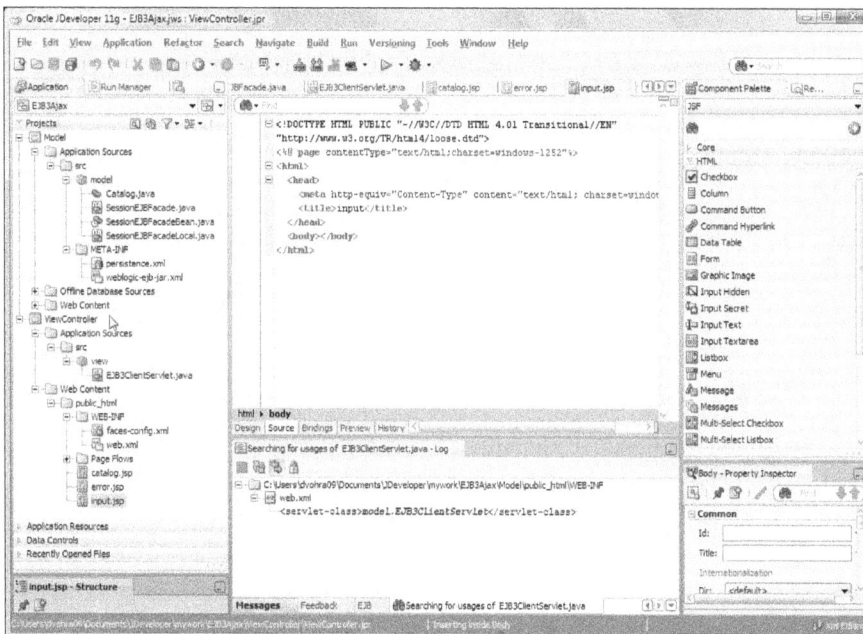

The input form requires a unique catalog id to be specified to create a new catalog entry. The input catalog id in the form is validated against the database content to see if it is already specified.

Sending an Ajax request

The catalog id data added to the HTML form is sent to the server as the catalog id is added (not when the form is completed) and an HTTP servlet returns an XML response that contains information about the validity of the catalog id. In the `input.jsp`, the `XMLHttpRequest` response from the server is processed and if the instructions indicate that the catalog id is valid, a message "Catalog Id is Valid" is displayed. An `XMLHttpRequest` is sent to the server and a response received with each modification in the input field.

The procedure to send an `XMLHttpRequest` request and process the XML response is as follows:

1. Invoke a JavaScript function from an HTML event such as onkeyup.

2. Create an `XMLHttpRequest` object in the JavaScript function.

3. Open an `XMLHttpRequest` request, which specifies the servlet URL, the HTTP method, and whether the request is asynchronous.

4. Register a callback event handler that gets invoked when the request is complete.

5. Send an `XMLHttpRequest` request asynchronously.

6. Retrieve the XML response and modify the HTML page.

To initiate an `XMLHttpRequest`, register a JavaScript function, `validateCatalogId()`, with an event, `onkeyup` event for example, generated from the HTML form's input field `CatalogId`, which is required to be validated:

```
<form name="validationForm" action="ejb3clientservlet" method="post">
  <table>
    <tr>
      <td>Catalog Id:</td>
      <td><input type="text" size="20" id="catalogId"
          name="catalogId" onkeyup=validateCatalogId();></td>
      <td>
        <div id="validationMessage"></div>
      </td>
    </tr>…..
  </table>
</form>
```

In the JavaScript function `validateCatalogId()`, create a new `XMLHttpRequest` object. If a browser supports the `XMLHttpRequest` object as an ActiveX object (as in IE 6), the procedure to create an `XMLHttpRequest` object is different than when the `XMLHttpRequest` object is a window object property (as in IE 7 and Netscape).

```
<script type="text/javascript">
  function validateCatalogId(){
    var xmlHttpRequest=init();
    function init(){
      if (window.XMLHttpRequest) {
        return new XMLHttpRequest();
      } else if (window.ActiveXObject) {
        return new ActiveXObject("Microsoft.XMLHTTP");
      }
    }
  }
</script>
```

Next, we need to construct the URL to which the `XMLHttpRequest` will be sent. As we shall invoke a servlet, `EJB3ClientServlet`, which is mapped to servlet URL `validateForm` as specified in `web.xml`, specify the URL as `ejb3clientservlet?catalogId=encodeURIComponent(catalogId.value)`. The parameter `catalogId` specifies the value of `CatalogId` input in the HTML form. The `encodeURIComponent(string)` method is used to encode the `CatalogId` value. The HTTP method specified is `GET`, which invokes the `doGet()` method of the servlet. Next, open the `XMLHttpRequest` object using the `open()` method in which specify the HTTP method as `GET`, the URL that we constructed, and the `asysnchronous` boolean as `true`:

```
var catalogId = document.getElementById("catalogId");
    xmlHttpRequest.open(«GET»,»ejb3clientservlet?catalogId=»+
encodeURIComponent(catalogId.value), true);
```

We need to register a callback event handler with the `XMLHttpRequest` object using the `onreadystatechange` property. The callback method is the JavaScript function `processRequest`:

```
xmlHttpRequest.onreadystatechange=processRequest;
```

We need to send an HTTP request using the `send()` method. As the HTTP method is `GET`, data sent with the `send()` method is set to `null`:

```
xmlHttpRequest.send(null);
```

As the callback event handler is `processRequest`, the `processRequest()` function gets invoked when the value of the `readyState` property changes. In the `processRequest()` function, the `readyState` property value is retrieved. If the request has loaded completely, corresponding to `readyState` value 4, and HTTP status is "OK", we invoke a JavaScript function to process the response from the server:

```
function processRequest(){
if(xmlHttpRequest.readyState==4){
   if(xmlHttpRequest.status==200){
      processResponse();
    }
  }
}
```

Processing the server response

In the `processRequest()` JavaScript function, if the HTTP request has loaded completely, which corresponds to `readyState` property value 4, and the HTTP status is "OK", which corresponds to `status` property value 200, the `processResponse()` JavaScript function gets invoked. In the `processResponse()` function, obtain the value of the `responseXML` property. This contains the XML string that was set in the `doGet()` method of `EJB3ClientServlet`.

```
var xmlMessage=xmlHttpRequest.responseXML;
```

The `responseXML` property contains instructions in XML form about the validity of the `CatalogId` value specified in the input form. Obtain the value of the `<valid/>` element using the `getElementsByTagName(string)` method:

```
var valid=xmlMessage.getElementsByTagName("valid")[0].firstChild.
nodeValue;
```

If the `<valid/>` element is set to `true`, set the HTML `validationMessage` div to "Catalog Id is Valid", and enable the **Submit** button in the input form, as shown below:

```
if(valid=="true"){
  var validationMessage=document.getElementById("validationMessage");
  validationMessage.innerHTML = "Catalog Id is Valid";
  document.getElementById("submitForm").disabled = false;
}
```

Also, set the values of all the fields to an empty string. For example, the `journal` field value is set as follows:

```
var journalElement = document.getElementById("journal");
journalElement.value = «»;
```

If the `<valid/>` element value is set to `false`, set the HTML of the `validationMessage` div in the `CatalogID` field row to `"Catalog Id is not Valid"`, and disable the **Submit** button. Set the values of the other input fields as shown for the `journal` field below. Setting the values of the other fields corresponding to a `CatalogId` is an example of auto-completion with AJAX.

```
if(valid=="false"){
var validationMessage=document.getElementById("validationMessage");
validationMessage.innerHTML = "Catalog Id is not Valid";
document.getElementById("submitForm").disabled = true;
var journal=xmlMessage.getElementsByTagName("journal")[0].firstChild.
nodeValue;
var journalElement=document.getElementById("journal");
journalElement.value = journal;
}
```

The Ajax user interface JSP

The Ajax user interface `input.jsp` is listed next:

```
<%@ page language="java" contentType="text/html; charset=ISO-8859-1"
    pageEncoding="ISO-8859-1"%>
<!DOCTYPE html PUBLIC "-//W3C//DTD HTML 4.01 Transitional//EN"
                    "http://www.w3.org/TR/html4/loose.dtd">
<html>
  <head>
    <script type="text/javascript">
      function validateCatalogId() {
        var xmlHttpRequest = init();
        function init() {
          if (window.XMLHttpRequest) {
            return new XMLHttpRequest();
          } else if (window.ActiveXObject) {
            return new ActiveXObject("Microsoft.XMLHTTP");
          }
        }
        var catalogId = document.getElementById("catalogId");
        xmlHttpRequest.open("GET", "ejb3clientservlet?catalogId="
                            + encodeURIComponent(catalogId.value), true);
```

```
xmlHttpRequest.onreadystatechange = processRequest;
xmlHttpRequest.send(null);

function processRequest() {
  if (xmlHttpRequest.readyState == 4) {
    if (xmlHttpRequest.status == 200) {
      processResponse();
    }
  }
}
function processResponse() {
  var xmlMessage = xmlHttpRequest.responseXML;
  var valid = xmlMessage.getElementsByTagName("valid")[0].
                                  firstChild.nodeValue;

  if (valid == "true") {
    var validationMessage =
                document.getElementById("validationMessage");
    validationMessage.innerHTML = "Catalog Id is Valid";
    document.getElementById("submitForm").disabled = false;
    var journalElement = document.getElementById("journal");
    journalElement.value = "";
    var publisherElement = document.
                                getElementById("publisher");
    publisherElement.value = "";
    var editionElement = document.getElementById("edition");
    editionElement.value = "";
    var titleElement = document.getElementById("title");
    titleElement.value = "";
    var authorElement = document.getElementById("author");
    authorElement.value = "";
  }
  if (valid == "false") {
    var validationMessage =
                document.getElementById("validationMessage");
    validationMessage.innerHTML = "Catalog Id is not Valid";
    document.getElementById("submitForm").disabled = true;
```

```
        var journal = xmlMessage.
          getElementsByTagName("journal")[0].firstChild.nodeValue;
        var publisher = xmlMessage.getElementsByTagName(
                          "publisher")[0].firstChild.nodeValue;
        var edition = xmlMessage.getElementsByTagName(
                          "edition")[0].firstChild.nodeValue;
        var title = xmlMessage.getElementsByTagName(
                          "title")[0].firstChild.nodeValue;
        var author = xmlMessage.getElementsByTagName(
                          "author")[0].firstChild.nodeValue;

        var journalElement = document.getElementById("journal");
        journalElement.value = journal;
        var publisherElement = document.
                              getElementById("publisher");
        publisherElement.value = publisher;
        var editionElement = document.getElementById("edition");
        editionElement.value = edition;
        var titleElement = document.getElementById("title");
        titleElement.value = title;
        var authorElement = document.getElementById("author");
        authorElement.value = author;
      }
    }
  }
  </script>
</head>
<body>
  <h1>Form for Catalog Entry</h1>
  <form name="validationForm"
        action="ejb3clientservlet" method="post">
    <table>
      <tr>
        <td>Catalog Id:</td>
        <td><input type="text" size="20" id="catalogId"
                name="catalogId" onkeyup=validateCatalogId();>
        </td>
        <td>
          <div id="validationMessage"></div>
        </td>
      </tr>
      <tr>
        <td>Journal:</td>
        <td><input type="text" size="20" id="journal"
                name="journal"></td>
      </tr>
```

```
          <tr>
            <td>Publisher:</td>
            <td><input type="text" size="20" id="publisher"
                  name="publisher"></td>
          </tr>
          <tr>
            <td>Edition:</td>
            <td><input type="text" size="20" id="edition"
                      name="edition"></td>
          </tr>
          <tr>
            <td>Title:</td>
            <td><input type="text" size="20" id="title" name="title">
            </td>
          </tr>
          <tr>
            <td>Author:</td>
            <td><input type="text" size="20" id="author"
                      name="author"></td>
          </tr>
          <tr>
            <td><input type="submit" value="Create Catalog"
                      id="submitForm" name="submitForm"></td>
          </tr>
        </table>
      </form>
    </body>
  </html>
```

The `catalog.jsp`, which gets redirected to if a catalog entry gets created, is listed below:

```
<%@ page language="java" contentType="text/html; charset=ISO-8859-1"
    pageEncoding="ISO-8859-1"%>
<!DOCTYPE html PUBLIC "-//W3C//DTD HTML 4.01 Transitional//EN"
                      "http://www.w3.org/TR/html4/loose.dtd">
<html>
  <head>
  </head>
  <body>
    <%
      out.println("Database Updated");
    %>
  </body>
</html>
```

The `error.jsp`, which gets redirected to if an error is generated in creating a catalog entry, is listed below:

```
<%@ page language="java" contentType="text/html; charset=ISO-8859-1"
```

```
        pageEncoding="ISO-8859-1"%>
<!DOCTYPE html PUBLIC "-//W3C//DTD HTML 4.01 Transitional//EN"
                    "http://www.w3.org/TR/html4/loose.dtd">
<html>
  <head>
  </head>
  <body>
    <%
      out.println("Error in updating Database");
    %>
  </body>
</html>
```

Creating an application deployment descriptor

We also need to create an `application.xml` in the `META-INF` directory for the `EAR` application. Create the `application.xml` in the `META-INF` directory of the `Model` project and when we build the project in the next section we shall create a `META-INF` for the `EAR` file and copy the `application.xml` from the `META-INF` of the `Model` project to the `META-INF` of the `EAR` file. Select the **META-INF** directory node of the **Model** project in the **Application** navigator and select **File | New**. In the **New Gallery** window, select **General | Deployment Descriptors** in **Categories** and select **Java EE Deployment Descriptor** in **Items**. Click on **OK**.

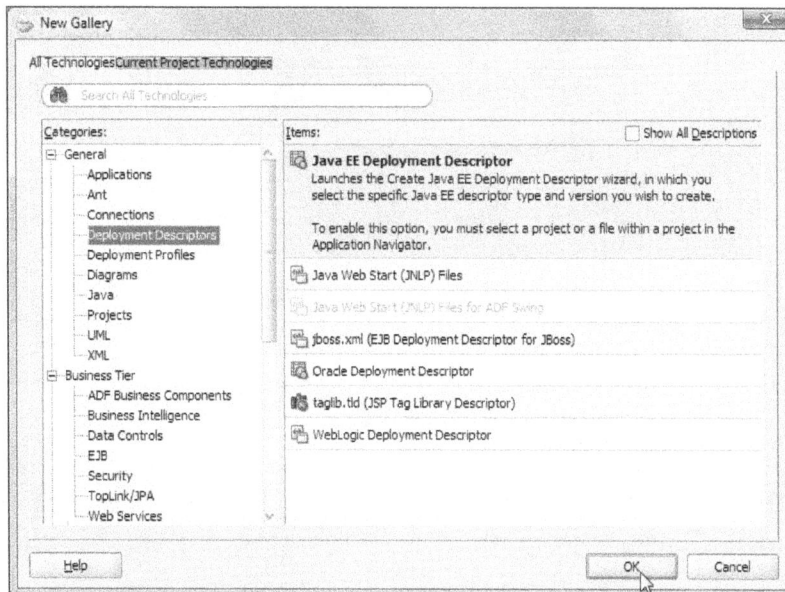

In the **Create Java EE Deployment Descriptor** window, select **application.xml** and click on **Next**:

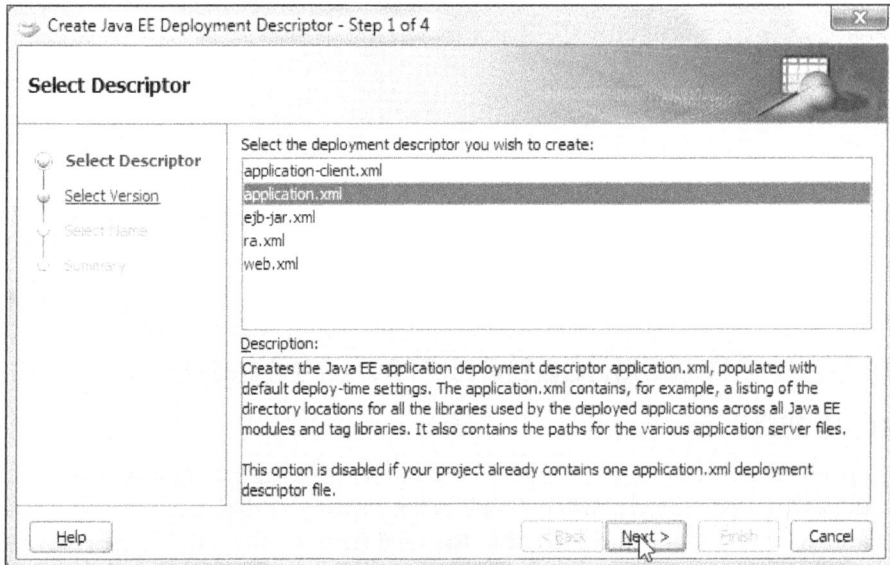

In the **Select Version** window, select **5.0** and click on **Next**:

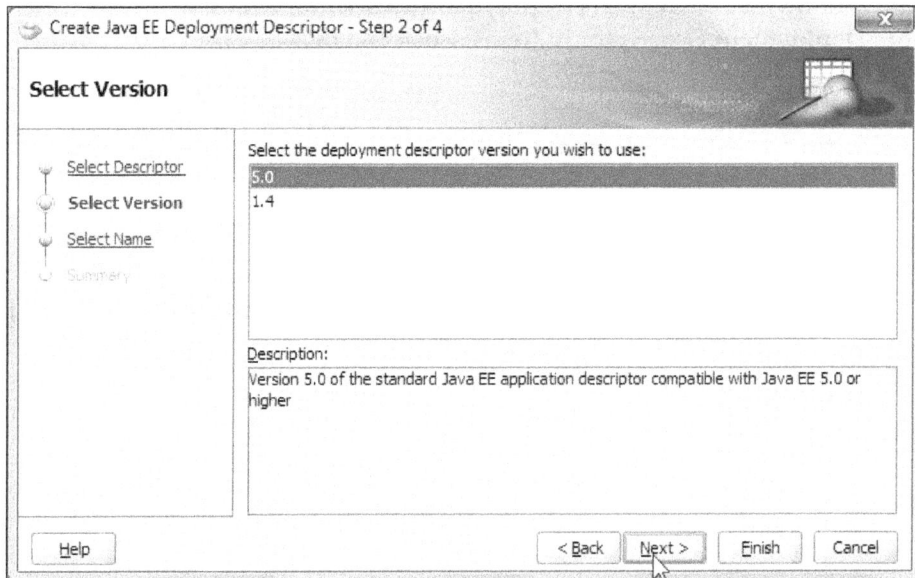

Click on **Finish**. An `application.xml` gets added to the `META-INF` directory of the `Model` project. In the `application.xml`, define an EJB module for the EJB `JAR` file and a web module for the client `WAR` file. The `application.xml` is listed next:

```
<?xml version = '1.0' encoding = 'windows-1252'?>
<application xmlns:xsi="http://www.w3.org/2001/XMLSchema-instance"
    xsi:schemaLocation="http://java.sun.com/xml/ns/javaee http://java.
sun.com/xml/ns/javaee/application_5.xsd"
    version="5" xmlns="http://java.sun.com/xml/ns/javaee">
    <display-name></display-name>
    <module>
        <ejb>ejb3.jar</ejb>
    </module>
    <module>
        <web>
                <web-uri>weblogic.war</web-uri>
                <context-root>weblogic</context-root>
        </web>
    </module>
</application>
```

Deploying the EJB 3 application to WebLogic Server

In this section we shall compile the EJB and Servlet classes, package the EJB classes in a JAR file, package the servlet class and the JSPs in a WAR file, and package the JAR and WAR files in an EAR file. We shall be using an Apache Ant `build.xml` script to compile and package the EJB 3.0 Ajax application.

Creating a build file

Create a `build.xml` in the `Model` project by selecting the **Model** project node in the
Application navigator and selecting **File | New**. In the **New Gallery** window, select
General | Ant in **Categories** and **Empty Buildfile** in **Items**. Click on **OK**:

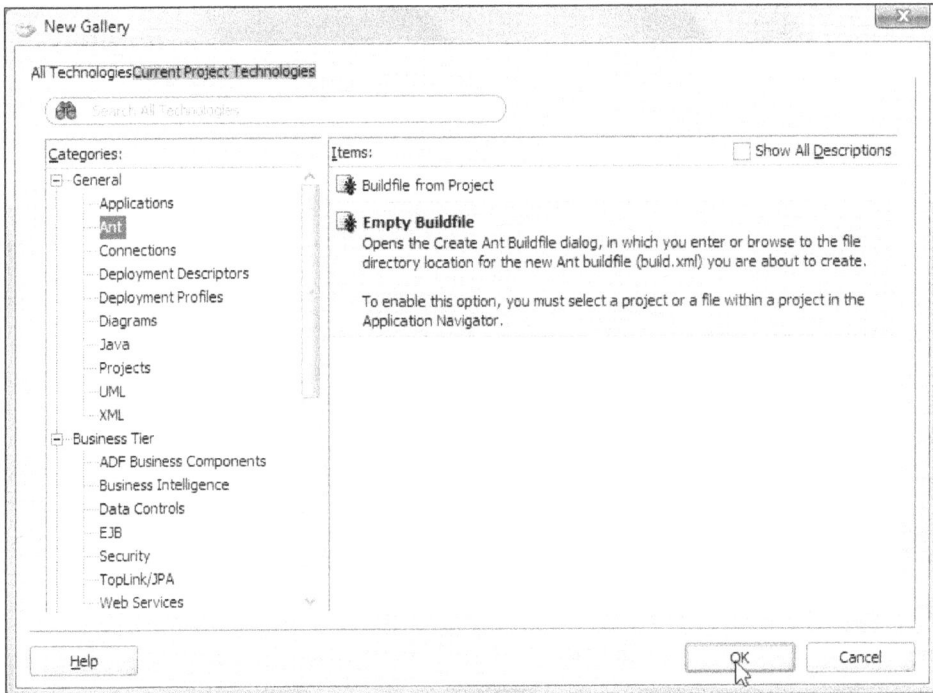

In the **Create Ant Buildfile** window, specify the **File Name** as **build.xml** and click
on **OK**:

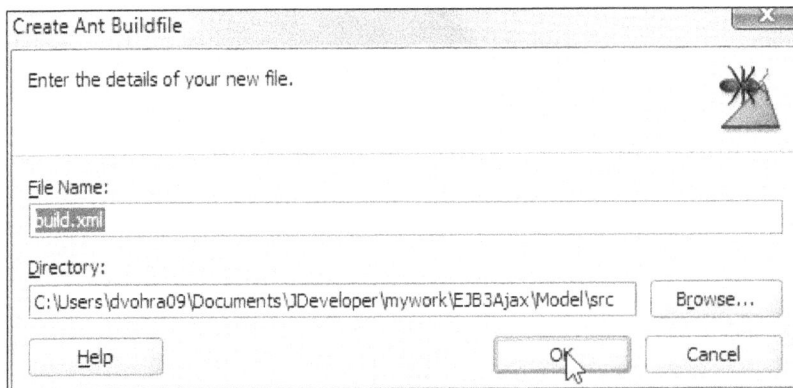

In the `build.xml`, specify properties for the different directory paths used for compiling and deploying the EJB 3.0 classes, the client servlet, and the JSPs. Specify a `path` element for the different JAR files in the classpath. Specify the `targets` listed in the following table:

Target	Description
prepare	Create the build directories.
compile	Compile the EJB 3.0 classes.
compileServlet	Compile the servlet class.
jar	Create a JAR file from the EJB 3.0 classes.
war	Create a WAR file from the servlet class and the JSPs.
assemble-app	Assemble the JAR and WAR files to an EAR file.
deploy	Deploy the EAR file to the WebLogic server autodeploy directory. In development mode, all the applications in the autodeploy directory get deployed to WebLogic server.
clean	Delete the JAR, WAR and EAR files if recompilation is required.

The `build.xml` file is listed below:

```xml
<?xml version="1.0" encoding="UTF-8"?>
    <!--
            WebLogic build file
    -->
<project name="EJB3Ajax" default="deploy" basedir="../..">
    <property name="src.dir" value="${basedir}/Model/src" />
    <property name="weblogic.home" value="C:/Oracle/Middleware/wls" />
    <property name="weblogic.server" value="${weblogic.home}/
wlserver_10.3/server" />
    <property name="web.module" value="${basedir}/ViewController" />
    <property name="build.dir" value="${basedir}/build" />
    <property name="build.classes.dir" value="${build.dir}/classes" />
    <property name="deploy.dir"
            value="${weblogic.home}/user_projects/domains/base_domain/
autodeploy" />
    <path id="classpath">
            <fileset dir="${weblogic.home}/modules">
                    <include name="*.jar" />
            </fileset>
            <fileset dir="${weblogic.server}/lib">
                    <include name="*.jar" />
            </fileset>
            <pathelement location="${build.classes.dir}" />
    </path>
    <property name="build.classpath" refid="classpath" />
    <target name="prepare">
```

```
                    <mkdir dir="${build.dir}" />
                    <mkdir dir="${build.dir}/META-INF" />
                    <mkdir dir="${build.classes.dir}" />
        </target>
        <target name="compile" depends="prepare">
                    <javac srcdir="${src.dir}/model" destdir="${build.classes.
dir}"
                            debug="on" includes="**">
                            <classpath refid="classpath" />
                    </javac>
        </target>
        <target name="compileServlet" depends="compile">
                    <javac srcdir="${web.module}/src/view" destdir="${build.
                                    classes.dir}" debug="on" includes="**">
                            <classpath refid="classpath" />
                    </javac>
        </target>
        <target name="jar" depends="compileServlet">
                    <jar destfile="${build.dir}/ejb3.jar">
                            <fileset dir="${build.classes.dir}">
                                    <include name="**/*.class" />
                                    <exclude name="**/EJB3ClientServlet.class" />
                            </fileset>
                            <fileset dir="${src.dir}/">
                                    <include name="META-INF/persistence.xml" />
                            </fileset>
                    </jar>
        </target>
        <target name="war" depends="jar">
                    <copy todir="${web.module}/public_html/WEB-INF/classes">
                            <fileset dir="${build.classes.dir}">
                                    <include name="view/EJB3ClientServlet.class"
                                    />
                            </fileset>
                    </copy>
                    <war destfile="${build.dir}/weblogic.war" webxml="${web.
                                    module}/public_html/WEB-INF/web.xml">
                            <fileset dir="${web.module}/public_html">
                                    <include name="*.jsp" />
                            </fileset>
                            <fileset dir="${web.module}/public_html">
                                    <include name="WEB-INF/classes/view/
                                            EJB3ClientServlet.class" />
                            </fileset>
                    </war>
        </target>
        <target name="assemble-app" depends="war">
                    <copy todir="${build.dir}/META-INF">
                            <fileset dir="${src.dir}/META-INF">
```

```
                    <include name="application.xml" />
            </fileset>
        </copy>
        <jar destfile="${build.dir}/ejb3.ear">
                <metainf dir="${build.dir}/META-INF">
                        <include name="application.xml" />
                </metainf>
                <fileset dir="${build.dir}" includes="*.jar,*.war" />
        </jar>
    </target>
    <target name="deploy" " depends="assemble-app">
            <copy file="${build.dir}/ejb3.ear" todir="${deploy.dir}" />
    </target>
    <target name="clean">
            <delete file="${build.dir}/ejb3.ear" />
            <delete file="${build.dir}/ejb3.jar" />
            <delete file="${build.dir}/weblogic.war" />
    </target>
</project>
```

The directory structure of the EJB 3.0 application, including the `build.xml` file, is shown below:

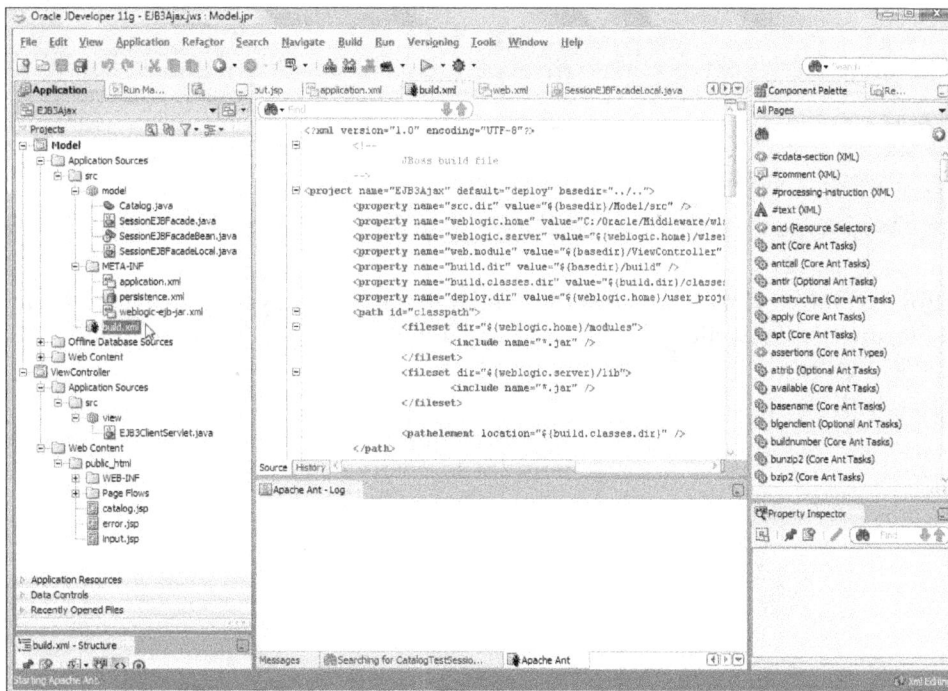

Deploying the EJB 3.0 application

Start the WebLogic server before deploying the EAR application to the WebLogic server. To compile and deploy the EJB 3.0 Ajax application, right-click on the `build.xml` and select **Run Ant Target | deploy**. As the `target`s have dependencies on the preceding `target`s, all the targets except the `clean target` get run in the sequence defined in the table.

The EJB 3.0 and servlet classes get compiled, the application gets packaged into an EAR file, and the EAR file gets deployed to WebLogic server, as shown in the `build.xml` output.

In the WebLogic server Administration Console, the EJB 3.0 EAR application is shown as deployed to the server:

Testing the Ajax input form

Next, we shall test the input form, which sends Ajax requests to the WebLogic server. Display the form with the URL `http://localhost:7001/weblogic/input.jsp`. URL pattern `weblogic` is included in the URL, as the context root of the WAR file is specified as `weblogic` in the `application.xml` file:

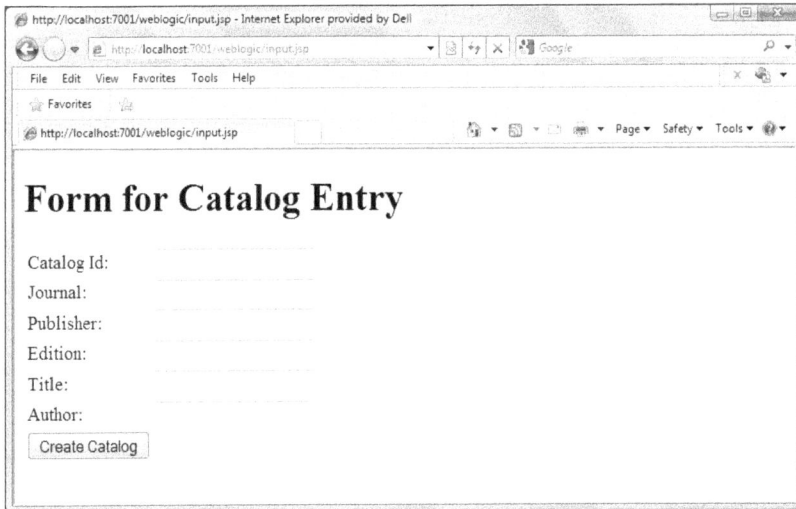

Start to specify a catalog id value. An Ajax request is sent to the server and a validation message "Catalog Id is Valid" gets displayed. For the validity of a catalog id, we have used just the business logic that a catalog id is not specified in the database, but other business logic may be added, such as regular expression matching.

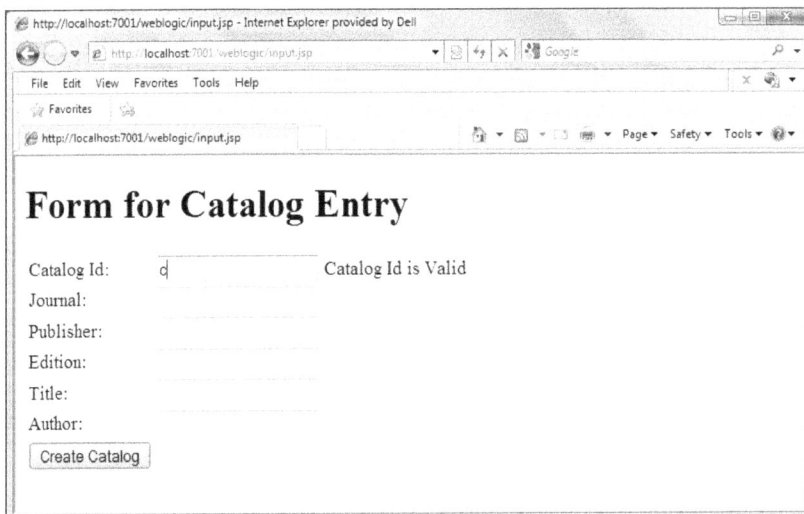

An Ajax request is sent with each modification to the input field and a server response returned to indicate the validity of the catalog ID.

If a catalog id is specified that is already specified in the database, a server response indicates that the catalog id is not valid. For example, specify catalog id as `catalog1`. The validation message "Catalog Id is not Valid" gets displayed. The form fields get filled with column values for the `catalog1` catalog entry and the **Submit** button gets disabled. Field values getting filled is an example of auto-completion.

To create a new catalog entry, specify a catalog that is not already in the database, `catalog3` for example. The validation message is **Catalog Id is Valid**. Specify field values for the catalog id and click on **Create Catalog**.

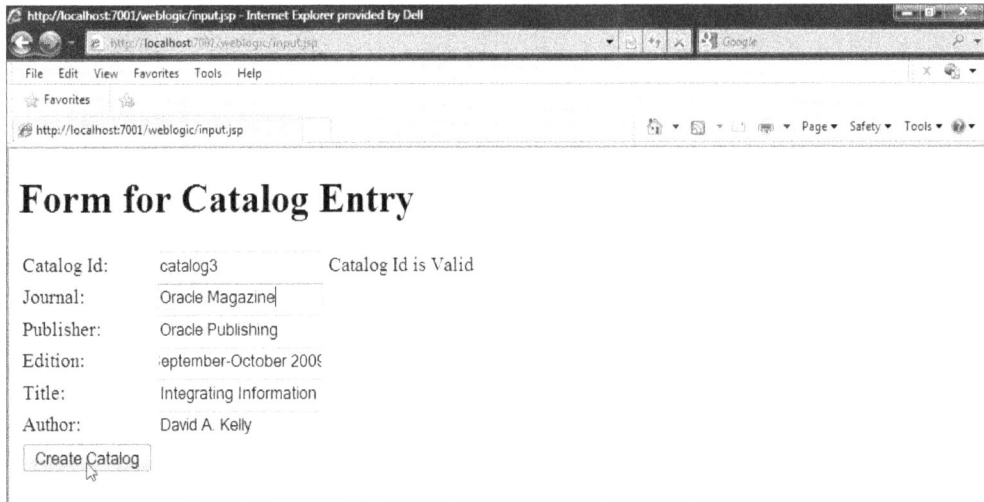

A new catalog entry gets created and the `catalog.jsp` displays the message that the database has been updated:

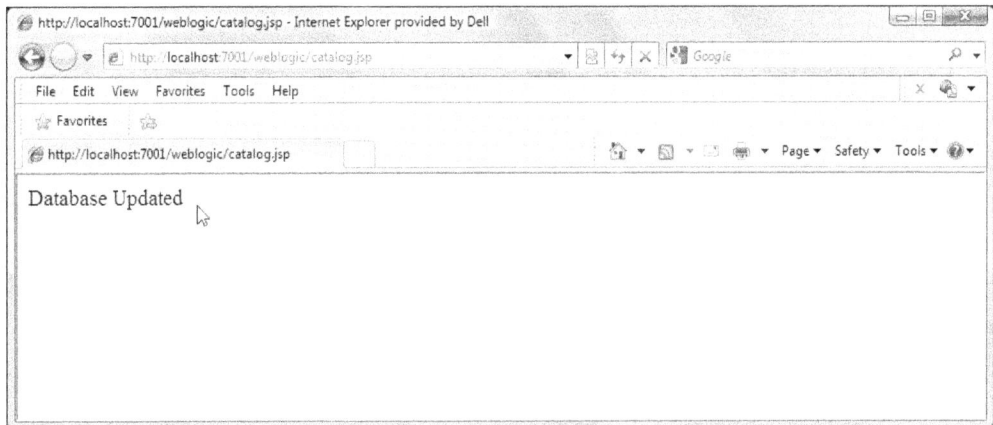

If, subsequently, the `catalog3` catalog id is respecified, the validation message is **Catalog Id is not Valid**, because we had previously created a catalog entry with `catalog3` catalog id.

Summary

In this chapter, we created a EJB 3.0 entity bean that maps to the Oracle Database XE table CATALOG. We created a wrapper session bean. We created a client servlet to lookup the session bean and invoke methods on the session bean. We created an input form to create a new catalog entry. An Ajax request is sent from the input form to the server to validate a catalog id value and if the catalog id is valid, a new catalog entry is created. In the next chapter, we add JSF user interfaces to create EJB 3.0 entity relationships.

9
Using JSF with Entity Relationships

In *Chapter 7, Creating EJB 3.0 Entity Relationships*, we discussed creating one-to-many and many-to-many relationships between entity EJBs. We added data by hard coding the data in the session bean. However, hardcoded data is rarely what is required. In this chapter, we shall create EJB 3.0 entity relationships and add data from JSF user interfaces. JSF UIs are the most commonly used interfaces for inputting data. JSF provides a range of UI components including select lists and event handling for those components. JSF also has the provision to create custom components. In this chapter, we shall discuss the following:

- Creating Oracle database tables
- Creating entity beans from database tables
- Creating the Edition, Section, and Article entities
- Creating a session bean façade
- Creating JSF user interfaces for creating entities and mapping entity relationships
- Adding JSF components to the user interfaces
- Defining managed beans for the JSF user interfaces
- Adding JSF page navigation
- Running the JSF user interfaces to create and persist entities

Setting the environment

We need to install Oracle Fusion Middleware 11*g* (http://www.oracle.com/technology/software/products/middleware/index.html), which includes WebLogic Server 11*g* and JDeveloper 11*g*. Also install Oracle database 10*g* XE Edition (http://www.oracle.com/technology/software/products/database/xe/index.html) including the sample schemas. In this chapter, we won't be using the standalone WebLogic Server, but shall test the application in the WebLogic server that is integrated in JDeveloper 11g. However, an EAR file may be created and deployed to the standalone version using a build script, which is discussed in some of the other chapters. If the application is deployed to the standalone version, a data source is required to be configured in WebLogic Server with Oracle database, which is also explained in some of the other chapters, such as *Chapter 8, EJB 3.0 Database Persistence with Ajax in the UI*.

Creating database tables

We shall be creating EJB 3.0 entity beans from database tables. Therefore, first we need to create the database table Oracle database XE. Connect to the Oracle database XE with the OE schema and create tables ARTICLE, SECTION, and EDITION using the following SQL scripts:

```
CREATE TABLE EDITION (id VARCHAR(100) PRIMARY KEY NOT NULL,
   journal VARCHAR(100), publisher VARCHAR(100), edition VARCHAR(100));
CREATE TABLE SECTION (id VARCHAR(100) PRIMARY KEY NOT NULL,
   section VARCHAR(100));
CREATE TABLE ARTICLE (id VARCHAR(100) PRIMARY KEY NOT NULL,
   title VARCHAR(100), author VARCHAR(100));
```

We shall be modifying two of these tables later when we map EJB 3.0 relationships between entities. We shall add an EDITION_ID column to the SECTION table, because the Edition entity has one-to-many mapping with the Section entity. And, we shall add the SECTION_ID and EDITION_ID columns to the ARTICLE table, as Section and Edition entities have one-to-many mappings with the Article entity.

Creating an EJB 3.0 application

In this section, we create an EJB 3.0 application in JDeveloper 11*g*. Start JDeveloper 11*g* and select the **New Application** link in the **Application** navigator. In the **Create Java EE Web Application** window, specify an **Application Name**, EJB3RelationshipsJSF for example, select the **Java EE Web Application** template, and click on **Next**.

First, the view controller project is defined. In **Name you project**, select the default **Project Name ViewController**, and select the default project **Directory**. In the **Project Technologies** tab, shift the **EJB** technology from the **Available** column to the **Selected** column. Click on **Next**. Next, configure the Java Settings for the view controller project. Select the default **Package Name** view, in which the JSF backing bean classes get generated when we add JSFs. Select the default **Java Source Path** and **Output Directory** and click on **Next**. Select the default EJB 3.0 settings for the view project. The EJBs are created in the model project, but we shall be invoking the EJBs from the view controller project. Next, configure the **Model** project. Specify a **Project Name** (**Model** by default) and shift the **EJB** project technology from the **Available** to the **Selected** column in the **Project Technologies** tab. Click on **Next**. Select the default Java settings for the model project and click on **Next**. In the **Configure EJB Settings** window, select the default **EJB Version**, which is **EJB 3.0**. EJB 3.0 specification is based on annotations; therefore, **Using annotations** is selected by default. Click on **Next**.

A **Java EE Web Application** gets created; the application consists of two projects, the **ViewController** project and the **Model** project. We shall create entity and session beans in the **Model** project and the JSF UIs in the **ViewController** project. We shall add a dependency in the **ViewController** project on the **Model** project to run the JSF UIs in the WebLogic Server that is integrated with JDeveloper 11*g*:

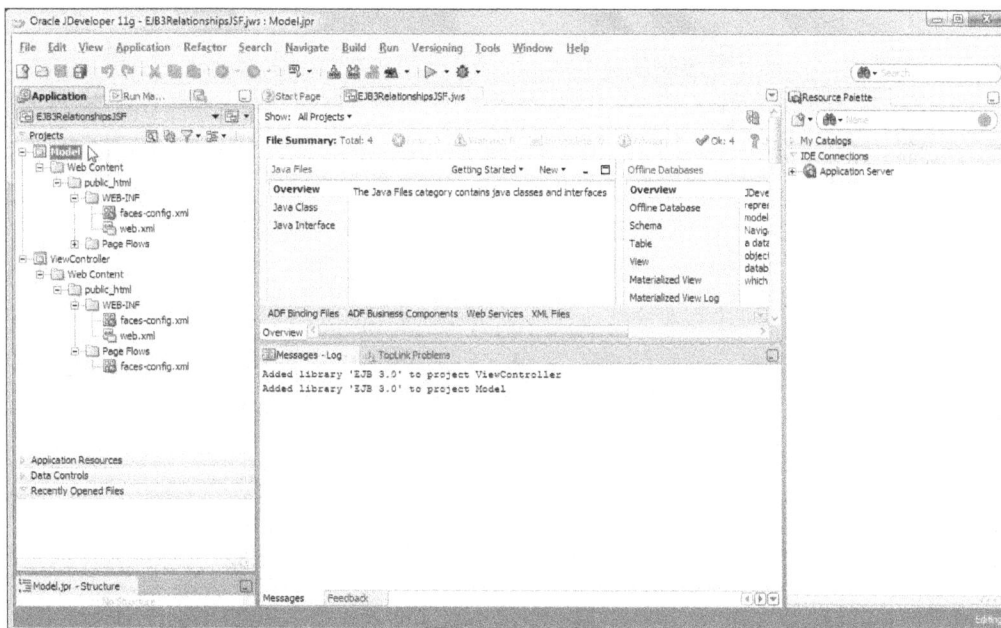

Creating a database connection

To generate entity beans from the database tables we created earlier, we need to create a database connection to Oracle database XE. As we are running the application in the integrated WebLogic Server, we shall also be using the connection for database persistence. Select the **Database Navigator,** right-click on the **EJB3RelationshipsJSF** application node, and select **New Connection**.

In the **Create Database Connection** window, specify a **Connection Name** (**OracleDBConnection**) and select **Connection Type** as **Oracle (JDBC)**. Specify **Username** as **OE**, as we created the database tables in the **OE** schema. Specify the **Password** for the **OE** schema. Select **Driver** type as **thin**, specify **Hostname** as **localhost**, and **SID** as **XE**. **JDBC Port** is **1521** by default. Click on **OK**:

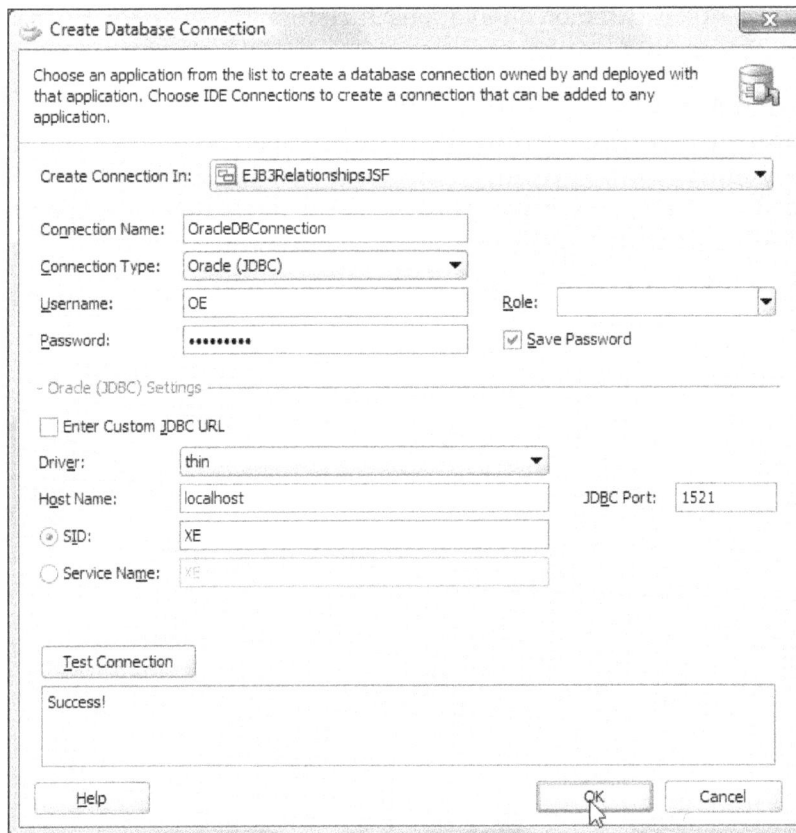

A database connection gets created and added to the **Database Navigator**. The **Tables** node displays the tables that we created:

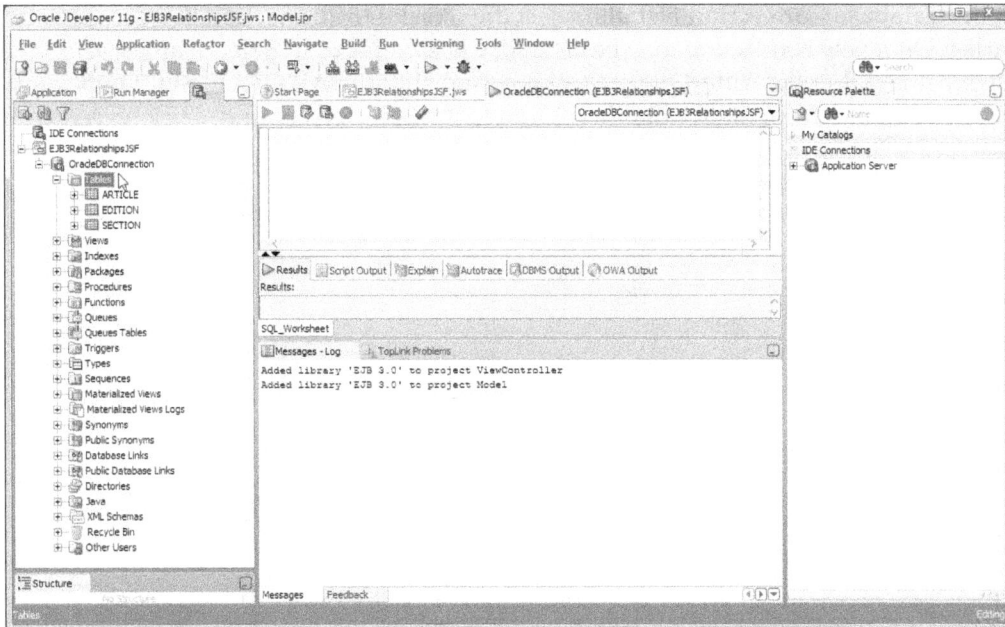

Creating entity beans from tables

In this section, we create EJB 3.0 entity beans from database tables. Right-click on the **Model** project node in the **Application** navigator and select **New**. In the **New Gallery** window, select **Business Tier | EJB** in **Categories** and **Entities from Tables** in **Items**. Click on **OK**. Next, we define the **Persistence Unit** for the entity beans. A **Persistence Unit** defines a data source, and other database persistence properties for creating and persisting entity beans. A persistence unit is defined in the META-INF/persistence.xml configuration file. Click on **New**. In the **New Persistence Unit** window, specify a persistence unit **Name** (**em** for example). Specify a **JTA Datasource Name**. Earlier we created a connection **OracleDBConnection**. A data source with JNDI name jdbc/OracleDBConnectionDS gets created by default when the connection is created. The data source name is of the format jdbc/ConnectionNameDS, in which ConnectionName is the variable; the connection name is what changes based on the database connection defined in JDeveloper. Specify **jdbc/OracleDBConnectionDS** as the **JTA Datasource Name**. The **TopLink/EclipseLink** is used as the JPA persistence provider. Select the **Default Database Platform** and the **Server Platform** as **WebLogic 10**. Click on **OK**. A new **Persistence Unit (em)** gets defined. Click on **Next**. In the **Type of Connection** window, a developer may select from an **Online Database Connection**, an **Offline Database Connection**, or a **Application Server Database Connection**. Select **Online Database Connection** and click on **Next**.

In the **Database Connection Details**, select the **OracleDBConnection** that we created earlier. Or, a new connection may be created. Click on **Next**. In **Select Tables**, select the **OE** schema, select the **Auto-Query** checkbox, and shift the **ARTICLE, SECTION**, and **EDITION** tables from the **Available** column to the **Selected** column. Click on **Next**:

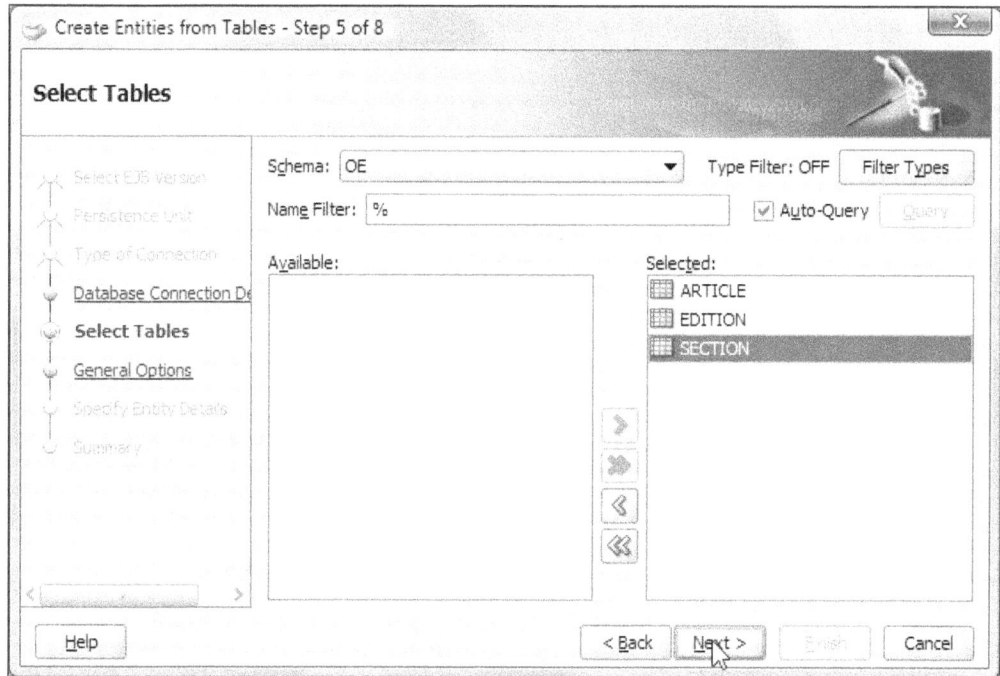

In the **General Options** window, specify the **Package Name** in which the entity beans are to be generated. The default package name is **model**. Select the default **Entity Class Options** and click on **Next**. Next, specify the Entity details: The **Table Name** from which an entity is to be generated, the **Entity name**, and the **Entity Class**. Click on **Next**. Mapping one database table maps all the other selected database tables similarly. The **Summary** page lists the entities that will be generated. Click on **Finish**. The entity classes `model.Article.java`, `model.Section.java`, and `model. Edition.java` get created:

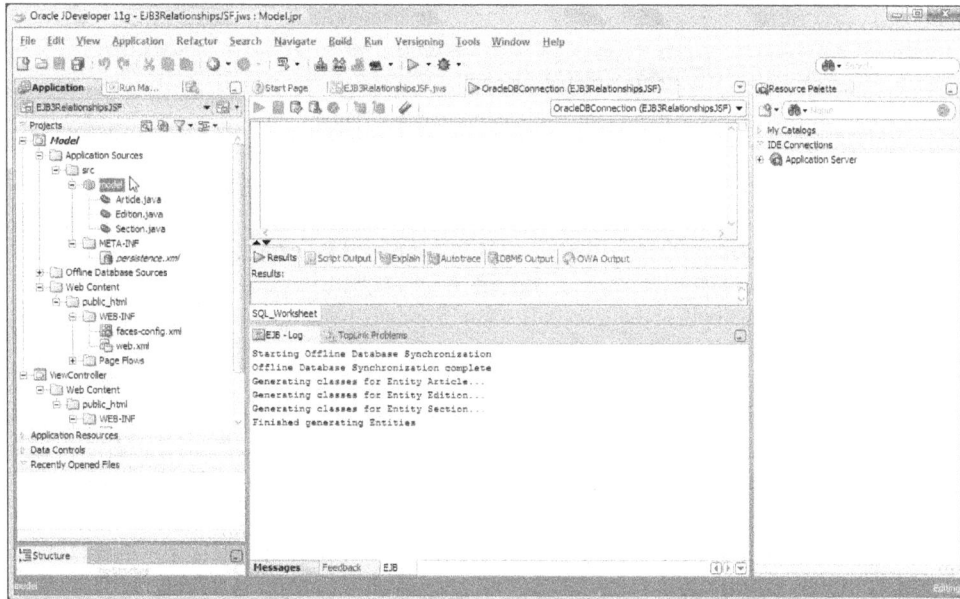

The default entities generated from the tables do not contain the complete code for the entities. We need to add named queries for finding entities by ID and finding all entities.

Edition entity

First, we modify the `model.Edition.java` entity. Add named queries to find all `Edition` entities and find an `Edition` entity by ID:

```
@NamedQueries( { @NamedQuery(name = "findEditionsAll",
                            query = "select o from Edition o"),
               @NamedQuery(name = "findEditionById",
                            query = "SELECT o from Edition o
                            WHERE o.id = :id")} )
```

The `Edition` entity implements the `Serializable` interface. An entity bean that is persisted by an entity manager uses caches to serialize the entity bean. Add a `static final` variable to associate the entity versions with a version number:

```
static final long serialVersionUID = 1;
```

As the `Edition` entity bean has a one-to-many relationship with the `Section` and `Article` entities, add parameterized variables of type `List` for the `Section` and `Article` entities:

```
private List<Section> sections;
private List<Article> articles;
```

Define a @OneToMany relationship to the Section entity. Set the cascade element to CascadeType.ALL to cascade all operations to the target of the association. The mappedBy element specifies the field that owns the relationship. In a one-to-many relationship the many-side must be the owning side of the relationship, which in the example is the Edition entity. The fetch element specifies the fetch strategy. The default strategy is LAZY, which does not fetch the associated entities when an entity is retrieved. LAZY fetching is useful if an entity has a number of associations, which further have associations and all that is required is a particular entity. But, as we require the associated entities too, set fetch strategy to EAGER, which fetches all the associated entities. Specify a join table for the one-to-many mapping using the @JoinTable annotation. The name element of the @JoinTable specifies the table name. The name element is optional and defaults to the concatenated names of the two associated primary entity tables The joinColumns element specifies the foreign key columns of the join table that are mapped to the primary table of the owning entity, and the inverseJoinColumns element specifies the foreign key columns of the join table that reference the table for the non-owning entity. The joinColumns and inverseJoinColumns are also optional and default values are used if not specified. The one-to-many mapping for the edition-section relationship is as follows:

```
@OneToMany(cascade = CascadeType.ALL, mappedBy = "edition",fetch =
        FetchType.EAGER)
  @JoinTable(name = "Edition_Section", joinColumns = {
     @JoinColumn(name = "edition_section_id",
              referencedColumnName = "id")} ,
           inverseJoinColumns = {
             @JoinColumn(name = "section_id",
                       referencedColumnName ="id")} )
```

Specify the getter/setter methods for the Section entity:

```
public List<Section> getSections() {
  return sections;
}
public void setSections(List<Section> sections) {
  this.sections = sections;
}
```

Also add methods to add and remove a Section entity:

```
public void addSection(Section section) {
  this.getSections().add(section);
  section.setEdition(this);
}
public void removeSection(Section section) {
  this.getSections().remove(section);
}
```

Specify the identifier property for the `Edition` entity. The `@GeneratedValue` annotation is not required if the ID value is set in the application and not generated automatically:

```
@Id
  @GeneratedValue
  public String getId() {
    return id;
  }
```

Similarly add a `@OneToMany` mapping to the `Article` entity. The `Edition` entity class is listed as follows:

```
package model;

import java.io.Serializable;
import java.util.List;
import javax.persistence.CascadeType;
import javax.persistence.Column;
import javax.persistence.Entity;
import javax.persistence.FetchType;
import javax.persistence.GeneratedValue;
import javax.persistence.Id;
import javax.persistence.JoinColumn;
import javax.persistence.JoinTable;
import javax.persistence.NamedQueries;
import javax.persistence.NamedQuery;
import javax.persistence.OneToMany;

@Entity
@NamedQueries( {
                @NamedQuery(name = "findEditionsAll",
                            query = "select o from Edition o"),
                @NamedQuery(name = "findEditionById",
                            query = "SELECT o from Edition o
                            WHERE o.id = :id") })
public class Edition implements Serializable {
  static final long serialVersionUID = 1;
  private List<Section> sections;
  private List<Article> articles;
  @Column(length = 100)
  private String edition;
  @Id
  @Column(nullable = false, length = 100)
  private String id;
  @Column(length = 100)
  private String journal;
  @Column(length = 100)
  private String publisher;
```

```
public Edition() {
}

public Edition(String edition, String id, String journal,
               String publisher) {
  this.edition = edition;
  this.id = id;
  this.journal = journal;
  this.publisher = publisher;
}

public String getEdition() {
  return edition;
}

public void setEdition(String edition) {
  this.edition = edition;
}

@Id
@GeneratedValue
public String getId() {
  return id;
}

public void setId(String id) {
  this.id = id;
}

public String getJournal() {
  return journal;
}

public void setJournal(String journal) {
  this.journal = journal;
}

public String getPublisher() {
  return publisher;
}

public void setPublisher(String publisher) {
  this.publisher = publisher;
}

@OneToMany(cascade = CascadeType.ALL, mappedBy = "edition",
           fetch = FetchType.EAGER)
@JoinTable(name = "Edition_Section", joinColumns = {
  @JoinColumn(name = "edition_section_id",
```

```
                     referencedColumnName = "id") },
     inverseJoinColumns = {
       @JoinColumn(name = "section_id",
                   referencedColumnName = "id") })
  public List<Section> getSections() {
    return sections;
  }

  public void setSections(List<Section> sections) {
    this.sections = sections;
  }

  public void addSection(Section section) {
    this.getSections().add(section);
    section.setEdition(this);
  }

  public void removeSection(Section section) {
    this.getSections().remove(section);
  }

  @OneToMany(cascade = CascadeType.ALL, mappedBy = "edition",
             fetch = FetchType.EAGER)
  @JoinTable(name = "Edition_Article", joinColumns = {
    @JoinColumn(name = "edition_id",
                referencedColumnName = "id") },
     inverseJoinColumns = {
       @JoinColumn(name = "article_id",
                   referencedColumnName = "id") })
  public List<Article> getArticles() {
    return articles;
  }

  public void setArticles(List<Article> articles) {
    this.articles = articles;
  }

  public void addArticle(Article article) {
    this.getArticles().add(article);
    article.setEdition(this);
  }

  public void removeArticle(Article article) {
    this.getArticles().remove(article);
  }
}
```

The property relates to the name of the table (entity) you query; the join takes the property returned by the getter method as the table name for the join at runtime.

Section entity

Similarly, to the `Section` entity add named queries to find all `Section` entities and find a `Section` entity by ID. As the `Section` entity has a one-to-many mapping with the `Article` entity define a parameterized variable of type `List` for the `Article` entity.

Specify a `@ManyToOne` relationship with the `Edition` entity. If we want to initiate merge, persist, refresh operations from the `Section` entity, we need to add a join table on the `Section` entity side. But, if we don't want the associated `Edition` to be deleted, then if the `Section` entity is deleted don't set the `cascade` element to `CascadeType.ALL`. Set the fetch strategy to `EAGER` as we want to retrieve associated entities when an entity is retrieved. The `mappedBy` element is not required to be set in a unidirectional relationship; the `mappedBy` element is set on the non-owning side of the relationship, which in the edition-section relationship is the `Edition` entity. However, if you want to make the `Section` entity as the owning side too, add the `mappedBy` element. The `@ManyToOne` relationship with the getter/setter methods for the `Edition` entity is defined as follows:

```
@ManyToOne(cascade ={ CascadeType.MERGE, CascadeType.PERSIST,
  CascadeType.REFRESH },fetch = FetchType.EAGER)
  @JoinTable(name = "Edition_Section", joinColumns = {
    @JoinColumn(name = "edition_id",
              referencedColumnName = "id")} ,
    inverseJoinColumns = {
      @JoinColumn(name = "section_id",
              referencedColumnName ="id")})
public Edition getEdition() {
  return edition;
}
public void setEdition(Edition edition) {
  this.edition = edition;
}
```

We also need to add a `@OneToMany` relationship to the `Article` entity. Set the `cascade` element to `CascadeType.ALL` as we want to cascade all operations to the `Article` entity. An `Article` entity without a `Section` entity wouldn't have much significance. Set the `mappedBy` element to `Section` as the `Section` entity is the non-owning side in the relationship. Add getter/setter methods for the `Article` entity and also add add/remove methods to add and remove an `Article` entity:

```
@OneToMany(cascade = CascadeType.ALL, mappedBy = "section",
          fetch = FetchType.EAGER)
  @JoinTable(name = "Section_Article", joinColumns = {
    @JoinColumn(name = "section_id",
              referencedColumnName = "id")} ,
    inverseJoinColumns = {
```

```
          @JoinColumn(name = "article_id",
                    referencedColumnName ="id")} )
    public List<Article> getArticles() {
      return articles;
    }
    public void setArticles(List<Article> articles) {
      this.articles = articles;
    }
    public void addArticle(Article article) {
      this.getArticles().add(article);
      article.setSection(this);
    }
    public void removeArticle(Article article) {
      this.getArticles().remove(article);
    }
```

The Section entity is listed as follows:

```
    package model;

    import java.io.Serializable;
    import java.util.List;
    import javax.persistence.CascadeType;
    import javax.persistence.Column;
    import javax.persistence.Entity;
    import javax.persistence.FetchType;
    import javax.persistence.GeneratedValue;
    import javax.persistence.Id;
    import javax.persistence.JoinColumn;
    import javax.persistence.JoinTable;
    import javax.persistence.ManyToOne;
    import javax.persistence.NamedQueries;
    import javax.persistence.NamedQuery;
    import javax.persistence.OneToMany;

    @Entity
    @NamedQueries( {
                   @NamedQuery(name = "findSectionsAll",
                              query = "select o from Section o"),
                   @NamedQuery(name = "findSectionById",
                              query = "SELECT o from Section o
                              WHERE o.id = :id") })
    public class Section implements Serializable {
      static final long serialVersionUID = 1;
      private Edition edition;
```

```java
  private List<Article> articles;
  @Id
  @Column(nullable = false, length = 100)
  private String id;
  @Column(length = 100)
  private String section;
  public Section() {
}

  public Section(String id, String section) {
    this.id = id;
    this.section = section;
  }

  @Id
  @GeneratedValue
  public String getId() {
    return id;
  }

  public void setId(String id) {
    this.id = id;
  }

  public String getSection() {
    return section;
  }

  public void setSection(String section) {
    this.section = section;
  }

  @ManyToOne(cascade = { CascadeType.MERGE, CascadeType.PERSIST,
    CascadeType.REFRESH }, fetch = FetchType.EAGER)
  @JoinTable(name = "Edition_Section", joinColumns = {
    @JoinColumn(name = "edition_id",
                referencedColumnName = "id") },
    inverseJoinColumns = {
      @JoinColumn(name = "section_id",
                  referencedColumnName = "id") })
  public Edition getEdition() {
    return edition;
  }

  public void setEdition(Edition edition) {
```

```
      this.edition = edition;
   }

   @OneToMany(cascade = CascadeType.ALL, mappedBy = "section",
              fetch = FetchType.EAGER)
   @JoinTable(name = "Section_Article", joinColumns = {
     @JoinColumn(name = "section_id",
                 referencedColumnName = "id") },
     inverseJoinColumns = {
       @JoinColumn(name = "article_id",
                   referencedColumnName = "id") })
   public List<Article> getArticles() {
     return articles;
   }

   public void setArticles(List<Article> articles) {
     this.articles = articles;
   }

   public void addArticle(Article article) {
     this.getArticles().add(article);
     article.setSection(this);
   }

   public void removeArticle(Article article) {
     this.getArticles().remove(article);
   }
}
```

Article entity

Similarly, in the Article entity, add named queries to find all Article entities and find an Article entity by ID. Add @ManyToOne annotations to define the many-to-one relationships between the Article entity and the Edition and Section entities. The Article entity is listed as follows:

```
package model;

import java.io.Serializable;
import javax.persistence.CascadeType;
import javax.persistence.Column;
import javax.persistence.Entity;
import javax.persistence.FetchType;
import javax.persistence.GeneratedValue;
import javax.persistence.Id;
```

```
import javax.persistence.JoinColumn;
import javax.persistence.JoinTable;
import javax.persistence.ManyToOne;
import javax.persistence.NamedQueries;
import javax.persistence.NamedQuery;

@Entity
@NamedQueries( {
                @NamedQuery(name = "findArticlesAll",
                            query = "select o from Article o"),
                @NamedQuery(name = "findArticleById",
                            query = "SELECT o from Article o
                            WHERE o.id = :id") })
public class Article implements Serializable {
  static final long serialVersionUID = 1;
  private Section section;
  private Edition edition;
  @Column(length = 100)
  private String author;
  @Id
  @Column(nullable = false, length = 100)
  private String id;
  @Column(length = 100)
  private String title;
  public Article() {
}

  public Article(String author, String id, String title) {
    this.author = author;
    this.id = id;
    this.title = title;
  }

  public String getAuthor() {
    return author;
  }

  public void setAuthor(String author) {
    this.author = author;
  }

  @Id
  @GeneratedValue
  public String getId() {
    return id;
  }
}
```

```
    public void setId(String id) {
      this.id = id;
    }

    public String getTitle() {
      return title;
    }

    public void setTitle(String title) {
      this.title = title;
    }

    @ManyToOne(cascade = { CascadeType.MERGE, CascadeType.PERSIST,
      CascadeType.REFRESH }, fetch = FetchType.EAGER)
    @JoinTable(name = "Section_Article", joinColumns = {
      @JoinColumn(name = "section_id",
                  referencedColumnName = "id") },
      inverseJoinColumns = {
        @JoinColumn(name = "article_id",
                    referencedColumnName = "id") })
    public Section getSection() {
      return section;
    }

    public void setSection(Section section) {
      this.section = section;
    }

    @ManyToOne(cascade = { CascadeType.MERGE, CascadeType.PERSIST,
      CascadeType.REFRESH }, fetch = FetchType.EAGER)
    @JoinTable(name = "Edition_Article", joinColumns = {
      @JoinColumn(name = "edition_id",
                  referencedColumnName = "id") },
      inverseJoinColumns = {
        @JoinColumn(name = "article_id",
                    referencedColumnName = "id") })
    public Edition getEdition() {
      return edition;
    }

    public void setEdition(Edition edition) {
      this.edition = edition;
    }
}
```

You may build the queries using the TopLink/Eclipse Link editing facilities, which you can access from the persistence.xml file.

Entity Persistence Configuration file

The `persistence.xml` file is the EJB 3.0 database persistence configuration file and gets generated when entities are created from database tables. But, the `persistence.xml` file as generated is not complete. The JTA data source JNDI name is specified and the entity classes are also specified. `EclipseLink` is used as the JPA persistence provider. The `javax.persistence.jtaDataSource` property is pre-specified and set to the JTA data source name. Add the following properties to `persistence.xml`:

Property	Value	Description
`eclipselink.target-server`	`WebLogic_10`	Specifies the target server as WebLogic Server 10.
`eclipselink.target-database`	`Oracle`	Specifies the target database.
`eclipselink.ddl-generation`	`create-tables`	Specifies the DDL generation strategy to create tables, but not to delete tables and re-create them.

The `persistence.xml` configuration file is listed as follows:

```xml
<?xml version="1.0" encoding="Cp1252" ?>
<persistence xmlns:xsi="http://www.w3.org/2001/XMLSchema-instance"
  xsi:schemaLocation="http://java.sun.com/xml/ns/persistence
    http://java.sun.com/xml/ns/persistence/persistence_1_0.xsd"
  xmlns="http://java.sun.com/xml/ns/persistence" version="1.0">
  <persistence-unit name="em">
  <provider>org.eclipse.persistence.jpa.PersistenceProvider</provider>
    <jta-data-source>
      java:/app/jdbc/jdbc/OracleDBConnectionDS
    </jta-data-source>
      <class>model.Article</class>
      <class>model.Edition</class>
      <class>model.Section</class>
      <properties>
        <property name="eclipselink.target-server"
                value="WebLogic_10" />
        <property name="eclipselink.target-database" value="Oracle" />
        <property name="eclipselink.ddl-generation"
                value="create-tables" />
        <property name="javax.persistence.jtaDataSource"
                value="java:/app/jdbc/jdbc/OracleDBConnectionDS" />
      </properties>
  </persistence-unit>
</persistence>
```

```
        </properties>
    </persistence-unit>
</persistence>
```

Creating a session bean

In this section, we create a `Stateless` session bean façade for the entity beans. Select the **Model** project node in **Application** navigator and select **File | New**. In the **New Gallery** window, select **Business Tier | EJB** and **Session Bean** in **Items**. Click on **OK**. In the **Create Session Bean** window, specify the session bean **EJB Name**, and select **Session Type** as **Stateless** and **Transaction Type** as **Container**. Specify a **Mapped Name**, which will be used to lookup the session bean from a client. Select a **Persistence Unit** and click on **Next**. Select the default session façade methods to generate and click on **Next**. Specify the **Bean Class** and click on **Next**. Specify the EJB interfaces to implement. Implement only one of the interfaces—local or remote. Select the **Implement a Remote Interface** checkbox, specify an interface name, and click on **Next**. In the **Summary** page, click on **Finish**. A session bean and a remote interface get created.

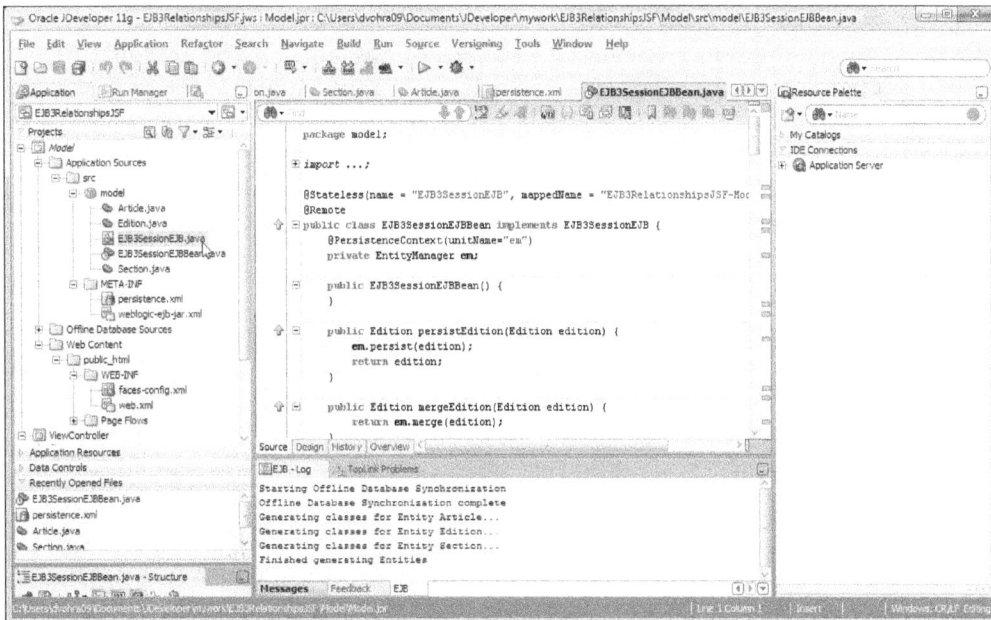

Session bean class

A stateless session bean is just a Java class annotated with the annotation `@Stateless`.

```
@Stateless(name = "EJB3SessionEJB",
           mappedName = "EJB3RelationshipsJSF-Model-EJB3SessionEJB")
```

The `mappedName` element specifies the mapped name for the session bean. The `mappedName` is used in the JNDI lookup of the session bean from a client. The `@Remote` annotation indicates that the class implements a remote interface:

```
@Remote
public class EJB3SessionEJBBean implements EJB3SessionEJB {
..
}
```

We shall be using an `EntityManager` for database persistence. Inject an `EntityManager` using dependency injection:

```
@PersistenceContext(unitName = "em")
    private EntityManager em;
```

Add `getAll<>` methods to retrieve all `Edition` entities, all `Section` entities, and all `Article` entities. By default, container-managed transactions do not require individual methods to be associated with transactions. Methods may be associated with transactions using the transaction attributes. Associate each of the `getAll` methods with a transaction attribute with `TransactionAttributeType` set to `REQUIRES_NEW`, which implies that a new transaction is required each time the method is invoked:

```
@TransactionAttribute(TransactionAttributeType.REQUIRES_NEW)
```

In each of the `getAll<>` methods, find all entities using the named query to find all entities. The `getAll<>` methods return a parameterized `List`. For example, the `getAllEdtions` method returns `List<Edition>`. In the `getAllEditions` method, create an `ArrayList<Edition>` type variable:

```
ArrayList<Edition> editions = new ArrayList<Edition>();
```

Create a `Query` object for the named query `findEditionsAll`, which was defined in the `Edition` entity class. A `Query` object is created using the `createNamedQuery` method of the `EntityManager` object that was created using dependency injection:

```
Query q = em.createNamedQuery("findEditionsAll");
```

Retrieve the query result `List` of `Edition` entity instances using the `getQueryList` method of the `Query` object and iterate over the result list using the `ForEach` loop. Add `Edition` entity instances to the `ArrayList` editions:

```
for (Object edition : q.getResultList()) {
  editions.add((Edition)edition);
}
```

Return the `ArrayList` constructed from the `getAllEditions` method, which is listed as follows:

```
@TransactionAttribute(TransactionAttributeType.REQUIRES_NEW)
  public List<Edition> getAllEditions() {
    ArrayList<Edition> editions = new ArrayList<Edition>();
    Query q = em.createNamedQuery("findEditionsAll");
    for (Object edition : q.getResultList()) {
      editions.add((Edition)edition);
    }
    return editions;
  }}
```

When the `getAllEditions` query is executed, it returns a `List` of type `<Edition>`. Similarly, define methods `getAllArticles` and `getAllSections`. We also need to add `get<>ById` methods to retrieve entity instances by ID. Annotate the `get<>ById` methods with the `@TransactionAttribute` with `TransactionAttributeType.REQUIRES_NEW`. The `get<>ById` methods return the corresponding entity instance. For example, the `getEditionById` returns an `Edition` object. The `getEditionById` method takes a `String` argument for the ID. Create a `Query` object from the named query `findEditionById`, which is defined in the `Edition` entity:

```
Query q = em.createNamedQuery("findEditionById");
```

Set the `Query` object parameter id using the `setParameter` method:

```
q.setParameter("id", id);
```

Retrieve the `Edition` entity instance from the `Query` object using the `getSingleResult` method:

```
Edition edition = (Edition)q.getSingleResult();
```

Return the `Edition` entity instance from the `getEdiitonById` method, which is listed as follows:

```
@TransactionAttribute(TransactionAttributeType.REQUIRES_NEW)
  public Edition getEditionById(String id) {
    Query q = em.createNamedQuery("findEditionById");
```

```
        q.setParameter("id", id);
        Edition edition = (Edition)q.getSingleResult();
        return edition;
    }
```

Similarly, add methods `getSectionById` and `getArticleById`. In order to create `Edition`, `Section`, and `Article` instances, add methods `createEdition`, `createSection`, and `createArticle`. The `createEdition` method takes `Edition` entity properties as arguments. In the `createEdition` method, create a `Edition` object and set the values of the different properties:

```
    Edition edition = new Edition();
    edition.setId(id);
    edition.setPublisher(publisher);
    edition.setJournal(journal);
    edition.setEdition(edition_date);
```

Persist the `Edition` entity object using the `persist` method of the `EntityManager`. The Entity instance data is synchronized with the database when the transaction with which the entity is associated commits. To synchronize an entity instance with the database, invoke the `flush` method, which explicitly commits the transaction. The `flush` method also synchronizes the entity data of the associated entities if the `cascade` element is set to `PERSIST` or `ALL`.

```
    em.persist(edition);
    em.flush();
```

Similarly, in the `createSection` method, create an instance of `Section` from the argument values and persist the `Section` instance to the database. However, creating a `Section` instance is different, because the `Section` entity has a many-to-one relationship with the `Edition` entity. Therefore, we need to add the section to the associated `Edition` entity instance. One of the `createSection` method's parameters is `editionId`. Retrieve the `Edition` entity instance using the `getEditionById` method:

```
    Edition edition = this.getEditionById(editionId);
```

Next, merge the state of the `Edition` entity into the current persistence context using the `merge()` method. Without merging the `Edition` entity instance, we won't be able to invoke methods on it.

```
    em.merge(edition);
```

Retrieve a parameterized `List` of `Section` entities from the `Edition` entities using the `getSections` method, which we defined in the `Edition` entity class. To add a new `Section` entity to the `List`, create an `ArrayList` from the `List`:

```
    List<Section> sections = edition.getSections();
    ArrayList<Section> sectionList =new ArrayList<Section>(sections.
    size());
```

Add the new `Section` instance to the `ArrayList` and flush the changes to the database:

```
sectionList.add(section);
em.flush();
```

Similarly, in the `createArticle` method create an `Article` entity object and persist and flush the entity instance to the database. As the `Article` entity has many-to-one relationships with the `Edition` entity and the `Section` entity, we also need to add the `Article` entity instance to the `Edition` and `Section` entities. The `createArticle` method has arguments for the edition ID and the section ID. Retrieve the `Edition` and `Section` entity objects using `getEditionById` and `getSectionById` methods and add the `Article` entity to the `Edition` and `Section` entities as explained for adding a `Section` entity instance to an `Edition` entity. The session bean class `EJB3SessionEJBBean` is listed as follows:

```
package model;

import java.util.ArrayList;
import java.util.List;
import javax.ejb.Remote;
import javax.ejb.Stateless;
import javax.ejb.TransactionAttribute;
import javax.ejb.TransactionAttributeType;
import javax.persistence.EntityManager;
import javax.persistence.PersistenceContext;
import javax.persistence.Query;

@Stateless(name = "EJB3SessionEJB",
            mappedName = "EJB3RelationshipsJSF-Model-EJB3SessionEJB")
@Remote
public class EJB3SessionEJBBean implements EJB3SessionEJB {
  @PersistenceContext(unitName = "em")
  private EntityManager em;

  public EJB3SessionEJBBean() {
  }

  @TransactionAttribute(TransactionAttributeType.REQUIRES_NEW)
  public List<Edition> getAllEditions() {
    ArrayList<Edition> editions = new ArrayList<Edition>();
    Query q = em.createNamedQuery("findEditionsAll");
    for (Object edition : q.getResultList()) {
      editions.add((Edition) edition);
    }
    return editions;
  }

  @TransactionAttribute(TransactionAttributeType.REQUIRES_NEW)
```

```java
  public List<Section> getAllSections() {
    ArrayList<Section> sections = new ArrayList<Section>();
    Query q = em.createNamedQuery("findSectionsAll");
    for (Object section : q.getResultList()) {
      sections.add((Section) section);
    }
    return sections;
  }
  @TransactionAttribute(TransactionAttributeType.REQUIRES_NEW)
  public List<Article> getAllArticles() {
    ArrayList<Article> articles = new ArrayList<Article>();
    Query q = em.createNamedQuery("findArticlesAll");
    for (Object article : q.getResultList()) {
      articles.add((Article) article);
    }
    return articles;
  }
  @TransactionAttribute(TransactionAttributeType.REQUIRES_NEW)
  public Edition getEditionById(String id) {
    Query q = em.createNamedQuery("findEditionById");
    q.setParameter("id", id);
    Edition edition = (Edition) q.getSingleResult();
    return edition;
  }
  @TransactionAttribute(TransactionAttributeType.REQUIRES_NEW)
  public Section getSectionById(String id) {
    Query q = em.createNamedQuery("findSectionById");
    q.setParameter("id", id);
    Section section = (Section) q.getSingleResult();
    return section;
  }
  @TransactionAttribute(TransactionAttributeType.REQUIRES_NEW)
  public Article getArticleById(String id) {
    Query q = em.createNamedQuery("findArticleById");
    q.setParameter("id", id);
    Article article = (Article) q.getSingleResult();
    return article;
  }
  public void createEdition(String id, String publisher, String journal,
    String edition_date) {
    Edition edition = new Edition();
    edition.setId(id);
    edition.setPublisher(publisher);
    edition.setJournal(journal);
    edition.setEdition(edition_date);
    em.persist(edition);
    em.flush();
  }
```

```
public void createArticle(String id, String title, String author,
  String sectionId, String editionId) {
  Article article = new Article();
  article.setId(id);
  article.setTitle(title);
  article.setAuthor(author);
  em.persist(article);
  em.flush();
  Section section = this.getSectionById(sectionId);
  em.merge(section);
  List<Article> articles = section.getArticles();
  ArrayList<Article> articleList = new arrayList<Article>(
                                      articles.size());
  articleList.add(article);
  em.flush();
  Edition edition = this.getEditionById(editionId);
  em.merge(edition);
  articles = edition.getArticles();
  articleList = new ArrayList<Article>(articles.size());
  articleList.add(article);
  em.flush();
}
public void createSection(String id, String section_name,
  String editionId) {
  Section section = new Section();
  section.setId(id);
  section.setSection(section_name);
  em.persist(section);
  em.flush();
  Edition edition = this.getEditionById(editionId);
  em.merge(edition);
  List<Section> sections = edition.getSections();
  ArrayList<Section> sectionList = new ArrayList<Section>(
                                      sections.size());
  sectionList.add(section);
   em.flush();
}
public Edition persistEdition(Edition edition) {
  em.persist(edition);
  return edition;
}
public Edition mergeEdition(Edition edition) {
  return em.merge(edition);
}
public void removeEdition(Edition edition) {
  edition = em.find(Edition.class, edition.getId());
  em.remove(edition);
}
public List<Edition> getEditionByCriteria(String jpqlStmt,
```

```
      int firstResult,int maxResults) {
    Query query = em.createQuery(jpqlStmt);
    if (firstResult > 0) {
      query = query.setFirstResult(firstResult);
    }
    if (maxResults > 0) {
      query = query.setMaxResults(maxResults);
    }
    return query.getResultList();
  }
  /** <code>select o from Edition o</code> */
  public List<Edition> findEditionAll() {
    return em.createNamedQuery("findEditionAll").getResultList();
  }
  /** <code>select o from Edition o</code> */
  public List<Edition> findEditionAllByRange(int firstResult,
                                             int maxResults) {
    Query query = em.createNamedQuery("findEditionAll");
    if (firstResult > 0) {
      query = query.setFirstResult(firstResult);
    }
    if (maxResults > 0) {
      query = query.setMaxResults(maxResults);
    }
    return query.getResultList();
  }
  /** <code>SELECT o from Edition o WHERE o.id = :id</code> */
  public List<Edition> findEditionById(String id) {
    return em.createNamedQuery("findEditionById").
      setParameter("id", id).getResultList();
  }
  /** <code>SELECT o from Edition o WHERE o.id = :id</code> */
  public List<Edition> findEditionByIdByRange(String id, int
firstResult,
                                              int maxResults) {
    Query query = em.createNamedQuery(
      "findEditionById").setParameter("id",id);
    if (firstResult > 0) {
      query = query.setFirstResult(firstResult);
    }
    if (maxResults > 0) {
      query = query.setMaxResults(maxResults);
    }
    return query.getResultList();
  }
  public Article persistArticle(Article article) {
    em.persist(article);
    return article;
  }
```

```
  public Article mergeArticle(Article article) {
    return em.merge(article);
  }
  public void removeArticle(Article article) {
    article = em.find(Article.class, article.getId());
    em.remove(article);
  }
  public List<Article> getArticleByCriteria(String jpqlStmt,
                                            int firstResult, int
maxResults) {
    Query query = em.createQuery(jpqlStmt);
    if (firstResult > 0) {
      query = query.setFirstResult(firstResult);
    }
    if (maxResults > 0) {
      query = query.setMaxResults(maxResults);
    }
    return query.getResultList();
  }
  /** <code>select o from Article o</code> */
  public List<Article> findArticlesAll() {
    return em.createNamedQuery("findArticlesAll").getResultList();
  }
  /** <code>select o from Article o</code> */
  public List<Article> findArticlesAllByRange(int firstResult,
                                              int maxResults) {
    Query query = em.createNamedQuery("findArticlesAll");
    if (firstResult > 0) {
      query = query.setFirstResult(firstResult);
    }
    if (maxResults > 0) {
      query = query.setMaxResults(maxResults);
    }
    return query.getResultList();
  }
  public Section persistSection(Section section) {
    em.persist(section);
    return section;
  }
  public Section mergeSection(Section section) {
    return em.merge(section);
  }
  public void removeSection(Section section) {
    section = em.find(Section.class, section.getId());
    em.remove(section);
  }
  public List<Section> getSectionByCriteria(String jpqlStmt,
                                            int firstResult,int
```

```
maxResults) {
   Query query = em.createQuery(jpqlStmt);
   if (firstResult > 0) {
     query = query.setFirstResult(firstResult);
   }
   if (maxResults > 0) {
     query = query.setMaxResults(maxResults);
   }
   return query.getResultList();
}
/** <code>select o from Section o</code> */
public List<Section> findSectionsAll() {
   return em.createNamedQuery("findSectionsAll").getResultList();
}
/** <code>select o from Section o</code> */
public List<Section> findSectionsAllByRange(int firstResult,
                                            int maxResults) {
   Query query = em.createNamedQuery("findSectionsAll");
   if (firstResult > 0) {
     query = query.setFirstResult(firstResult);
   }
   if (maxResults > 0) {
     query = query.setMaxResults(maxResults);
   }
   return query.getResultList();
}
}
```

The remote interface for the session bean is listed as follows. If you are not using a distributed environment, a local interface for the session bean may be used instead of a remote interface.

```
package model;

import java.util.List;
import javax.ejb.Remote;

@Remote
public interface EJB3SessionEJB {
  List<Edition> getAllEditions();

  List<Section> getAllSections();

  List<Article> getAllArticles();

  Edition getEditionById(String id);

  Section getSectionById(String id);

  Article getArticleById(String id);
```

```
void createEdition(String id, String publisher, String journal,
                    String edition_date);

void createArticle(String id, String title, String author,
                    String sectionId, String editionId);

void createSection(String id, String section_name, String
editionId);

Edition persistEdition(Edition edition);

Edition mergeEdition(Edition edition);

void removeEdition(Edition edition);

List<Edition> getEditionByCriteria(String jpqlStmt, int firstResult,
                                   int maxResults);

List<Edition> findEditionAll();

List<Edition> findEditionAllByRange(int firstResult, int
maxResults);

List<Edition> findEditionById(String id);

List<Edition> findEditionByIdByRange(String id, int firstResult,
                                     int maxResults);

Article persistArticle(Article article);

Article mergeArticle(Article article);

void removeArticle(Article article);

List<Article> getArticleByCriteria(String jpqlStmt, int firstResult,
                                   int maxResults);

List<Article> findArticlesAll();

List<Article> findArticlesAllByRange(int firstResult, int
maxResults);

Section persistSection(Section section);

Section mergeSection(Section section);

void removeSection(Section section);

List<Section> getSectionByCriteria(String jpqlStmt, int firstResult,
```

```
                              int maxResults);

   List<Section> findSectionsAll();

   List<Section> findSectionsAllByRange(int firstResult, int
maxResults);
}
```

Creating JSF user interfaces

We shall input data for the EDITION, SECTION, and ARTICLE tables from JSF interfaces. In this section, we shall create the edition.jsp, section.jsp and article.jsp JSFs. We shall use the backing beans from the JSFs as EJB 3.0 clients. In the backing beans, we shall lookup the session bean remote interface and invoke the createEdition, createSection, and createArticle methods to create and persist Entity, Section, and Article entities. First, we need to create the JSFs for the entities. We shall create the JSFs in the ViewController project. Select the **ViewController** project node and select **File | New**. In the **New Gallery** window, select **Web Tier | JSF** in **Categories** and **JSF Page** in Items. Click on **OK**:

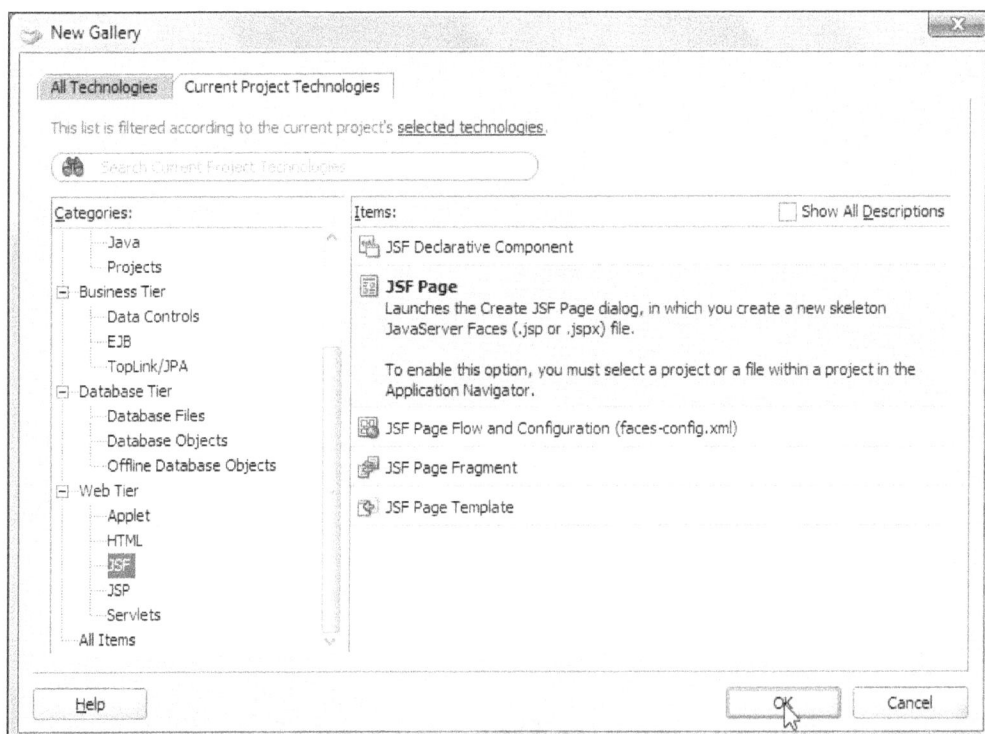

In the **Create JSF Page** window, specify a **File Name** (**article.jsp**). Expand the **Page Implementation** node and select **Automatically Expose UI Components in a New Managed Bean**. Specify the managed bean **Name**, which will be mapped to the `faces-config.xml` configuration file. Specify the managed bean **Class** (**Article.java**) and **Package** name (**view.backing**). Click on **OK**:

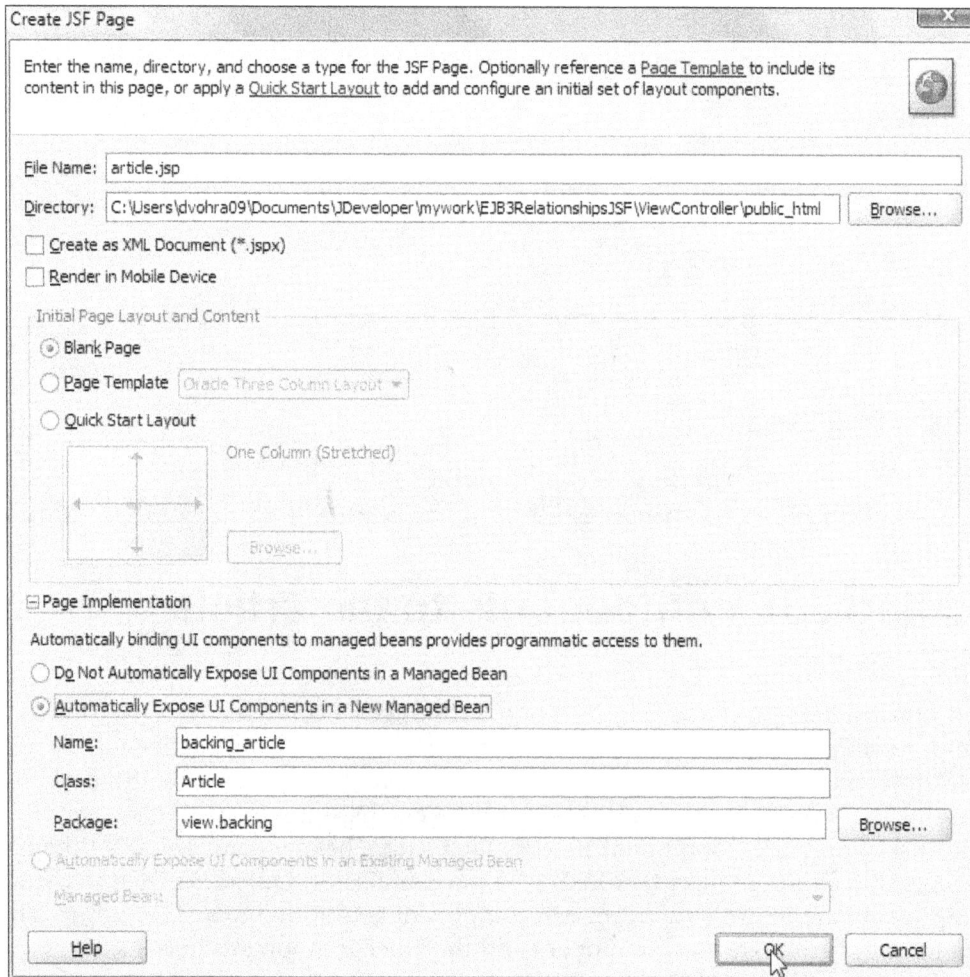

The `article.jsp` gets added to the **ViewController** project node. Similarly, add JSF pages `section.jsp` and `edition.jsp`.

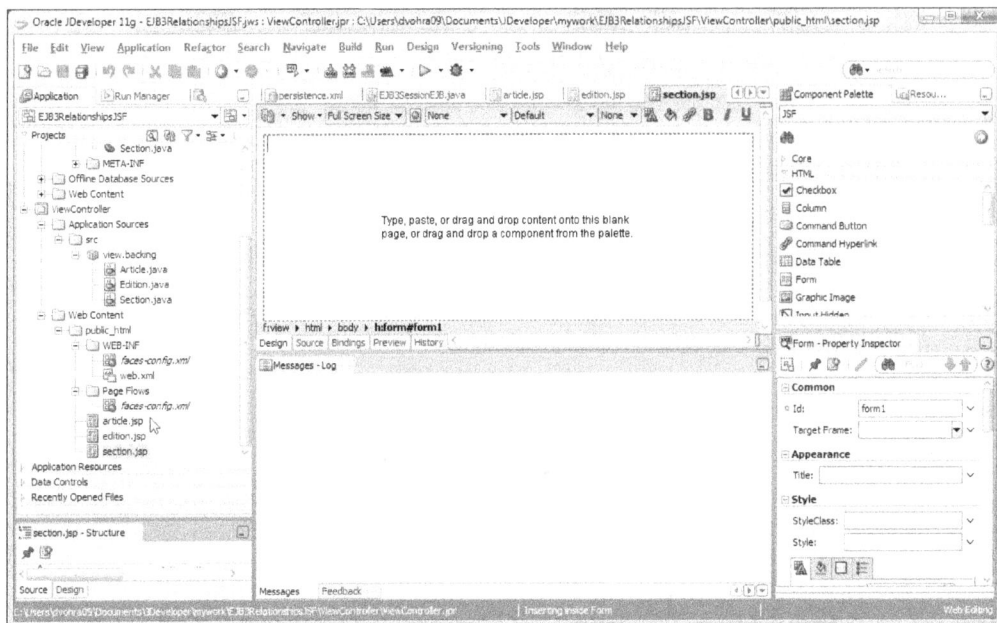

Adding JSF components to the article JSF page

Next, construct the `article.jsp` JSF page. Select **JSF** UI components from the **Component Palette** for JSF and add them to `article.jsp`. Components may be added in two ways: Either drag the components from the palette to the **JSF Page Design** view, or position the cursor on the **JSF Page Design** view and click on the component in the **Component Palette**. First, add a header component for the JSF page title. Position the cursor in the JSF page and select **Output Format** in the **Component Palette**. An `outputFormat` component gets added to `article.jsp`. The code for the **Output Format** component and the other components gets added to `article.jsp` automatically when the components are added to `article.jsp`.

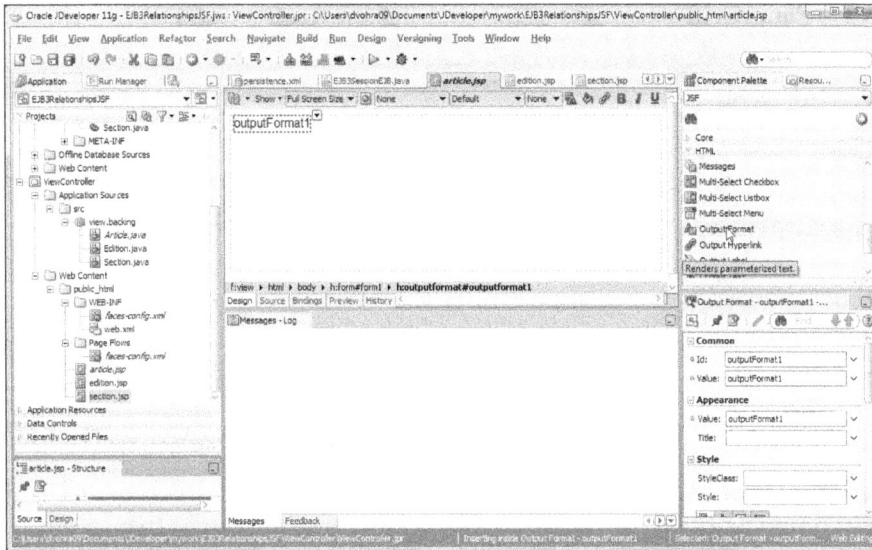

Set the **Value** for the `outputFormat` component in the **Property Inspector**. Next, we shall add **Output Label** and **Input Text** components for the `Article` entity properties `id`, `title`, and `author`. We shall also add **Menu** components for the `Section` id and `Edition` id. A `Section` id and an `Edition` id may be selected when creating an `Article` entity. And we would need a **Command Button** component to submit the JSF page values to a method in the managed bean class `Article.java`. We shall layout the different JSF UI components in a **Panel Grid**. Add a **Pane Grid** to the JSF page `article.jsp` in the **Design** view.

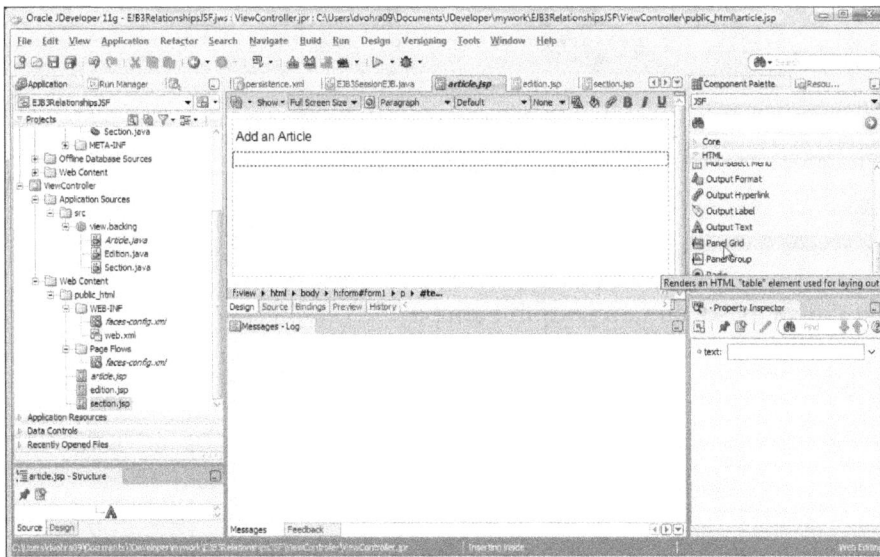

The **Create PanelGrid** wizard gets started. Click on **Next**:

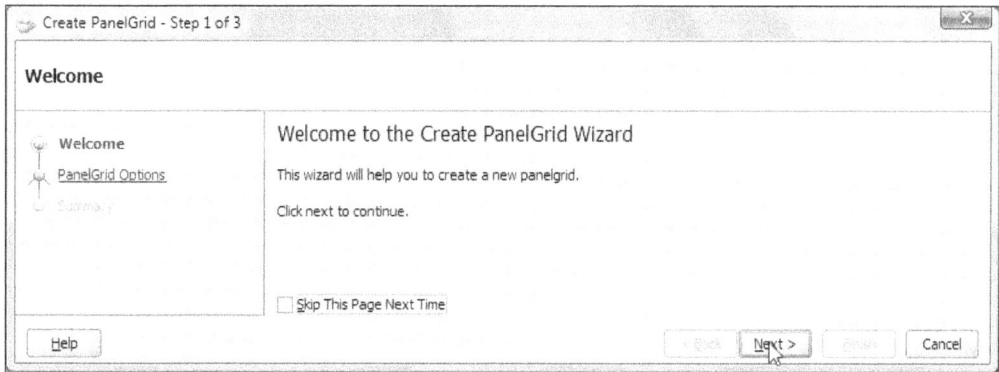

In **PanelGrid Options**, select **Create empty panel grid**. Specify **Number of Columns** as **2**. The components that we add to the panel grid get laid out in two columns. Click on **Next**:

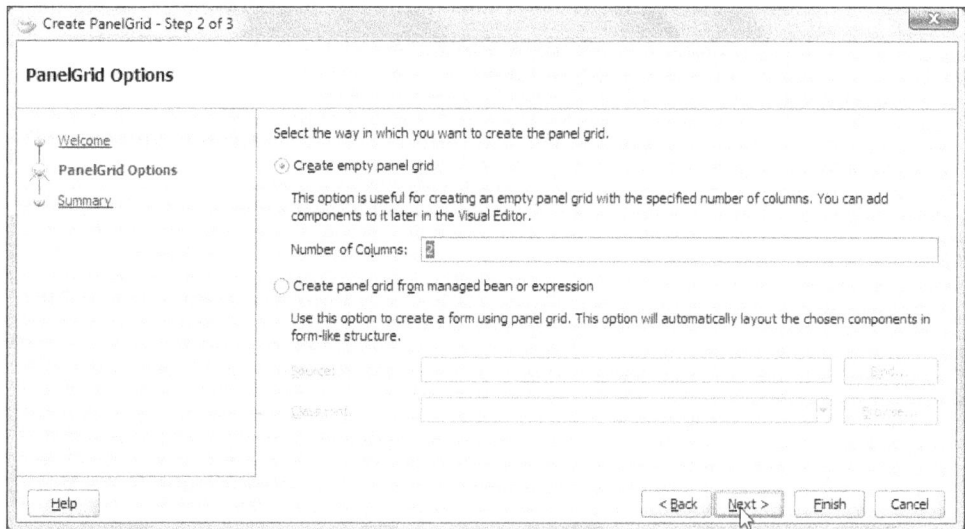

Click on **Finish**. Next, add an **Output Label** to the panel grid:

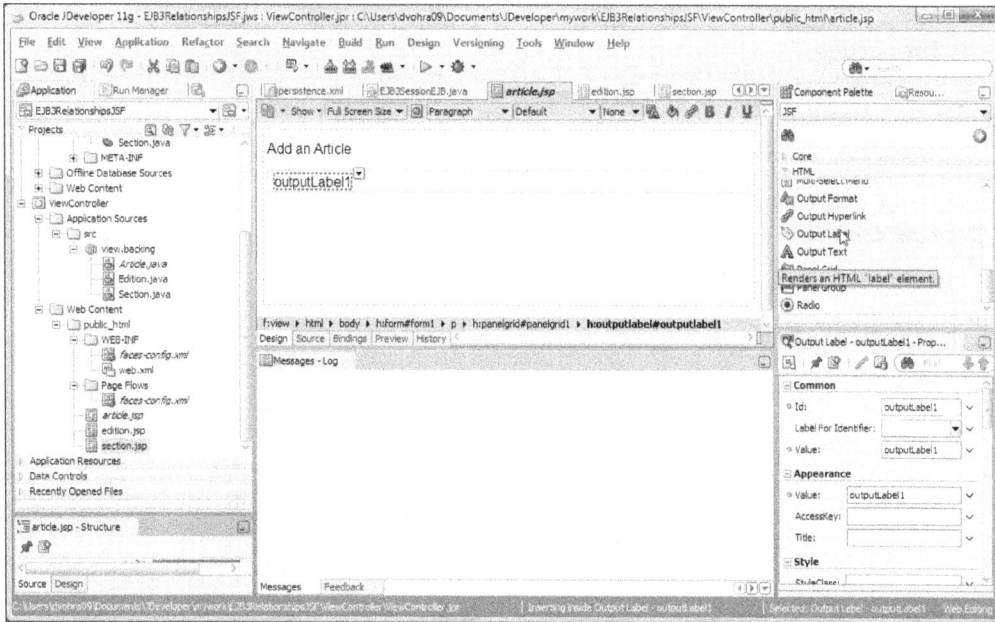

Set the **Value** of the **Output Label** to **Id** in the **Property Inspector**. Position the cursor to the right of the **Output Label** in the **Design** view and add an **Input Text** component from the Component Palette:

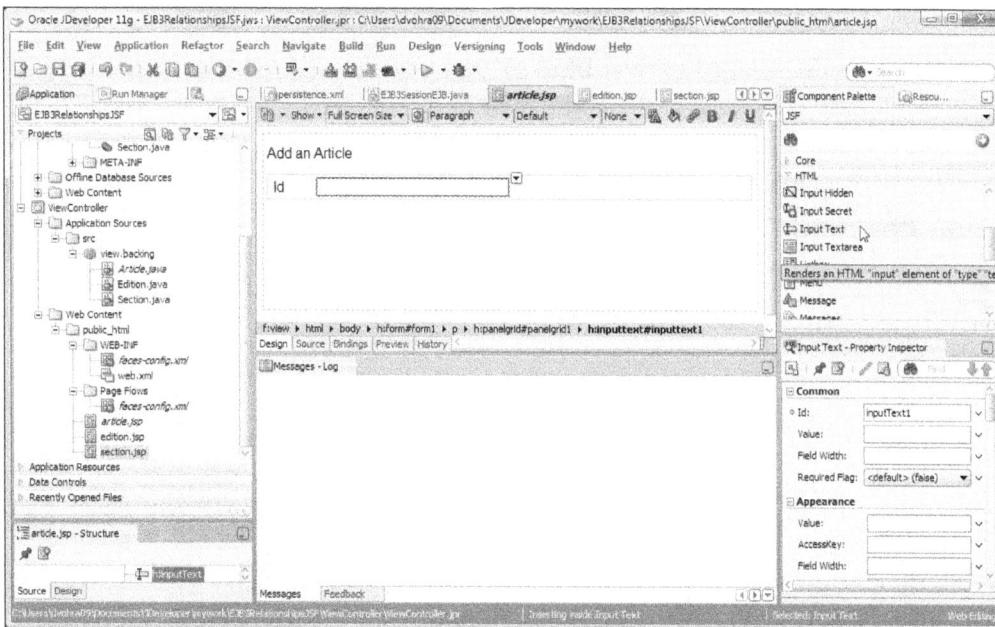

Similarly, add **Output Label** and **Input Text** components for the `title` and `author` entity properties. Next, add an **Output Label** for **Section Id**. We shall add a **Menu** for selecting a **Section Id**. A **Menu** consists of a list of values from which a value may be selected. Position the cursor to the right of the **Section Id** label and select **Menu** in the Component Palette:

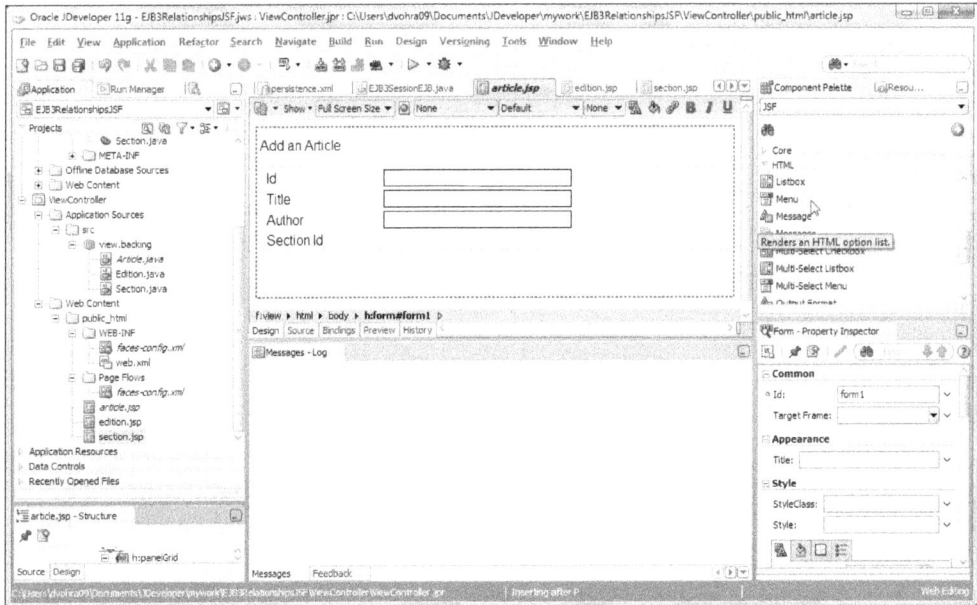

In the **Insert Menu** window, select **Bind to list (select items)** to bind the **Menu** to a list. Select the **Bind** button for the **Value** field:

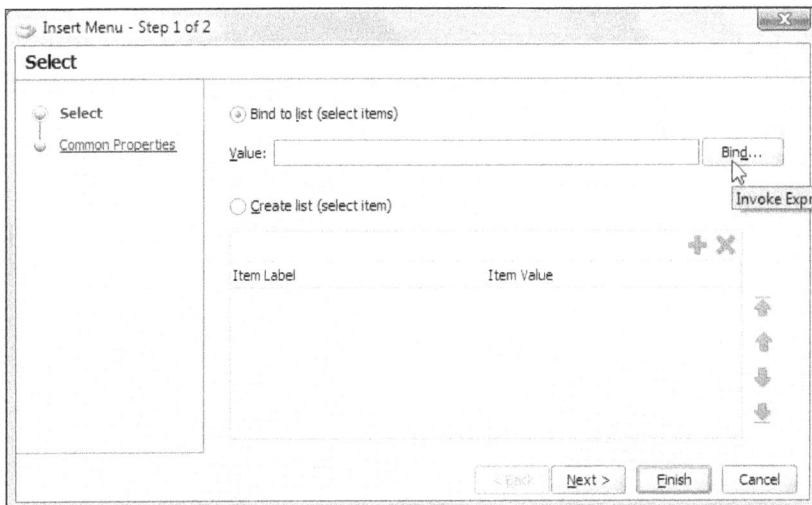

We shall bind the **Menu** to a parameterized `ArrayList` of type `SelectItem` in the managed bean class `view.backing.Article`. In the **Expression Builder**, specify the EL expression **#{backing_article.sectionItems}**. In the expression, **backing_Article** refers to the managed bean name and **sectionItems** refers to a `ArrayList` of type `SelectItem` that we shall define later in the section. Click on **OK**:

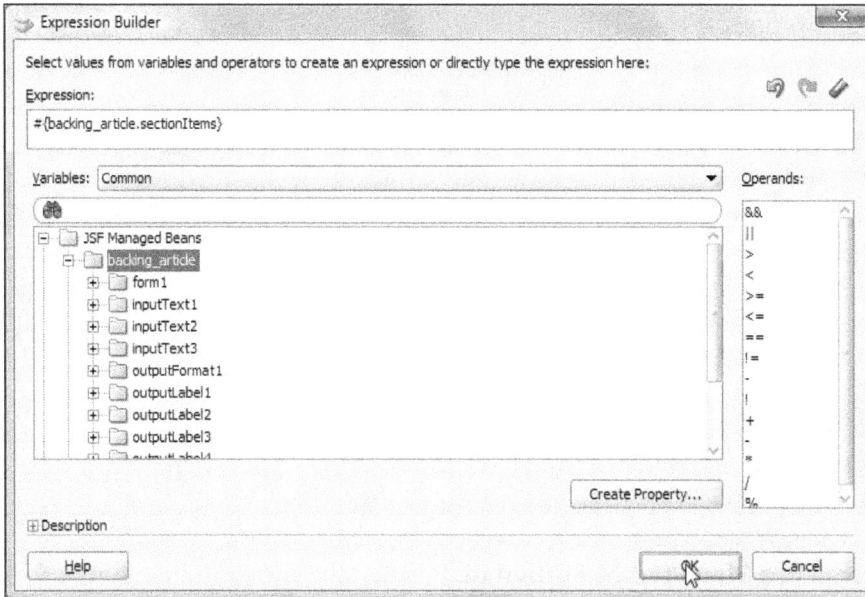

The EL expression gets specified in the **Value** field of the **Insert Menu** window. Click on **Next**:

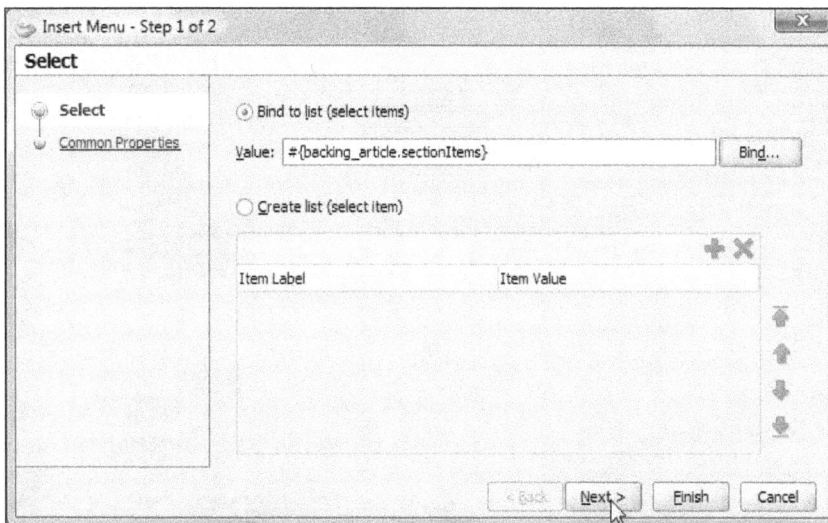

Specify a **Label** for the **Menu** and click on **Finish**. The **Menu** gets added to the **Panel Grid** to the right of the label **Section Id**:

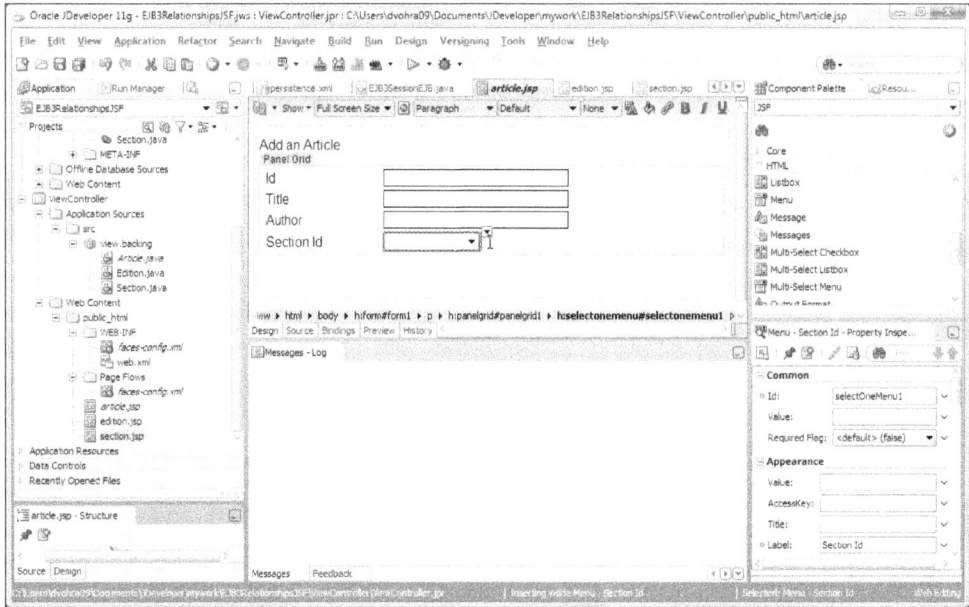

Similarly, add a **Menu** for the **Edition Id**. Position the cursor to the right of the **Menu** for the **Edition Id** and select **Command Button** in the Component Palette:

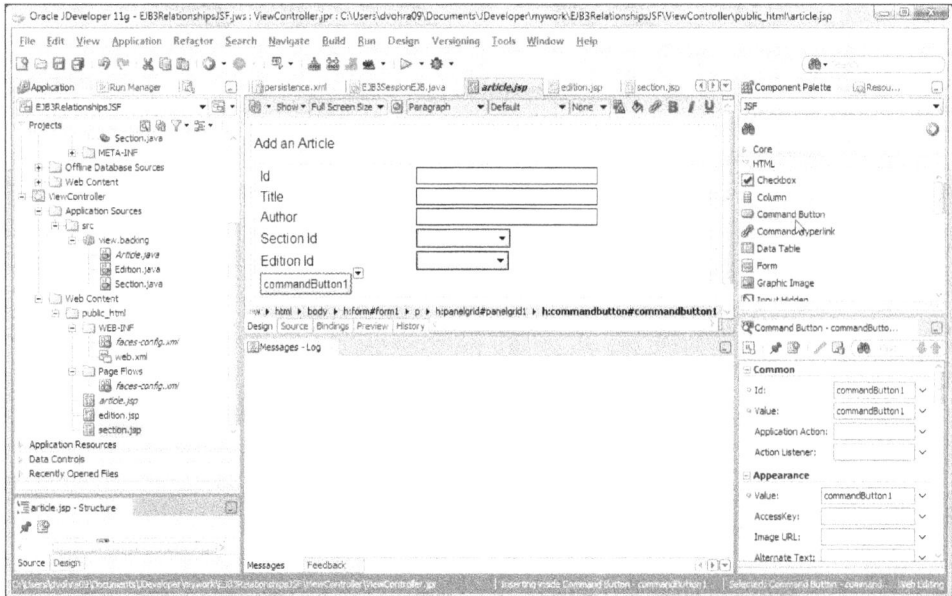

Set the value for the **Command Button** to **Submit** in the **Property Inspector**:

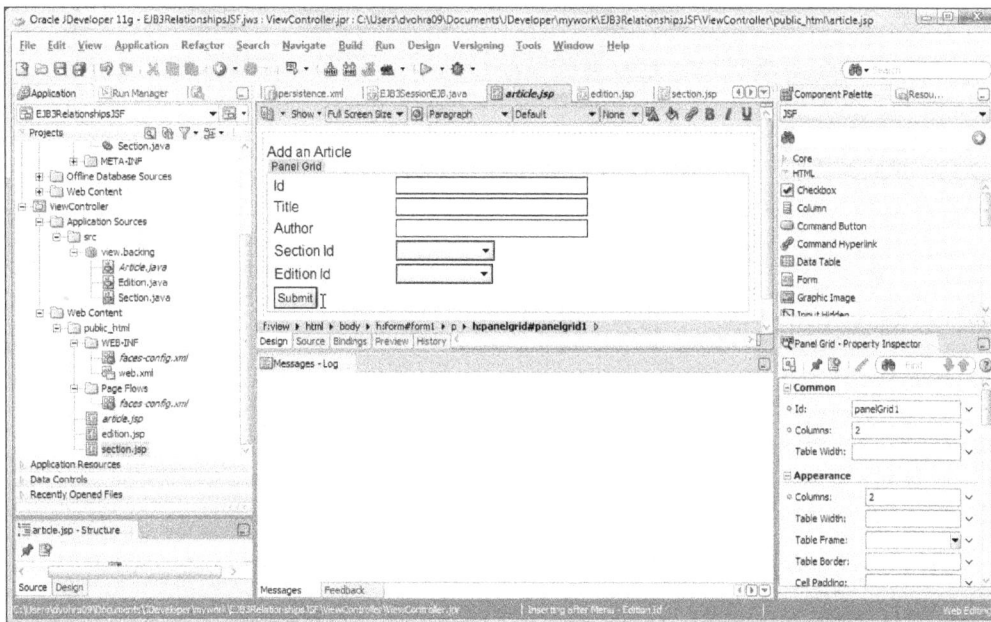

Next, bind the **Submit** button to a managed bean method so that when the **Submit** button is clicked, the managed bean method gets invoked. Double-click on the **Submit** button in the **Design** view:

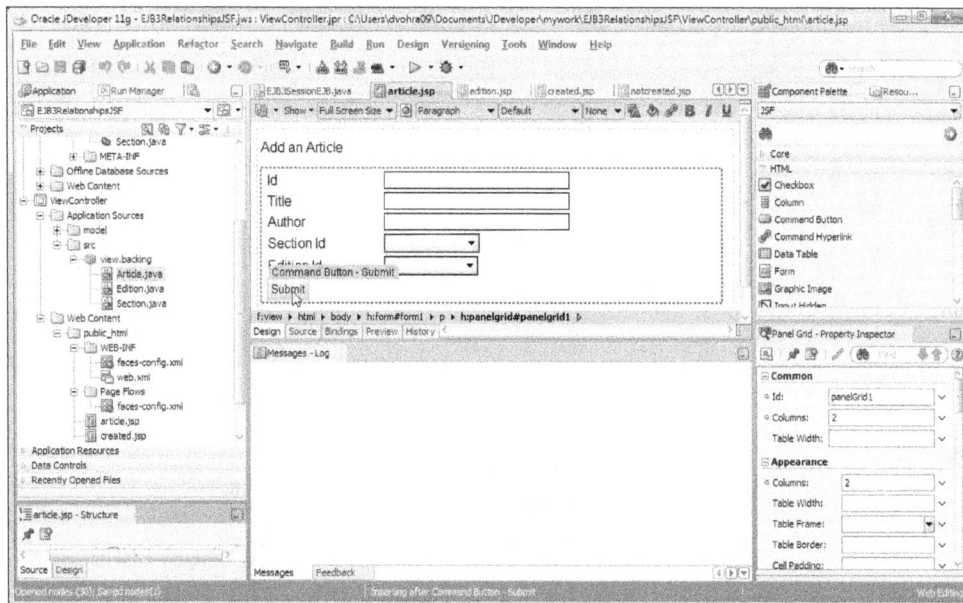

In the **Bind Action Property** window, select the **Managed Bean** to bind to, and select a **Method** to bind to. Click on **OK**:

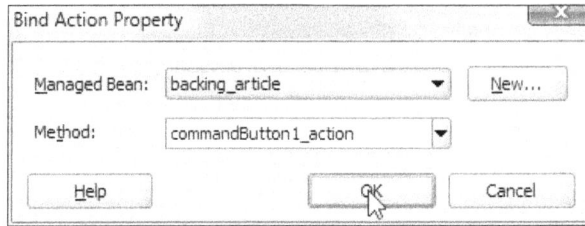

The `article.jsp` JSF page is listed as follows:

```
<!DOCTYPE HTML PUBLIC "-//W3C//DTD HTML 4.01 Transitional//EN"
"http://www.w3.org/TR/html4/loose.dtd">
<%@ page contentType="text/html;charset=windows-1252"%>
<%@ taglib uri="http://java.sun.com/jsf/core" prefix="f"%>
<%@ taglib uri="http://java.sun.com/jsf/html" prefix="h"%>
<f:view>
  <html>
    <head>
      <meta http-equiv="Content-Type"
            content="text/html; charset=windows-1252"/>
      <title>article</title>
    </head>
    <body>
      <h:form binding="#{backing_article.form1}" id="form1">
        <p>
          <h:outputFormat value="Add an Article"
                          binding="#{backing_article.outputFormat1}"
                          id="outputFormat1"/>
        </p>
        <p>
          <h:panelGrid columns="2"
             binding="#{backing_article.panelGrid1}"
                       id="panelGrid1">
            <h:outputLabel value="Id"
                           binding="#{backing_article.outputLabel1}"
                           id="outputLabel1"/>
            <h:inputText binding="#{backing_article.inputText1}"
                         id="inputText1"/>
            <h:outputLabel value="Title"
                           binding="#{backing_article.outputLabel2}"
                           id="outputLabel2"/>
```

```
                <h:inputText binding="#{backing_article.inputText2}"
                        id="inputText2"/>
                <h:outputLabel value="Author"
                        binding="#{backing_article.outputLabel3}"
                        id="outputLabel3"/>
                <h:inputText binding="#{backing_article.inputText3}"
                        id="inputText3"/>
                <h:outputLabel value="Section Id"
                        binding="#{backing_article.outputLabel4}"
                        id="outputLabel4"/>
                <h:selectOneMenu label="Section Id"
                        binding="#{backing_article.
                            selectOneMenu1}"
                        id="selectOneMenu1">
                  <f:selectItems value="#{backing_article.sectionItems}"
                        binding="#{backing_article.selectItems1}"
                        id="selectItems1"/>
                </h:selectOneMenu>
                <h:outputLabel value="Edition Id"
                        binding="#{backing_article.outputLabel5}"
                        id="outputLabel5"/>
                <h:selectOneMenu label="Edition Id"
                        binding="#{backing_article.
                            selectOneMenu2}"
                        id="selectOneMenu2">
                  <f:selectItems value="#{backing_article.editionItems}"
                        binding="#{backing_article.selectItems2}"
                        id="selectItems2"/>
                </h:selectOneMenu>
                <h:commandButton value="Submit"
                        binding="#{backing_article.
                            commandButton1}"
                        id="commandButton1"
                        action="#{backing_article.
                            commandButton1_action}"/>
          </h:panelGrid>
        </p>
      </h:form>
    </body>
  </html>
</f:view>
<%-- oracle-jdev-comment:auto-binding-backing-bean-name:backing_
    article--%>
```

Managed bean for the article JSF page

As we need to display all of the Section id and Edition id IDs in the article. jsp JSF page when the page is run, we have added a value binding in the selectOneMenu labels in article.jsp to SelectItem ArrayLists in the managed bean. To display the Section id and Edition id IDs, we shall retrieve all the Section id and Edition id IDs in the managed bean and bind the id values to the **Menu** lists. Define parameterized ArrayList variables of type SelectItem for the Section id **Menu** and the Edition id **Menu**:

```
private ArrayList<SelectItem> sectionItems;
private ArrayList<SelectItem> editionItems;
```

Next, retrieve all the Section id IDs and add the id values to the sectionItems ArrayList, which is of type SelectItem. Add the method getAllSections() to retrieve and bind all the Section id IDs. In the getAllSections() method, create an InitialContext object and lookup the session bean via its remote interface:

```
InitialContext context = new InitialContext();
EJB3SessionEJB
beanRemote=(EJB3SessionEJB)context.lookup(
  "EJB3RelationshipsJSF-Model-EJB3SessionEJB#model.EJB3SessionEJB");
```

Retrieve all the Section entities in the database with the getAllSections method:

```
List<Section> sections =beanRemote.getAllSections();
```

Initialize the sectionItems ArrayList with its size set to the size of the List<Section> retrieved:

```
sectionItems = new ArrayList<SelectItem>(sections.size());
```

Using a ForEach loop, iterate over the List<Section> object sections and retrieve the Section id IDs for the Section entity instances. For each of the Section id IDs, create a SelectItem object and add the SelectItem object to sectionItems ArrayList<SelectItem>, which has a value binding to the Section id **Menu** list in article.jsp:

```
for (Section section : sections) {
  String sectionId = section.getId();
  SelectItem selectItem=new SelectItem(sectionId,sectionId);
  sectionItems.add(selectItem);
}
this.setSectionItems(sectionItems);
```

The first `sectionId` argument is displayed as the label of the list and the second argument is for the value. Similarly, create a parameterized `ArrayList` of type `SelectItem` for the `Edition` id IDs. In the managed bean method `commandButton1_action`, retrieve the values for the `id`, `title`, and `author`:

```
String id = (String)inputText1.getValue();
String title = (String)inputText2.getValue();
String author = (String)inputText3.getValue();
```

The **Menu** components have a binding with UI components of type `HtmlSelectOneMenu` in the managed bean, and the **Menu** list items have a binding with UI components of type `UISelectItems` in the managed bean. Retrieve the `ArrayList` objects for the **Menu** items.

```
java.util.ArrayList sectionUIComponents =
    (java.util.ArrayList)selectItems1.getValue();
java.util.ArrayList editionUIComponents =
    (java.util.ArrayList)selectItems2.getValue();
```

Because, we bound the select items in the Menus to `ArrayLists` of type `SelectItem`, the items in the `ArrayList` lists retrieved are of type `SelectItem`. As only one value is returned to the managed bean when a **Menu** item is selected, the retrieved `ArrayList` lists have only one item in each of the lists. Retrieve the list item from `ArrayList` using the `get` method with index value as 0, as `ArrayList` lists are 0 based. As the list item is of type `SelectItem`, cast the retrieved object to `SelectItem`.

```
SelectItem sectionItem=(SelectItem)sectionUIComponents.get(0);
SelectItem editionItem=(SelectItem)editionUIComponents.get(0);
```

Retrieve the `Section` id and `Edition` id values from the `SelectItem` objects using the `getValue` method:

```
String sectionId=(String)sectionItem.getValue();
String editionId=(String)editionItem.getValue();
```

Next, create an `InitialContext` object and lookup the session bean through the JNDI name for its remote interface:

```
InitialContext context = new InitialContext();
EJB3SessionEJB beanRemote = (EJB3SessionEJB)context.lookup(
    "EJB3RelationshipsJSF-Model-EJB3SessionEJB#model.EJB3SessionEJB");
```

Invoke the `createArticle` method of the session bean to create and persist an `Article` entity:

```
beanRemote.createArticle(id, title, author, sectionId,editionId);
```

The `view.backing.Article` class is listed as follows:

```
package view.backing;

import model.*;
import java.util.ArrayList;
import java.util.List;
import javax.faces.model.SelectItem;
import javax.faces.component.UISelectItems;
import javax.faces.component.html.HtmlCommandButton;
import javax.faces.component.html.HtmlForm;
import javax.faces.component.html.HtmlInputText;
import javax.faces.component.html.HtmlOutputFormat;
import javax.faces.component.html.HtmlOutputLabel;
import javax.faces.component.html.HtmlPanelGrid;

import javax.faces.component.html.HtmlSelectOneMenu;

import javax.naming.InitialContext;
import javax.naming.NamingException;

public class Article {
  private HtmlForm form1;
  private HtmlOutputFormat outputFormat1;
  private HtmlPanelGrid panelGrid1;
  private HtmlOutputLabel outputLabel1;
  private HtmlInputText inputText1;
  private HtmlOutputLabel outputLabel2;
  private HtmlInputText inputText2;
  private HtmlOutputLabel outputLabel3;
  private HtmlInputText inputText3;
  private HtmlOutputLabel outputLabel4;
  private HtmlSelectOneMenu selectOneMenu1;
  private UISelectItems selectItems1;
  private HtmlOutputLabel outputLabel5;
  private HtmlSelectOneMenu selectOneMenu2;
  private UISelectItems selectItems2;
  private HtmlCommandButton commandButton1;
  private ArrayList<SelectItem> sectionItems;
  private ArrayList<SelectItem> editionItems;
  private String sectionItem;
  private String editionItem;

  public Article() {
    getAllEditions();
    getAllSections();
  }
```

```
public void setSectionItems(ArrayList<SelectItem> sectionItems) {
  this.sectionItems = sectionItems;
}

public ArrayList<SelectItem> getSectionItems() {
  return sectionItems;
}

public void setEditionItems(ArrayList<SelectItem> editionItems) {
  this.editionItems = editionItems;
}

public ArrayList<SelectItem> getEditionItems() {
  return editionItems;
}

public void setSectionItem(String sectionItem) {
  this.sectionItem = sectionItem;
}

public String getSectionItem() {
  return sectionItem;
}

public void setEditionItem(String editionItem) {
  this.editionItem = editionItem;
}

public String getEditionItem() {
  return editionItem;
}

public void setForm1(HtmlForm form1) {
  this.form1 = form1;
}

public HtmlForm getForm1() {
  return form1;
}

public void setOutputFormat1(HtmlOutputFormat outputFormat1) {
  this.outputFormat1 = outputFormat1;
}

public HtmlOutputFormat getOutputFormat1() {
  return outputFormat1;
```

```
    }

    public void setPanelGrid1(HtmlPanelGrid panelGrid1) {
      this.panelGrid1 = panelGrid1;
    }

    public HtmlPanelGrid getPanelGrid1() {
      return panelGrid1;
    }

    public void setOutputLabel1(HtmlOutputLabel outputLabel1) {
      this.outputLabel1 = outputLabel1;
    }

    public HtmlOutputLabel getOutputLabel1() {
      return outputLabel1;
    }

    public void setInputText1(HtmlInputText inputText1) {
      this.inputText1 = inputText1;
    }

    public HtmlInputText getInputText1() {
      return inputText1;
    }

    public void setOutputLabel2(HtmlOutputLabel outputLabel2) {
      this.outputLabel2 = outputLabel2;
    }

    public HtmlOutputLabel getOutputLabel2() {
      return outputLabel2;
    }

  public void setInputText2(HtmlInputText inputText2) {
      this.inputText2 = inputText2;
    }

    public HtmlInputText getInputText2() {
      return inputText2;
    }

    public void setOutputLabel3(HtmlOutputLabel outputLabel3) {
      this.outputLabel3 = outputLabel3;
    }

    public HtmlOutputLabel getOutputLabel3() {
```

```
    return outputLabel3;
  }

public void setInputText3(HtmlInputText inputText3) {
  this.inputText3 = inputText3;
}

public HtmlInputText getInputText3() {
  return inputText3;
}

public void setOutputLabel4(HtmlOutputLabel outputLabel4) {
  this.outputLabel4 = outputLabel4;
}

public HtmlOutputLabel getOutputLabel4() {
  return outputLabel4;
}

public void setSelectOneMenu1(HtmlSelectOneMenu selectOneMenu1) {
  this.selectOneMenu1 = selectOneMenu1;
}

public HtmlSelectOneMenu getSelectOneMenu1() {
  return selectOneMenu1;
}

public void setSelectItems1(UISelectItems selectItems1) {
  this.selectItems1 = selectItems1;
}

public UISelectItems getSelectItems1() {
  return selectItems1;
}

public void setOutputLabel5(HtmlOutputLabel outputLabel5) {
 this.outputLabel5 = outputLabel5;
}

public HtmlOutputLabel getOutputLabel5() {
  return outputLabel5;
}

public void setSelectOneMenu2(HtmlSelectOneMenu selectOneMenu2) {
  this.selectOneMenu2 = selectOneMenu2;
}
```

```java
public HtmlSelectOneMenu getSelectOneMenu2() {
  return selectOneMenu2;
}

public void setSelectItems2(UISelectItems selectItems2) {
  this.selectItems2 = selectItems2;
}

public UISelectItems getSelectItems2() {
  return selectItems2;
}

public void setCommandButton1(HtmlCommandButton commandButton1) {
  this.commandButton1 = commandButton1;
}

public HtmlCommandButton getCommandButton1() {
  return commandButton1;
}

public ArrayList<SelectItem> getAllSections() {
  try {
    InitialContext context = new InitialContext();
    EJB3SessionEJB beanRemote = (EJB3SessionEJB) context.lookup(
      "EJB3RelationshipsJSF-Model-EJB3SessionEJB#model.
        EJB3SessionEJB");
    List<model.Section> sections = beanRemote.getAllSections();
    sectionItems = new ArrayList<SelectItem>(sections.size());
    for (model.Section section : sections) {
      String sectionId = section.getId();
      SelectItem selectItem = new SelectItem(sectionId, sectionId);
      sectionItems.add(selectItem);
    }
      this.setSectionItems(sectionItems);
  } catch (NamingException e) {
    System.err.println(e.getMessage());
  }
  return sectionItems;
}

public ArrayList<SelectItem> getAllEditions() {
  try {
    InitialContext context = new InitialContext();
    EJB3SessionEJB beanRemote = (EJB3SessionEJB) context.lookup(
      "EJB3RelationshipsJSF-Model-EJB3SessionEJB#model.
        EJB3SessionEJB");
    List<model.Edition> editions = beanRemote.getAllEditions();
```

```
      editionItems = new ArrayList<SelectItem>(editions.size());
      for (model.Edition edition : editions) {
        String editionId = edition.getId();
        SelectItem selectItem = new SelectItem(editionId, editionId);
        editionItems.add(selectItem);
      }
      this.setEditionItems(editionItems);
    } catch (NamingException e) {
      System.err.println(e.getMessage());
    }
    return editionItems;
  }

  public String commandButton1_action() {
    // Add event code here...
    try {
      String id = (String) inputText1.getValue();
      String title = (String) inputText2.getValue();
      String author = (String) inputText3.getValue();
      java.util.ArrayList sectionUIComponents = (java.util.ArrayList)
        selectItems1.getValue();
      java.util.ArrayList editionUIComponents = (java.util.ArrayList)
        selectItems2.getValue();
      SelectItem sectionItem = (SelectItem) sectionUIComponents.
get(0);
      SelectItem editionItem = (SelectItem) editionUIComponents.
get(0);
      String sectionId = (String) sectionItem.getValue();
      String editionId = (String) editionItem.getValue();
      InitialContext context = new InitialContext();
      EJB3SessionEJB beanRemote = (EJB3SessionEJB) context.lookup(
        "EJB3RelationshipsJSF-Model-EJB3SessionEJB#model.
          EJB3SessionEJB");
      beanRemote.createArticle(id, title, author, sectionId,
editionId);
    } catch (NamingException e) {
      System.err.println(e.getMessage());
      return "notcreated";
    }
    return "created";
  }
}
```

Adding JSF components to the section JSF page

Similar to the `article.jsp` JSF page, construct the `section.jsp` JSF page, which has a binding with the managed bean `backing_section`. The `section.jsp` JSF has two **Input Text** fields for **Id** and **Section Name** labels and a **Menu** for the **Edition Id** label. When a `Section` entity is to be created and persisted, the `Edition id` of the associated `Edition` entity is also required to be specified, because `Edition` entity has a one-to-many relationship with the `Section` entity. Create a binding to a managed bean method `commandButton1_action` for the **Submit** button:

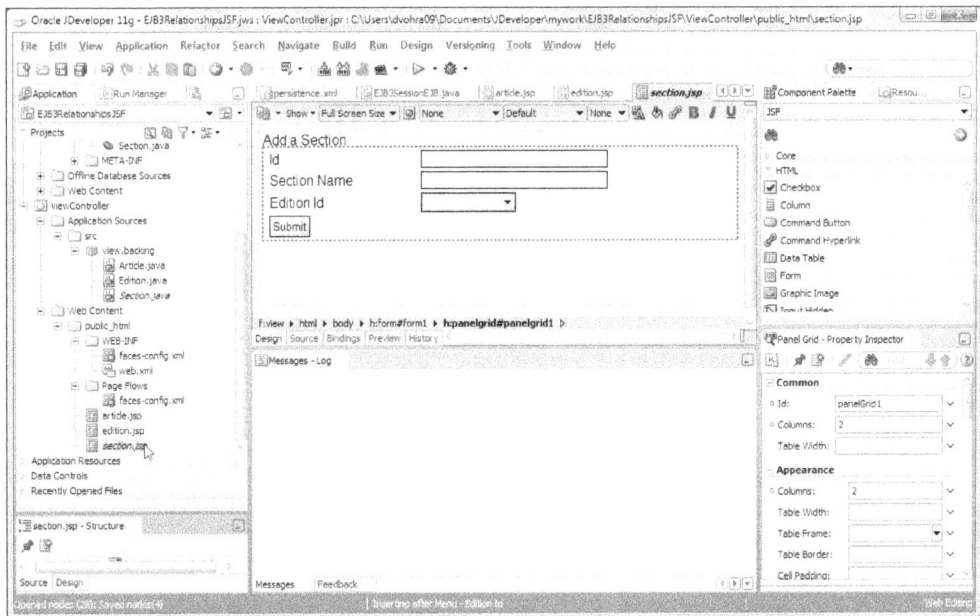

The `section.jsp` is listed as follows:

```
<!DOCTYPE HTML PUBLIC "-//W3C//DTD HTML 4.01 Transitional//EN"
"http://www.w3.org/TR/html4/loose.dtd">
<%@ page contentType="text/html;charset=windows-1252"%>
<%@ taglib uri="http://java.sun.com/jsf/core" prefix="f"%>
<%@ taglib uri="http://java.sun.com/jsf/html" prefix="h"%>
<f:view>
  <html>
    <head>
      <meta http-equiv="Content-Type"
            content="text/html; charset=windows-1252"/>
      <title>section</title>
```

```
    </head>
    <body>
      <h:form binding="#{backing_section.form1}" id="form1">
        <h:outputFormat value="Add a Section"
                        binding="#{backing_section.outputFormat1}"
                        id="outputFormat1"/>
        <h:panelGrid columns="2" binding="#{backing_section.
                                            panelGrid1}"
                     id="panelGrid1">
          <h:outputLabel value="Id"
                         binding="#{backing_section.outputLabel1}"
                         id="outputLabel1"/>
          <h:inputText binding="#{backing_section.inputText1}"
                       id="inputText1"/>
          <h:outputLabel value="Section Name"
                         binding="#{backing_section.outputLabel2}"
                         id="outputLabel2"/>
          <h:inputText binding="#{backing_section.inputText2}"
                       id="inputText2"/>
          <h:outputLabel value="Edition Id"
                         binding="#{backing_section.outputLabel3}"
                         id="outputLabel3"/>
          <h:selectOneMenu label="Edition Id"
                           binding="#{backing_section.selectOneMenu1}"
                           id="selectOneMenu1">
            <f:selectItems value="#{backing_section.editionItems}"
                           binding="#{backing_section.selectItems1}"
                           id="selectItems1"/>
          </h:selectOneMenu>
          <h:commandButton value="Submit"
                           binding="#{backing_section.commandButton1}"
                           id="commandButton1"
                           action="#{backing_section.commandButton1_
                               action}"/>
        </h:panelGrid>
      </h:form>
    </body>
  </html>
</f:view>
<%-- oracle-jdev-comment:auto-binding-backing-bean-name:backing_
    section--%>
```

Managed bean for the section JSF page

In the managed bean class `view.backing.Section`, add a method `getAllEditions()` to retrieve all the `Edition` entities, retrieve the `Edition` entity ids, and create a parameterized `ArrayList` of type `SelectItem`, which has a value binding with the **Menu** component for the **Edition Id** label in the `section.jsp` JSF page, from the `Edition` ids.

In the `commandButton1_action` method, retrieve the values for the `Section id`, `Section name`, and `Edition id` with the procedure discussed for the `view.backing.Article` managed bean class. Create an `InitialContext` object and lookup the session bean with its remote interface, and create and persist a `Section` entity object. The `view.backing.Section` class is listed as follows:

```
package view.backing;

import model.*;
import java.util.ArrayList;
import java.util.List;
import javax.faces.model.SelectItem;
import javax.faces.component.UISelectItems;
import javax.faces.component.html.HtmlCommandButton;
import javax.faces.component.html.HtmlForm;
import javax.faces.component.html.HtmlInputText;
import javax.faces.component.html.HtmlOutputFormat;
import javax.faces.component.html.HtmlOutputLabel;
import javax.faces.component.html.HtmlPanelGrid;
import javax.faces.component.html.HtmlSelectOneMenu;
import javax.naming.InitialContext;
import javax.naming.NamingException;

public class Section {
  private HtmlForm form1;
  private HtmlOutputFormat outputFormat1;
  private HtmlPanelGrid panelGrid1;
  private HtmlOutputLabel outputLabel1;
  private HtmlInputText inputText1;
  private HtmlOutputLabel outputLabel2;
  private HtmlInputText inputText2;
  private HtmlOutputLabel outputLabel3;
  private HtmlSelectOneMenu selectOneMenu1;
  private UISelectItems selectItems1;
  private HtmlCommandButton commandButton1;
  private ArrayList<SelectItem> editionItems;
  private String editionItem;

  public Section() {
    getAllEditions();
  }
```

```
public void setEditionItems(ArrayList<SelectItem> editionItems) {
  this.editionItems = editionItems;
}

public ArrayList<SelectItem> getEditionItems() {
  return editionItems;
}

public void setEditionItem(String editionItem) {
  this.editionItem = editionItem;
}

public String getEditionItem() {
  return editionItem;
}

public void setForm1(HtmlForm form1) {
  this.form1 = form1;
}

public HtmlForm getForm1() {
  return form1;
}

public void setOutputFormat1(HtmlOutputFormat outputFormat1) {
  this.outputFormat1 = outputFormat1;
}

public HtmlOutputFormat getOutputFormat1() {
  return outputFormat1;
}

public void setPanelGrid1(HtmlPanelGrid panelGrid1) {
  this.panelGrid1 = panelGrid1;
}

public HtmlPanelGrid getPanelGrid1() {
  return panelGrid1;
}

public void setOutputLabel1(HtmlOutputLabel outputLabel1) {
  this.outputLabel1 = outputLabel1;
}

public HtmlOutputLabel getOutputLabel1() {
  return outputLabel1;
}

public void setInputText1(HtmlInputText inputText1) {
```

```
    this.inputText1 = inputText1;
  }

  public HtmlInputText getInputText1() {
    return inputText1;
  }

  public void setOutputLabel2(HtmlOutputLabel outputLabel2) {
    this.outputLabel2 = outputLabel2;
  }

  public HtmlOutputLabel getOutputLabel2() {
    return outputLabel2;
  }

  public void setInputText2(HtmlInputText inputText2) {
    this.inputText2 = inputText2;
  }

  public HtmlInputText getInputText2() {
    return inputText2;
  }

  public void setOutputLabel3(HtmlOutputLabel outputLabel3) {
    this.outputLabel3 = outputLabel3;
  }

  public HtmlOutputLabel getOutputLabel3() {
    return outputLabel3;
  }

  public void setSelectOneMenu1(HtmlSelectOneMenu selectOneMenu1) {
    this.selectOneMenu1 = selectOneMenu1;
  }

  public HtmlSelectOneMenu getSelectOneMenu1() {
    return selectOneMenu1;
  }

  public void setSelectItems1(UISelectItems selectItems1) {
    this.selectItems1 = selectItems1;
  }

  public UISelectItems getSelectItems1() {
    return selectItems1;
  }

  public void setCommandButton1(HtmlCommandButton commandButton1) {
    this.commandButton1 = commandButton1;
  }
```

```
  public HtmlCommandButton getCommandButton1() {
    return commandButton1;
  }

  public ArrayList<SelectItem> getAllEditions() {
    try {
      InitialContext context = new InitialContext();
      EJB3SessionEJB beanRemote = (EJB3SessionEJB) context.lookup(
        "EJB3RelationshipsJSF-Model-EJB3SessionEJB#model.
          EJB3SessionEJB");
      List<model.Edition> editions = beanRemote.getAllEditions();
      editionItems = new ArrayList<SelectItem>(editions.size());
      for (model.Edition edition : editions) {
        String editionId = edition.getId();
        SelectItem selectItem = new SelectItem(editionId, editionId);
        editionItems.add(selectItem);
      }
      this.setEditionItems(editionItems);
    } catch (NamingException e) {
      System.err.println(e.getMessage());
    }
    return editionItems;
  }

  public String commandButton1_action() {
    // Add event code here...
    try {
      String id = (String) inputText1.getValue();
      String sectionName = (String) inputText2.getValue();
      java.util.ArrayList editionUIComponents = (java.util.ArrayList)
        selectItems1.getValue();
      SelectItem editionItem = (SelectItem) editionUIComponents.
get(0);
      String editionId = (String) editionItem.getValue();
      InitialContext context = new InitialContext();
      EJB3SessionEJB beanRemote = (EJB3SessionEJB) context.lookup(
        "EJB3RelationshipsJSF-Model-EJB3SessionEJB#model.
          EJB3SessionEJB");
      beanRemote.createSection(id, sectionName, editionId);
    } catch (NamingException e) {
      System.err.println(e.getMessage());
      return "notcreated";
    }
    return "created";
  }
}
```

Adding JSF components to the Edition JSF page

Construct an `edition.jsp` JSF page, which has **Input Text** fields corresponding to the `id`, `journal`, `publisher`, and `edition` properties of the `Edition` entity. Create a binding from the **Submit** button to the `commandButton1_action` method in the managed bean class `backing_edition` so that when the **Submit** button is clicked, the managed bean method gets invoked.

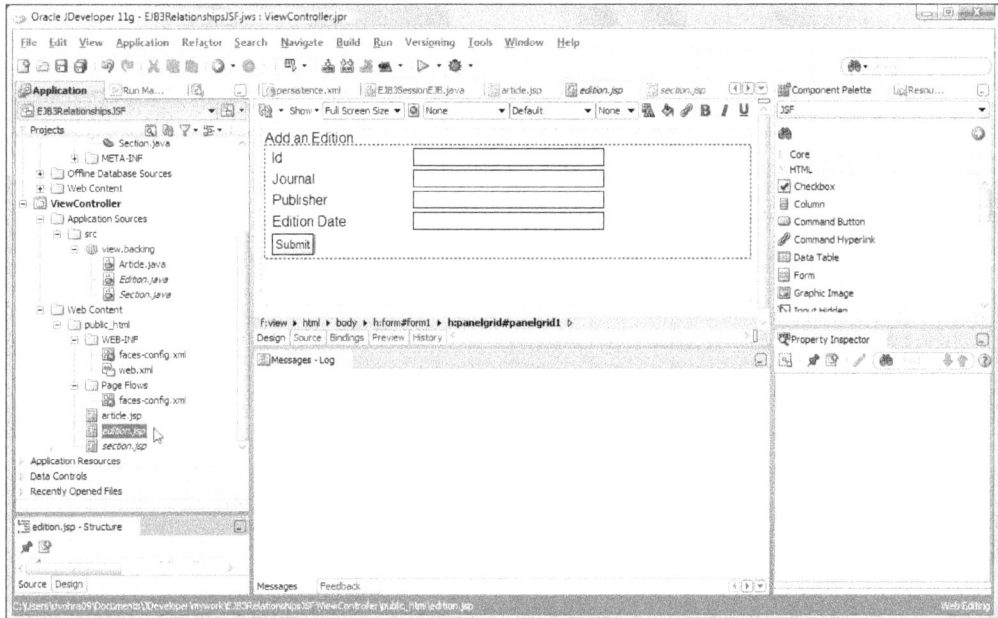

The `edition.jsp` is listed as follows:

```
<!DOCTYPE HTML PUBLIC "-//W3C//DTD HTML 4.01 Transitional//EN"
"http://www.w3.org/TR/html4/loose.dtd">
<%@ page contentType="text/html;charset=windows-1252"%>
<%@ taglib uri="http://java.sun.com/jsf/core" prefix="f"%>
<%@ taglib uri="http://java.sun.com/jsf/html" prefix="h"%>
<f:view>
  <html>
    <head>
      <meta http-equiv="Content-Type"
            content="text/html; charset=windows-1252"/>
      <title>edition</title>
    </head>
    <body>
```

```
        <h:form binding="#{backing_edition.form1}" id="form1">
          <h:outputFormat value="Add an Edition"
                          binding="#{backing_edition.outputFormat1}"
                          id="outputFormat1"/>
          <h:panelGrid columns="2" binding="#{backing_edition.
panelGrid1}"
                       id="panelGrid1">
            <h:outputLabel value="Id"
                           binding="#{backing_edition.outputLabel1}"
                           id="outputLabel1"/>
            <h:inputText binding="#{backing_edition.inputText1}"
                         id="inputText1"/>
            <h:outputLabel value="Journal"
                           binding="#{backing_edition.outputLabel2}"
                           id="outputLabel2"/>
            <h:inputText binding="#{backing_edition.inputText2}"
                         id="inputText2"/>
            <h:outputLabel value="Publisher"
                           binding="#{backing_edition.outputLabel3}"
                           id="outputLabel3"/>
            <h:inputText binding="#{backing_edition.inputText3}"
                         id="inputText3"/>
            <h:outputLabel value="Edition Date"
                           binding="#{backing_edition.outputLabel4}"
                           id="outputLabel4"/>
            <h:inputText binding="#{backing_edition.inputText4}"
                         id="inputText4"/>
            <h:commandButton value="Submit"
                             binding="#{backing_edition.commandButton1}"
                             id="commandButton1"
                             action="#{backing_edition.commandButton1_
                                 action}"/>
          </h:panelGrid>
        </h:form>
      </body>
    </html>
</f:view>
<%-- oracle-jdev-comment:auto-binding-backing-bean-name:backing_
    edition--%>
```

Managed bean for the Edition JSF page

In the `view.backing.Edition` managed bean class, the `commandButton1_action()` method is invoked when the **Submit** button is clicked. In the `commandButton1_action()` method, retrieve the **Input Text** values, create an `InitialContext` object and lookup the session bean via its remote interface, and create and persist a `Edition` entity object. The `Edition` managed bean is listed as follows:

```
package view.backing;

import model.*;
import javax.faces.component.html.HtmlCommandButton;
import javax.faces.component.html.HtmlForm;
import javax.faces.component.html.HtmlInputText;
import javax.faces.component.html.HtmlOutputFormat;
import javax.faces.component.html.HtmlOutputLabel;
import javax.faces.component.html.HtmlPanelGrid;
import javax.naming.InitialContext;
import javax.naming.NamingException;

public class Edition {
  private HtmlForm form1;
  private HtmlOutputFormat outputFormat1;
  private HtmlPanelGrid panelGrid1;
  private HtmlOutputLabel outputLabel1;
  private HtmlInputText inputText1;
  private HtmlOutputLabel outputLabel2;
  private HtmlInputText inputText2;
  private HtmlOutputLabel outputLabel3;
  private HtmlInputText inputText3;
  private HtmlOutputLabel outputLabel4;
  private HtmlInputText inputText4;
  private HtmlCommandButton commandButton1;

  public void setForm1(HtmlForm form1) {
    this.form1 = form1;
  }

  public HtmlForm getForm1() {
    return form1;
  }

  public void setOutputFormat1(HtmlOutputFormat outputFormat1) {
    this.outputFormat1 = outputFormat1;
  }

  public HtmlOutputFormat getOutputFormat1() {
    return outputFormat1;
```

```
  }

  public void setPanelGrid1(HtmlPanelGrid panelGrid1) {
    this.panelGrid1 = panelGrid1;
  }

  public HtmlPanelGrid getPanelGrid1() {
    return panelGrid1;
  }

  public void setOutputLabel1(HtmlOutputLabel outputLabel1) {
    this.outputLabel1 = outputLabel1;
  }

  public HtmlOutputLabel getOutputLabel1() {
    return outputLabel1;
  }

  public void setInputText1(HtmlInputText inputText1) {
    this.inputText1 = inputText1;
  }

  public HtmlInputText getInputText1() {
    return inputText1;
  }

  public void setOutputLabel2(HtmlOutputLabel outputLabel2) {
    this.outputLabel2 = outputLabel2;
  }

  public HtmlOutputLabel getOutputLabel2() {
    return outputLabel2;
  }

  public void setInputText2(HtmlInputText inputText2) {
    this.inputText2 = inputText2;
  }

  public HtmlInputText getInputText2() {
    return inputText2;
  }

  public void setOutputLabel3(HtmlOutputLabel outputLabel3) {
    this.outputLabel3 = outputLabel3;
  }

  public HtmlOutputLabel getOutputLabel3() {
    return outputLabel3;
```

```
    }

    public void setInputText3(HtmlInputText inputText3) {
      this.inputText3 = inputText3;
    }

    public HtmlInputText getInputText3() {
      return inputText3;
    }

    public void setOutputLabel4(HtmlOutputLabel outputLabel4) {
      this.outputLabel4 = outputLabel4;
    }

    public HtmlOutputLabel getOutputLabel4() {
      return outputLabel4;
    }

    public void setInputText4(HtmlInputText inputText4) {
      this.inputText4 = inputText4;
    }

    public HtmlInputText getInputText4() {
      return inputText4;
    }

    public void setCommandButton1(HtmlCommandButton commandButton1) {
      this.commandButton1 = commandButton1;
    }

    public HtmlCommandButton getCommandButton1() {
      return commandButton1;
    }

    public String commandButton1_action() {
      // Add event code here...
      try {
        String id = (String) inputText1.getValue();
        String journal = (String) inputText2.getValue();
        String publisher = (String) inputText3.getValue();
        String edition_date = (String) inputText4.getValue();
        InitialContext context = new InitialContext();
        EJB3SessionEJB beanRemote = (EJB3SessionEJB) context.lookup(
          "EJB3RelationshipsJSF-Model-EJB3SessionEJB#model.
            EJB3SessionEJB");
        beanRemote.createEdition(id, journal, publisher, edition_date);
      } catch (NamingException e) {
        System.err.println(e.getMessage());
        return "notcreated";
```

```
    }
    return "created";
  }
}
```

Adding JSF page navigation

All of the JSF pages navigate to a JSF page `created.jsp`, which displays a message to indicate that the database has been updated if an error is not generated in creating and persisting an entity. The `created.jsp` JSF page is listed as follows:

```
<!DOCTYPE HTML PUBLIC "-//W3C//DTD HTML 4.01 Transitional//EN"
"http://www.w3.org/TR/html4/loose.dtd">
<%@ page contentType="text/html;charset=windows-1252"%>
<%@ taglib uri="http://java.sun.com/jsf/core" prefix="f"%>
<%@ taglib uri="http://java.sun.com/jsf/html" prefix="h"%>
<f:view>
  <html>
    <head>
      <meta http-equiv="Content-Type"
            content="text/html; charset=windows-1252"/>
      <title>created</title>
    </head>
    <body>
      <h:form><%out.println("Created"); %></h:form>
    </body>
  </html>
</f:view>
```

And if an error is generated, the JSF pages navigate to a JSF page `notcreated.jsp`, which is listed as follows:

```
<!DOCTYPE HTML PUBLIC "-//W3C//DTD HTML 4.01 Transitional//EN"
"http://www.w3.org/TR/html4/loose.dtd">
<%@ page contentType="text/html;charset=windows-1252"%>
<%@ taglib uri="http://java.sun.com/jsf/core" prefix="f"%>
<%@ taglib uri="http://java.sun.com/jsf/html" prefix="h"%>
<f:view>
  <html>
    <head>
      <meta http-equiv="Content-Type"
            content="text/html; charset=windows-1252"/>
      <title>notcreated</title>
    </head>
    <body>
        <h:form><%out.println("Not created"); %></h:form>
    </body>
  </html>
</f:view>
```

The `created.jsp` and `notcreated.jsp` JSF pages are not associated with managed beans. The JSF page navigation and the managed beans are defined in the configuration file `faces-config.xml`, which is listed as follows:

```
<?xml version="1.0" encoding="windows-1252"?>
<faces-config version="1.2" xmlns="http://java.sun.com/xml/ns/javaee">
    <managed-bean>
        <managed-bean-name>backing_article</managed-bean-name>
        <managed-bean-class>view.backing.Article</managed-bean-class>
        <managed-bean-scope>request</managed-bean-scope>
        <!--oracle-jdev-comment:managed-bean-jsp-link:1article.jsp-->
    </managed-bean>
    <managed-bean>
        <managed-bean-name>backing_edition</managed-bean-name>
        <managed-bean-class>view.backing.Edition</managed-bean-class>
        <managed-bean-scope>request</managed-bean-scope>
        <!--oracle-jdev-comment:managed-bean-jsp-link:1edition.jsp-->
    </managed-bean>
    <managed-bean>
        <managed-bean-name>backing_section</managed-bean-name>
        <managed-bean-class>view.backing.Section</managed-bean-class>
        <managed-bean-scope>request</managed-bean-scope>
        <!--oracle-jdev-comment:managed-bean-jsp-link:1section.jsp-->
    </managed-bean>
    <navigation-rule>
        <from-view-id>/edition.jsp</from-view-id>
        <navigation-case>
            <from-outcome>created</from-outcome>
            <to-view-id>/created.jsp</to-view-id>
        </navigation-case>
        <navigation-case>
            <from-outcome>notcreated</from-outcome>
            <to-view-id>/notcreated.jsp</to-view-id>
        </navigation-case>
    </navigation-rule>

    <navigation-rule>
        <from-view-id>/section.jsp</from-view-id>
        <navigation-case>
            <from-outcome>created</from-outcome>
            <to-view-id>/created.jsp</to-view-id>
        </navigation-case>
        <navigation-case>
            <from-outcome>notcreated</from-outcome>
```

```
            <to-view-id>/notcreated.jsp</to-view-id>
        </navigation-case>
    </navigation-rule>

    <navigation-rule>
        <from-view-id>/article.jsp</from-view-id>
        <navigation-case>
            <from-outcome>created</from-outcome>
            <to-view-id>/created.jsp</to-view-id>
        </navigation-case>
        <navigation-case>
            <from-outcome>notcreated</from-outcome>
            <to-view-id>/notcreated.jsp</to-view-id>
        </navigation-case>
    </navigation-rule>

</faces-config>
```

Web configuration file

In the WEB-INF/web.xml, we need to add a servlet mapping for the javax.faces.
webapp.FacesServlet, which is required to invoke the JSF framework. When the /
faces/* URL pattern is included when running a JSF page, the Faces Servlet
gets invoked:

```
<servlet>
    <servlet-name>Faces Servlet</servlet-name>
    <servlet-class>javax.faces.webapp.FacesServlet</servlet-class>
    <load-on-startup>1</load-on-startup>
</servlet>
<servlet-mapping>
    <servlet-name>Faces Servlet</servlet-name>
    <url-pattern>/faces/*</url-pattern>
</servlet-mapping>
```

Running the JSF user interfaces

In this section, we shall run the JSF pages and add data to the database tables using the EJB 3.0 entity beans for database persistence. We need to re-create the database tables SECTION and ARTICLE to include columns that map to the join tables of the EJB 3.0 relationships. The join tables are automatically generated when the EJB 3.0 entity beans are invoked. Drop the SECTION and ARTICLE tables and re-create the tables with the following SQL script:

```
CREATE TABLE ARTICLE (id VARCHAR(100) PRIMARY KEY NOT NULL,
    title VARCHAR(100), author VARCHAR(100),
    SECTION_ID VARCHAR(100), EDITION_ID(100));
CREATE TABLE SECTION (id VARCHAR(100) PRIMARY KEY NOT NULL,
    section VARCHAR(100), EDITION_ID VARCHAR(100));
```

First, we need to add a project dependency in the ViewController project on the Model project. Right-click on the ViewController project node and select **Project Properties**:

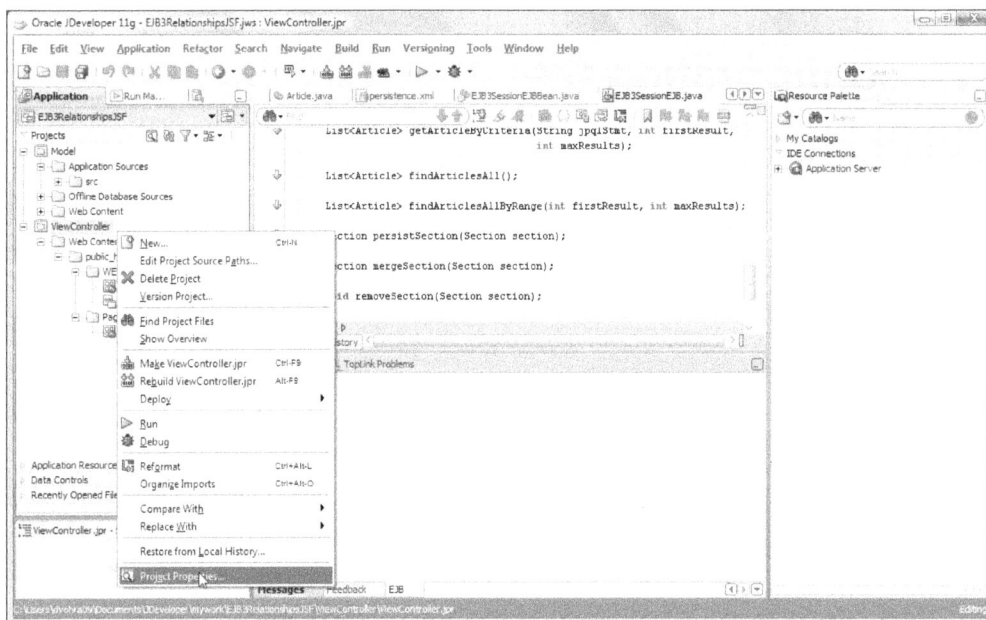

In the **Project Properties** window, select the **Dependencies** node and select **Edit Dependencies**. In **Edit Dependencies**, select the **Model** project **Build Output** and click on **OK**. In the **Dependencies** window, click on **OK**. Before creating a Section entity, we need to create an Edition entity and before creating an Article entity, we need to create a Section entity, because the JSF pages are so designed.

Creating an Edition entity

To create and persist an `Edition` entity, right-click on **edition.jsp** and select **Run**:

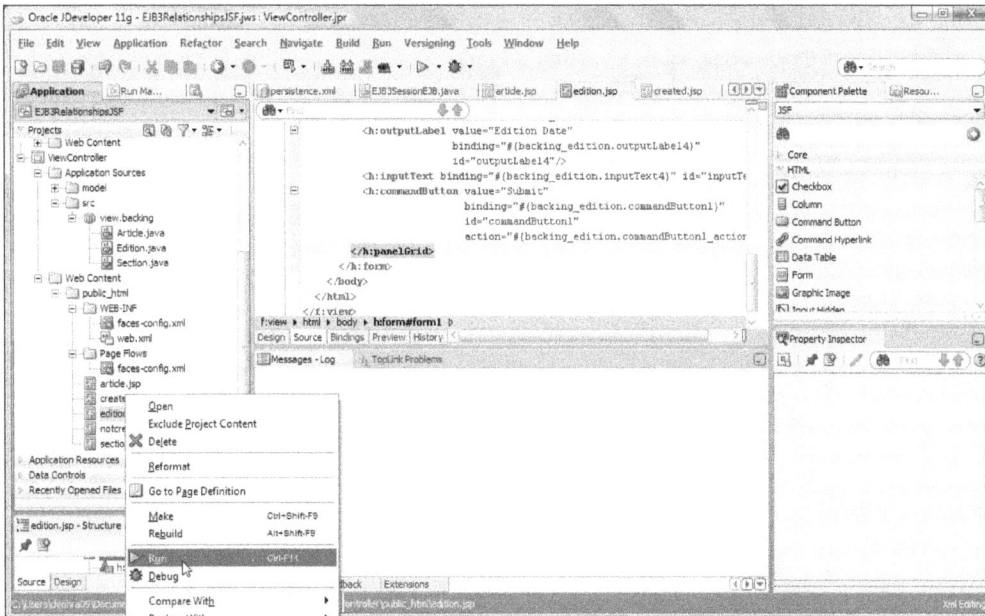

In the `edition.jsp` JSF page, specify values for **Id**, **Journal**, **Publisher**, and **Edition Date** and click on **Submit**:

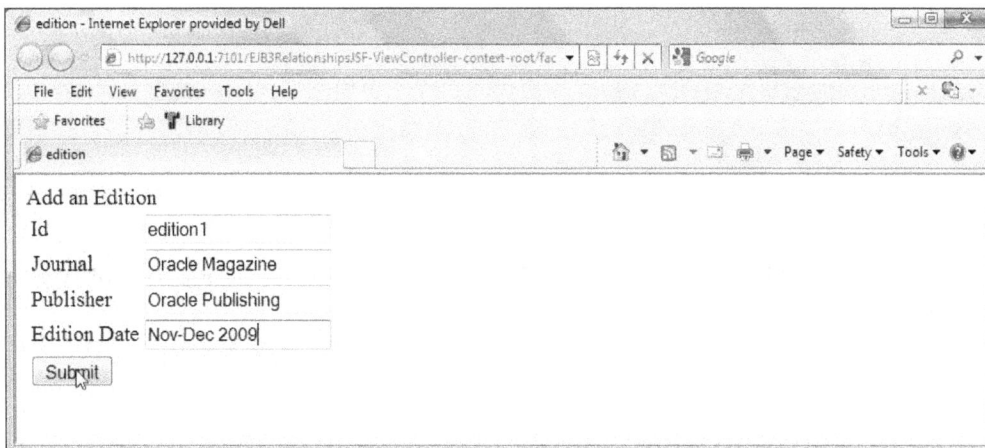

Creating a Section entity

Next, right-click on the **section.jsp** JSF and select **Run**. In the `section.jsp` JSF page specify **Id**, **Section Name** and select an **Edition Id** from the **Menu** select items:

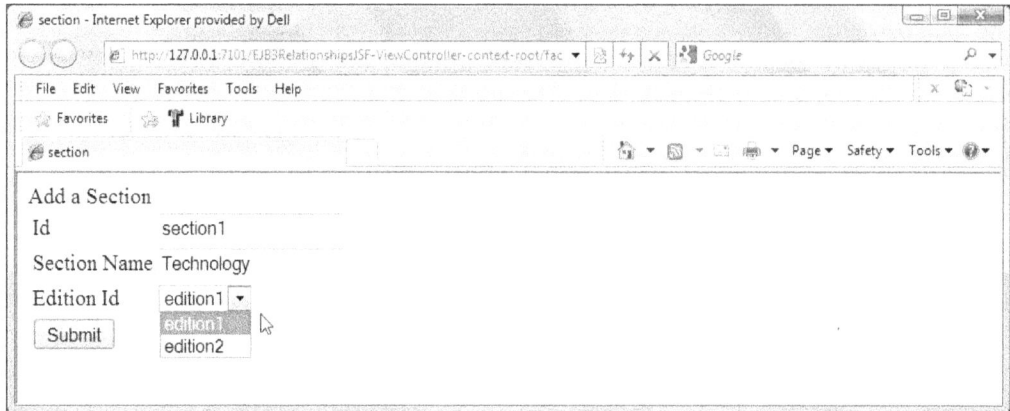

Click on **Submit**:

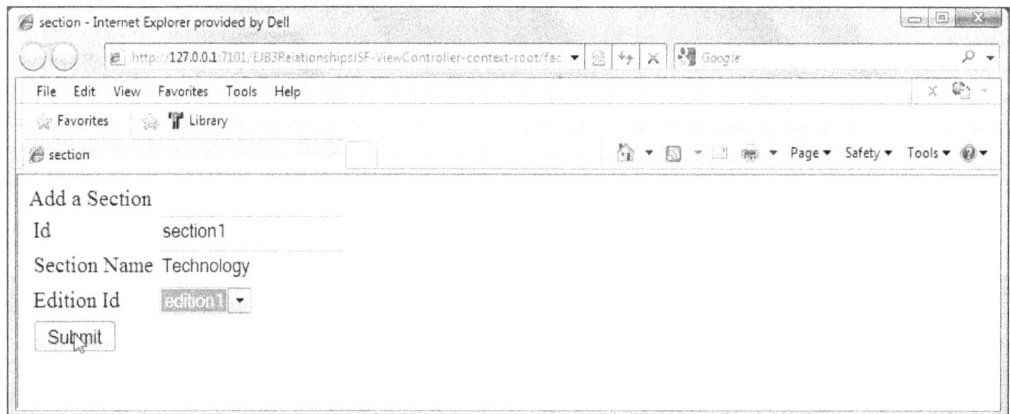

A `Section` entity gets created and persisted to the database. The `Section` entity gets associated with an `Edition` entity.

Creating an Article entity

To create and persist an `Article` entity, right-click on **article.jsp** and select **Run**. Specify values for the **Id**, **Title**, and **Author** fields and select a **Section Id** and an **Edition Id** from the **Menu** select items:

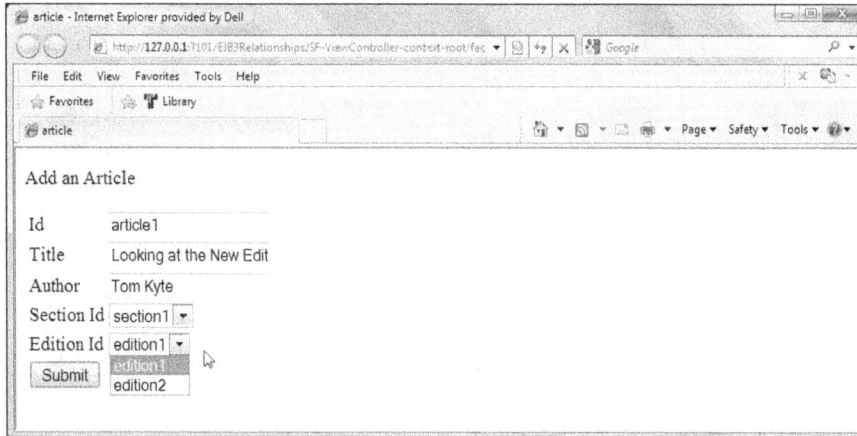

Click on **Submit**:

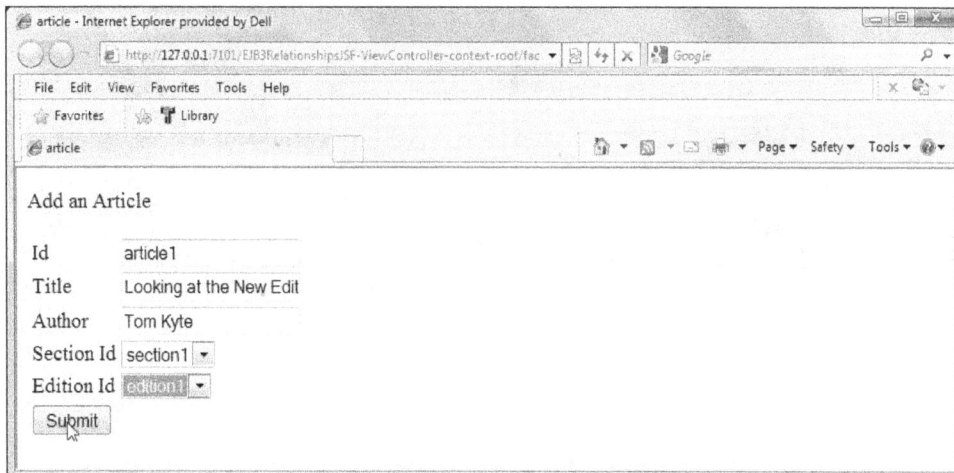

`Edition`, `Section`, and `Article` entities get created and persisted to the Oracle database. We ran the JSF UIs separately, but, alternatively, the session façade may be exposed as a data control, and a page flow with JSF navigation may be created for the JSF user interfaces. Subsequently, a Master-Detail JSF page, which has a binding with the data control, may be created, as discussed in a tutorial (http://www.oracle.com/technology/obe/obe1013jdev/10131/ejb_and_jpa/master-detail_pagewith_ejb.htm#t4).

The database persisted entities

A SELECT query on the Edition table lists the two editions added:

A SELECT query on the SECTION table lists the two sections added:

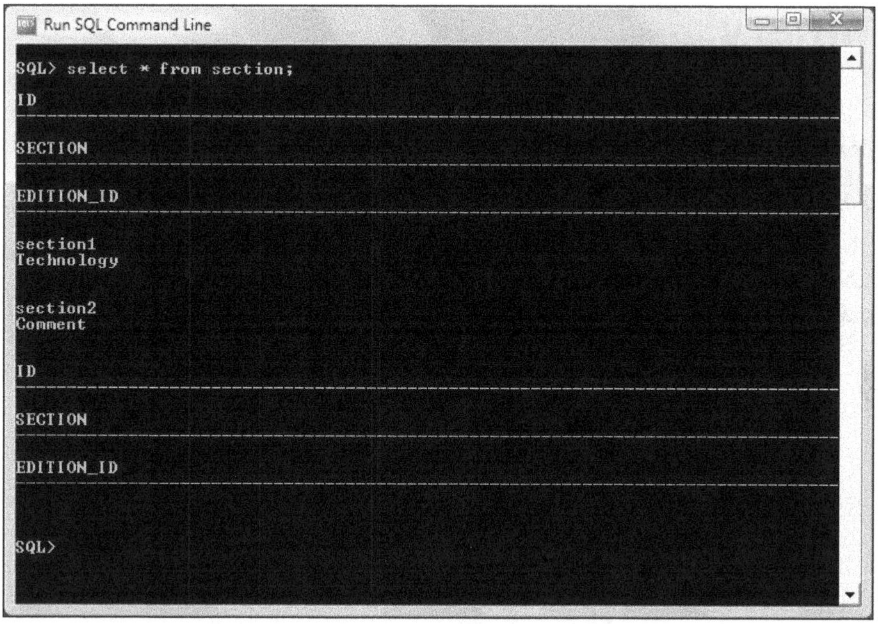

A `SELECT` query on the `ARTICLE` table lists the article added:

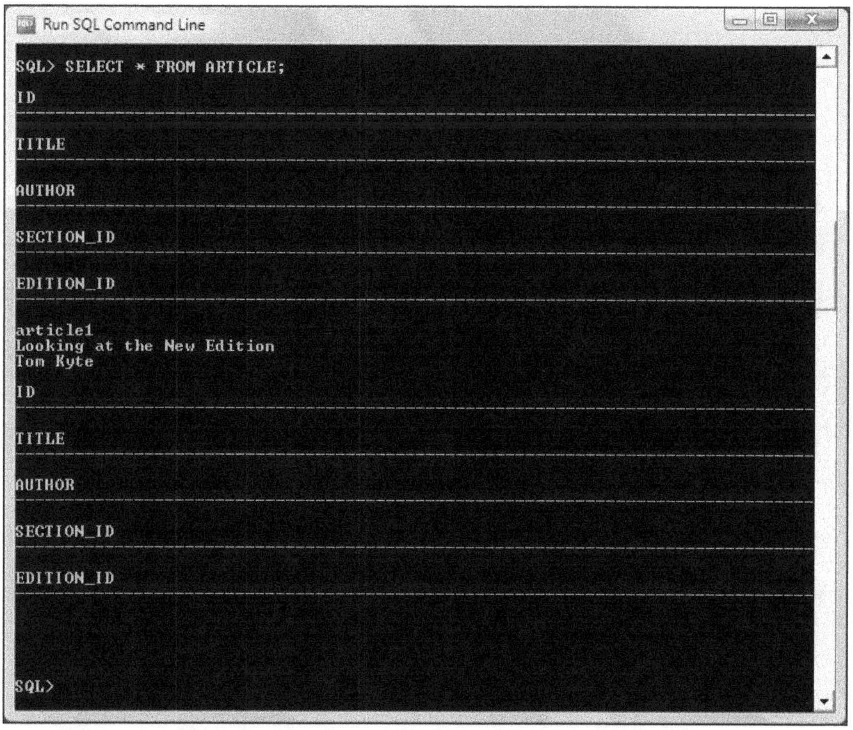

Summary

We had discussed entity EJB 3.0 entity relationships in *Chapter 7, Creating EJB 3.0 Entity Relationships*, too. In this chapter, we discussed how the EJB 3.0 entity relationships may be mapped using JSF user interfaces to input data. We created three entities Edition, Section, and Article with one-to-many relationships between the Edition and Section entities, and one-to-many relationships between the Section and Article entities. Subsequently, we created JSF user interface pages to create Edition, Section, and Article entity instances. When creating the entities, we also added the mappings between the entities.

10

Creating an EJB 3.0 Web Service

JAX-WS is an API to create web applications and web services using the XML-based web services functionality. A web service consists of a Service Endpoint Implementation (SEI) class, which must satisfy the following points:

- It's annotated with the `javax.jws.WebService` annotation
- It must not be abstract or final
- It must contain a default public constructor
- A web service provides operations, which are public methods, that are made available to web service clients

The business methods must not be `static` or `final` and, though not required, may be annotated with the `javax.jws.WebMethod` annotation. By default, all `public` methods are made available as web service operations.

In this chapter, we shall create an EJB 3.0 web service with JDeveloper 11*g*, WebLogic Server 11*g*, and Oracle Database. We shall discuss the following topics in this chapter:

- Creating a data source in WebLogic Server
- Creating an entity bean
- Creating a session bean façade
- Creating a Web Service class
- Creating a web service client
- Testing the web service

Setting the environment

We need to download and install JDeveloper 11*g* Studio edition and WebLogic Server 11*g*, both of which are components of Oracle Fusion Middleware 11*g* (`http://www.oracle.com/technology/software/products/middleware/index.html`). We will also need to create a new WebLogic domain with the Fusion Middleware Configuration Wizard. As for the entity bean persistence, we need to download and install Oracle Database 10*g* XE (`http://www.oracle.com/technology/software/products/database/index.html`). Create a user OE with the following SQL commands:

```
CREATE USER OE IDENTIFIED BY pw;
GRANT CREATE SESSION, DBA to OE;
```

Create a test table `CATALOG` in database schema `OE` with the following SQL script:

```
CREATE TABLE Catalog (id INTEGER PRIMARY KEY NOT NULL,
                      journal VARCHAR(100), publisher VARCHAR(100),
                      edition VARCHAR(100), title VARCHAR(100),
                      author VARCHAR(100));
```

Creating a JDeveloper application

First, we create an EJB 3.0 Application in JDeveloper. Here is how to do it:

1. Select **New Application**.

2. Specify an **Application Name** (**EJB3WebService**), select the **Java EE Web Application** template, which consists of a **Model** project and a **ViewController** project, and click on **Next**.

3. Next, specify the name (**ViewController**) for the View and Controller project.

4. In the **Project Technologies** tab, transfer the **EJB** project technology from the **Available** list to the **Selected** list using the **>** button.

5. Click on **Next**.

6. Select the default Java settings for the View project and click on **Next**.

7. Configure the **EJB Settings** for the View project.

8. Select **EJB Version** as **Enterprise JavaBeans 3.0** and select **Using Annotations**.

9. Click on **Next**.

10. Next, create the Model project. Specify the **Project Name** (**EJB3Model**, for example) and in the **Project Technologies** tab, transfer the **EJB** project technology from the **Available** list to the **Selected** list using the **>** button. Click on **Next**.

11. Select the default Java settings for the Model project and click on **Next**.

12. Configure the EJB settings for the Model project similar to the View project. Select **EJB Version** as **Enterprise JavaBeans 3.0**, select **Using Annotations**, and click on **Finish**.

An EJB 3.0 application, which consists of a **Model** project and a **ViewController** project, gets added in the **Application** tab:

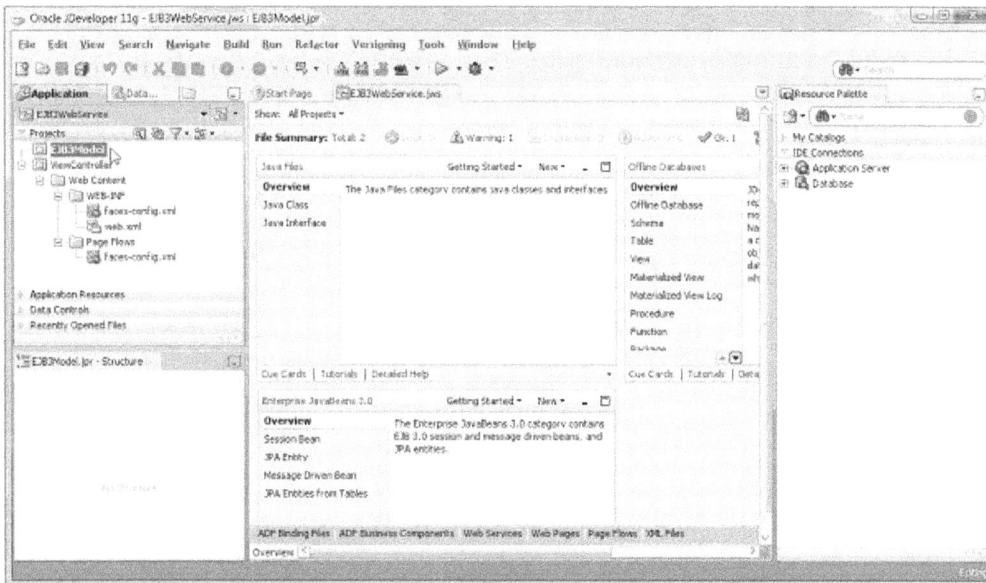

Creating a database connection

Next, we need to create a JDBC connection in JDeveloper with the Oracle database. Here is how we go about it:

1. Open the **Database Navigator** with **View | Database | Database Navigator** or select the **Database Navigator** tab if already open.

2. Right-click on the **IDE Connections** node and select **New Connection**.

3. In the **Create Database Connection** window, specify a **Connection Name**.

4. Select **Connection Type** as **Oracle (JDBC)**.

5. Specify **Username** as **OE**, which is the schema in which the Catalog table is created.

6. Specify the password for the **OE** schema.

7. Select **Driver** as **thin**, **Host Name** as **localhost**, **SID** as ORCL, and **JDBC Port** as **1521**.

8. Click on the **Test Connection** button to test the connection.

9. If the connection gets established, click on **OK**.

10. The **OracleDBConnection** gets added to the **Database Navigator** view.

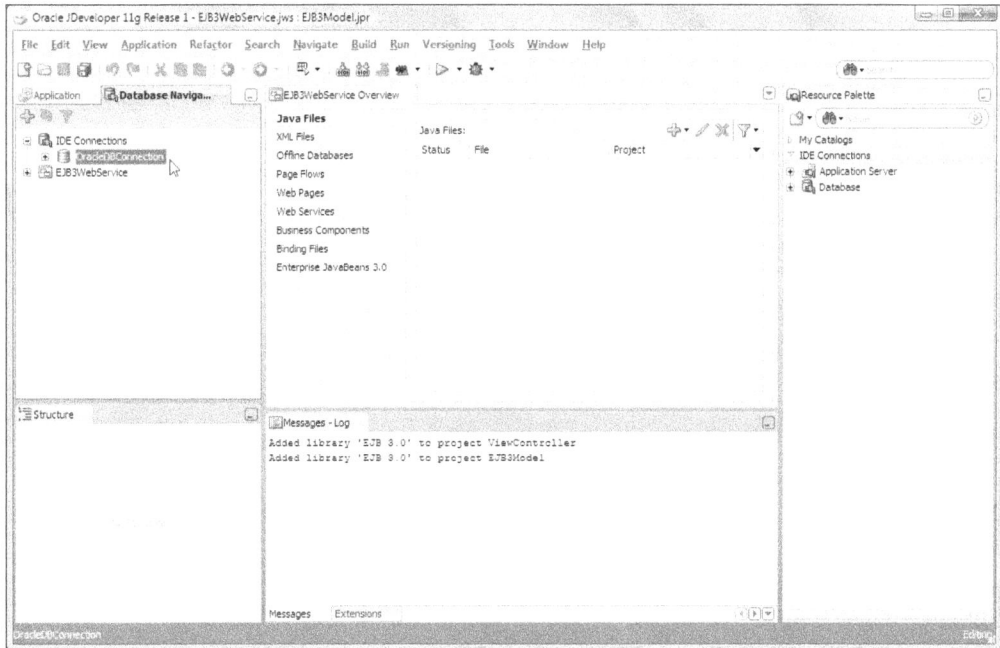

Creating a data source in the WebLogic server

In order to create a data source in the WebLogic server, follow these steps:

1. Start the WebLogic server and navigate to the Administration Console with the URL `http://localhost:7001/console`.

2. Select the **Services | JDBC** node and select the **Data Sources** section.

3. In the **Data Sources** table, click on **New** to create a new data source.

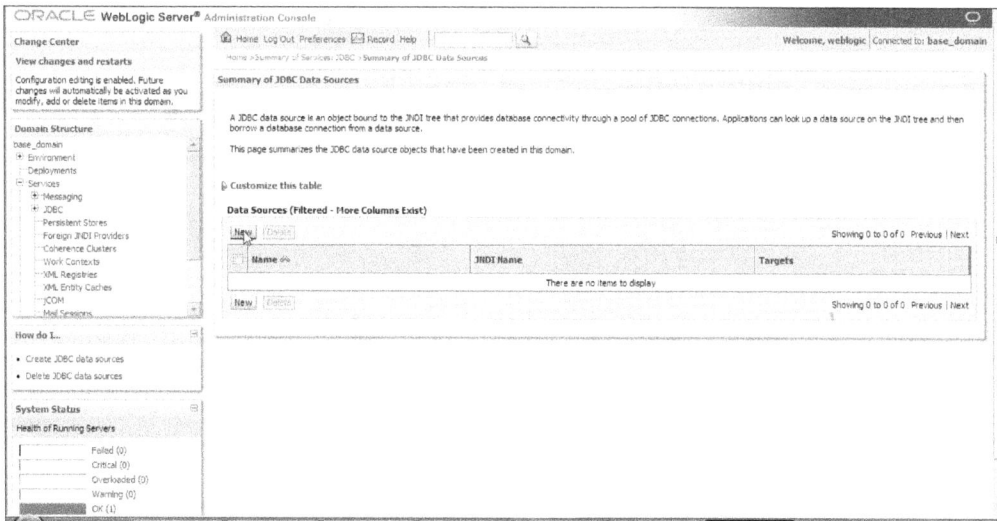

4. Specify the data source **Name** and the **JNDI Name** (`jdbc/OracleDBConnectionDS`) for the data source.

5. Select **Database Type** as **Oracle** and click on **Next**:

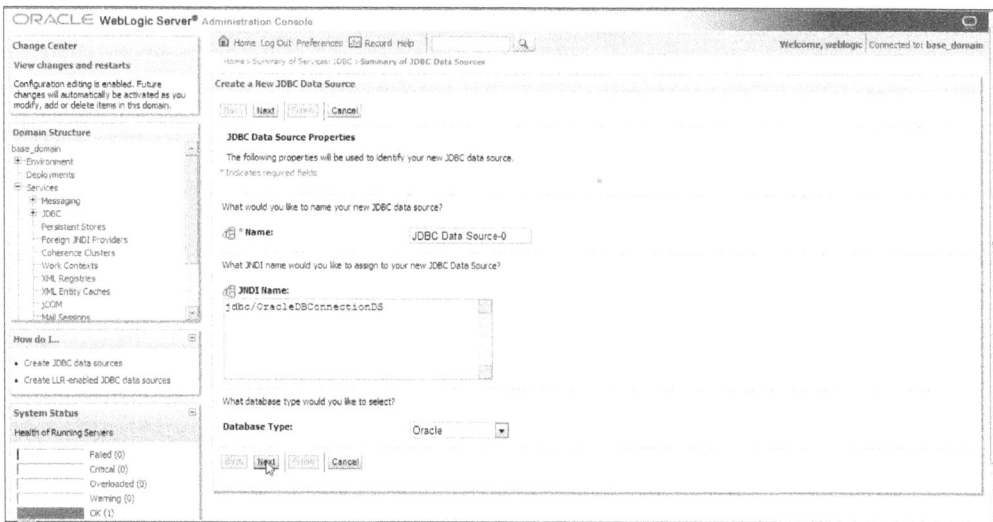

6. Select the default **Database Driver, Oracle's Driver (Thin XA)**, and click on **Next**:

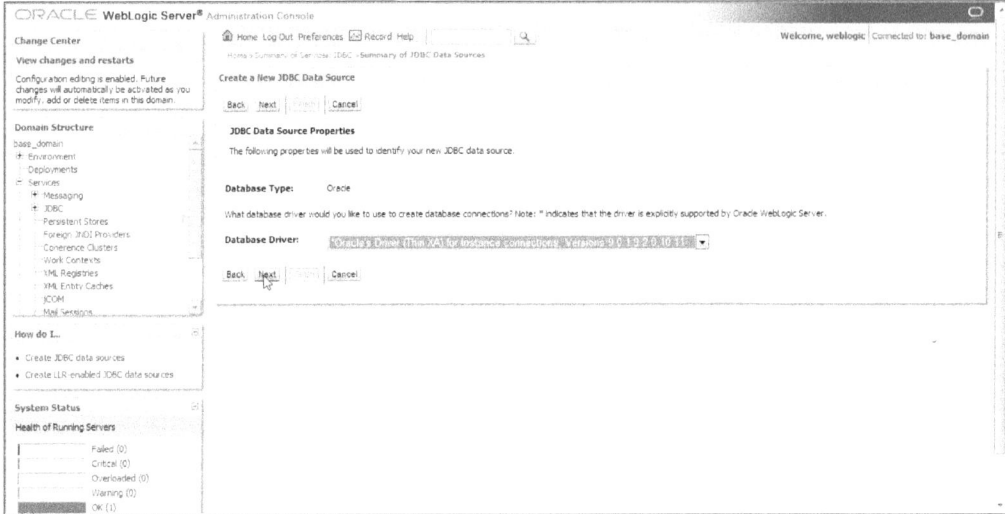

7. With the XA JDBC driver, the default transaction options are to support global transactions and the Two-Phase Commit global transaction protocol. Click on **Next**:

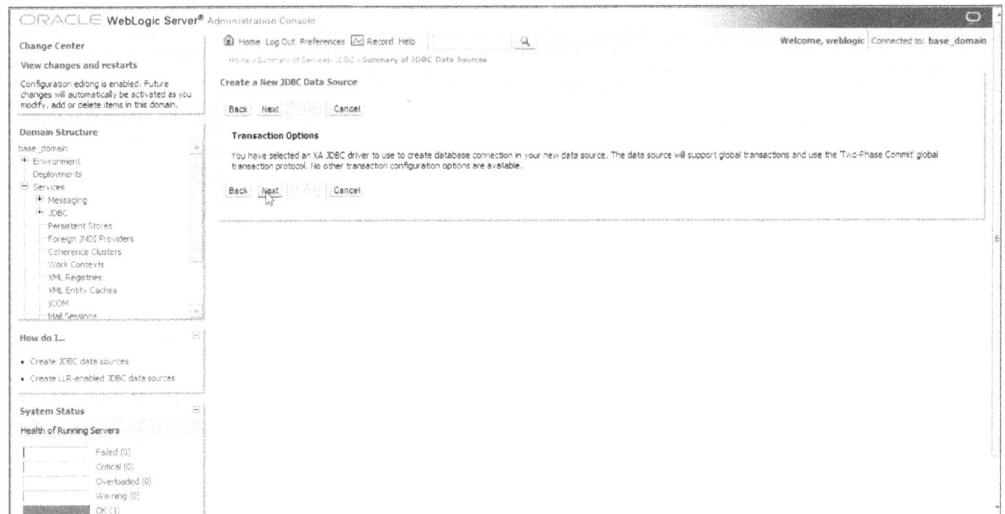

8. In the **Connection Properties** window, specify:

   ° **Database Name** as **XE**

- ° **Host Name** as **localhost**, **Port** as **1521**
- ° **Database User Name** as **OE**
- ° The **Password**

9. Click on **Next**:

10. Click on **Test Configuration** to test the database connection. If the connection gets established, click on **Next**:

11. Select the **AdminServer** as the target server to deploy the data source and click on **Finish**:

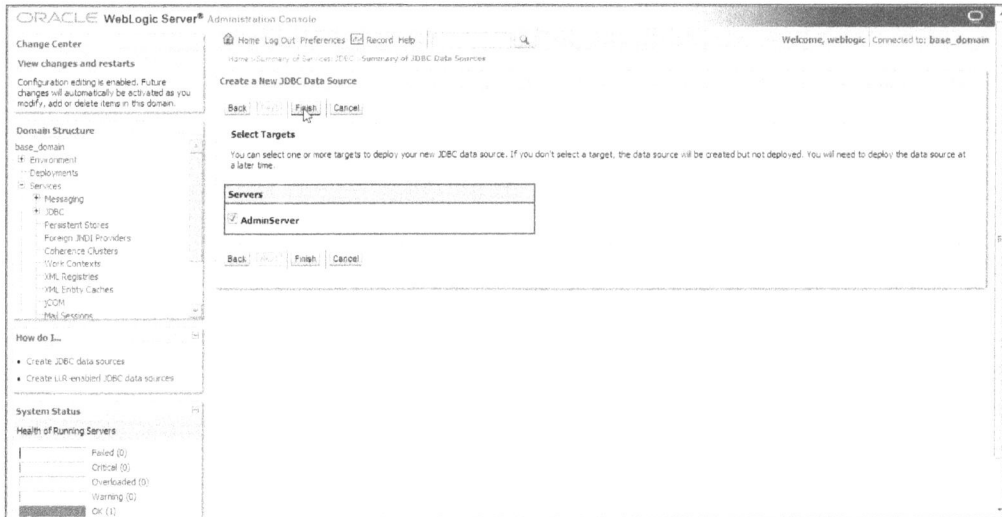

12. A data source gets added to the **Data Sources** table:

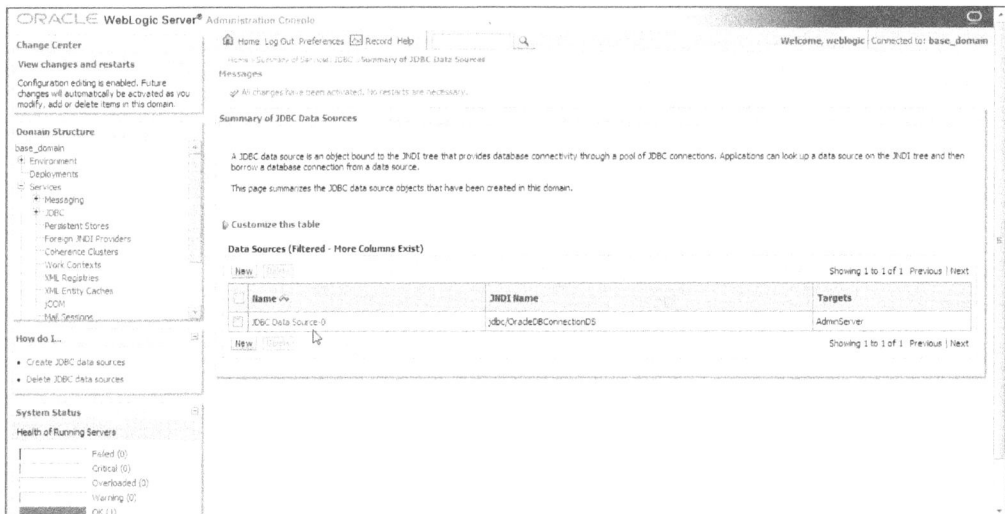

Creating an entity bean

Next, we create an EJB 3.0 entity bean from the Oracle database table CATALOG that we created earlier. Here's how to go about it:

1. Select the **EJB3Model** project in the **Application** navigator and select **File | New**.

2. In the **New Gallery** window, select **Categories | Business Tier | EJB** and **Items | Entities from Tables** and click on **OK**.

3. In the **Persistence Unit** window, select **New** to create a new persistence unit. In the **New Persistence Unit** window, specify a persistence unit name (**em**).

4. Specify **JTA DataSource Name** as **jdbc/OracleDBConnectionDS**, which is the data source name corresponding to the OracleDBConnection connection.

5. Select the settings for **Toplink; Database Platform** as **Oracle** and **Server Platform** as **WebLogic 10**. Click on **OK**.

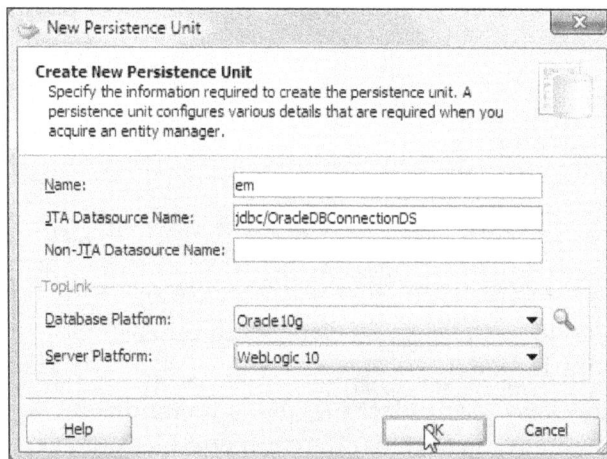

6. The **em Persistence Unit** gets created. Click on **OK** in the **Persistence Unit** window.

7. Select **Type of Connection** as **Online Database Connection** and click on **Next**.

8. In the **Database Connection Details** window, select the **OracleDBConnection** and click on **Next**.

9. In the **Select Tables** window, select **Schema** as **OE**, **Name Filter** as %, and check the **Auto-Query** checkbox.

10. Select the **CATALOG** table and click on **Next**:

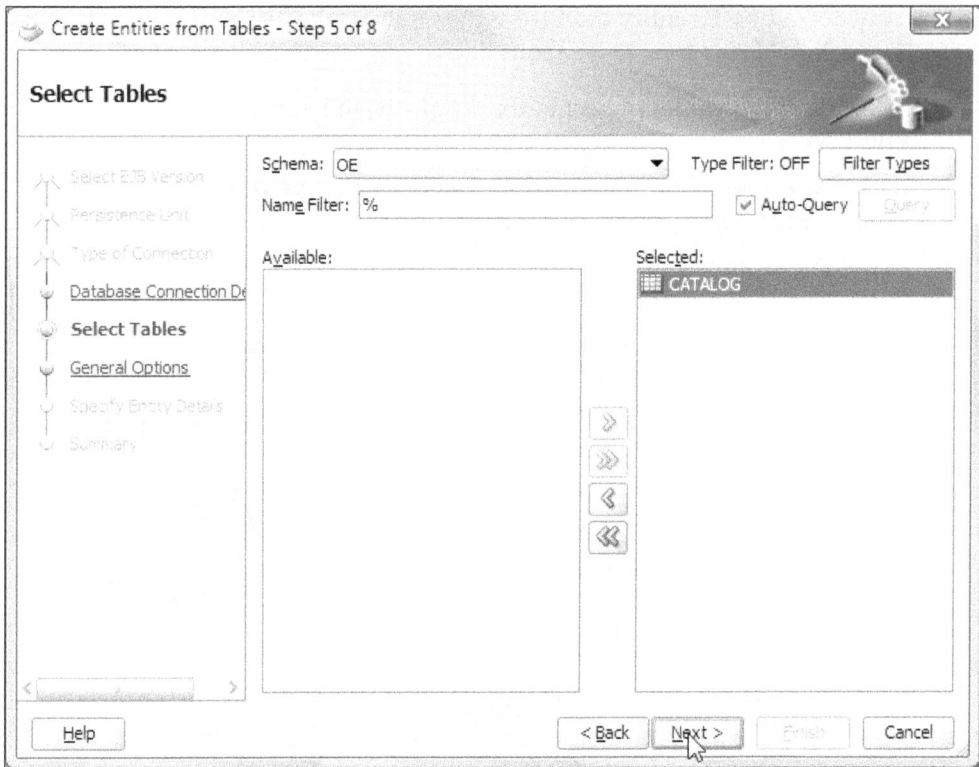

11. Select the default settings in the **General Options** window. The default package name is **model**.

12. In the **Entity Class**, select **Place member annotations on Fields**, and select the **Implement java.io.Serializable** checkbox. Click on **Next**.

13. In the **Specify Entity Details** window, select **Table Name** as **OE.CATALOG**. Specify **Entity Name** as **Catalog** and **Entity Class** as **model.Catalog**. Click on **Next**.

14. In the **Summary Page**, click on **Finish**. The entity bean class `model.Catalog` gets created. The `persistence.xml` deployment descriptor gets created in the `META-INF` directory:

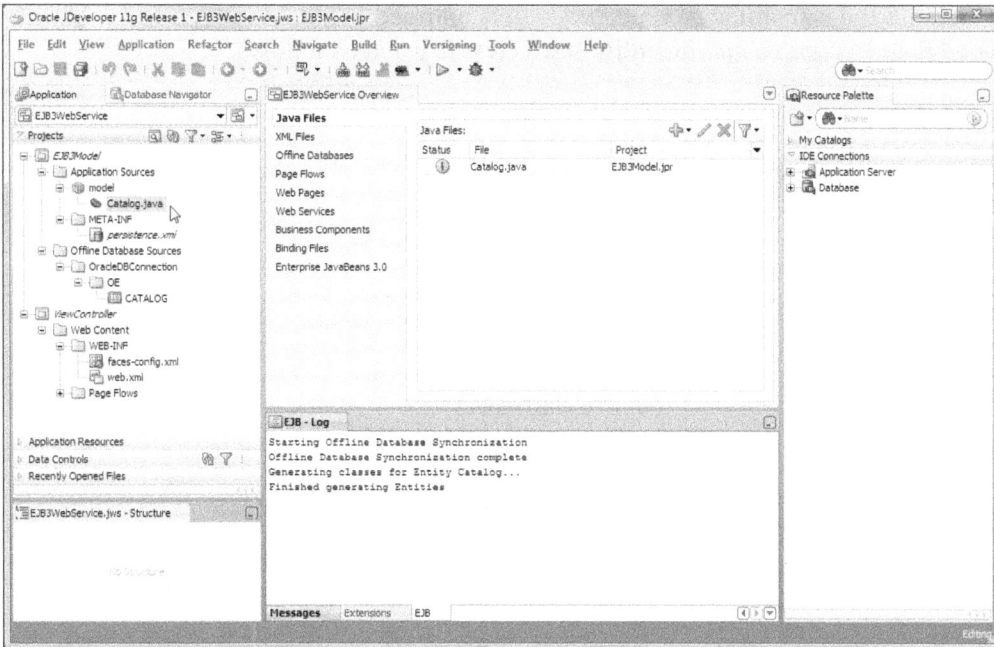

The Entity class

The entity bean class is just a POJO class annotated with the `@Entity` annotation. A `@NamedQuery` specifies a `findAll` query, which selects all the entity instances. An entity bean, which is persisted to a database, that has caching enabled, is serialized by caches. Therefore, the entity bean class implements the `java.io.Serializable` interface. Specify a `serialVersionUID` variable, which is used by serialization runtime to associate a version number with the serializable class:

```
private static final long serialVersionUID = 7422574264557894633L;
```

The database columns are mapped to entity bean properties, which are defined as private variables. The getter setter methods for the properties are also defined. The identifier property is specified with the `@Id` annotation. The `@Column` annotation specifies that the `id` column is not `nullable`:

```
@Id
@Column(nullable = false)
private long id;
```

By default, the id column of type INTEGER is mapped to a field of type Long. Modify the id field to type long. The entity bean class is listed as follows:

```java
package model;
import java.io.Serializable;
import javax.persistence.Column;
import javax.persistence.Entity;
import javax.persistence.Id;
import javax.persistence.NamedQueries;
import javax.persistence.NamedQuery;

@Entity
@NamedQueries({
  @NamedQuery(name = "Catalog.findAll",
              query = "select o from Catalog o")
})
public class Catalog implements Serializable {
  private String author;
  private String edition;
  private static final long serialVersionUID = 7422574264557894633L;
  @Id
  @Column(nullable = false)
  private long id;
  private String journal;
  private String publisher;
  private String title;

  public Catalog() {super();
  }
  public Catalog(String author, String edition, long id,
                 String journal, String publisher, String title) {
    super();
    this.author = author;
    this.edition = edition;
    this.id = id;
    this.journal = journal;
    this.publisher = publisher;
    this.title = title;
  }
  public String getAuthor() {
    return author;
  }
  public void setAuthor(String author) {
    this.author = author;
```

```
  }
  public String getEdition() {
    return edition;
  }
  public void setEdition(String edition) {
    this.edition = edition;
  }
  public long getId() {
    return id;
  }
  public void setId(long id) {
    this.id = id;
  }
  public String getJournal() {
    return journal;
  }
  public void setJournal(String journal) {
    this.journal = journal;
  }
  public String getPublisher() {
    return publisher;
  }
  public void setPublisher(String publisher) {
    this.publisher = publisher;
  }
  public String getTitle() {
    return title;
  }
  public void setTitle(String title) {
    this.title = title;
  }
}
```

The entity Persistence Configuration file

The `persistence.xml` file is used to define the persistence unit/s, which includes a JTA data source that is used for database persistence. The persistence provider is specified as `org.eclipse.persistence.jpa.PersistenceProvider`. The `jta-data-source` is defined as `java:/app/jdbc/jdbc/OracleDBConnectionDS`. The `eclipselink.target-server` property is specified as `WebLogic_10`. The `javax.persistence.jtaDataSource` property is specified as `java:/app/jdbc/jdbc/OracleDBConnectionDS`. The `java:/app/jdbc` prefix gets added to the JTA Data Source specified when creating the persistence unit. Remove the `java:/app/jdbc` prefix as we are using an external WebLogic server, not the integrated WebLogic server. The `persistence.xml` configuration file is listed as follows:

```xml
<?xml version="1.0" encoding="windows-1252" ?>
<persistence xmlns="http://java.sun.com/xml/ns/persistence"
  xmlns:xsi="http://www.w3.org/2001/XMLSchema-instance"
  xsi:schemaLocation="http://java.sun.com/xml/ns/persistence
  http://java.sun.com/xml/ns/persistence/persistence_1_0.xsd"
  version="1.0">
  <persistence-unit name="em">
    <provider>org.eclipse.persistence.jpa.PersistenceProvider
    </provider>
    <jta-data-source>jdbc/OracleDBConnectionDS</jta-data-source>
    <class>model.Catalog</class>
    <properties>
      <property name="eclipselink.ddl-generation" value="none" />
      <property name="eclipselink.target-server"
                value="WebLogic_10" />
      <property name="javax.persistence.jtaDataSource"
                value="jdbc/OracleDBConnectionDS" />
      <property name="eclipselink.target-database"
                value="Oracle10g" />
    </properties>
  </persistence-unit>
</persistence>
```

Creating a stateless session bean

As we already discussed, it's always a good practice to create a session bean façade for an entity bean. This is done to ensure that the entity bean is not directly accessed by a client. To create a session bean, follow the given steps:

1. Select the **EJB3Model** project and select **File | New**.

2. In the **New Gallery** window, select **Categories | Business Tier | EJB** and **Items | Session EJB**. Click on **OK**.

3. Specify the **EJB Name** as **CatalogSessionEJB**. Select **Session Type** as **Stateless** and **Transaction Type** as **Container**. Specify a mapped name (**EJB3-SessionEJB**). The **Generate Session Façade Methods** checkbox is selected by default. The **Entity Implementation** is **JPA Entities** by default. The persistence unit is **em**. Click on **Next**.

4. Select the default **JPA Entity Methods** to create and click on **Next**.

5. Specify the **Bean Class** (`model. CatalogSessionEJBBean`) and click on **Next**.

6. Select the EJB business interface to implement. Select the **Implement a Remote Interface** checkbox, and specify the **Remote interface** (`model. CatalogSessionEJB`). Click on **Next**.

7. In the **Summary** window, click on **Finish**.

A session bean class `CatalogSessionEJBBean` gets added to the entity bean model project. The remote business interface for the session bean, `CatalogSessionEJB`, also gets created.

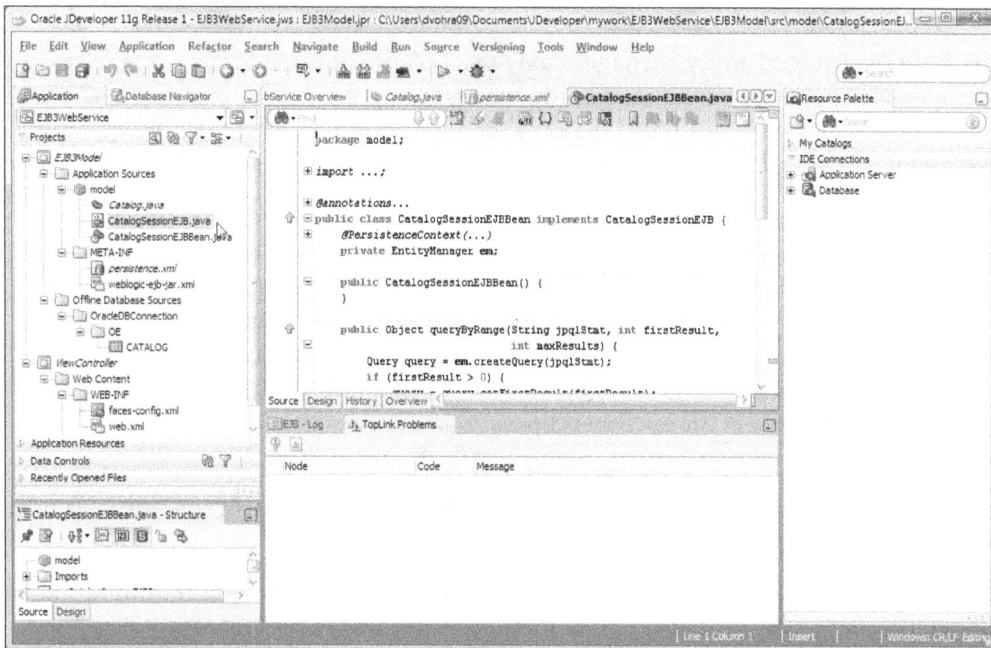

The session bean class

The `CatalogSessionEJBBean` class is annotated with the annotation `@Stateless`. The `mappedName` attribute specifies the global JNDI for the session bean. We shall use the mapped name in the web service to look up the session bean and invoke method/s on it. The `@Remote` annotation indicates that the session bean is a remote interface:

```
@Stateless(name = "CatalogSessionEJB", mappedName = "EJB3-SessionEJB")
@Remote
public class CatalogSessionEJBBean implements CatalogSessionEJBRemote
{ }
```

Two types of `EntityManager`s are supported by the JPA: application-managed `EntityManager` and container-managed `EntityManager`.

Container-managed `EntityManager`s always use JTA transactions, which are managed by the EJB container and are created by injecting using the `@PersistenceContext` annotation or by direct lookup of the **entity manager** in the JNDI namespace.

Application-managed entity managers may use JTA or resource-local transactions. Application-managed entity managers are created by injecting an `EntityManagedFactory` with the `@PersistenceUnit` annotation and subsequently invoking the `createEntityManager()` method on the `EntityManagedFactory` object.

We are using a container-managed entity manager. In the session bean, inject an `EntityManager` using the `@PersistenceContext` annotation. One of the value-added features of WebLogic Server 10.3 is that if the injected variable's name is the same as the persistence unit, the `unitName` attribute of the `@PersistenceContext` or `@PersistenceUnit` is not required to be specified, though we have specified it. The type attribute is set to `PersistenceContextType.TRANSACTION`, which implies that the persistence context is transaction-scoped.

```
@PersistenceContext(unitName = "em",
                    type = PersistenceContextType.TRANSACTION)
EntityManager em;
```

Add a method `persistEntity()` and a method `test()` to the session bean and the remote interface. The `persistEntity` method is used to persist an entity using the `persist()` method. Subsequent to persisting an entity instance, invoke the `flush()` method to synchronize the entity manager with the database:

```
em.persist(entity);
em.flush();
```

In the `test()` method, we shall create a `Catalog` entity instances and persist the entities to the database. We shall also query the entity instances. In the `test()` method, set the flush mode to `COMMIT`, which implies that the changes to the entity manager are synchronized to the database when the transaction commits:

```
em.setFlushMode(FlushModeType.COMMIT);
```

Create a `Catalog` entity instance and persist it to the database. We need to merge the entity instance with the entity manager using the `merge()` method before persisting it.

```
Catalog catalog1 =new Catalog("Kimberly Floss", "Nov-Dec 2004",
    new Integer(1), Oracle Magazine", "Oracle Publishing",
    "Database Resource Manager");
Catalog c1 = em.merge(catalog1);
persistEntity(c1);
```

Similarly, create and persist two more entity instances. An entity instance may be found with the Java persistence query language. For example, find a catalog entity instance by author name. First, create an instance of the `Query` object using the `createQuery` method to run a Java persistence query language statement. Bind the author name to a named parameter `name` using the `setParameter` method of the `Query` object and run the Java persistence query statement using the `getResultList` method, which returns a `List`:

```
List catalogList =em.createQuery("SELECT c from Catalog c
                            where c.author=:name").setParameter
                        ("name","Jonas Jacobi").
                                    getResultList();
```

Iterate over the `List`, which is actually just one catalog entry, to retrieve the `Catalog` entity instance. Create a `String`, which will be returned by the `test()` method, from the `Catalog` instance properties:

```
for (Iterator iter = catalogList.iterator(); iter.hasNext(); )
{
  Catalog element = (Catalog)iter.next();
  catalogEntry =catalogEntry + " Journal:  " + element.getJournal()
            + "Publisher:  " + element.getPublisher() + " Edition:  "
            + element.getEdition() + " Title:  "
            + element.getTitle() + " Author:  "
            + element.getAuthor();
}
```

Similarly, all the titles may be listed and all the `Catalog` entity instances may be listed. An entity instance may be removed using the `remove()` method. To remove an entity instance, create the entity instance, merge the entity instance with the entity manager using the `merge()` method, and remove the entity instance using the `remove()` method:

```
Catalog catalog2 =new Catalog("Jonas Jacobi", "Nov-Dec 2004",
    new Integer(2),"Oracle Magazine", "Oracle Publishing",
    "From ADF UIX to JSF");
Catalog c2 = em.merge(catalog2);
em.remove(c2);
em.flush();
```

Annotate the `test()` method with the `@TransactionAttribute` annotation with type set to `REQUIRES_NEW`, which implies that a new transaction is created for the `test()` method in the session bean:

```
@TransactionAttribute(TransactionAttributeType.REQUIRES_NEW
```

The session bean class is listed as follows:

```
package model;

import java.util.Iterator;
import java.util.List;
import javax.ejb.Remote;
import javax.ejb.Stateless;
import javax.ejb.TransactionAttribute;
import javax.ejb.TransactionAttributeType;
import javax.persistence.EntityManager;
import javax.persistence.EntityManagerFactory;
import javax.persistence.EntityTransaction;
import javax.persistence.FlushModeType;
import javax.persistence.PersistenceContext;
import javax.persistence.PersistenceContextType;
import javax.persistence.PersistenceUnit;
import javax.persistence.Query;

import javax.transaction.UserTransaction;

@Stateless(name = "CatalogSessionEJB", mappedName = "EJB3-SessionEJB")
@Remote
public class CatalogSessionEJBBean implements CatalogSessionEJB {

  @PersistenceContext(unitName = "em",
                      type = PersistenceContextType.TRANSACTION)
  EntityManager em;

  public CatalogSessionEJBBean() {
```

```
    }
    @TransactionAttribute(TransactionAttributeType.REQUIRES_NEW)
    public String test() {
        String catalogEntry = "A catalog entry: ";
        try {
            em.clear();
            em.setFlushMode(FlushModeType.COMMIT);
            Catalog catalog1 =
                new Catalog("Kimberly Floss", "Nov-Dec 2004", new Integer(1),
                            "Oracle Magazine", "Oracle Publishing",
                            "Database Resource Manager");
            Catalog c1 = em.merge(catalog1);
            persistEntity(c1);
            Catalog catalog2 =new Catalog("Jonas Jacobi", "Nov-Dec 2004",
                            new Integer(2),"Oracle Magazine",
                            "Oracle Publishing",
                            "From ADF UIX to JSF");
            Catalog c2 = em.merge(catalog2);
            persistEntity(c2);
            Catalog catalog3 =new Catalog("Steve Muench", "March-April 2005",
                                new Integer(3),"Oracle Magazine",
                                "Oracle Publishing",
                                "Starting with Oracle ADF");
            Catalog c3 = em.merge(catalog3);
            persistEntity(c3);
            /*     catalog2 =new Catalog("Jonas Jacobi", "Nov-Dec 2004",
                            new Integer(2),"Oracle Magazine",
                            "Oracle Publishing","From ADF UIX to JSF");
                c2 = em.merge(catalog2);
                em.remove(c2);
                em.flush();
                catalog3 =new Catalog("Steve Muench", "March-April 2005",
                                new Integer(3),"Oracle Magazine",
                                "Oracle Publishing",
                                "Starting with Oracle ADF");
                c3 = em.merge(catalog3);
                em.remove(c3);
                em.flush();*/
            List catalogList = em.createQuery("SELECT c from Catalog c
                                where c.author=:name").setParameter
                                ("name","Jonas Jacobi").getResultList();
            for (Iterator iter = catalogList.iterator(); iter.hasNext(); ) {
                Catalog element = (Catalog)iter.next();
```

```
        catalogEntry =catalogEntry + " Journal:   " +
                    element.getJournal() + " Publisher:   " +
                    element.getPublisher() + " Edition:   " +
                    element.getEdition() + " Title:   " +
                    element.getTitle() + " Author:   " +
                    element.getAuthor();
      }
      catalogEntry = catalogEntry + " All Titles: ";
      List allTitles =em.createQuery("SELECT c from Catalog c").
                                            getResultList();
      for (Iterator iter = allTitles.iterator(); iter.hasNext(); ) {
        Catalog element = (Catalog)iter.next();
        catalogEntry = catalogEntry + " Title:   " +
                                        element.getTitle();

      }
      catalogEntry = catalogEntry + "  All catalog entity instances: ";
      List allCatalogEntries = em.createQuery("SELECT c from
                                    Catalog c").getResultList();
      for (Iterator iter = allCatalogEntries.iterator();
          iter.hasNext(); ) {
        Catalog element = (Catalog)iter.next();
        catalogEntry = catalogEntry + " Catalog Entry:   " + element;

      }
    } catch (Exception e) {
      catalogEntry = e.getMessage();
    }
    em.clear();

    return catalogEntry;
  }
  public void persistEntity(Catalog entity) {
    em.persist(entity);
    em.flush();

  }
}
```

The corresponding remote interface is listed as follows:

```
package model;

import java.util.List;

import javax.ejb.Remote;
```

```
@Remote
public interface CatalogSessionEJB {
    String test();
    void persistEntity(Catalog entity);


}
```

Creating a Web Service class

In this section, we take a look at the Java Web Service (JWS) file, which is simply a Java class annotated with the `@WebService` annotation (`http://java.sun.com/ javase/6/docs/api/javax/jws/WebService.html`), for implementing a JAX-WS Web Service. *JSR 181: Web Services Metadata for the Java Platform* defines the standard annotations that can be used in a Java Web Service. The `javax.jws.WebService` annotation specifies that a class implements a web service. All the attributes of the `@ WebService` annotation are optional. First, create a Java class by selecting **Java Class** in the **New Gallery**. In the **Create Java Class** window, specify the class name as `EJB3WSImpl`. A Web Service class gets added to the EJB 3.0 project. The Entity class may also be made a web service by annotating it with the `@WebService` annotation. However, creating a separate Web Service class provides the advantage of de-coupling the Entity bean from the web service; if modifications are required to the web service, the entity does not have to be modified.

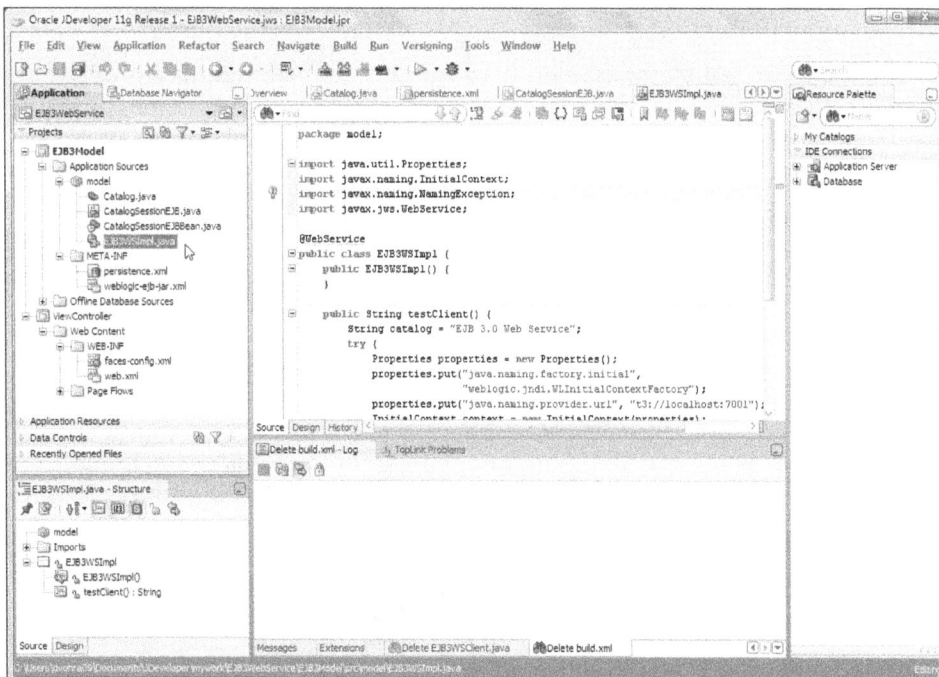

Add a Web Service method, `testClient()` that returns a `String` message. By default, all `public` methods are exposed as web service operations. If you want to explicitly mark methods as web service methods for maintainability, add the annotation `@WebMethod` to them. The `operationName` and action of attributes may be specified in the `@WebMethod` annotation. The `operationName` attribute maps the operation name as mapped to the `wsdl:operation` element in the WSDL. The default value is the same as the method name.

For SOAP bindings, the `action` attribute maps to the `SoapAction` header in the SOAP messages. In the `testClient()` method, create an `InitialContext` object using the WebLogic Server properties for initial context factory and provider URL. As the web service is running directly on the WebLogic server instance, the properties are not required to be specified. However, we have added the properties for the setting in which the web service is not directly running on theWebLogic Server instance:

```
Properties properties = new Properties();
properties.put("java.naming.factory.initial",
             "weblogic.jndi.WLInitialContextFactory");
properties.put("java.naming.provider.url", "t3://localhost:7001");
InitialContext context = new InitialContext(properties);
```

Two methods are available to look up a session bean using the remote business interface:

- Look up the session bean remote interface using the mapped name. The global JNDI name for a session bean remote business interface is derived from the remote business interface name. The format of the global JNDI name is `mappedName#qualified_name_of_businessInterface`.

- Specify the business interface JNDI name in the `weblogic-ejb-jar.xml` deployment descriptor. The global JNDI name is specified as follows:

```
<weblogic-enterprise-bean>
  <ejb-name>CatalogSessionEJB</ejb-name>
  <stateless-session-descriptor>
    <business-interface-jndi-name-map>
      <business-remote>CatalogSessionEJBRemote</business-remote>
      <jndi-name>EJB3-SessionEJB</jndi-name>
    </business-interface-jndi-name-map>
  </stateless-session-descriptor>
</weblogic-enterprise-bean>
```

We shall use the first method. Create a remote business interface instance using lookup with the mapped name:

```
CatalogSessionEJBRemote beanRemote =(CatalogSessionEJBRemote)context.
                lookup("EJB3-SessionEJB#model.CatalogSessionEJBRemote");
```

Invoke the `test()` method of the session bean and return the `String` value returned from the `testClient` method, which is a web service operation:

```
catalog=beanRemote.test();
```

The Web Service class is listed as follows:

```
import javax.jws.WebService;
@WebService
public class EJB3WSImpl {
  public EJB3WSImpl() {
  }
  public String testClient() {
    String catalog = "EJB 3.0 Web Service";
      try {
        Properties properties = new Properties();
        properties.put("java.naming.factory.initial",
                    "weblogic.jndi.WLInitialContextFactory");
        properties.put("java.naming.provider.url",
                    "t3://localhost:7001");
        InitialContext context = new InitialContext(properties);
        CatalogSessionEJB beanRemote =
                        (CatalogSessionEJB)context.lookup(
                        "EJB3-SessionEJB#model.CatalogSessionEJB");
        catalog=beanRemote.test();
      } catch (NamingException e) {catalog=e.getMessage();
    }
    return catalog;
  }
}
```

Creating a web service client

Next, we create a JAX-RPC Java client for the web service. First, create a Java class `EJB3WSClient`. In the Java client application, create an instance of the `EJB3WSImplService` service:

```
EJB3WSImplService service = new EJB3WSImplService();
```

Obtain a proxy to the service from the service using the `getEJB3WSImplPort()` method:

```
EJB3WSImpl port = service.getEJB3WSImplPort();
```

Invoke the `testClient()` web service method of the service:

```
String result = port.testClient();
```

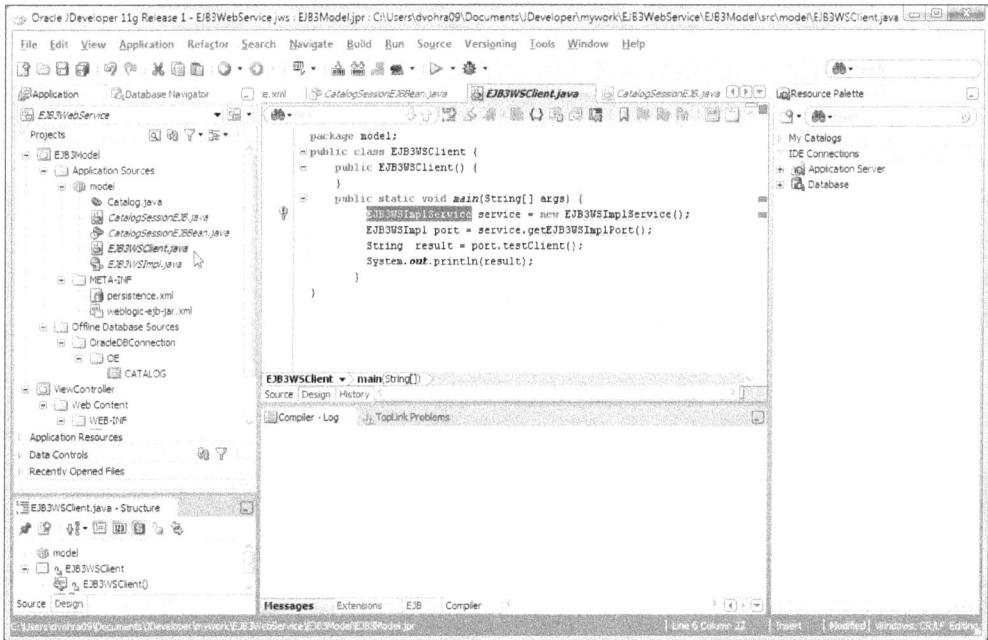

The Web Service Client class is listed as follows:

```
package model;
import java.util.Properties;
import javax.naming.InitialContext;
import javax.naming.NamingException;
package model;
public class EJB3WSClient {
  public EJB3WSClient() {
  }
  public static void main(String[] args) {
    EJB3WSImplService service = new EJB3WSImplService();
    EJB3WSImpl port = service.getEJB3WSImplPort();
    String  result = port.testClient();
    System.out.println(result);
  }
}
```

Creating and packaging Web Service classes

Next, create a `build.xml` Apache Ant script in the `Application Sources` directory by selecting **Categories:General | Ant** and **Items:Empty Buildfile** in the **New Gallery** window. The `build.xml` file is created to compile the EJB 3.0 classes and Web Service classes, and package the classes to an EAR file.

Deploy the EAR file to the WebLogic server. In the `build.xml` file, specify properties for various directories that are used for development and deployment of the web service.

Property	Description
`src.dir`	The source directory for the EJB 3.0 classes and the web service classes.
`deploy.dir`	The deploy directory of the WebLogic server: `C:/Oracle/Middleware/wlserver_10.3/samples/domains/wl_server/autodeploy`.
`build.dir`	The build directory for developing the web service application classes.
`build.classes.dir`	The directory for the compiled classes.

Specify the project classpath with the `path` element:

```
<path id="project.classpath">
  <pathelement location="C:/Oracle/Middleware/wlserver_10.3/server/
                         lib/weblogic.jar"/>
  <pathelement path="C:/Oracle/Middleware/jdk160_05/lib/tools.jar"/>
</path>
```

Specify a `target` for various stages of the application development.

Target	Description
`clean`	Deletes the directories and JAR/WAR/EAR files generated from the previous compilation.
`prepare`	Create the required build directories.
`compile`	Compile the EJB 3.0 classes using the `javac` task. Has dependency on the `prepare` target.
`jar`	Create a EJB JAR file for the EJB 3.0 classes, including `persistence.xml`. Has dependency on the `compile` target.

Target	Description
build-service	Compile the Web Service class using the jwsc task, which generates a WAR file. Has dependency on the jar target.
assemble-app	Create an EAR file from the EJB JAR file and the web service WAR file. Has dependency on the build-service target.
deploy	Deploy the EAR file to the WebLogic server. Has dependency on the assemble-app target.
build-client	Compile the web service client class with the clientgen task. Has dependency on the build-client target.
run	Run the web service client class.

WebLogic Server provides a task for compiling a Web Service class: jwsc. We shall be compiling the EJB3WSImpl class with the jwsc task, which uses the weblogic.wsee.tools.anttasks.JwscTask class. Create a taskdef for the jwsc task:

```
<taskdef name="jwsc" classname="weblogic.wsee.tools.anttasks.
JwscTask">
  <classpath>
    <path refid="project.classpath"/>
  </classpath>
</taskdef>
```

The jwsc Ant task (http://download.oracle.com/docs/cd/E12840_01/wls/docs103/webserv_ref/anttasks.html#wp1069899) takes an annotated JWS file as input and generates all the artifacts required to create a web service. When the jwsc-generated WAR file is deployed, the application server and the JAX-WS runtime generate the WSDL file and any additional artifacts required to invoke the web service from a client. The following artifacts get generated:

- Java Source files that implement a standard web service, such as the Service Endpoint Interface (SEI). For a JWS class EJB3WSImpl, an SEI EJB3WSImplPortType.java gets created.

- Standard and WebLogic-specific deployment descriptors. The standard webservices.xml deployment descriptor and the JAX-RPC mapping files get created. The WebLogic-specific web services deployment descriptor weblogic-webservices.xml also gets created.

- The WSDL file that describes the web service.

- The XML Schema representation of any Java user-defined types used as parameters or return values of web service methods.

A `jws` subelement of the `jwsc` element specifies a JWS file. The only required attribute of the `jws` element is file, which specifies the JWS file. By default `jwsc` generates a JAX-RPC 1.1 Web Service. To generate a JAX-WS 2.0 Web Service, specify the type attribute of the `jws` element as `type="JAXWS"`. Subsequent to generating the web service artifacts, `jwsc` compiles the JWS and Java files and packages the generated artifacts and classes into a web application WAR file. `Jwsc` also creates an enterprise application directory structure. `Jwsc` generates a WAR file corresponding to each `jws` elements. JWS files may be grouped by adding the `jws` elements to a `module` element, which is a direct subelement of the `jwsc` element. If a `module` element is specified, only one WAR file is generated.

WebLogic server provides the `clientgen` task for compiling a Web Service Client class. We shall be compiling the `EJB3WSClient` class with the `clientgen` class. The `clientgen` task uses the `weblogic.wsee.tools.anttasks.ClientGenTask` class for which we need to add a `taskdef` to the `build.xml`:

```
<taskdef name="clientgen"
         classname="weblogic.wsee.tools.anttasks.ClientGenTask">
  <classpath>
    <path refid="project.classpath"/>
  </classpath>
</taskdef>
```

The `clientgen` task generates the following artifacts:

- The client-side copy of the WSDL file.

- The Java source code for the Stub and Service interface implementations for the web service.

- Java classes for any user-defined XML Schema data types defined in the WSDL file.

- `JAX-RPC` deployment descriptor that describes the mapping between the Java data types and the corresponding XML Schema types in the WSDL file.

The only required attribute of the `clientgen` task (http://download.oracle.com/docs/cd/E12840_01/wls/docs103/webserv_ref/anttasks.html#wp1039270) is one of `destDir` or `destFile` and `wsdl`. The `build.xml` file is listed as follows:

```
<?xml version="1.0" encoding="windows-1252" ?>
<project name="ejb3-webservices" basedir="." default="deploy">
  <property name="src.dir" value="${basedir}" />
  <property name="deploy.dir"
            value="C:/Oracle/WLS11g/user_projects/domains/base_domain/
                   autodeploy" />
  <property name="build.dir" value="${basedir}/build" />
```

```xml
<property name="build.classes.dir" value="${build.dir}/classes" />
<path id="project.classpath">
  <pathelement location="C:/Oracle/WLS11g/wlserver_10.3/server/lib/
                          weblogic.jar" />
  <pathelement path="C:/Oracle/WLS11g/jdk160_18/lib/tools.jar" />
</path>
<taskdef name="jwsc" classname="weblogic.wsee.tools.anttasks.
                                                          JwscTask">
  <classpath>
    <path refid="project.classpath" />
  </classpath>
</taskdef>
<taskdef name="clientgen"
         classname="weblogic.wsee.tools.anttasks.ClientGenTask">
  <classpath>
    <path refid="project.classpath" />
  </classpath>
</taskdef>
<target name="clean">
  <delete file="${build.dir}/model/EJB3WSImpl.war" />
  <delete dir="${build.classes.dir}" />
  <delete dir="${build.dir}/clientclass/model" />
  <delete file="${build.dir}/ejb3.jar" />
  <delete file="${build.dir}/ejb3webservice.ear" />
  <delete file="${deploy.dir}/ejb3webservice.ear" />
</target>
<target name="prepare">
  <mkdir dir="${build.dir}" />
  <mkdir dir="${build.classes.dir}" />
</target>
<target name="compile" depends="prepare">
  <javac srcdir="${src.dir}" destdir="${build.classes.dir}"
         debug="on">
    <classpath refid="project.classpath" />
    <exclude name="model/EJB3WSImpl.java" />
    <exclude name="model/EJB3WSClient.java" />
    <include name="**/**.java" />
  </javac>
</target>
<target name="jar" depends="compile">
  <jar destfile="${build.dir}/ejb3.jar">
    <metainf dir="META-INF">
      <include name="persistence.xml" />
```

```
      </metainf>
      <fileset dir="${build.classes.dir}">
        <include name="**/**.class" />
      </fileset>
    </jar>
  </target>
  <target name="build-service" depends="jar">
    <echo>Compiling Web Service</echo>
    <jwsc srcdir="${src.dir}" destdir="${build.dir}">
      <jws file="model/EJB3WSImpl.java" type="JAXWS" />
      <classpath refid="project.classpath" />
    </jwsc>
  </target>

  <target name="assemble-app" depends="build-service">
    <jar destfile="${build.dir}/ejb3webservice.ear">
      <metainf dir="META-INF">
        <include name="application.xml" />
      </metainf>
      <fileset dir="${build.dir}/model" includes="EJB3WSImpl.war" />
      <fileset dir="${build.dir}" includes="ejb3.jar" />
    </jar>
  </target>
  <target name="deploy" depends="assemble-app">
    <copy file="${build.dir}/ejb3webservice.ear"
          todir="${deploy.dir}" />
  </target>
  <target name="build-client" depends="deploy">
    <clientgen type="JAXWS"
               wsdl="http://localhost:7001/EJB3WSImpl/
                                        EJB3WSImplService?wsdl"
               destdir="${build.dir}/clientclass"
               packagename="model" />
    <javac srcdir="${build.dir}/clientclass"
           destdir="${build.dir}/clientclass"
           includes="**/*.java" />
    <javac srcdir="${src.dir}" destdir="${build.dir}/clientclass"
           includes="model/EJB3WSClient.java" />
  </target>
  <path id="client.class.path">
    <pathelement path="${build.dir}/clientclass" />
  </path>
  <target name="run">
    <java fork="true" classname="model.EJB3WSClient">
```

```
        <classpath refid="client.class.path" />
    </java>
  </target>
</project>
```

The directory structure of the EJB 3.0 web service is shown in the following screenshot:

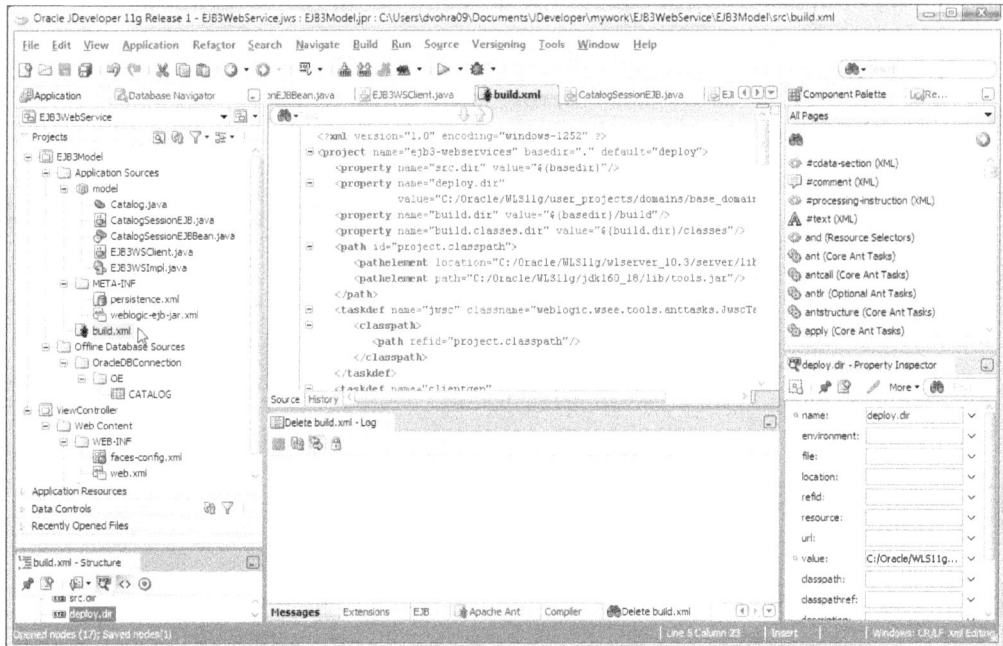

Testing the web service

Next, we test the web service. Start the **WebLogic** server if not already started. First, we run the `build-client` target, which also runs the preceding targets. Subsequently, we run the `run target` to run the client.

Building the client

To build the client, right-click on the **build.xml** file and select **Run Ant Target | build-client**:

The EJB 3.0 classes and the web service classes get compiled, the EAR file gets
deployed to the WebLogic Server, and the client gets built:

When the EAR application is deployed, the WebLogic Server and the JAX-WS runtime generate the WSDL file, which may be accessed with the given URL: `http://localhost:7001/EJB3WSImpl/EJB3WSImplService?WSDL`.

Select the **EJB3Model** project and select **View | Refresh**. The compiled classes for the EJB 3.0 entity and session beans, the compiled classes for the Web Service class, and the `jwsc` generated `EJB3WSImpl.war` get displayed in the Application navigator. The `ejb3.jar` and the `ejb3webservice.ear` also get displayed.

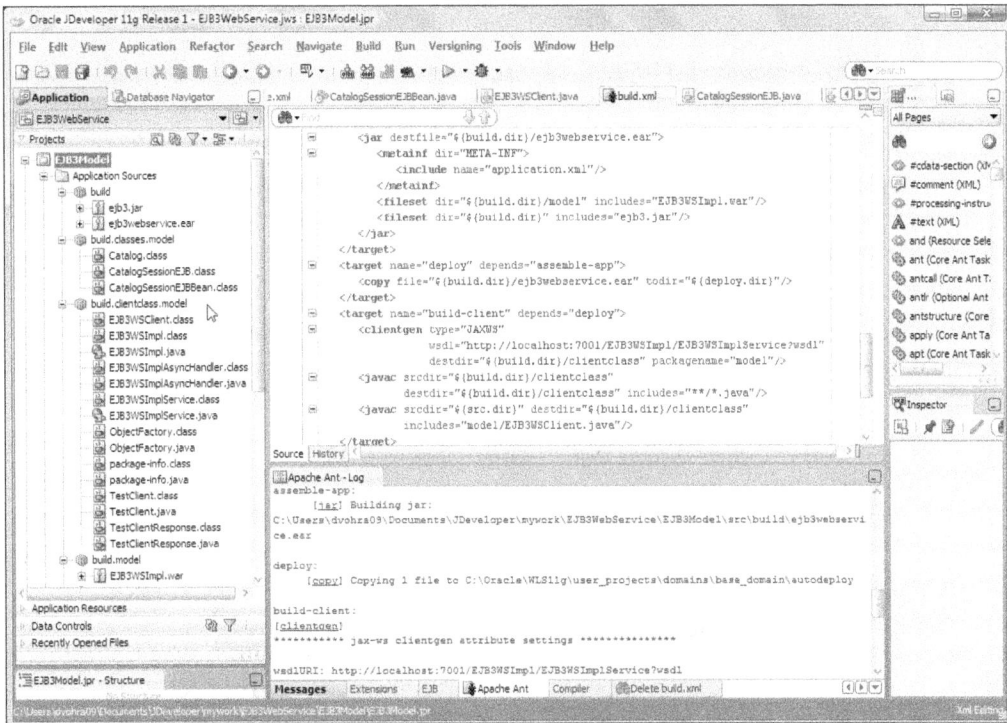

The complete output from the `build.xml` script is listed as follows:

```
Buildfile: C:\Users\dvohra09\Documents\JDeveloper\mywork\
EJB3WebService\EJB3Model\src\build.xml

prepare:
    [mkdir] Created dir: C:\Users\dvohra09\Documents\JDeveloper\
mywork\EJB3WebService\EJB3Model\src\build\classes

compile:
    [javac] Compiling 3 source files to C:\Users\dvohra09\Documents\
JDeveloper\mywork\EJB3WebService\EJB3Model\src\build\classes

jar:
     [jar] Building jar: C:\Users\dvohra09\Documents\JDeveloper\
mywork\EJB3WebService\EJB3Model\src\build\ejb3.jar

build-service:
    [echo] Compiling Web Service
    [jwsc] JWS: processing module /model/EJB3WSImpl
    [jwsc] Parsing source files
    [jwsc] Parsing source files
    [jwsc] 1 JWS files being processed for module /model/EJB3WSImpl
```

```
        [jwsc] JWS: C:\Users\dvohra09\Documents\JDeveloper\mywork\
EJB3WebService\EJB3Model\src\model\EJB3WSImpl.java Validated.
        [jwsc] Processing 1 JAX-WS web services...
        [jwsc] warning: Annotation types without processors: [javax.
xml.bind.annotation.XmlRootElement, javax.xml.bind.annotation.
XmlAccessorType, javax.xml.bind.annotation.XmlType, javax.xml.bind.
annotation.XmlElement]
1 warning
        [jwsc] Compiling 3 source files to
                C:\Users\dvohra09\AppData\Local\Temp\_oij0g71
        [jwsc] Building jar:
                C:\Users\dvohra09\Documents\JDeveloper\mywork\
EJB3WebService\
                EJB3Model\src\build\model\EJB3WSImpl.war
        [jwsc] Created JWS deployment outputFile:
                C:\Users\dvohra09\Documents\JDeveloper\mywork\
EJB3WebService\
                EJB3Model\src\build\model\EJB3WSImpl.war
        [jwsc] [EarFile] Application File :
                C:\Users\dvohra09\Documents\JDeveloper\mywork\
EJB3WebService\
                EJB3Model\src\build\META-INF\application.xml
[AntUtil.deleteDir] Deleting directory
                C:\Users\dvohra09\AppData\Local\Temp\_oij0g71

assemble-app:
        [jar] Building jar:
                C:\Users\dvohra09\Documents\JDeveloper\mywork\
EJB3WebService\
                EJB3Model\src\build\ejb3webservice.ear

deploy:
        [copy] Copying 1 file to
                C:\Oracle\WLS11g\user_projects\domains\base_domain\
autodeploy

build-client:
[clientgen]
*********** jax-ws clientgen attribute settings ***************

wsdlURI: http://localhost:7001/EJB3WSImpl/EJB3WSImplService?wsdl
packageName : model
destDir :
        C:\Users\dvohra09\Documents\JDeveloper\mywork\EJB3WebService\
        EJB3Model\src\build\clientclass

*********** jax-ws clientgen attribute settings end ***************

[clientgen] Consider using <depends>/<produces> so that wsimport won't
do
                                                    unnecessary
compilation
[clientgen] parsing WSDL...
```

```
[clientgen]
[clientgen]
[clientgen] generating code...
[clientgen]
[clientgen]
[clientgen] compiling code...
[clientgen]
    [javac] Compiling 1 source file to
            C:\Users\dvohra09\Documents\JDeveloper\mywork\
EJB3WebService\
            EJB3Model\src\build\clientclass

BUILD SUCCESSFUL
Total time: 33 seconds
```

Testing the client

Next, we run the client:

1. Right-click on `build.xml` and select **Run Ant Target | run**:

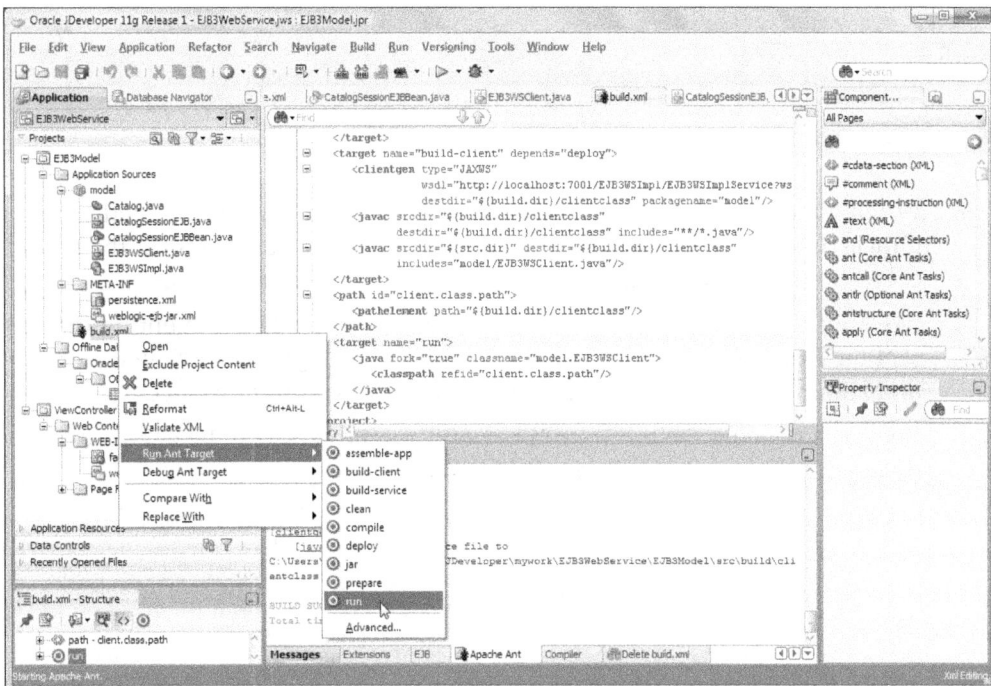

2. The `Catalog` entity instances get created. The query results get listed as follows:

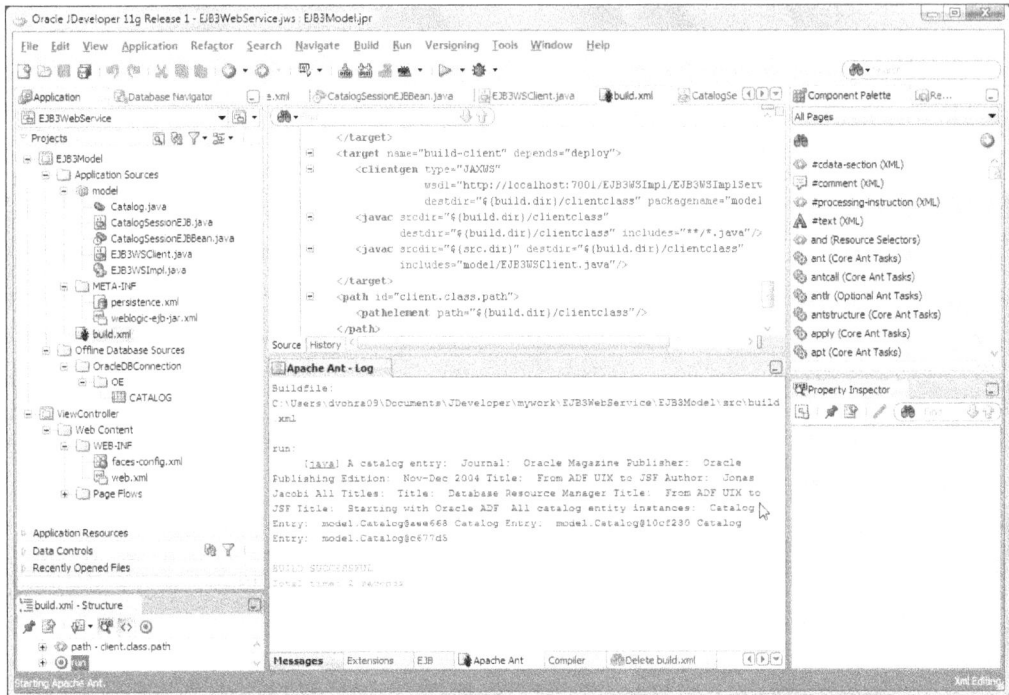

3. When the transaction is completed, the entity instances get persisted to the Oracle database. If a SQL query on the CATALOG table does not list the rows corresponding to the entity instances, restart the XE database service.

4. Next, we shall remove two of the entity instances by de-commenting the code section for removing entity instances in the `CatalogSessionEJBBean` class and commenting out the code section for creating entity instances.

5. Before re-running the `build-client` and `run` targets, run the `clean` target to delete the files generated from the previous run.

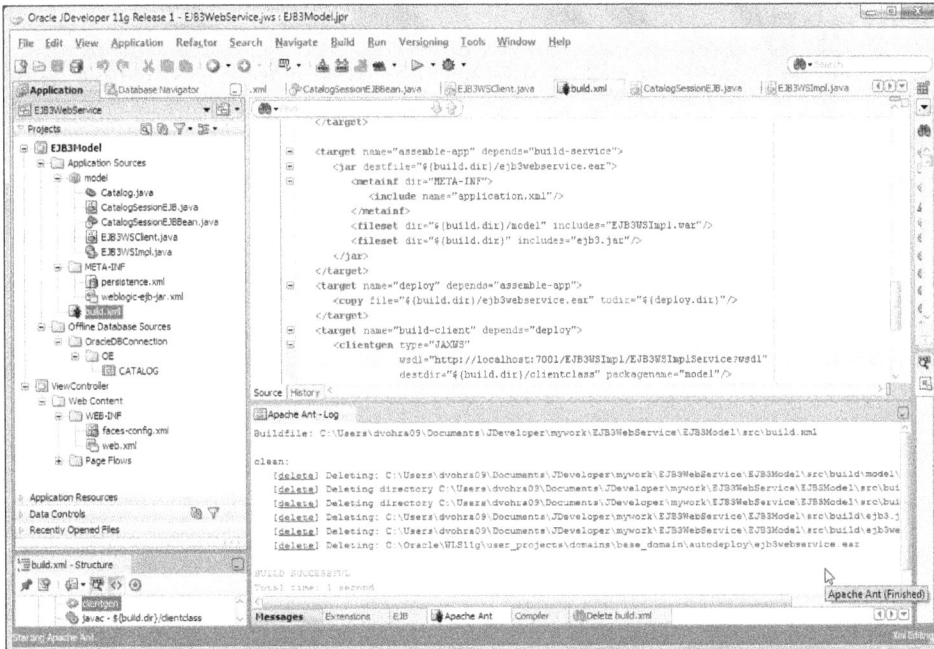

6. Rerun the `build-client` target followed by the `run` target in the `build.xml` script. As we deleted two of the entity instances, the query results list only one entity instance.

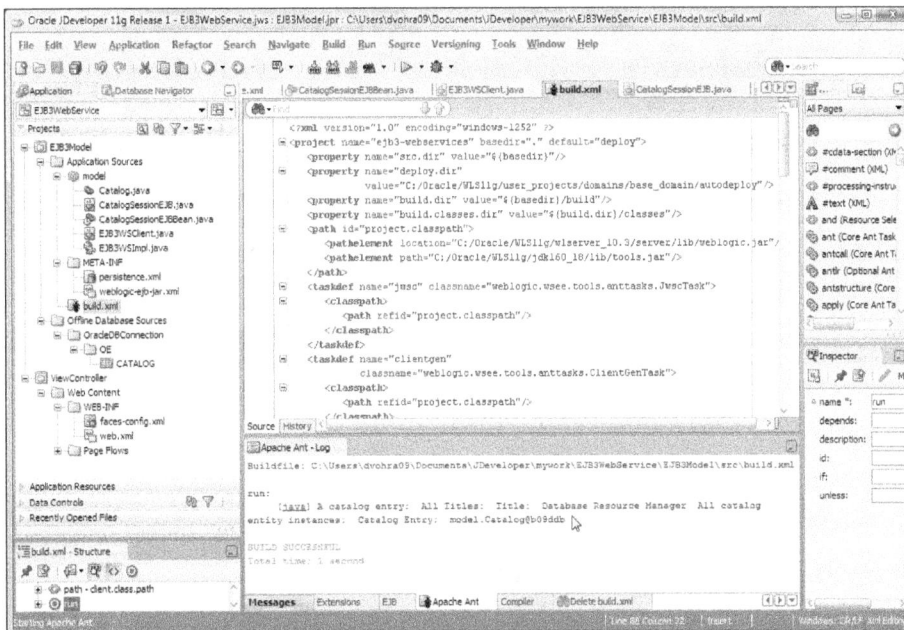

Summary

In this chapter, we created an EJB 3.0 database persistence application and a web service for the EJB 3.0 application in JDeveloper 11*g*. We deployed the EJB 3.0 web service to WebLogic server 11*g* and tested the web service with Oracle Database.

Index

@JoinTable annotation 228
@ManyToOne annotation 228
NamedQueries findArticleAll 228
article JSF page
  managed bean for 354, 355, 361
article.jsp 344
article.jsp JSF page 352, 353
Asynchronous JavaScript And
    XML (AJAX) 259

B

build.classes.dir property 407
build.dir property 407
Business Tier | EJB in Categories 317

C

callback interfaces 22
CatalogBean entity bean 18
CatalogBean session bean 14
Catalog class 279
CATALOGEDITIONS 221
Catalog entity bean 131
catalog entity class
  about 220
  cascade element 221
  CATALOGEDITIONS 221
  Edition entity 221
  findCatalogByJournal(), adding 220
  id property 220
  journal property 220
  @ManyToMany annotation 221
  many-to-many relationship 221
  NamedQueries findCatalogAll(),
    adding 220
Catalog entity instance 99, 262, 399
catalog entry JSF page 190-194
catalogentry.jsp JSF page 204
catalogId 48
catalogId parameter 173
Catalog object 193
CatalogSessionEJBBean class 173, 236, 398
CatalogTestRemote interface 135
CatalogTestSessionEJBBean class 99
cb1_action method 188
checked exceptions 22
client

  creating 103, 104, 105, 246, 247
  testing 106, 107, 249-252
clientgen task 409
CMP (Container Managed Persistence) 15
CMR (Container Managed Relationships)
    field methods 15
commandButton1_action 362
commandButton1_action method 364, 368
commandButton1_action() method 370
configuration defaults, EJB 10
container-managed entity manager 66
Container-Managed Transaction (CMT)
  uses 10
context-param elements 200
createArticle method 335, 342, 355
Create Database Connection window 316
createEdition method 334, 342
createEntityManager() method 66, 398
Create.java managed bean 187
create.jsp JSF page 183, 187
create() method 14, 15, 18, 48
createNamedQuery method 19, 332
createNamedQuery() method 48
createNamedQuery(String queryName),
    EntityManager method 47
createQuery method 99, 399
createQuery() method 136
createQuery(String ejbQlString),
    EntityManager method 47
createSection method 334, 342
createTestData() method 234, 246

D

database connection
  creating 316
database persisted entities 380, 381
database tables
  creating 212, 314
data source
  creating, in WebLogic server 271-276,
    386-390
datasource
  creating, in JDeveloper 78, 80, 156, 157
DeclareRoles annotation 9
deleteSomeData() method 236, 247
DELETE statement 21

DenyAll annotation 9
deploy.dir property 407
desc command 111
Document Object Model (DOM) 259
doGet method 261
doGet() method 288
doPost method 262

E

Eclipse
   Java Persistence API (JPA) project,
      creating 117-126
Eclipse IDE 109
eclipselink.application-location 73
eclipselink.create-ddl-jdbc-file-name 73
eclipselink.ddl-generation 73
eclipselink.ddl-generation.output-mode 73
eclipselink.ddl-generation property 133, 330
eclipselink.drop-ddl-jdbc-file-name 73
eclipselink.exception-handler 69
eclipselink.jdbc.batch-writing 69
eclipselink.jdbc.bind-parameters 69
eclipselink.jdbc.cache-statements 69
eclipselink.jdbc.cache-statements.size 69
eclipselink.jdbc.driver 70
eclipselink.jdbc.exclusive-connection.
      is-lazy 69
eclipselink.jdbc.native-sql 69
eclipselink.jdbc.password 70
eclipselink.jdbc.read-connections.max 70
eclipselink.jdbc.read-connections.min 70
eclipselink.jdbc.read-connections.shared 70
eclipselink.jdbc.url 70
eclipselink.jdbc.user 70
eclipselink.jdbc.write-connections.max 71
eclipselink.jdbc.write-connections.min 71
EclipseLink JPA
   about 67
   entity identity 68
   entity relationships 68
   metadata annotations 67
   XML mapping metadata 67
EclipseLink JPA documentation
   URL 61
eclipselink.logging.exceptions 72
eclipselink.logging.file 72

eclipselink.logging.level 71
eclipselink.logging.timestamp 71
EclipseLink persistence provider
   specifying 62
eclipselink.target-database 72
eclipselink.target-database property 330
eclipselink.target-server 72
eclipselink.target-server property 169, 330
EclispeLink JPA
   persistence unit properties 69-73
Edition entities 319
edition entity
   creating 377
Edition entity 319
Edition entity class
   @ManyToMany annotation 223
   Edition entity 223
   edition property 223
   editions field 223
   findEditionByEdition() 223
   id property 223
   mappedBy element 223
   NamedQueries findEditionAll() 223
   one-to-many relationship 223
edition JSF page
   managed bean for 370, 373
edition.jsp 368
Edition managed bean 370
EditionSections method 253
editions field 223
EJB
   about 7
   callback interfaces 22
   checked exceptions 22
   configuratin defaults 10
   environment, setting 23
   interceptor 21
   simplified entity beans 15, 17
EJB 2.0
   session facade, developing 47, 49
EJB 2.0 entity to EJB 3.0 entity, conversion
   about 31-33
   application, adding 24, 25
   environment, setting 23
   Style Sheets, creating 27-29
   XML deployment descriptor, creating 26
   XSLT stylesheet 33-41

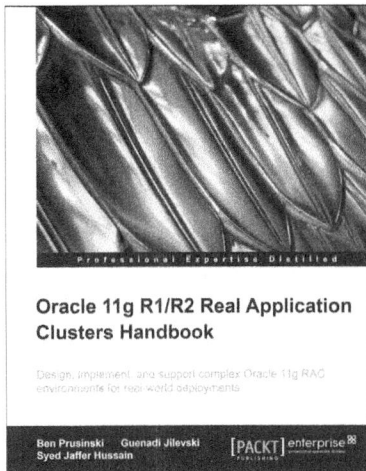

Oracle 11g R1 / R2 Real Application Clusters Handbook

ISBN: 978-1-847199-62-1   Paperback: 676 pages

Design, implement and support complex Oracle 11g RAC environments for real world deployments

1. Design, implement and support complex Oracle 11g RAC environments

2. Understand sophisticated components that make up your Oracle RAC environment such as the role of High Availability, the required RAC architecture, the RAC installation and upgrade process and much more!

3. Bonus Oracle 11g RAC R2 information included

Oracle 11g R1/R2 Real Application Clusters Handbook

Design, implement, and support complex Oracle 11g RAC environments for real-world deployments

Ben Prusinski   Guenadi Jilevski
Syed Jaffer Hussain   [PACKT] enterprise 🕸

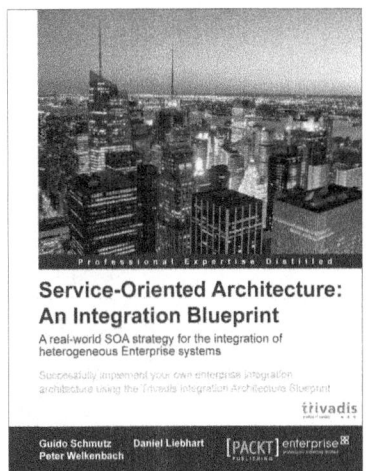

Service Oriented Architecture: An Integration Blueprint

ISBN: 978-1-849681-04-9   Paperback: 240 pages

Successfully implement your own enterprise integration architecture using the Trivadis Integration Architecture Blueprint

1. Discover and understand the structure of existing application landscapes from an integration perspective

2. Get to grips with fundamental integration concepts and terminology while learning about architecture variants

3. Fully comprehend all the individual layers and components that make up the Trivadis Integration Architecture Blueprint

Service-Oriented Architecture: An Integration Blueprint

A real-world SOA strategy for the integration of heterogeneous Enterprise systems

Successfully implement your own enterprise integration architecture using the Trivadis Integration Architecture Blueprint

trivadis

Guido Schmutz   Daniel Liebhart
Peter Welkenbach   [PACKT] enterprise 🕸

Please check **www.PacktPub.com** for information on our titles

www.ingramcontent.com/pod-product-compliance
Lightning Source LLC
Chambersburg PA
CBHW080134220326
41598CB00032B/5069